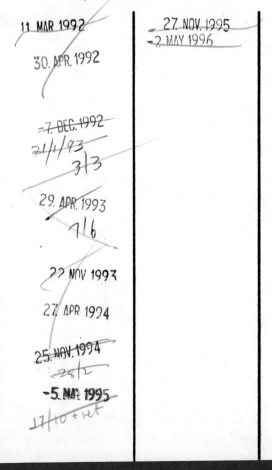

Hope and Independence

Hope and Independence
Blacks' Response
to Electoral and Party Politics

Patricia Gurin
Shirley Hatchett
James S. Jackson

Russell Sage Foundation   New York

The Russell Sage Foundation

The Russell Sage Foundation, one of the oldest of America's general purpose foundations, was established in 1907 by Mrs. Margaret Olivia Sage for "the improvement of social and living conditions in the United States." The Foundation seeks to fulfill this mandate by fostering the development and dissemination of knowledge about the political, social, and economic problems of America. It conducts research in the social sciences and public policy and publishes books and pamphlets that derive from this research.

The Board of Trustees is responsible for oversight and the general policies of the Foundation, while administrative direction of the program and staff is vested in the President, assisted by the officers and staff. The President bears final responsibility for the decision to publish a manuscript as a Russell Sage Foundation book. In reaching a judgment on the competence, accuracy, and objectivity of each study, the President is advised by the staff and selected expert readers. The conclusions and interpretations in Russell Sage Foundation publications are those of the authors and not of the Foundation, its Trustees, or its staff. Publication by the Foundation, therefore, does not imply endorsement of the contents of the study.

Library of Congress Cataloging-in-Publication Data

Gurin, Patricia.
  Hope and independence : Blacks' response to electoral and party
politics / Patricia Gurin, Shirley Hatchett, James S. Jackson.
    p.   cm.
  Includes bibliographical references.
  ISBN 0-87154-374-5
  1. Afro-Americans—Politics and government. 2. United States—
Politics and government—1945- 3. Jackson, Jesse, 1941– .
4. Presidents—United States—Election—1984. 5. Political parties—
United States. 6. Afro-Americans—Suffrage. I. Hatchett,
Shirley. II. Jackson, James S. (James Sidney), 1944– .
III. Title.
E185.615.G86 1989
323.1'196073—dc20   89-39277
                                                              CIP

Cover and text design: William Bennett

Contents

Preface

Black participation in American political life has been a recurrent subject of analysis and scholarship. Its import increased manyfold when the 1965 Voting Rights Act began to loosen the political chains that had bound southern blacks ever since the 1890s. By the 1970s, scholars had begun to talk of a New Black Politics that fused protest and electoral forms and had a strong base in organizations spawned by the Civil Rights and Black Power movements of the 1960s. New Black Politics were putting blacks in office and mobilizing blacks to register and vote in numbers unimaginable since the days of Reconstruction. A rich new scholarship began to analyze these developments—little of it, however, from the perspective of the national black electorate. We thought the lack of attention to the reactions and attitudes of individual blacks a serious gap in the literature on black politics. It seemed to us that the 1984 election offered a special opportunity to shed light on a long history of black politics by going directly to black Americans in a broad-scale national survey.

The year 1984 was crucial for black politics. Blacks had responded to the conservative political climate in the nation and to the Reagan administration's retreat from civil rights with renewed vigor, not political resignation. Since 1982, mobilization efforts had brought nearly two million new black voters onto the registration lists. As of May, 1983, blacks were mayors of sixteen cities with a population of over 100,000—largely because of the black vote. The black electorate was already on the move when on November 3, 1983, Jesse Jackson announced that he would seek the Democratic party's nomination for president. Reaction in the black community was mixed. Most elected black officials and party regulars were initially opposed; most endorsed Walter Mondale's candidacy. Many predicted that Jackson's inevitable failure to win the nomination would turn blacks away from electoral politics—a prediction that proved unfounded when black turnout in the November election increased nearly 6 percent over 1980. As in other periods of history, the black electorate was not following the advice of its political leaders. Jackson was drawing large and responsive black audiences all across the country. This was an election, we felt, that might reveal how these independent-minded black citizens saw the issues and their relationship to electoral and party politics.

We were fortunate that three foundations—the Ford Foundation, the Rockefeller Foundation, and the Carnegie Corporation—responded to our concern. With their financial support, we were able to mount a nationally representative sample survey of voting-age black Americans. Of course, blacks have always been included in national political surveys in numbers reflecting their proportion in the nation's population. Typically, however, these surveys yield too few black respondents to give trustworthy estimates of the attitudes of this important segment of the electorate or to study variation within it. Our survey, which interviewed 1,150 blacks before and 871 after the election, covered a wide range of political and personal topics.

This book changed as it was being written. As we began to look at the data, we uncovered issues that have deep roots in black history. The dilemma facing the 1984 black electorate was not new. Blacks have always struggled with party dependency—with the question of how to get their votes taken seriously by the one party (earlier the Republicans, now the Democrats) that even approximately represents their interests. We realized our data on blacks' reactions to the Jackson candidacy and to the possibility of organizing a separate black party needed to be placed in a broader context than that of a single election. As no one of us is an historian, we turned to studies carried out by other scholars to bring an historical perspective to the book. It was a daunting assignment, one we doubtless have not fulfilled as well as a professional historian would have. We feel, nonetheless, that we have taken an important step in bringing together historical and survey materials. One of the great unfinished tasks in the social sciences is to do just that.

We found four major themes embedded in our data and in the history of blacks' relationship to the parties and the electoral and party system—*hope* for eventual inclusion as full citizens and influential members of the parties, *perseverance* despite exclusion and expectations of *betrayal*, and *independence*, not as an end but as a strategy to win incorporation. These four themes, expressed by black political leaders, found their way into black political culture through sermons in black churches and the talk and songs of ordinary people. In some periods, one theme was in the forefront; in other periods, another took the lead. There is no doubt that these themes are with us still.

As this book goes to press, the 1988 presidential primaries, the Democratic National Convention, and the election have concluded. We must leave to others the task of looking at the 1988 black electorate with the depth and care we brought to our analysis of the 1984 election. But our early reading of 1988 does suggest that the basic themes we have identified play on.

Most would agree that Jackson's victories in 1988 were more impressive than those in 1984. He won 6.6 million votes and placed first in the primaries or caucuses of ten states and the District of Columbia, Puerto Rico, and the Virgin Islands. In 1984, he won 3.5 million votes and took first place only in Louisiana and the District of Columbia. This time around, the support of the black electorate and of black leaders was virtually consensual. Fully 92 percent of the black primary voters cast ballots for Jackson and nearly all nationally known black political figures endorsed him. White support increased from 5 percent in 1984 to 12 percent in 1988, and one-third of his delegates to the 1988 Democratic National Convention were white. Jackson's negotiators at the convention delivered for his constituency an increased share of membership on the Democratic National Committee and its executive committee. These achievements will make Jackson's 1988 presidential bid an historic step in the ongoing developments in black politics.

It is incontestable that hope was part of the 1988 campaign. Jackson made it his central message: "Keep hope alive," Jackson told his audiences. But even with the achievements of the Jackson candidacy, there was throughout the campaign "an abiding skepticism born . . . of painful experience that progress is fitful and alliances are tenuous" (*New York Times*, April 5, 1988). Long before Governor Michael Dukakis selected Senator Lloyd Bentsen as his running mate, blacks expressed misgivings about how Jackson was being treated by the press and by party leaders. The repeated questions—What does Jesse want? and Is Jesse electable?—symbolized for blacks their continuing dilemma in the racial politics and ideological climate of America. Our word, *betrayal*, may be too strong to define the sentiments of the black electorate. Only time will tell how blacks on balance evaluated the successes and failures of 1988. Even now it is clear, however, they they will persevere—as they have in the past—in electoral and party politics, searching for strategies that combine participation with enough independence to press the Democratic party in a progressive direction. We suspect that these themes will endure for decades to come.

The development of this book has had certain consequences. Its concern is with blacks' reactions *to* the party system, not with blacks *in* the party system. In keeping with our disciplinary training, we focus on social psychological questions—what black citizens think about national politics, how they evaluate candidates, what political independence means to them, and whether they saw Jackson's candidacy in 1984 and a separate black party as expressions of independence. This focus means, of course, that the book is not about many other things. It does not provide a detailed contrast between blacks and whites or between blacks and other groups currently struggling for inclusion in party politics: we hope that other scholars use our findings in comparative studies of groups in American politics. Nor does the book cover local politics or institutional issues that we all know are important: we do not analyze black participation in local and state parties, the evolution of the primaries or of trends in support for the Democratic party, and we do not examine the coalitional strategies of black and non-black party leaders vis-à-vis black voters, southern whites, or other groups. This book is about blacks and individuals.

As in any complex collaborative project, there has been much interaction among the authors. Virtually all aspects of the project reflect a joint effort, but at some points there was a certain division of labor. Preparation of the manuscript itself was the primary responsibility of the senior author, Patricia Gurin. Shirley Hatchett was largely responsible for the methodological aspects of the study, which she describes in Appendix A; she also drafted significant portions of the introductory and concluding chapters. James Jackson conceived of the idea of conducting the 1984 survey, and the data analysis and writing were carried out within his Program on Black Americans at the University of Michigan's Institute for Social Research. All of us contributed to the discussions and critical exchanges that led to the final story.

Acknowledgments

M ANY INDIVIDUALS AND ORGANIZATIONS supported our research and the writing of this book. The 1984 national survey of the black electorate was funded by the Ford Foundation, the Rockefeller Foundation, and the Carnegie Corporation, and was conducted at the University of Michigan's Institute for Social Research. We acknowledge with appreciation the efforts of the Institute's sampling and field sections, the helpful advice of colleagues in the Institute's Center for Political Studies, the research assistance of Karin Clissold, and the library assistance of Adye Bel Evans. We are deeply indebted to three close associates, Ronald Brown, Debbie Robinson, and Catherine Tate, who worked on the survey from conception through analysis, and to other Michigan colleagues who read early versions of the manuscript, especially Aldon Morris, Walter Allen, Jr., Gerald Gurin, and Michael Dawkins.

A national commitee of political scientists guided the survey, responded to analyses of the data, and critiqued the book manuscript. This committee included Charles V. Hamilton, Robert B. Hill, Matthew Holden, Jr., Jewell Prestage, Michael Preston, Ernest Wilson III, Ronald Walters, Althea Simmons, Diane M. Pinderhughes, Milton Morris, James D. McGhee, Sherill Ismael, and Shirley Chisholm. We acknowledge with gratitude their continuing collaboration over the course of the study. We are also indebted to three anonymous reviewers of the manuscript and to Thomas Cavanaugh and Hanes Walton, Jr., for penetrating questions and criticisms. The responsibility for the final content of the book of course rests with us.

Preparation of the book manuscript was made possible by the Russell Sage Foundation's support of the senior author as a Resident Scholar. Among many generous colleagues at the Foundation, we are especially grateful to Robert K. Merton, who unstintingly responded to the book's substance, recommended revisions of organization and content, and edited the entire manuscript. Fellow scholars Jonathan Rieder, Theodore Marmor, Fay Cook, Tom Cook, and Kathleen Gerson were provocative critics who more than occasionally put aside their own work to read and make suggestions about ours. So, too, did Priscilla Lewis and Peter de Janosi, the Foundation's Director of Publications and Vice-President, who together made the potentially adversarial relationship between authors and publisher a partnership of mutual respect. These two understand people as well as books. Special thanks are also due to Marshall Robinson and Eric Wanner, who served as the Foundation's presidents during the senior author's residency and made the Foundation an exciting, intellectual community of social scientists. The Foundation's Director of Information Services Pauline Rothstein, secretaries Corrine Rosenthal and Camille Yezzi, and Managing Editor Charlotte Shelby provided invaluable assistance as the book was being written and edited. So, too, did Ann Watson and Mary Rubin, whose collaboration and friendship are deeply valued.

Finally, this book has depended on the cooperation and openness of hundreds of black citizens who talked with our interviewers before and after the 1984 presidential election. A report highlighting the study's basic results was sent to each of them in appreciation for their participation. We dedicate this book to them and to other black Americans who have persistently kept hope alive.

Introduction

. . . The shape of the world today does not permit us the luxury of an anemic democracy. The price America must pay for the continued exploitation of the Negro and other minority groups is the price of its own destruction. . . . Now more than ever before, America is challenged to bring her noble dream into reality, and those who are working to implement the American dream are the true saviors of democracy.*

I<small>T IS IRONIC THAT</small> although originally brought to the American colonies by force and in servitude, Americans of African descent—much like members of other groups, who emigrated more or less voluntarily and in search of freedom, equality, and opportunity—came to view the United States as a land of promise. Frederick Douglass, an escaped slave who educated himself and later became one of the first great leaders of American blacks, wrote in his autobiography:

> After a time, a careful reconsideration of the subject convinced me that there was no necessity for dissolving the union between the northern and southern States; that to seek this dissolution was no part of my duty as an abolitionist; that to abstain from voting was to refuse to exercise a legitimate and powerful means of abolishing slavery; and that the Constitution of the United States not only contained no guarantees in favor of slavery,

* Martin Luther King, Jr., "The American Dream" speech, Commencement Address, Lincoln University, Lincoln, Pennsylvania, 1961.

1

but on the contrary, was in its letter and spirit an anti-slavery instrument, demanding the abolition of slavery as a condition of its own existence, as the supreme law of the land.[1]

Douglass was well aware that the Constitution of the United States was never intended to be seen as a freedom manifesto for blacks. He recognized, however, that this document, with its egalitarian tone and at times ambiguous language, provided a tool that could be used to abolish slavery. He went on to regard the legislation and constitutional amendments enacted after emancipation as a further basis for the hope that freed blacks would enjoy the full protection and privileges afforded other citizens.

Nearly seventy years after Douglass's death, another black leader voiced similar hope. This came at a time when blacks were emerging from a long, bleak period during which the promises of the founding documents and legislation passed immediately after emancipation were betrayed by judicial interpretation in federal courts and by legislation passed in southern states. Cognizant of this history, Martin Luther King, Jr., underscored the inherent contradiction in American democracy in his famous "I Have a Dream" speech: ". . . America is essentially a dream, a dream as yet unfilled." Referring to the Declaration of Independence, he observed:

> One of the first things we notice in this dream is an amazing universalism. It does not say some men, but it says all men. . . . And there is another thing we see in this dream that ultimately distinguishes democracy and our form of government from all of the totalitarian regimes that emerge in history. It says that each individual has certain basic rights neither conferred by nor derived from the state.[2]

Unlike the history of other groups that came to this country, the history of blacks in the United States has been one of seemingly endless cycles of hope and betrayal. From the beginning to the present, the inclusion of blacks in the American democracy has been thwarted by attitude, law, and action. The remarkable aspect of this history is the perseverance of black Americans in their struggle to achieve citizenship and political influence.

The founding documents of American democracy formed the wellspring of their hope and perseverance. Harding, a historian, writes: ". . . During the War for Independence—in petitions to legislatures, freedom cases in the courts, and speeches—black people resolutely turned the professed revolutionary faith of their captors into outright challenges to the system of American slavery. . . . Eventually this sort of protest, based on American democratic principles . . . became the broadest single element—the mainstream—in the river of black struggle in America."[3]

Not all blacks had access to information about the existence and meaning of the founding documents. Freed and educated blacks, however, were in a position to recognize that the contradiction between the principles of democracy and the institution of slavery was a basis for hope. They communicated this idea to others by means of black churches and communal gatherings of various sorts. Then, as now, many black leaders were ministers, and the black church became the normative hub of the emerging black community.

From its beginnings, the black Christian tradition fused religious ends (the eschatology of social justice) and sociopolitical ends. In this tradition Christian service and social activism are viewed as one and the same. The idea of Christian hope and the necessity of perserverance were conveyed to the black masses through sermons and songs. Howard Thurman, noted theologian and black leader, pointed to the spiritual "Balm in Gilead" as a prototype of these themes:[4]

> There is a balm in Gilead,
> To make the spirit whole.
> There is a balm in Gilead,
> To heal the sin-sick soul.

Relating this spiritual to the prophet Jeremiah's spiritual depression, Thurman argued that the slaves who sang this song answered Jeremiah's question optimistically and assertively. There must be a balm in Gilead; there *is* a balm in Gilead. Was their faith naive? Commenting on Thurman's analysis, Young addresses this question: "In this example of Christian hope, the basic insight is an optimism that grows out of the pessimism of life; it uses the pessimism of life as raw material, transcends it, and creates its own strength."[5]

Together the principles of democracy and the black Christian tradition nourished blacks' hopes for freedom and inclusion. But with the specter of betrayal ever present, the political struggle of blacks has required independence. In order to define their own political goals and to control decisions about the strategies to achieve them, blacks have often had to operate outside of conventional political institutions.

This book focuses on black reaction to electoral and party politics in which independent strategies have been used to gain access and influence policy. We examine how the themes of hope, betrayal, perseverance, and independence have been expressed historically and, most particularly, in the 1984 presidential bid by Jesse Jackson.

We take up one aspect of the persistent involvement of black citizens in the political process: their struggle to participate in the electoral system and use the party system to make government accountable to their interests. A review of the history of party politics from the perspectives of black leaders and the black electorate finds that parties have always treated blacks as pawns in their bids for electoral power. As such, blacks have been used tactically, and their interests often were sacrificed. Indeed, even their status as pawns has been tenuous. At any time, only one party (first the Whigs, later the Republicans, and now the Democrats) has come even close to representing their interests, and that party often shunned them. More often than not, the opposing party attempted to remove blacks from the game completely, through disfranchisement. Black leaders have persistently searched for strategies to use in their attempts to gain greater influence in party politics; they have worried about dependency on a single party; and they have advocated independence when they believed it would enhance the group's political effectiveness. Independence is examined in this book through historical materials and survey responses in 1984 to questions about the Jackson candidacy and the possibility of organizing a black party and black strategy in national politics.

HOPE AND BETRAYAL

The first recorded arrival of blacks in the thirteen colonies was in 1619, a year before the *Mayflower* landed: a Virginia planter is said to have received "twenty Negars" from a Dutch ship.[6] Jordan, in a historical analysis of early attitudes of whites toward blacks, argues that although initially no legal differences existed between black indentured servants and white indentured servants, blacks were always perceived and treated differently from their white counterparts. These differences, he suggests, derived from attributions made by the English about the nature and character of Africans and other dark people on the basis of their color. In seventeenth-century Europe, this was "an emotionally partisan color, the handmaid and symbol of baseness and evil, a sign of danger and repulsion."[7] Blacks were seen as less than ordinary men and treated accordingly. During the height of the slave trade, blacks were captured like animals in their homeland, packed tightly on shelves in the cargo holds of ships, and transported to the colonies to be sold like other commodities in the markets of the New World.

The American system of perpetual slavery evolved in the course of

time. As many as twenty years before perpetual slavery became codi-
fied in law, black servants were being kept in servitude longer and
treated more harshly than white servants. Other practices presaged the
impending enslavement of blacks: "Indications of perpetual service,
the very nub of slavery, coincided with indications that English set-
tlers discriminated against Negro women, withheld arms from Negroes, and . . . reacted unfavorably to interracial sexual union."[8] Between 1660 and 1664, legislation in Virginia and Maryland prescribed
that blacks were to serve *durante vita*; after the early 1700s, slave trade
increased notably, and slavery spread throughout the colonies.

A long period of degradation and despair prevailed between this
initial betrayal and the first sign of hope that emerged when white
Americans revolted against colonial rule. Commenting on the Declaration of Independence, Quarles, a historian, writes, "This was revolutionary language and it was but natural that Negroes would interpret
the Declaration as a freedom manifesto to mankind rather than merely
an attack on a King across the water."[9] The promise of freedom led
blacks to fight on both sides. Although only the British explicitly offered blacks their freedom, the rebels welcomed the enlistment of free
blacks and often pressed slaves into service. Yet the expectation of
freedom was crushed when the defeated British were unable to act on
their promise and the independent Americans founded a nation that
excluded blacks from the basic rights endowed to "all men" and which
tolerated the institution of slavery for nearly another century.

Hope emerged again with the beginning of the white Abolitionist
movement in the 1830s. Free blacks in the North had always agitated
for the abolition of slavery, with little success. The actions of white
abolitionists had greater influence and received wider notice. The initial positive reactions of black abolitionists gave way to disappointment as white leaders instituted separate conventions for white activists and black activists and proved reluctant to agitate for full
citizenship and equality for blacks. Martin R. Delany, a black
abolitionist and newspaper editor, expressed this new sense of betrayal: ". . . And thus did we expect much. But in all this, we were
doomed to disappointment, sad, sad disappointment. Instead of realiz-
ing what we had hoped for, we find ourselves occupying the very same
position in relationship to our Anti-Slavery friends, as we do in relation to the proslavery part of the community—a mere secondary,
underling position."[10]

Foreshadowing a response to betrayal that would recur throughout
the political history of black Americans, black leaders emerged from
this failed coalition to pursue an independent course. Delany and sev-

eral other black abolitionists embraced more militant stances and eventually formulated an emigrationist, separatist movement. Frederick Douglass, equally disappointed but not wholly disillusioned, broke with William Lloyd Garrison, a leading white abolitionist, and argued that the spirit of the Constitution provided the hope for the eventual freedom and equal treatment of blacks. On the eve of the Civil War, that prospect dimmed when the Dred Scott decision struck down the Missouri Compromise, which forbade slavery in the territories. In deliberating this decision, several Justices (though a minority) held the view that blacks who were descended from slaves had no rights as American citizens and thus no recourse in the courts.

The outbreak of the Civil War ended this second period of disappointment, and the subsequent signing of the Emancipation Proclamation in 1863 signaled the third period of hope for blacks. In the first summer of freedom, blacks all across the nation lay special claim to the revolutionary significance of the Fourth of July. It was their jubilee. Harding describes the event in Louisville, Kentucky. A procession was formed by thousands of marchers, led by eight hundred black soldiers (the Blues and Blacks as they were called). They were joined by nearly 100,000 people when they arrived at Johnson's Woods, the site of the celebration. It seemed that every black person from Kentucky and lower Ohio was there when the Declaration of Independence was read. These former slaves "were declaring, creating, and acting out their own freedom" in the best revolutionary tradition.[11]

After the war and the freeing of the slaves, a series of civil rights bills were enacted and three amendments to the Constitution—the Thirteenth, Fourteenth, and Fifteenth—were passed to ensure the freedom of blacks and to protect their rights as citizens. Nevertheless, an intense struggle ensued between the executive branch, Congress, and the southern states over the new rights. For the most part, the new laws were rarely enforced, and blacks enjoyed only a brief period of full suffrage and participation in the political system. The decision in the famous Slaughterhouse cases (1873)[12] initiated a period of restricted judicial interpretation of the three new constitutional amendments, which led to a new concept of "dual citizenship," one national and one state, and bolstered Jim Crow practices in the South.

The Civil Rights Act of 1875, passed to curtail these practices, was quickly declared unconstitutional. Nineteen years later, the dual citizenship concept was finely tuned in *Plessy* v. *Ferguson*. This decision functioned to relegate blacks to a second class citizenship and to protect those who used the courts, law, and violence to deny blacks their rights as citizens. "Separate but equal" became the legal fiction that regulated the lives of blacks until the mid-1950s.

As the Supreme Court evolved, the three amendments enacted after emancipation—in particular, the Fourteenth—again provided a basis for the incorporation of blacks into the nation as first class citizens. In 1954, the landmark decision of *Brown v. Board of Education of Topeka* struck down the doctrine of separate but equal. Along with progress on the judicial front, a ground swell of protest against segregation was building among blacks in the South. Organization and experienced leadership in the black community—legacies of previous struggles to gain rights afforded other citizens—together with a changing political economy in the South brought about a historic mobilization of blacks in the late 1950s and in the 1960s. The modern Civil Rights movement successfully challenged the nation's conscience and again secured legal promises of full citizenship and equal opportunity.

PERSEVERANCE AND INDEPENDENCE

Hope and betrayal provide the persisting context in which black politics take place; perseverance and independence are the dominant characteristics. From the Abolitionist movement and the post-emancipation days of the Afro-American League to the Niagara movement, which spawned the National Association for the Advancement of Colored People (NAACP) and the Urban League, through the political movements of the 1950s and 1960s, blacks have persistently tried to participate in the political system. They have used a wide range of political mechanisms: moral suasion, litigation, political parties, pressure groups and lobbying, both violent and nonviolent direct action, and, when they had it, the vote.

In periods when they were denied the vote, they tried to influence the outcome of elections through other forms of politics. In the 1860s, black leaders used abolitionist meetings, informal gatherings, and the black press as forums for their opinions on policies and presidential candidates. During and after Reconstruction, blacks engaged in the entire repertoire of political acts that characterizes nineteenth- and twentieth-century politics in Europe and the United States.[13] They organized their own political conventions and formed factions in the Republican party; they developed race-advancement groups; and they launched protests and demonstrations to curb terrorism and protect or regain the vote.

The black women's club movement provides an example of the breadth of black politics in the late nineteenth and early twentieth centuries. Before women achieved suffrage in 1920, black women's clubs organized demonstrations and petition drives to gain the vote for women and end the disfranchisement of black men; they protested the racism of white leaders in the woman suffrage movement; and they provided leaders for the movements against lynching and police brutality. After the Nineteenth Amendment gave women the right to vote, the members of these clubs continued to take part in a wide range of political activities. Brooks describes how they continued to work for the anti-lynching cause and began to take part in the political activities made possible by woman suffrage: they organized voter-registration drives; published articles in the black press on registration, voting, and election issues; and worked in the Colored Women's Department of the Republican National Committee.[14]

Recent theories of political mobilization define politics much as blacks have always construed it: Any effort made by individuals or groups to affect the distribution of power and resources in a community or state. Both the orderly and disorderly sides of politics are considered instrumental and rational. Thus, according to Gamson, "Rebellion in this view is simply politics by other means. It is not some kind of irrational behavior. It is as instrumental in its nature as a lobbyist trying to get special favors for his group or a major political party conducting a presidential campaign."[15] White racism and the structural position of blacks usually limited blacks' political struggles to protest; although they employed protest to gain incorporation, not to destroy the political system.

Blacks have expressed the theme of independence, fundamental to their participation in politics, in numerous ways: by supporting the opposing party (though its ideology was rarely congenial to their interests), by running independent candidates, by taking part in third parties, by forming separate black parties or factions within the major parties, or by deciding not to vote in a particular election, and by abandoning party politics altogether. In presidential politics, complete independence in the form of a separate party has had little chance of success, since the black electorate is too small to control a significant number of votes in the electoral college. Usually blacks have pursued less extreme strategies of independence to protest exclusion, gain influence in a party, and raise policy issues ignored by the major parties. The spirit of independence is evident in a 1924 editorial in Crisis, the NAACP magazine edited by the black political leader and sociologist W. E. B. Du Bois. It warns blacks to "watch the candidates for Congress and the state legislature. . . . Defeat your enemies even if they are Republicans. Vote for your friends even if they are Democrats."[16]

Much has changed in recent years. Blacks now participate in electoral politics—voting and winning offices in both government and the Democratic party—in numbers unimaginable before the Voting Rights

Act of 1965. But dependency on one party and limited influence over the direction of that one party's policies remain as critical to the black electorate as in the earliest period of party politics.

THE BLACK ELECTORATE'S VIEW

Studies of black politics generally have neglected the participation of blacks in party politics as viewed from the perspective of the black electorate. This neglect, which derives mostly from a lack of adequate data, has had serious implications for scholarship on black parties. An emphasis on black political elites can produce misleading expectations, since the black electorate has generally ignored the advice of its leaders to withhold their vote from the Grand Old Party in days of loyalty to the Republicans or from the Democrats in recent times. The voting patterns of blacks reveal extraordinary loyalty to either one party or the other at any given time in history.

The view of the black electorate presented in this book is based on the 1984 National Black Election Study (NBES), which was conducted at the Institute for Social Research (ISR) of the University of Michigan. Following the design of the well-known National Election Studies (NES), which have been carried out at the ISR for more than thirty years, respondents were contacted before and after the November presidential election. Altogether 1,150 black respondents of voting age were interviewed by telephone, and 871 were reinterviewed later in the post-election survey. The sample for the NBES was drawn using random-digit-dial methods. (Details of the methodology are presented in Appendix A.)

We use these survey data to explore the black electorate's support for the candidacy of Jesse Jackson and for an independent black political voice. Support for Jackson is gauged by an index indicating preference for him over other candidates in the Democratic primaries, belief that his candidacy was a good idea, and willingness to have voted for him even if he had run independently. Advocacy of an independent black political voice is measured by an index indicating approval of a separate black party and of a strategy of always voting for black candidates. These two expressions of independence might be construed as "insider" and "outsider" strategies, although we will show that this distinction is overly simplified.

Our analysis of support for Jackson and for an independent political voice makes possible the exploration of two related sets of questions.

First, what does this support reveal about the relationship of the black electorate to the major parties? Were those who strongly supported Jackson more critical than others of the Democratic as well as the Republican party? How did the supporters evaluate other candidates and symbols of the two parties? Were the advocates of a separate black party thinking of long-term separation from two-party politics or only reacting to the current policy positions of the major parties? Were they negatively disposed toward both parties or more favorable toward the Democratic party, perhaps wishing to be loyal should it respond to their needs?

Second, how do blacks view their political options outside the major parties? Although the Jackson bid was waged within the Democratic party, the possibility of an independent candidacy was always present in 1984. Did his supporters see Jackson's candidacy as a strategy of political independence? In supporting a separate party and a strategy of voting black, did the advocates of an independent black voice believe that significant electoral impact could be achieved outside the two major parties? Did they lose faith in two-party politics and in the electoral system as a means of affecting government policy?

A LANDMARK ELECTION

The 1984 election and Jackson's candidacy must be set in the contemporary context of hope and betrayal—the far-reaching political accomplishments wrought by the modern Civil Rights and Black Power movements and the disappointments blacks experienced during the first four years of the Reagan administration.

As Chapter One documents, the political struggle of the 1960s and 1970s resulted in remarkable political gains.[17] Between 1964 and 1980, registration of blacks increased 40 percent in the nation at large, and the number of black elected officials increased 840 percent.[18] Black independent political organizations flourished, and black interest groups attained greater visibility and effectiveness as lobbyists in Washington.[19] The black vote proved pivotal in the elections of President Jimmy Carter and numerous senators and congresspersons. Following reforms in the Democratic party, more blacks became delegates to its national conventions. In 1968, blacks comprised only 5 percent of the national convention delegates, but in 1972 they comprised 15 percent and in 1980, 19 percent. (Throughout this period, they never exceeded 4 percent of the Republican party delegates.)[20] The Civil Rights and Black Power movements also strengthened racial solidarity and provided a cohesive base for black electoral politics in the 1980s and for the black electorate's response to the Jackson candidacy.

In the 1980s, these achievements were threatened by attacks on the Voting Rights Act and affirmative-action legislation and, more broadly, on the role of the federal government. The contemporary struggle among the three branches of government and between conservative and liberal groups is to a degree reminiscent of the struggles that took place during the period following the Civil War. But there is a difference. As a consequence of the movements of the 1960s, the black vote is now a formidable factor in many political contests. Its impact has been felt in elections for particular offices and in rebuffs to President Reagan's judicial appointments and legislative agenda.

The continuity of assault on black rights over the course of American history suggests that the underpinning of betrayal is an intractable desire on the part of white Americans to maintain the racial status quo. The differing perceptions of Reagan's performance as president among black and white Americans mirror a general reorientation of national politics along racial lines that began in the aftermath of the modern Civil Rights movement, particularly among the working class and southerners. A similar reorientation had occurred after the Civil War.

Race is now the best demographic predictor of Americans' policy evaluations and of the vote for the Democratic and Republican presidential candidates.[21] Since 1968, racial differences in the vote have never been less than 48 percentage points and usually were between 55 and 60 points.[22] Moreover, although a four-decade analysis of trends in racial attitudes shows that whites have become more progressive in supporting the principle of racial equality, they have barely increased their support for policies that would implement these principles.[23] Over the same period, blacks continued to favor an activist national government that would implement racial equality through Supreme Court decisions, congressional legislation, and executive orders. On the eve of the 1984 presidential election, Cavanagh contended that the political perceptions and attitudes of blacks and whites still could be characterized by the famous, twenty-year-old conclusion of the Kerner Commission on Civil Disorders—that there are essentially two Americas, one white and one black.[24]

Again, as in the past, blacks reacted with increased political activity rather than resignation to the conservative political climate, curtailment of civil rights action by the federal government under the Reagan administration, and that administration's failure to bring a significant number of blacks into the senior executive service and federal judiciary. Some observers credit the Reagan administration's negative record on racial issues with having spurred the political mobilization of blacks in the early 1980s. Between the 1980 and 1984 presidential

elections, the number of black elected officials in the nation at large
increased by more than 14 percent.[25] Between 1982 and 1984, numerous organizations—the A. Philip Randolph Institute, the NAACP, Op-
eration Big Vote, the Voter Education Project, People United to Save
Humanity (PUSH) and Jesse Jackson's Southern Crusade—enrolled another 1.9 million blacks on the registration lists.[26] As the primary
campaigns of 1984 unfolded and Jesse Jackson entered the fray, optimism thus ran high that the black electorate would vote in unprece-
dented numbers and influence hotly contested Senate and House races
as well as the presidential vote in key states.

But there was no question that a sense of betrayal was also part of
the 1984 political context for blacks. With Jesse Jackson and Ronald
Reagan both in the contest, this nomination and election process symbolized more than any previous one the basic themes of black politics:
hope and betrayal, perseverance and independence.

DIVERSITY AND SOLIDARITY

In exploring the themes of hope and betrayal, perseverance and independence, we address three major controversies in the black electorate's relationship to electoral and party politics. All three relate to
diversity and solidarity.

First is the homogeneity/heterogeneity of this electorate's political
attitudes and reactions. There is a tendency in the literature to talk
about a black point of view and to exaggerate homogeneity. Thus in
using the survey data to explore the reactions of the black electorate,
we continually emphasize social, economic, and political variations
within the black community.[27] We find considerable agreement across
many different sectors. But we also find diversity, especially in matters
of strategy.

The second controversy concerns the historical and current role of
social class in black politics. By and large, social class has not been a
decisive political factor historically in either electoral or protest politics. Some analysts suggest, however, that the increasing economic
polarization of the black community is likely to produce stronger
class-based political cleavages now and in the future. Most of the discussion about the political implications of class division is not based
on solid research evidence. The debate revived by Wilson on the importance of class division among blacks[28] depends almost entirely
on studies of income, occupation, and educational disparities. The
few studies, including ours, that have investigated the impact of class
division on the black electorate's political attitudes find more consen-

sus than division.[29] We find solidarity across class in this electorate's policy preferences and evaluations of the candidates and parties. Blacks who are faring well economically are quite aware of the educational, economic, health, and housing problems that continue to affect most of the black community.

The third controversy also involves solidarity. We find an electorate with strong group solidarity, defined in this book multidimensionally as comprised of group identification and group political consciousness. The critical political question is whether group solidarity discourages coalitions and a commitment to inclusiveness. We find that subtle but important distinctions must be drawn within solidarity to understand when it may have divisive effects. Two types of solidarity are revealed in the survey analysis, one quite rare, the other widespread. Only the former is potentially divisive. In general, the racial solidarity of the black electorate is pro-black, not anti-white, and solidarity is a positive source of engagement in politics.

THE ORGANIZATION OF THIS BOOK

Chapter One places the black electorate's support for Jackson and for an independent political voice in historical perspective. It finds that these political sentiments are contemporary expressions of long-standing issues in national politics. It begins in the early days of the new American state, when parties were quite weak, proceeds through the nineteenth century, when their strength increased, and ends with the twentieth century, when party strength waned. Through each period, we examine how the parties treated blacks and how blacks tried to solve two continuing problems; that of participation—how to gain access to the major parties and have a meaningful role in them; and that of accountability—how to utilize electoral and party politics in order to make government policies and programs responsive to the social and economic needs of the black community.

Chapter Two delineates five types of political motivations and resources that help individuals take part in electoral politics. These are structural advantages, organizational experience, group solidarity, partisanship and political beliefs, and psychological qualities. From the survey data, we derive a profile of the black electorate that exhibits strong political motivation and reveals both agreement and diversity in political opinions.

Chapters Three, Four, and Five focus on support for Jackson and advocacy of an independent black political voice. The supporters of Jackson and the advocates of a black voice came from different sectors of the black community and expressed different types of group solidarity, but both were Democratic partisans. Neither were political outsiders in the usual sense of the term. Independence in 1984 was consistent with the longer view of history according to which black political independence has always been aimed at political incorporation.

Chapter Six discusses the survey results in light of the three major controversies involving diversity and solidarity. Chapter Seven returns to the book's major themes and relates the survey's findings to hope and betrayal, perseverance and independence.

Notes

1. Douglass 1881, 266.
2. King 1986, 208.
3. Harding 1981, 42.
4. Thurman 1945, cited in Young 1979, 51.
5. Ibid.
6. Jordan 1970, 65.
7. Ibid., 57.
8. Ibid., 72.
9. Quarles 1969, 53.
10. Martin R. Delany 1852, cited in Litwak 1970, 167–168.
11. Harding 1981, 301.
12. Although this litigation did not involve blacks, the decision rendered null and void a clause in the Fourteenth Amendment that states, "no state shall make or enforce any law which abridges the privileges and immunities of citizens of the United States." See Logan 1957.
13. Tilly 1981.
14. Brooks 1989.
15. Gamson 1975, 139.
16. Editorial, *Crisis* 28 (July 1924), reprinted in Hamilton 1973, 260.
17. Cruse (1987) argues that these political movements have had little impact on the quality of life for most blacks; citizenship and the vote have not brought about the elimination of poverty. He faults black leaders for pursuing political goals without sufficient attention to economic problems. But he goes further, criticizing them for concentrating on integration, which he claims is an impossible goal in America. He advocates separate organizations for self-determination, self-sufficiency, and the consolidation of resources.
18. Cavanagh 1985a, Table 4, 20; Williams 1982, 75.
19. Smith 1981.
20. Mitofsky and Plissner 1980, 37–43. See also Miller and Jennings, 1986.
21. Kinder and Sears 1985; Shapiro and Patterson 1986.

22. Miller 1984, 6.
23. Schuman, Steeh, and Bobo 1985; Shapiro et al. 1987a and 1987b.
24. Cavanagh 1985a.
25. Ibid., Table 22.
26. Ibid., Table 4. Although accurate national statistics are not kept, the Census Bureau surveys summarized by Cavanagh show that the registration rate for blacks rose from 60 to 66 percent, whereas white registration increased only slightly, from 68.4 to 69.6 between 1980 and 1984. This resulted, of course, in a significant narrowing of the race gap: from 8.4 points in 1980 to 3.3 points in 1984 (Cavanagh 1985a, 12).
27. Another national survey, conducted by the Gallup Organization for the Joint Center for Political Studies, interviewed some nine hundred black respondents during the 1984 presidential campaign. See Cavanagh 1985a.
28. Wilson 1978.
29. Daniels 1981; Dillingham 1981; Gilliam 1986.

CHAPTER ONE

Blacks and Electoral and Party Politics: A Historical Overview

T HE PROBLEMATIC RELATIONSHIP BETWEEN blacks and the major national political parties has long been a critical facet of black politics. A brief historical overview of the treatment accorded blacks by these parties and their responses to them during five periods from the early 1800s up to the 1980s will help place in a broad context the 1984 reactions of the black electorate to two-party politics. This overview is limited to the role of parties in state making, the relationship between blacks and major and third parties, and the formation of separate and satellite black parties, with occasional observations on developments in protest and pressure or interest-group politics, especially those that influenced the ways blacks have used electoral and party politics.

The two-party system, as we know it, was firmly established by 1840, performing the functions of mobilizing voters, organizing government, and linking citizens to government. Although third parties have emerged from time to time, institutional biases in the United States, including the single-member district plurality system, state control over party access to the ballot, and campaign finance rules, have proved discouraging. In general, third parties have performed three functions: they have served as an outlet for political discontent, as a medium for raising issues and policies that the major parties ignored, and as a means for keeping voters linked to the electoral system and the government when they would otherwise have "sat out" an election. Instead of threatening two-party politics, third parties have had an integrative, stabilizing effect.[1]

Black political parties have served the same functions for blacks as the nation's minor third parties have served for Americans in general. They have also been based on and reinforced by the group solidarity of blacks. They have emerged when blacks, rebuffed by other parties, have seen their own party as the only effective mechanism for addressing problems of participation and accountability. Walton categorizes black political parties as either satellite or separate parties.[2] Satellite parties are new political organizations seeking, through acceptance of local voters, the national party's recognition that it is a valid local organ. The goal of a satellite party is to win a place in a major national party. The goal of a separate party, on the other hand, is to achieve electoral victories, usually at city, county, or state levels, for candidates representing black interests. Unlike satellite parties, separate parties are entirely independent of any existing party. Using different strategies, both types of parties have sought entry into—not reconstruction of—the party system.[3]

THE PRE–CIVIL WAR PERIOD

The formation of the party system in the United States has been rocky. In the early 1800s, when the American state was characterized by power diffused among the localities, a weak central apparatus, and only a few national institutions, such as land offices, post offices, and custom houses, parties—along with the courts—were the major political means by which the procedural dimension of the state was handled. Skowronek describes the procedural role of the parties and the courts, which "tied together this state's peculiar organizational determinants and established its effective mode of operations. They coordinated action from the bottom to the top of this radically deconcentrated government scheme. Under a Constitution designed to produce institutional conflicts and riddled with jurisdictional confusions, they came to lend order, predictability, and continuity to government activity."[4]

Yet, it was not immediately evident how the parties might provide the procedures that would facilitate governing under the Constitution. The early parties were largely collections of local elites whose capacity for governing was limited by their patrician character. In fact, the Jeffersonians and the Federalists initially distrusted formal parties and hoped for a consensus among enlightened men. Nonetheless, a fragile, two-party system slowly emerged as the different interests represented by them resulted in electoral competition.[5]

Early Experiences: The Continual Threat of Disfranchisement

Around the turn of the eighteenth century, most blacks aligned with the Federalists (later to become the Whigs). According to Walton, Free Negroes in the North, especially in New York, supported the Federalists because of their stance on slavery.[6] The New York Federalists had passed a law in 1799 calling for the gradual abolition of slavery. While the Federalists were winning black support, the Jeffersonian Republicans were pushing blacks away from their party and thus helping to establish black allegiance to the Federalists. In 1811, for instance, the Jeffersonian Republicans, who controlled the New York State legislature, attempted to disfranchise the Free Negroes and then in 1821 succeeded in passing an amendment to the state constitution limiting their vote. Southern Free Negroes, of whom there were a considerably smaller number, related to the political parties differently. For them, the politics of particular candidates from specific locations were more important than the parties they represented.[7]

Party organizations were strong on local and state levels but still weak nationally during the first two decades of the nineteenth century. They were beginning to "define a clear and irresistible discipline for gaining and manipulating political power,"[8] however, and during the 1830s they gradually took hold of the national government. Thereafter "the regimen of voter mobilization, party coalition building, and two-party competition provided the extra constitutional framework necessary for channeling the ambitions of officials in government" and handling the operational problems of governing.[9] By the 1840 election, the two-party system had achieved its final form. The Whig and Democratic parties were balanced and competitive and able to contest both state and national elections. Voters everywhere identified themselves with one party or the other.[10]

After 1830, when the parties were stronger, Free Negroes in the North voted and were politically significant in some elections. For example, they influenced the election of William Seward, New York's Whig candidate for Senate in 1838. Nonetheless, northern blacks maintained a problematic relationship with the parties because in some states they were still threatened with disfranchisement. In Pennsylvania, the Democrats pressed for their disfranchisement in order to avoid electoral losses to the Whigs. Southern Free Negroes, able to vote in some counties, continued to identify more with candidates than with parties. Even so, the party that failed to receive their votes fought vigorously for disfranchisement.[11]

Strategies for Independence

Blacks, like other Americans, supported third parties during the 1840s and 1850s. This was one of three distinct periods of third-party strength (the other two were 1904–1924, and 1968–1980).[12] Between 1848 and 1860, third parties lured some 5 percent of the popular vote away from the major parties in all but one presidential election. The slavery issue produced a third party in five elections, two of which found black support (in 1840 the moderately anti-slavery Liberty party and in 1848 its successor, the Free-Soil party). By the mid-1850s, however, third parties were no longer affecting blacks' involvement in electoral politics; by then, blacks were virtually disfranchised in both the North and the South.

Other forms of black political independence also emerged in this period. Blacks organized their own abolitionist and pressure groups between 1830 and the Civil War, because they were kept from playing meaningful roles in the American Anti-Slavery Society. Only three blacks were invited to co-sign its original Declaration of Sentiments drafted by William Lloyd Garrison, and no blacks were officers of the society.[13] These groups, usually called "vigilance committees," agitated for abolition and assisted runaway slaves.

Hope for freedom dimmed when the Compromise of 1850 strengthened the Fugitive Slave Act and the Kansas-Nebraska Act of 1854 extended slavery into the western plains territories. As a consequence, political independence began to take the form of sentiments favoring separation and emigration. Martin R. Delany, the ardent abolitionist and newspaper editor who felt betrayed by the subordination of black abolitionists in the Anti-Slavery Society and by the general political climate of the nation, led an expedition to what is now western Nigeria. He obtained a land grant from the Yoruba for what was to become an Afro-American colony.[14] The idea of emigration was similar to the political analysis that lay behind the formation of maroons, politically autonomous black communities. Fifty of these had come into existence in the South by the time of the Civil War. Emigration and maroons were political responses based on a belief that the survival of blacks required physical and/or political disengagement from the white supremacist state.[15] Yet compared with blacks' commitment to participation in the American political system, these extreme forms of independence were minor political responses.

No formal black political party emerged in the period preceding the Civil War. The first National Negro Convention, however, called by black leaders in 1830 to protest disfranchisement, did create the semblance of a party by approving a permanent national convention and local and state auxiliaries. Reconvening periodically until 1853, the convention as a political organization did not survive, partly because dissension over tactics (emigration, moral suasion, and direct political action) was too strong, but ultimately because disfranchisement prevented the translation of convention proposals into bloc voting.[16]

THE CIVIL WAR AND RECONSTRUCTION

During Reconstruction, blacks were more active as voters and more successful in electoral politics than they had been before or would be again until the passage of the Voting Rights Act of 1965. Between 1868 and 1876, blacks were elected to 255 state and federal offices and were active in the Republican party in both the North and the South. (The modern Republican party, emerging from the Whig party, and the Democratic party, emerging from the Democratic Republicans, first appeared as contestants in the 1856 election.) Sixteen blacks won seats in Congress before Reconstruction was over.[17] Even in the 1880s, blacks sent one congressman from each of two states to the four Congresses convened in that decade. Black participation in Republican party affairs was also more extensive than would be seen in either political party until the 1960s. The temporary chairman of the 1884 Republican convention, John R. Lynch, a state legislator from Mississippi, was black. In 1892, 13 percent of the delegates to the national Republican convention were black—a record never again achieved.[18]

Still, there were warnings as early as 1872 that Republicans would eventually retreat from Reconstruction. "A revolt within the Republican ranks foreshadowed the end of Reconstruction. A group calling itself the Liberal Republicans bolted the party and nominated Horace Greeley, the well-known editor of the *New York Tribune,* for president . . . they often spoke of a more lenient policy toward the South."[19] Although the Liberal Republicans did not defeat Ulysses S. Grant, they presaged the southern strategy the Republicans would adopt from the 1870s onward. Their challenge reinforced Grant's concern with avoiding confrontation with white southerners. Grant used troops very sparingly thereafter and in 1875 refused a desperate request for troops from the governor of Mississippi.[20]

The death knell of Reconstruction sounded in the election of 1876. ". . . It was obvious to most political observers that the North was no longer willing to pursue the goals of Reconstruction. The results of a disputed presidential election confirmed this fact."[21] The presidential candidate Samuel J. Tilden, Democratic governor of New York, with

184 electoral votes, needed only one more electoral vote to defeat Republican Rutherford B. Hayes. Both parties disputed votes from Louisiana, South Carolina, and Florida, and one vote from Oregon was undecided due to a technicality. With no constitutional guidance for the resolution of such a situation, Congress appointed an electoral commission, which reached a compromise. Hayes was elected, and southern Democrats could look forward to sharing patronage and to the withdrawal of all federal troops from the South.

Of course, the outcome of this election did not stop some Republicans from trying to keep alive the promises of Reconstruction. Most notable was Henry Cabot Lodge, who introduced the Federal Election Bill of 1890. A conceptual predecessor of the 1965 Voting Rights Act, it would have placed federal officials on election boards in any district where a prescribed number of voters signed a petition requesting them.

> The officials would have been authorized to inspect and verify returns, pass upon qualifications of voters, and receive ballots refused by local officials. . . . The Republicans had a three-vote edge in the House and got the bill through narrowly. When it went to the Senate, opponents staged a thirty-three-day filibuster. . . . Ultimately, Democrats and free silver Republicans found enough tactical grounds in common. The Lodge Bill never came to a vote.[22]

POST-RECONSTRUCTION TO THE NEW DEAL

Turn-of-the-century politics reconstructed the early American state. According to Skowronek, the weak springs of the state apparatus before 1900 were traceable to the operational vitality of courts and parties; by 1920, a stronger central government had emerged from the state-building activities that attacked and weakened the political parties.[23]

American history between 1877 and 1920 has been variously described as a movement from social simplicity to complexity, or the destruction of the isolated, local community and the concomitant growth of cities and cosmopolitanism; as the triumph of conservatism; as the beginning bureaucratization of government that resulted from intellectual advisors' pushing scientific principles of management and attacking the party machine; and as a time when the administrative apparatus and legislatures became more accessible to pressure groups, in turn increasing the importance of interest-group politics.[24] During this time, citizens increasingly supported an independent national administrative apparatus, limiting the role of parties in handling the procedural dimension of government, and involvement in politics through direct primaries and referenda.

The Loss of Political Influence

Blacks, however, were not included in the broadening of direct participation in government. In the South, they were almost totally disfranchised. The Fifteenth Amendment prohibited states from denying the vote "on account of race, color, or previous condition of servitude," but southern state legislators found methods of excluding black voters. Mississippi led the way in 1890 when it instituted literacy tests that applied higher standards for blacks than for whites. In 1898, Louisiana enacted the first grandfather clause; registration dropped from some 130,000 in 1896 to 5,000 in 1900 and 1,700 in 1916. The number of localities or parishes in which blacks represented a majority of voters declined from twenty-six in 1896 to zero in 1900.[25] By the early 1900s, blacks had effectively lost the right to vote in every southern state except Tennessee.[26]

Northern blacks, generally denied access to elective office, had to form clientage relationships, usually with the Republican party, to have any political influence. Nor did the stronger central administration provide channels for black political involvement. In fact, black representation in the federal government was restricted to only a few appointive positions.[27]

Efforts at Independence: In Response to Exclusion

Political independence was a major theme in discussions among black leaders struggling to gain influence in post-Reconstruction national and local politics. Historians have documented the independent posture of numerous blacks who rose to prominence during and after Reconstruction. Among them was Edwin G. Walker, a former slave who became a member of the Massachusetts House of Representatives in 1866. Walker's watchword was "union among ourselves, division between the two political parties."[28]

At a convention held in Louisville, Kentucky, in 1883, leaders "assert[ed] the political independence of the Negro at a time when the Republican party was discarding the issues on which it had based its Reconstruction policies. The Democratic party, not yet dominated by the South, had made consequential inroads into northern state governments."[29] It seemed a propitious time to reappraise blacks' loyalty to the Republican party (in the South, Republicans were gaining support for a new "lily white" Republicanism). As Hamilton emphasizes, how-

ever, there were blacks who disapproved of the convention's advocacy
of independence, fearing it would alienate white Republican friends.[30]
In their attempts to gain access to electoral politics and to see their
grievances and needs addressed, blacks engaged in debates among
themselves concerning possible allies, how hard they should push to
get their needs addressed, the issues they should raise, and when they
should compromise. These debates hastened as the allegiance of blacks
to the Republican party waned and as they sought to use major, third,
and black parties to gain a voice in politics.

Blacks responded to the decreasing influence in several ways. In the
South, some argued that the solution to disfranchisement was migra-
tion to the North. A few advocated emigration. Two hundred South
Carolinian blacks left the United States for Liberia in 1878. The principal spokesman for emigration in the late nineteenth century was
Henry M. Turner, a bishop in the African Methodist Church and a
Georgia state legislator after the Civil War.[31] The most common response, however, was to try to gain an effective political voice in the
Republican party. As "lily white" Republicanism grew, southern
blacks formed Black and Tan Republican factions. These satellite
black political organizations attempted to operate as Republican organs at the local level and to gain recognition and acceptance by the
national Republican party.[32] Some Black and Tan factions survived
beyond the 1890s, like those in Texas and Louisiana counties, where
they existed until the 1920s, but most of them faded as disfranchisement brought black voting to a halt.

In the 1880s and 1890s, southern blacks also tried third parties,
specifically the People's party of the Populist movement, which grew
out of the Farmers' Alliances, a network of organizations that included
the Colored Farmers' Alliance of approximately one million members.[33] These rural blacks were active in the People's party in locales
where its leaders were committed to an interracial class-conscious
organization, but that goal was not realized in most areas because
racial prejudice overshadowed class bonds. Furthermore, the intense
competition between the Populists and the planter elite, who formed
the core of the white supremacist Democratic party, led both to conclude that it was "much better to have clear-cut constitutional disenfranchisement of the Negro and to leave the white group to fight elections out among themselves."[34]

At the turn of the century, northern blacks fared little better than
southern blacks in national politics. They were more successful, however, in participating in the major parties at the local level, usually
through a clientage relationship. Southern blacks had begun migrating

to northern cities, although the migration was small compared with the exodus from the South that would occur in the 1930s, '40s, and '50s. Nevertheless, the 10 percent of the black population living outside the South in 1900 were located primarily in urban areas (thirty-two cities had ten thousand or more blacks).[35] Their concentration was a political asset in local politics.

Even though their numbers were significant in many cities, the black migrants were treated differently from the European immigrants who had descended on these same northern cities earlier in the nineteenth century. Much of the European immigration had occurred when the urban, party machines were quite strong and were attempting to woo each new group to strengthen their competitive party position. In contrast, the large migration from the South occurred after the parties had been weakened. Furthermore, party elites were unwilling to challenge the racial status quo, and so blacks were excluded from decision-making and leadership roles in the parties. They were relegated to buffer organizations that the parties could take advantage of without being accountable to black voters or giving leaders an equitable share of patronage, services, and contracts.[36]

As for national politics, blacks in the North were increasingly shunned by the Republican party, owing to its candidates' preoccupation with the South. The Republican party treated black Republicans as expendable, since a relatively small number of blacks lived in the North, and southern blacks generally could not vote. Holden concludes that after 1900 and for more or less the first third of the century, "Presidents and Congresses were in agreement in accepting racial stratification, whether as preference or merely as fact. The white Southern victory was virtually total, and government was conducted as if the prior Afro-American participation was to be wiped from institutional memory."[37]

Growing Disaffection with the Republican Party

Blacks became more and more alienated from the national Republican party. Although Theodore Roosevelt at first seemed to be responsive to blacks, relying on Booker T. Washington's advice and appointing some blacks to federal office during his first term, in his second term he alienated many blacks when he summarily discharged three companies of black infantrymen who had refused to inform on fellow soldiers accused of shooting up the town of Brownsville, Texas. "All denied complicity. Roosevelt ordered the men—including at least one Medal of Honor holder—discharged without honor, an action that predictably engendered much anger in Black communities across the country."[38] Later, when Roosevelt ran for president on the Progressive party ticket, he cultivated a "lily white" constituency in the South. Disenchantment with him was complete when his Progressive party refused seats to blacks at its national convention and would not even consider an equal rights plank drafted by W. E. B. Du Bois.[39]

Although the Republican southern strategy had proved completely unable to win over white southern Democrats, both Roosevelt and William Howard Taft paid special attention to the sensitivities of the white South. Weiss notes that Taft's policy of not appointing to federal office people whom local communities found objectionable was particularly offensive to blacks.[40] This policy essentially excluded blacks from federal posts in the South. His inattention to problems of segregation, discrimination, disfranchisement, and racial violence also troubled blacks.

In 1912, this negligence on the part of the Republican administrations led some blacks to support Woodrow Wilson. This was the first election in which blacks indicated any substantial interest in the national Democratic party. *Crisis*, edited by Du Bois, endorsed Wilson, largely as a choice of desperation and with many misgivings:

> The Republican party emphasizes its past relations with the Negro, the recent appointments to office, and warns against the disfranchisement and caste system of the Democratic South. The weak point in this argument is that without the consent of the Republican Supreme Court, Southern disfranchisement could not survive a single day. The Progressive party stresses its platform of social reform, so admirable in many respects, and points to the recognition given in its party councils to the Northern Negro voter. The weak point here is the silence over the fact that Theodore Roosevelt, the perpetrator of the Brownsville outrage, has added to that blunder the Chicago disfranchisement and is appealing to the South for white votes on this platform . . . even in the face of promises disconcertingly vague, and in the face of the solid caste-ridden South, it is better to elect Woodrow Wilson President of the United States and prove once for all if the Democratic party dares to be Democratic when it comes to black men. It has proven that it can be in many Northern states and cities. Can it be in the nation? We hope so and we are willing to risk a trial.[41]

The hope was not realized. In the Wilson administration, patronage to blacks was meager, and segregation in federal departments, which began during the Roosevelt years, spread greatly.[42] The volume of anti-black legislation during the first Wilson Congress was greater than during any other session in congressional annals. "No less than twenty bills were proposed that would segregate Negroes on public carriers in the District of Columbia, exclude them from commissions in the army and navy, and set up segregated accommodations for white and Negro federal employees."[43] Moreover, in some cases presidential action rendered legislation unnecessary. Shortly after his inauguration, Wilson ordered segregation in the Department of Treasury and the Post Office. Later he extended the prohibition to race mixing in work areas, toilet facilities, and food services.[44] Commenting on Wilson's racism in 1913, Booker T. Washington wrote, "I have never seen the colored people so discouraged and bitter as they are at the present time."[45] Blacks who supported Wilson "deceived themselves and were . . . utterly disappointed. Wilson was the Southern president of a Southern party. Racial stratification had become so normal that Harding, Coolidge and Hoover had little about which even to think."[46]

Despite blacks' disillusionment with the Republicans and their disappointment with the first limited turn toward the Democrats, few supported a third party during the second period of third-party strength (1904–1924.)[47] They rejected not only Roosevelt's Progressive party but Robert La Follette's Progressive party as well. In 1924, most blacks supported the Republican candidate, Calvin Coolidge, and had a visible role in his campaign. Black women united to form the National League of Republican Colored Women in an effort to mobilize black women voters in support of Coolidge after female suffrage was instituted. Brooks details the generally positive responses to this mobilization on the part of both the Women's Division of the National Republican Committee and the state Republican organizations, except in the South.[48] Nonetheless, not all black leaders supported Coolidge; several began to emphasize the importance of independence and of having parties compete for the black vote. Writing in *The Messenger*, A. Philip Randolph endorsed La Follette in 1924 for just that reason:

> What is the significance of the La Follette–Progressive Movement to the Negro? The paramount value lies in the fact that it puts another political party in the field to compete for Negroes' votes. This enables the Negro to bargain more effectively . . . the rise of the strong third party makes both old parties less secure and sure of themselves. Hence, they begin to make bids to any and every group of citizens that have votes in order to retain those followers they have and to get back those that have left.[49]

The theme of independence was even more prominent in the election of 1928, when Alfred E. Smith, a Democrat opposed by the anti-Catholic and anti-wet Democratic South, ran against the Republican

Herbert Hoover. Even before Smith's nomination, his supporters had planned a campaign to gain black voters. They approached Walter White, head of the NAACP, for campaign help. White argued that by breaking away from the Republican party, blacks would strike a blow against party dependency. Independence was all the more important, he reasoned, when a Democratic victory could be no worse than a Republican one. Democrats gave blacks little reason for support, however, when Smith chose a senator from Arkansas, Joseph T. Robinson, as his running mate. Furthermore, their convention had no black delegates, and the party platform failed to address the concerns of blacks.[50]

Despite the Democrats' failure to be more responsive to black voters, it has been estimated that in the predominantly black precincts of Harlem and Chicago Smith won 28 percent of the black vote, up from 3 percent for the Democratic candidate in 1920 and 11 percent in 1924. This was clear evidence of growing disillusionment with the Republican party.[51] During the 1928 campaign, Hoover was so determined to win white southern votes that he tolerated racial invective in the campaign. Black leaders, including nine officials of national black organizations, three bishops of black churches, four public officials, four college presidents, and two editors, spoke out harshly against the racist campaign strategies of Hoover's friends.[52]

Hoover had further widened the breach by 1932 with the appointments or attempted appointments of his first term. Blacks especially resented the successful appointment of William N. Doak, head of a trade union that explicitly excluded blacks, to the post of Secretary of Labor, and the unsuccessful appointment of John J. Parker, a North Carolinian who had opposed suffrage rights for blacks, to the position of Justice of the Supreme Court.[53] Black leaders complained that Hoover ignored racial violence and disfranchisement, had a mediocre record on black appointments, and acted in ways that blacks interpreted as deliberately insulting—for example, allowing the War Department to send black mothers and white mothers on separate ships to visit the graves of their sons buried in Europe.[54]

Thus while arguments for independence had been common throughout the post-Reconstruction period, they gained special currency in 1932 because of the Depression and Hoover's racial record. Blacks had good reason to reevaluate their Republican alliance. Many were ready to support Franklin Roosevelt.

Non-electoral Action

Before moving on to a discussion of the New Deal, note should be made of other organized efforts by blacks to gain political influence and protest their economic subordination and physical harassment. Two important pressure groups came on the political scene in the late nineteenth century, the National Afro-American League, formed in 1890, and the Equal Rights League, formed in 1894. Separate black parties were also formed in some states: the Coloured Independent party of Pennsylvania in 1883, the Negro Protection party of Ohio in 1897, and the National Liberty party in 1904.[55] Hamilton contends that the post-Reconstruction period was particularly consequential for the process of racial consolidation, since "communal bonds among blacks in politically and economically vulnerable communities had to be forged if many people were to survive."[56] These solidarity organizations and black parties protested disfranchisement, lynching, mob violence, and discrimination.

Yet with black participation in the Populist movement increasing and with Booker T. Washington's philosophy promoting self-help institutions for blacks, black pressure-group agitation designed to gain the vote and to achieve a role in the electoral system waned, at least until the Niagara movement, formed in 1905, led to the creation of the NAACP in 1909. The early efforts at organizational coordination, seen in the Negro Convention movement, resurfaced in 1924 with the Great Sanhedrin, an elite council called by Dean Kelly Miller of Howard University to achieve unity among black organizations.

This period also saw the reemergence of emigrationist and separatist movements. In fact, more black Americans, mostly from poor and working class communities, were attracted to Marcus Garvey's United Negro Improvement Association (UNIA) in the early 1920s than to any other nationalist organization in black political history. The aims of UNIA, an example of Pan-Africanism, were similar to those of earlier emigration movements, except that UNIA also stressed connections among all peoples of African descent and the importance of liaisons among nationalist organizations in the Caribbean, the United States, and Canada.

Several political and economic factors fostered responsiveness to Garvey's appeals to "give the blood you have shed for the white man to make Africa a republic for the Negro."[57] Marable stresses the high level of post–World War I conservatism and violence against blacks, the mushrooming of the Ku Klux Klan, the failure of political organizations like the NAACP to obtain significant economic and political gains for blacks during a period of national economic expansion and prosperity, and the rejection of the political aspirations of blacks by both parties.[58] Garvey's achievement was short-lived, however. Leaders of most black political organizations denounced Garvey's rhetoric as racist and fascist and UNIA's business ventures as gigantic swindles. After Garvey's imprisonment in 1925 and his deportation to Jamaica in 1927, UNIA rapidly fell apart—another testament to the dominance of the political goal of incorporation.[59]

Summary

The history of blacks' relationship to electoral and party politics during this period is characterized by rebuff. Blacks persistently tried to participate in the electoral system through the Republican party. They were shunned and rebuffed. They searched for ways to make the party respond. They formed separate black factions within the party, turned to Populism until it, too, proved inhospitable, and began to support Democratic candidates. But they found no strategy that gave them significant political influence. It is not a story of unswerving loyalty to the Republicans but one of growing disillusionment with the party that, since the days of the early Federalists and on through the Whigs, had been the most sensitive to black concerns.[60] It is not only that blacks lost a role in the Republican party, but that the threat of disfranchisement, which had plagued their relationship to party politics from its beginning, became a hard political reality.

Thus at the very time in American political history when the opportunities provided by referenda and direct primaries brought most citizens greater involvement in governance, blacks' opportunities for political participation and influence were severely diminished. Disfranchisement destroyed the ability of blacks to use a balance-of-power strategy at the local level to bargain with competing segments of the white electorate for political and economic gains and fostered violence against blacks who could no longer threaten electoral reprisal. Since 90 percent of the black population lived in the South, disfranchisement rendered the small, northern black vote easily expendable as northern Republican industrialists increasingly saw their interests aligned with the anti-black agriculturalists of the Democratic South.[61]

It was not disfranchisement alone that rendered blacks politically powerless. McAdam argues that their decline in national influence was quite as much the product of party affiliation, sectional political alignments, and population distribution.[62] Identified with the Republican party, blacks could exert little political leverage in the Democratic South, where they were overwhelmingly concentrated. And in the North, their votes carried so little weight that voting Democratic could not have persuaded white Democrats to pressure the party for changes in racial policy. Furthermore, nationwide party competition had decreased dramatically between 1896, when thirty-six states had a competitive two-party system, and 1903, when there were only six.

Thus, McAdam notes, for the extended period from 1896 to 1928 "the geographical alignment of political loyalties, coupled with disenfranchisement, destroyed whatever chance blacks might have had of mobilizing any semblance of national electoral leverage."[63]

Yet another difference between the political experience of blacks and that of other Americans was consequential in this period. As the central state apparatus grew, opportunities for political influence through federal appointments increased but remained largely unavailable to blacks. Legislation honoring local authority over the appointments of federal bureaucrats in regional agencies effectively blocked the appointment of blacks in the South.

Finally, the federal government's policy of noninvolvement in racial matters during this period was replaced by aggressive anti-black legislative and executive action. McAdam concludes that "cumulatively, the evidence is impressive. In less than 40 years the federal government had been transformed from an advocate of black equality to a force buttressing the southern racial status quo."[64]

THE NEW DEAL TO THE 1960S

The changes that characterized the Progressive era—the growth of bureaucracy, the withering of party machines, and the lifting of judicial restriction on state action—accelerated during the New Deal years. Skowronek describes the sealing of the fate of the courts and parties during this period:

> The second round of the 20th century state-building left the courts to search for a new domain in which to exercise judicial creativity. It left party government to degenerate as a remnant of an earlier state of things. . . . The major constructive contribution of the New Deal to the operations of the new American state lay in the sheer expansion of bureaucratic services and supports. Pushing courts and party organizations further out of the center of government operations, the New Deal turned bureaucracy itself into the extraconstitutional machine so necessary for the continuous operation of the constitutional system. Like party patronage in the old order, bureaucratic goods and services came to provide the fuel and the cement of the new institutional politics.[65]

Black participation and influence in the Democratic party thus began to increase at a time when parties became much less critical in governance. Blacks faced the same political question—How could their participation in electoral politics make the government respond to their needs? Kept from an active role when parties were crucial to government operations, blacks entered a new phase of electoral participation and allegiance to a new party at a time when institutional politics were less dependent on party machinery.

Although this disjunction in timing put blacks at a political disadvantage, other economic and political factors enhanced their political significance. As the Depression ended the dominant role of cotton in the South's economy, the structure of blacks' political opportunities changed. McAdam explains how the demise of "King Cotton" improved political prospects for blacks.[66] First, the demand for black labor increased in the North at the same time that the economic basis of the powerful alliance between northern industrialists and southern planters—which had precluded change in the racial status quo for many years—was undermined. Second, black insurgency became more feasible as the need of planters to control the cotton economy's labor pool decreased and the risks associated with protest were somewhat reduced. Third, the collapse of cotton tenancy in the South triggered a massive migration from countryside to city that enabled blacks to organize a stronger base for political action. Fourth, along with labor demands in the North, three other factors—legislation restricting immigration, two world wars, and the changed economy of the South—combined to send large numbers of blacks north and west. Moreover, as McAdam shows, the particular pattern of that migration had political consequences. Blacks moved especially *from* states where their political participation was most restricted (Mississippi, Alabama, South Carolina, and Georgia) *to* seven key northern and western industrial states that were the most influential in presidential elections (New York, New Jersey, Pennsylvania, Ohio, Michigan, Illinois, and California). This migration greatly enlarged the electoral importance of blacks. Fifth and, for the moment, finally, the federal government began to reverse its discriminatory policies, thus creating a place for blacks in the central governing apparatus that was becoming increasingly powerful in American politics. In the late 1930s, the Supreme Court invalidated many of its narrow interpretations of the constitutional safeguards provided by the Fourteenth and Fifteenth Amendments. Of the decisions handed down before 1931, only 43 percent supported civil rights for blacks; the comparable figure for 1931–1955 was 91 percent.[67] In due course, presidential action also became more responsive to blacks' concerns.

Roosevelt and the New Deal: Black Leaders Ambivalent; The Electorate Supportive

The treatment of blacks by the New Deal and the responses of blacks to Franklin Roosevelt and the Democratic party were complicated matters. During Roosevelt's first two terms, blacks were not assured that he would act on racial issues of concern to them, especially when his action would alienate southern Democrats whose support he needed to achieve his economic aims. Anti-lynching proposals are an example. Pressure began mounting to do something about lynching in 1935, when northern Democrats joined Republican sponsors of anti-lynching bills. Holden analyzes the new support among northern Democrats as an effort primarily to heighten public consciousness. They knew that their party leader, the president, was determined not to take a favorable position on the legislation. Walter White of the NAACP was turned down flat when he asked for Roosevelt's help on the anti-lynching legislation. "The President was express in his rationale that he could not let his economic program become hostage."[68] When Roosevelt was asked to send a courtesy message to the 1937 convention of the National Urban League, negotiations took place to ensure that the message contained no reference to lynching.[69]

Eventually people within the administration who were committed to government being used to help blacks won a more open stance on racial issues. Roosevelt began to respond to such cabinet members and agency heads as Harold Ickes and Aubry Williams and to his wife, Eleanor, these being the most concerned with racial matters among the New Dealers. Unique in United States history was the presence within the administration of a Black Cabinet, a group of black bureaucrats in federal agencies who advised agency heads and the White House on racial matters. Never before had there been so many black advisers to the White House or so many highly trained professionals in high-level government jobs. This group included William H. Hastie and Robert C. Weaver, both of whom had advanced degrees from Harvard and served in the Department of the Interior; Mary McLeod Bethune, president of what became Bethune-Cookman College and director of the Division of Negro Affairs of the National Youth Administration; Lawrence A. Oxley, a social worker who served in both the Departments of Commerce and Labor; Eugene Kinckle Jones, executive secretary of the National Urban League; and Ralph Bunche, Ira De A. Reid, Abram H. Harris, and Layford Logan, social scientists who acted as government consultants.[70] Whatever their actual influence on the administration, their appointments had important symbolic meaning to the black electorate. The Black Cabinet stood, according to Holden, as a critical "break with previous Administrations, the hallmark of which was their regard for the untouchability of race."[71]

In the election of 1936, however, black leaders were not without misgivings about Roosevelt. Emmett J. Scott, the secretary of Howard

University, urged blacks to vote for Roosevelt but noted in an *Opportunity* editorial that

> it is not to be overlooked, however, that while the Democratic administration has provided this large number of representative positions for Negroes, it has stood by and permitted the most outrageous discriminations. Under its Bankhead Cotton Control Bill, the AAA, and in the dispensation of relief, colored people, that is, the masses, have been held to the lowest levels and have been treated in many communities as groups entitled to but scant consideration.[72]

Instead of benefiting black tenant farmers and sharecroppers, the Agricultural Adjustment Administration (AAA) had forced many off their land.[73] So, too, an editorial in *Crisis* just before the November election concluded that "no matter who wins in November, [the] most vexing problems will still face the colored people. For that reason it is well not to get too partisan for Mr. Roosevelt and Mr. Landon so that we will have energy and a measure of unity in tackling the post-election tasks."[74]

Whatever the advice of such leaders, practically all blacks who could vote had shifted allegiance from the Republican to the Democratic party in 1936 for Roosevelt's second election. Since official voting records are not kept by race, historical studies usually estimate the candidate preference of blacks on the basis of the vote in predominantly black precincts. Using that procedure for eight northern and border cities with large black populations, Weiss found increases between the 1932 and the 1936 elections in favor of Roosevelt: 138 percent in Philadelphia, 84 percent in Harlem, 96 percent in Chicago, 233 percent in Cleveland, 83 percent in Pittsburgh, 124 percent in Cincinnati, 119 percent in Detroit, and 67 percent in Knoxville.[75]

Numerous explanations have been given for this dramatic shift after the first Roosevelt administration. Reflecting the importance that blacks attribute to an activist government, Kelly Miller, writing in the *Pittsburgh Courier* in 1936, emphasized that the changed position of the major parties on centralist and states' power were critical in the candidate preference of blacks. "Today, the Republican party has shifted its position from the advocacy of a strong Federal Government to that of defender of States Rights, unmindful of the incidental sacrifice of the Negro by the exchange. The exchange of positions of the two great parties on the issue of Federal authority versus State sovereignty" is the basis of the black electorate's support for Roosevelt and the Democratic party.[76]

Present-day political analysts disagree, however, about the specific role of the New Deal record on race in the conversion of blacks to the

Democratic party.[77] Sitkoff believes that the positive racial record of the first Roosevelt administration did affect that change, while others argue that blacks supported Roosevelt *despite* the fact that some New Deal agencies and programs functioned in ways that were hostile to blacks. Among those that are faulted, in addition to the AAA, are the Federal Housing Administration, which refused to guarantee mortgages on houses purchased by blacks in white neighborhoods; the United States Housing Authority, which financed segregated housing projects; and the Civilian Conservation Corps, which was racially segregated, as was much of the Tennessee Valley Authority, which "constructed all-white towns, handed out skilled jobs to whites first, and segregated its labor crews."[78] Also, the bulk of the unskilled and service jobs that blacks filled—as waiters, cooks, hospital orderlies, janitors, farm workers, and domestics—were excluded from Social Security coverage and from minimum-wage provisions of the Fair Labor Standards Act of 1938.

Weiss concludes that the conversion of blacks to the Democratic party occurred despite their not receiving a fair share of New Deal benefits, largely because they did receive some share. John Dancy, director of the Detroit Urban League in the 1930s, provides a case in point. Dancy was a man with conservative views who before 1936 had been opposed to federal action. He had always voted Republican. He shifted to the Democratic party, however, because he saw blacks in Detroit being helped by relief programs as the Depression worsened.[79]

The Roosevelt of the last two terms was considered a friend of the race by many blacks. Nonetheless, his limited support for their racial interests was reluctant, won primarily when blacks brought pressure. They increasingly undertook direct action as a means of exerting political influence. Sometimes blacks joined with whites in class-based political activity, as for example when they formed the Southern Tenant Farmers' Union. More often they joined with other blacks in Don't Buy Where You Can't Work campaigns, in demonstrations for Jobs for Negroes, and in forming tenants' unions to fight high rents. The most dramatic of these protest actions is represented by a proposal made in 1941 by A. Philip Randolph, president of the Brotherhood of Sleeping Car Porters, for a March on Washington to demand access to jobs in the defense industry. People of influence within the administration, including Mrs. Roosevelt, tried to convince Randolph to call off the march. Randolph refused, and Roosevelt himself responded to the pressure by negotiating a cancellation of the march in return for issuing an executive order (Number 8802) establishing the Fair Employment Practices Committee.

Throughout Roosevelt's tenure, black leaders were divided: many supported him; some urged independence and nonpartisanship; and others backed Republican candidates. In 1944, two prominent black organizations, the Chicago Citizen's Committee of 1,000 and the National Negro Council, opposed Roosevelt's race for a fourth term.[80] But in spite of such exhortations for independence and party competition, the black electorate was strongly behind Roosevelt: in every city Weiss examined (except Chicago), two-thirds or more voted for Roosevelt in 1940, as they had in 1936.[81] And in 1944, blacks provided the key margin of victory for Roosevelt in Pennsylvania, Maryland, Michigan, Missouri, New York, Illinois, and New Jersey.[82] South Carolinian blacks were so eager to support Roosevelt in 1944 that they formed a black party for that purpose. The South Carolina Progressive Democratic party emerged from a statewide organization (the Negro Citizens' Committee) that had been challenging the legality of wholly white primaries since the mid-1930s. Since South Carolina had a one-party system, this law proscribing white primaries in effect disfranchised the few blacks who managed to register. Determined to vote for Roosevelt, these activists established a satellite party, held a party convention, elected state and national delegations, adopted a constitution, and sent twenty-one delegates to the 1944 Democratic National Convention.[83]

The Black Electorate and the Post-war Democratic Party: Unstable Loyalty

There was genuine competition for the black vote in the 1948 election. Blacks had improved their economic status during the war years. They had gathered political strength from NAACP legal victories in *Smith* v. *Allwright* (1944), a decision by the Supreme Court outlawing the whites-only primaries held by the Democratic party in some southern states, and in *Morgan* v. *Virginia* (1946), a Supreme Court decision declaring segregation in interstate bus transportation unconstitutional, as well as from the willingness of the Justice Department in 1947 to submit friend-of-the-court briefs on behalf of the Civil Rights movement. Social attitudes had changed somewhat as the nation dismantled the machinery of a war effort aimed at destroying Nazism and the racism it represented. The Cold War also benefited blacks, since the Soviet Union pointed to human rights problems in the United States.[84]

Harry S Truman knew he would need black support in urban-industrial states like California, Illinois, Michigan, Ohio, Pennsylvania, and New York. Some Republicans also cultivated the black vote.

The Republican presidential candidate, Thomas E. Dewey, as governor of New York, had pushed successfully for a fair employment commission and had won large margins in Democratic Harlem in his 1942 and 1946 races.[85] Henry Wallace, who ran on the independent Progressive party ticket, argued for racial desegregation and seemed to be making significant inroads in his bid for black votes until Truman, persuaded that he had to preempt the civil rights issue, took actions that eventually won black support. Truman appointed a committee on civil rights, which submitted its report, *To Secure These Rights,* in early 1948. The report recommended federal anti-lynching, anti-segregation, anti-brutality, and anti-poll tax laws. It also called for laws guaranteeing voting rights and equal employment opportunity and for the establishment of a permanent commission on civil rights and a civil rights division of the Justice Department. Truman's own civil rights proposals, submitted in a special message to Congress in February 1948, were less far-reaching than the committee's recommendations.[86] But they were controversial enough. "Some Southerners told Truman that with such a civil rights program, 'You won't be elected dog catcher in 1948.' "[87] Truman did not push for enactment of his proposals, no action was taken, and the civil rights fight erupted at the Democratic National Convention.

The controversy surfaced over what the party's platform should say about civil rights. The platform committee, dominated by the Democratic leadership of the Senate, merely called for Congress to work for protection of equal rights. The southern Democrats presented a minority plank demanding that Truman's proposals be rejected and states' rights be upheld. The northern liberal minority called for the convention to support the rights of equal political participation, equal employment opportunity, and equal treatment in the service and defense of the nation. The liberals won with the help of big-city bosses, who argued that "we've got to stir up the interest of the minority groups in this election; otherwise we're dead."[88] The story is well-known. Many southern Democrats bolted the convention, formed the Dixiecrat party, and won control of the Democratic party in four southern states.

Truman's surprise victory in 1948 is attributed to many factors, among them economic prosperity; peace; his appearance of moderation between Wallace on the left and the Dixiecrats on the right; the presence on the ticket of formidable Democrats, such as Adlai E. Stevenson and Hubert H. Humphrey, who were running for office that year; the critical farm vote; and the survival of the New Deal coalition of the big cities, blacks, and labor. In three key states (Ohio, Illinois, and California), black support was influential in Truman's victory.[89]

In the 1950s, the loyalty of blacks to the Democratic party, built up during the New Deal and solidified in the 1948 election, proved unstable. Some southern blacks voted for Dwight Eisenhower to protest the Dixiecrat influence in the Democratic party in the South. Legal victories for blacks under the first Eisenhower administration led to further turning from the Democratic to the Republican party. It was President Eisenhower who in 1953 appointed Earl Warren, Republican governor of California, Chief Justice of the Supreme Court. The liberal and activist course of the Warren Court with respect to minority group rights was quite apparent by the time of the 1956 presidential election.

In 1954, in the landmark case of *Brown* v. *Board of Education of Topeka* the court unanimously decided that racial segregation in public schools violates the Fourteenth Amendment. In 1955, the court empowered federal district courts to supervise state and local authorities to see that school desegregation was achieved with "all deliberate speed." President Eisenhower himself did relatively little in the civil rights arena;[90] but through his appointment of the Republican Warren as Chief Justice, he was perceived by blacks as responsive to their concerns (especially in the South, where the court decision struck a blow against legally enforced separation of the races). The later black vote reflected these widespread feelings. Support for Eisenhower rose from 20 percent in 1952 to 38 percent in 1956, in particular as a result of the southern black vote. According to an NAACP survey cited by Henderson,[91] the black vote for Eisenhower increased 37 points in twenty-three southern cities, but only 10 points in forty non-southern cities.

Separate black parties were not a significant political phenomenon, nor were separatist movements, in the period from the New Deal through the 1950s.[92] Bracey notes that the "proliferation of nationalist movements and ideologies in the 1920s was followed by a period in which nationalism as a significant theme in black thought was at a low ebb." Except for the religious nationalism that flowered in Father Divine's Peace Mission movement, Noble Drew Ali's Moorish Science Temple of America, and Elijah Muhammad's Nation of Islam, and except for the economic nationalism that was expressed in Don't Buy Where You Can't Work campaigns, "black nationalism was clearly on the defensive during the Depression."[93]

Protest and Pressure

Important developments did take place in protest and pressure-group politics during the 1950s. As we have seen, the political and demographic results of the demise of "King Cotton" affected both electoral results and protest politics. Morris details the precursors of the famous 1960 Greensboro sit-in, organizational bases of these developments, such as the movement of blacks from rural to urban areas in the South, and the lessening of constraints on black insurgency due to the white agriculturalists' weakened control of the black labor force:

> During the mid-fifties the extensive internal organization of the Civil Rights movement began to crystalize in communities in the South. During this period "direct action" organizations were being built by local activists. Community institutions—especially the black church—were becoming political. The "mass meeting" with political oratory and protest music became institutionalized. During the same period, CORE (Congress of Racial Equality) entered the South with intentions of initiating protest, and NAACP Youth Councils were reorganized by young militant adults who desired to engage in confrontational politics.[94]

As Morris emphasizes, the great migration of blacks to the cities produced many new black churches. These urban black churches were much larger, better financed, and led by better-educated ministers than the rural churches. They became, in Morris's words, "local movement centers." These centers coordinated local individual and group activities, perfected strategies of confrontation, led marches, organized voter drives, radicalized members of the community, and built on the personal and organizational networks of the activists. Since the centers were already in place, they provided the needed internal organization through which information could be rapidly passed to groups preparing for direct political action, as with the sit-ins and other protest activities of the 1960s. The organizational developments in the 1950s provided a critical, though unheralded, foundation for the Civil Rights movement. The Montgomery Improvement Association, formed to carry out the bus boycotts in December 1955 is the most widely known of this type of organization. But many others were making connections with civil rights groups in the 1950s. The movement centers, civil rights organizations, and students from black colleges found themselves part of a regional organization when the Southern Christian Leadership Conference (SCLC) was formed in 1957 by activist clergymen from across the South.

Summary

Four facts concerning black national electoral politics between the New Deal and the 1960s are especially prominent. First, the black vote became significant as the size of the northern black community increased in the 1930s and, especially, in the two decades thereafter. In 1936, blacks gained more attention than ever before from the two major parties. Weiss points out that although neither party's platform included a civil rights plank, there were clear, positive signs of new responsiveness to the potential importance of the black vote.[95] The Democratic party repealed the two-thirds rule for nomination of the presidential candidate, thereby reducing the influence of the South. They seated ten black delegates and twenty-two alternates from twelve states at the 1936 convention. The national committees of both parties went on to provide resources for "colored divisions" to organize the campaign among blacks.

Second, blacks' allegiance to the Democratic party created by the New Deal marked the beginning of a new phase of one-party dependency. Black leaders argued against this new dependency, but, once again, the leadership exhibited more diverse viewpoints on electoral strategies than was apparent from the majority vote for one party.

Third, although this majority reached 78 percent by 1952, the period did not end with unswerving loyalty to the Democratic party. A significant minority voted the Republican ticket as Republicans associated with the Eisenhower administration proved responsive to minority rights.

Fourth, organizational and political resources among blacks developing in the South would galvanize the protest politics of the Civil Rights and Black Nationalist movements and relate these to electoral politics in the 1960s and 1970s.

THE 1960S

During Eisenhower's second term, blacks witnessed numerous examples of inaction on civil rights issues. Garrow details the significant events that changed the opinions of blacks and brought defectors back to the Democratic party for the 1960 election.[96] The first civil rights act since Reconstruction, which had been passed in September 1957, was neither quickly nor fully implemented. Little was done about its provisions for creating a civil rights commission and permitting the Justice Department to file suits against southern registrars who discriminated against blacks. The president paid little attention to the appeals of black leaders that he make a strong statement insisting on compliance with federal law in the Little Rock school crisis. It was a federal district judge, not the president, who finally demanded obedience to federal authority in school desegregation. As resistance to the court's 1954 desegregation order grew in the South, Eisenhower pronounced his decision of appointing Warren the Chief Justice

> "the biggest damn fool mistake I ever made." The president had hoped to avoid a confrontation over desegregation, for he tended to side with white southerners. Indeed, he had approached the chief justice at a White House dinner while the Court was considering the *Brown* case. Referring to the white South, Eisenhower had said, "These are not bad people. All they are concerned about is to see that their sweet little girls are not required to sit in school alongside some big over-grown Negroes." . . . In the absence of a clear public commitment by the president, [Governor] Faubus doubtless believed he could ignore the Court.[97]

Eventually, when there was no recourse, Eisenhower did federalize the guard and dispatch paratroopers to Little Rock to quell the white resistance to school desegregation. Even then he did not respond to repeated requests for a meeting with black leaders. Indeed, during his first five years as president Eisenhower never invited black leaders to the White House to discuss race relations. When a meeting was finally held in June 1958, those who attended (Martin Luther King, Jr., A. Philip Randolph, Roy Wilkins, and Lester Granger) expressed disappointment at the president's noncommittal response to their requests. They asked Eisenhower to make a public statement saying that federal law on school desegregation would be enforced, to call a White House conference on peaceful desegregation, to support stronger civil rights laws, to order the Justice Department to take a more active role in combating voting discrimination, and to extend the only temporarily established Civil Rights Commission.[98]

The reactions of Martin Luther King, Jr., illustrate the ambivalence of blacks toward the candidates in the upcoming 1960 presidential election. King repeatedly denounced President Eisenhower and the executive branch for apathy and silence on racial matters. King felt better about Richard Nixon. Nixon had met with King in 1957 and two years later invited him to speak at a conference on employment discrimination. King went on to meet twice with John F. Kennedy during the early part of the campaign. With misgivings about the extent of Kennedy's understanding of civil rights issues, King thought neither candidate better than the other and urged blacks to recognize that they were not bound to either party. Later in the campaign, when Kennedy telephoned Coretta Scott King to express concern over her husband's imprisonment in a Georgia state prison, the King family's ambivalence about Kennedy lessened. Without actually endorsing him, King expressed personal appreciation for Kennedy's expression of concern.[99]

Solid Support for Democratic Presidential Candidates

As it turned out, nearly all of the 1956 defectors to the Republican ticket returned to the Democratic fold, with the black vote contributing substantially to Kennedy's small margin of 110,000 votes over Nixon. The "pivotal role of the black vote in the 1960 presidential election elated civil rights leaders and notified political strategists that black votes were no longer of minor political significance."[100]

Analysts attribute the support of black voters for Kennedy to the candidate's responsiveness to the King family and to his promise to sign an executive order forbidding segregation in federally subsidized housing. But despite the importance of the black vote to his victory, Kennedy was slow to act in behalf of blacks. The actions he took were forced on him by the momentum and the course of the Civil Rights movement. In September 1962, with violence erupting, he ordered United States marshals to protect James Meredith, the first black student admitted to the University of Mississippi. The following summer, with Alabama Governor George Wallace in defiance of federal authority, federal officials under court order forced the desegregation of the University of Alabama. In June 1963, Kennedy finally requested legislation to outlaw segregation in public accommodations. Not discounting the significance of these actions, Holden questions why blacks were so favorable to Kennedy, given his lack of vigor in the civil rights arena.

> It is rather remarkable that John F. Kennedy's presidency should have yielded him such strong symbolic dividends in the Afro-American political community. There was, of course, a broad public perception of a moral-psychological crisis associated with race. If there were such a crisis, however, it was one with which John Kennedy was very reluctant to entangle himself. He was perhaps more cautious than anyone except FDR and he was reluctant to act administratively. The housing order was long delayed. . . . The ultimate reality was that Kennedy, with his remarkable political caution and his strong sense of exposure to Southern pressure in Congress, deemed himself obligated to act in ways that were equivalent to a posture of a stand-still.[101]

In Lyndon Johnson blacks finally had a president firmly committed to civil rights. He made it his top priority. He told a joint session of Congress five days after Kennedy's assassination that "no memorial oration or eulogy could more eloquently honor President Kennedy's memory than the earliest passage of the civil rights bill."[102] Within months Johnson signed into law the Civil Rights Act of 1964. This act outlawed segregation in public accommodations and job discrimination against blacks and women, authorized the government to withhold funds from public agencies that discriminated on the basis of race, and gave the attorney general power to guarantee voting rights and to end school segregation. The Voting Rights Act was passed the following year, and, as we shall see, has had an enormous effect in reducing political inequality and enlarging the size of the registered and voting sector of the black population. Blacks gave Johnson nearly 100 percent of their votes in 1964.[103]

Pressure on the Democrats: Satellite and Separate Parties

Throughout the 1960s, voter-education and voter-registration organizations and satellite political parties that emerged from these organizations were an important feature of black electoral politics. The Mississippi Freedom Democratic party (MFDP) and the National Democratic Party of Alabama (NDPA) illustrate how satellite parties function when the participation of blacks in the major parties is restricted. In both cases, these organizations worked to gain acceptance from the national Democratic party by showing that the regular state party was not representative of all the people in the state and therefore not committed to democratic procedures.

The MFDP grew out of the Council of Federated Organizations (COFO), a political organization that was formed in the early 1960s to coordinate and unify the voter-education and registration activities of all national, state, and local organizations—the Congress of Racial Equality (CORE), the SCLC, the Student Non-Violent Coordinating Committee (SNCC), and the NAACP.[104] In 1963, COFO held a statewide mock election. They ran Aaron Henry, state chairman of the NAACP, and Edwin King, chaplain at Mississippi's Tougaloo College, to demonstrate, as a technique for mobilizing registration, that blacks would vote in large numbers if allowed to register. Approximately ninety thousand blacks took part in the election. Robert Moses, the SNCC field secretary in Mississippi, then made a strong case for a political party not only to strengthen registration but to translate registration into meaningful political action in cases where state regulars of the Democratic party excluded blacks and resisted their enfranchisement.

The new party held its first freedom vote in June 1964, electing delegates to the Democratic National Convention in Atlantic City. Their challenge to unseat the state regulars failed, and this failure was a critical factor in the growth of sentiments favoring what came to be called Black Power. Many members of the MFDP became convinced by the response of the convention's Credentials Committee that the interests of blacks would always be denied by white liberals. Four years later, however, a second challenge at the 1968 Chicago convention was successful. This later challenge was mounted not by the MFDP alone but by a coalition, called the Loyal Democrats of Mississippi, that included the NAACP, the American Federation of Labor and Congress of Industrial Organizations (AFL-CIO), the Young Democrats, and other liberal groups.

Between 1964 and 1968, what had been a block of united Mississippi leaders underwent fragmentation. Beginning in November 1964, just after the first seating challenge, the MFDP ran its own candidates for city, county, and state offices. Then, in 1965, SNCC leaders adopted a separatist political strategy and severed itself from the MFDP. This was an embittered response to the failure of the Democratic party to seat the MFDP delegates at the national convention and to the growing convictions that the liberal establishment could not be trusted and the rural poor could not be reached with tactics congenial to their other partners in the MFDP. SNCC ran candidates in the 1966 and 1967 elections. Taking conflicting views on voter-registration strategies and modes of representing different class sectors of the black population, the MFDP and the NAACP ran separate candidates in the summer of 1965.[105]

Although the MFDP candidates for national offices were not successful (no black would win a congressional seat from Mississippi until 1986), the party achieved other successes. It won the 1968 seating challenge at the Democratic National Convention, a victory that eventually opened the state party somewhat to black participation. As an expression of independent black politics in Mississippi, the MFDP (along with other political organizations) also helped mobilize voter registration, which increased greatly, from a mere 6.7 percent in 1964 to 32.9 percent in 1966 and 67.4 percent in 1976,[106] and ran candidates when blacks could not run on the Democratic ticket. The 1970s ended with seventeen black state legislators and over four hundred county, municipal, and city officials.[107] Although the MFDP disbanded as a formal coalition, it was nevertheless instrumental in establishing an independent political pattern that is still characteristic of black politics in Mississippi. To this day, black Democrats work through the Democratic state party when this is possible and efficacious but mount independent candidacies when it is not.

The history of the NDPA is similar in that it developed because blacks were excluded from the regular state party.[108] At the time of the 1965 Voting Rights Act, the regular party's constitution included a white supremacy clause. Frustrated by efforts to work with the state party and by the clause itself, civil rights groups and politically active individuals urged the strongest and most predominant black political organization, the Alabama Democratic Conference (ADC), to form a statewide interracial third party. Initially the ADC refused to commit itself, offering the executive committee of the Democratic party a chance to delete the exclusionary clause and to institute practices that would increase black participation in the state party. The noxious clause was struck. Some blacks, nonetheless, felt that the party was still not responsive to the political aspirations of the state's blacks. Then, in 1967, when George Wallace engineered his wife's election as governor in order to maintain control of the state executive office, the ADC filed for a state charter to create a new political party, the NDPA.

Like the MFDP, the NDPA operated as a satellite party, trying to gain recognition and a meaningful role in the traditional state Democratic party. In 1968, having elected delegates to the national convention, it challenged the Credentials Committee to seat the NDPA delegates rather than state regulars. No NDPA delegates were seated, but the challenge led to a critical legal contest. The Supreme Court ruled that Alabama officials had to include the NDPA's slate on the 1969 November ballot. In 1970, one of its candidates was among the first blacks to serve in the Alabama state legislature since Reconstruction. The party eventually merged with the regular state party, having largely fulfilled the function of creating conditions for fuller black participation in the state Democratic party.

Separate black parties were also part of black electoral politics in the 1960s, but they were never electorally viable. In the South, the most notable example was the Lowndes County Freedom Organization (LCFO), which was formed to mobilize poor, rural blacks in one county.[109] The organization was given a severe blow when all seven of its candidates were defeated in the 1966 election. In 1969, LCFO merged with the NDPA.

In the North, the separate parties also failed decisively when they tried to win elections. The Freedom Now party, formed after the 1963 March on Washington, ran candidates in four states. It concentrated on Michigan, but its slate was so badly defeated that plans for the 1966 election were canceled.

Largely symbolic, two other parties ran black presidential candidates in the 1968 election. The Peace and Freedom party, a coalition of black nationalists and radical whites, ran Eldridge Cleaver, and the Freedom and Peace party ran Dick Gregory. Neither party survived beyond the election.

Black Power and the New Black Politics

Far more significant than black political parties was the formation of many new independent black organizations—an expression, according to Smith, of Black Power.[110] Of the 166 organizations having their dates of formation listed in Afram's *Directory of National Black Organizations*, 44 percent were founded between 1967 and 1969. The self-stated interests of these organizations ranged from business to culture, but most functioned explicitly as political interest groups lobbying in Washington. The black organizations as well as black caucuses within other organizations gave meaning to black power by articulating black interests in the national interest-group arena. This increase in black interest groups converged with an overall expansion of interest groups in Washington after 1960[111] and, along with the growing racial consciousness that resulted from the Civil Rights and Black Nationalist movements, helped blacks gain a more effective voice in the policy-making process.

Smith argues that the organizational development in the late 1960s was a new political phenomenon for blacks. Not only did the sheer number of organizations increase, but they were more successful than the older ones in providing sustained input into the federal policy-making process and lobbied on issues broader than just civil rights. Moreover, black elected and appointed officials formed caucuses to develop cohesive positions on policies under debate in Congress, state legislatures, and government agencies. Smith names the National Black Legislative Clearinghouse, founded in 1969 as an organization of black state legislators; the Congressional Black Caucus (CBC), founded in 1969 and made up of black members of the House of Representatives; the National Black Caucus of Local Elected Officials, founded in 1970; the Judicial Council of National Bar Associations, founded in 1971 as a group of elected and appointed black judges; the National Caucus of Black School Board Members, founded in 1971; the Southern Conference of Black Mayors, founded in 1972; and the National Association of Black County Officials, founded in 1975. Depending on organizational infrastructure to determine priorities and agree on strategies, these independent organizations were not separatist. They all aimed to increase black influence within government bodies and combine this influence with protest and electoral politics in order finally to produce a visible black presence in government. More than any other factor, this burst of political organizing in the late 1960s is the exemplar of what is now called the New Black Politics.

Summary

Black politics in the 1960s emphatically demonstrate the congeniality of political-protest and electoral action. The Civil Rights movement employed a wide range of activities to pressure the federal government to pass the legislation—the Voting Rights Act of 1965—that would force states to open up the electoral system to blacks. At the same time, protest mechanisms were being used for other political ends, including the institution of state policies that would soften inequalities in the marketplace and increase blacks' share of economic rewards—we should remember that the 1963 March on Washington was for jobs and freedom. Moreover, the state of the economy during the 1960s and government non-discrimination and affirmative-action policies together did produce large economic gains for the black population in that decade. A new black middle class was born, and black family income increased at a faster rate than that of whites. Most analysts would agree, however, that economic inequality in the black community was also beginning to increase and that the political instruments being used for economic ends would not keep a large sector of the black population from economic vulnerability when the economy slowed down in the 1970s.

The events of this period also verify the continued importance of strategies for independence. It was not only protest politics that wrestled protection of political rights from the state. Blacks organized separate and satellite parties to pressure the Democratic party for inclusion at both local and national levels. Arguably the most significant political achievement of the decade was the growth of independent black organizations—within political structures, but also in educational, professional, business, and other institutions—that became an effective presence in Washington interest-group politics and would become an influential infrastructure for local, state, and national electoral politics in the 1970s and 1980s.

1968–1984

The political climate did not change overnight. Support for the Civil Rights movement peaked early, sometime in 1965. Gallup polls show that civil rights was ranked as the country's most important problem

by approximately half of the general public from January 1963 through
January 1965. Later in 1965, only one-quarter ranked civil rights first,
and virtually no one did in 1970.[112] Black activists felt increasingly
betrayed by the attitudes and behavior of whites and, especially, by
growing evidence that mainstream political institutions would not
support their claims for inclusion. The 1964 Democratic National
Convention had disillusioned many civil rights activists who tried to
get the MFDP delegation approved by the convention's Credentials
Committee. SNCC and CORE volunteers to the 1964 Mississippi
Summer Project charged that FBI agents passively watched while
white mobs attacked them and that instead of providing protection for
the volunteers, Mississippi law enforcement officials assaulted and
arrested them. The thugs who killed James Chaney, Andrew Goodman, and Michael Schwerner included deputies of the sheriff.[113]

When political action moved to northern cities, black activists also
realized that the targets of their action would have to be broadened
beyond civil rights—to economic inequality and many forms of segregation and discrimination other than those in public accommodations
and voting. The North's was a different political climate, as the decade's first urban revolts in the summer of 1964 made clear. The angry
reactions of blacks in Harlem and Rochester, New York, and in several
cities in New Jersey would eventually be felt in over two hundred
American cities and towns. Whites and blacks increasingly evaluated
racial matters differently. Whites became more negative toward "black
militants"; blacks became more supportive of Black Power and of the
political necessity of blacks' forming their own organizations to be
independent of white control.

The decisive year was 1968. "As stormy and violent as the years
from 1963 through 1967 had been, many Americans were still trying to
downplay the nation's distress in hopes that it would go away. But in
1968 the sleepers awoke to a series of quakes."[114] Controversy over the
Vietnam War deepened after the January Tet offensive, the March My
Lai massacre, and the enormous increase in American deaths in the
first six months of the year (more than the previous year's total).[115] The
1968 presidential race was turned into an open competition when Lyndon Johnson announced on March 31 that he would not seek reelection. In the field for the Democratic nomination were Governor
George Wallace of Alabama, Senator Eugene McCarthy of Minnesota,
and Senator Robert Kennedy of New York.

The months leading up to the summer presidential nominating conventions were a time of agony. Martin Luther King, Jr., was assassinated on April 11. University-based protests over the Vietnam War

and the demands of students for a larger role in governance spread across the country. Robert Kennedy, celebrating his California Democratic primary victory, was assassinated on June 5. Then to the horror of many Americans, the Democratic convention itself was surrounded by violence as the Chicago police and National Guardsmen attacked demonstrators, newsmen, and innocent bystanders.

The 1968 election was symbolic of the state of the nation. Democrat Hubert H. Humphrey, a long-time advocate of civil rights but a supporter of the Vietnam War, was pitted against Republican Richard Nixon, also a supporter of the war, and George Wallace, the nominee of the American Independent party, who appealed for "law and order" at home (a euphemism for cracking down on protesters) and bombing North Vietnam to rubble. Wallace received more votes than any third-party candidate since 1924 (ten million, or 13.5 percent of the total), and Nixon was elected president with only 43 percent of a divided nation's popular vote.[116] The Nixon and Wallace votes together reflected a turn to the right from the liberal sentiments that had produced Johnson's landslide victory just four years before. The election studies of the Institute for Social Research (ISR) show that in 1968 as compared with 1964, 11 percent more of the public said that the "federal government was too powerful."[117]

The Retreat from Civil Rights

The first Nixon administration took steps that signaled to the black community that a major shift in federal civil rights policy was taking place. Instead of supporting a simple extension of the 1965 Voting Rights Act, the administration proposed amendments that would make the law apply to the entire nation. Many feared that the government's already limited resources for enforcement would prevent its effective implementation in the southern states, where the civil rights of blacks were most precarious. (Eventually the president signed a bill without the amendments.) Civil rights actions in employment and in extending the Civil Rights Commission came only after fights by civil rights groups, and the steps that were taken were considerably weaker than those desired.[118]

These were the political conditions that prevailed when representatives of both the older and the newer black organizations came together in Gary, Indiana, for a National Black Political Convention in 1972. Nixon, who was running for reelection, was not perceived as a supporter of civil rights. George Wallace was again on the ticket of the American Independent party. The political climate in the country had

become even more conservative. Black leaders, ranging from integra-
tionists to nationalists, reformers to radicals, and capitalists to Marxists, converged, doubting whether the major parties could resist racist
elements in the nation. They also felt a sense of collective power
following the mass mobilizations that had spanned the 1960s and especially as a consequence of the organizational developments that had
just taken place late in the decade. For the moment, they projected to
the nation the image of a strong, politically unified community when
they decided to initiate a party-building process by forming the National Black Political Assembly. Yet this decision to develop a black
party disintegrated within months. Some delegates endorsed George
McGovern for the Democratic nomination. The CBC issued a *Black
Bill of Rights* that was more moderate than the official document of
the Gary convention, *New Politics for Black People.*

The long-standing Republican efforts to win the South were finally
successful in 1972. Nixon followed a southern strategy that had already guided his first administration. His attorney general, John Mitchell, had courted southerners by trying to delay school desegregation in
Mississippi. Nixon was sensitive to the South in the nominations he
made to the Supreme Court. Then, during the 1972 campaign, he unabashedly wooed southern voters in policy areas that were marked by
strong black-white disagreement. For example, three days after Wallace won the Florida primary, Nixon proposed that Congress should
pass a moratorium on busing as a means of achieving desegregation.[119]
Of course, non-racial factors were also influential in Nixon's landslide
victory. His trips to China and the Soviet Union were well publicized
and popular; the Vietnam War was rumored to be near an end; and
McGovern took several positions that were too liberal to hold the old
Democratic coalition together. Nixon not only carried all of the Deep
South but a majority of the urban vote as well, including blue-collar
workers, Catholics, and ethnic whites.

Political conservatism dominated the 1970s. It was reflected in
opinion polls and in behavior across the country.[120]

> In Louisville in 1975, bumper stickers urged people to "Honk if you op-
> pose busing." The Ku Klux Klan stepped up its recruiting in Louisville,
> and violence soon erupted: over two days, one hundred people were in-
> jured and two hundred arrested. In Boston, where busing caused numer-
> ous riots, a group of white students protesting busing attacked a black
> passer-by outside City Hall. "Get the nigger; kill him," one shouted, and
> they ran at him with the sharp end of a flagstaff flying an American flag.
> Tension rose not only in Boston and Louisville, but across the nation.
> Membership in the Ku Klux Klan grew from about five thousand in 1978
> to ten thousand just two years later.[121]

The Democratic victory of Jimmy Carter over Gerald Ford in 1976 did not represent a resurgence of liberalism. Voters, disillusioned with corruption in government following the Watergate scandal, responded to the promise made by the fiscally conservative Carter to bring honesty back to government. They were not expressing the desire for a more active federal government. (It would not be until 1984 that public opinion would again reflect the 1964 level of support for action by the federal government.) Most political signs pointed to a desire for less government. In 1978, California voters approved Proposition 13 to cut property taxes and limit state spending on social programs. Nationally conservatives lobbied for a constitutional amendment to prohibit budget deficits; they also mobilized to run conservative candidates for office.

In preparation for the 1980 election, numerous conservative groups worked together to register new voters. The Moral Majority, a collection of groups and individuals who are Christian and politically conservative, managed under the leadership of the Reverend Jerry Falwell to register between two and three million new voters and raised $1.5 million to support conservative candidates.[122] Ronald Reagan was their candidate for president. The 1980 election between Reagan and Carter was predicted to be closer than it turned out to be. Blacks, responding to Carter's positive record of appointing them to positions in his administration and against Reagan's promises to slash federal spending, cut taxes, and increase the military budget, gave 95 percent of their votes to Carter.[123] They could not prevent Reagan's electoral sweep. He carried 51 percent of the vote; Carter, 41 percent; and Independent John Anderson, 7 percent. Reagan won all of the Deep South except Georgia, Carter's home state. Carter won only seven states and the District of Columbia.

The retreat from presidential support for civil rights was completed by Ronald Reagan. In his first administration, President Reagan indicated that he favored a "bail out" amendment to the Voting Act of 1964, a position opposed by civil rights groups, and a ten-year instead of a twenty-five-year extension of the 1965 Voting Rights Act (he eventually signed a bill providing for another twenty-five years); he attempted to confer a tax-exempt status on the South's segregated academies; and he opposed a national holiday for Martin Luther King's birthday. His administration narrowed affirmative action by joining a Memphis, Tennessee, court challenge to limit this relief only to individuals who can prove personal discrimination, and it reshaped the Civil Rights Commission from a six- to an eight-member group (four of whom were to be appointed by the president, four by Congress) and then joined with congressional Republicans to win control of the commission by appointing commissioners opposed by civil rights groups.[124] This administration disagreed with and thus tried to reverse prior civil rights policy.

Black conservatives argue that rather than being hostile to blacks, the Reagan administration has been trying to pursue racially neutral policies that would eventually benefit blacks as well as other Americans. The vast majority of the black population disagreed. They saw the Reagan administration systematically working to reverse the legal gains for which blacks had struggled throughout history and finally won in the 1960s. At least as important in the political thinking of blacks was the Reagan administration's cuts in social programs. These cuts disproportionately affected blacks, who are preponderantly in the low income population. Black opposition to Reagan, already widespread in 1980, grew over the course of his first administration. Black organizations responded not with cynicism but by launching a new effort to register new voters and to get out the vote in the 1982 congressional and the 1984 presidential races.

The Black Electorate's Response

From the Kennedy election on, approximately 90 percent of the black vote went to the Democratic presidential candidate. It was not until 1976, however, that the black vote would again be pivotal to the outcome. Johnson's victory in 1964 was so large that the black vote contributed little. Then, in 1968, Wallace's candidacy served as an antidote to the emerging strength of black voters. The antithesis of the 1964 election was the 1972 election, in which black voters could not reverse McGovern's landslide loss to Nixon. But in 1976 the black vote provided the margin of Carter's narrow victory in thirteen states. Moreover, it was black voters in the South who proved to be indispensable. Carter carried every southern state in the old Confederacy except Virginia, and although he did bring some southern whites back to the Democrats, it was the strength of his black vote in the South that was most consequential. Thus from the 1960 presidential election onward, two patterns stand out: black national electoral politics took place almost wholly in the Democratic party, and the black southern vote became increasingly important.

The growing significance of the black vote resulted from both bloc voting by blacks and the passage of the Voting Rights Act of 1965, which greatly increased their registration. In 1964, only 43 percent of blacks were registered; in 1972, 57 percent were.[125] Of course, registration increased most dramatically in the South, where practices and laws had disfranchised blacks for almost a century. Within just six years, registration increased seven-fold in Mississippi, doubled in Alabama and Louisiana, grew one and a half times in Georgia and Virginia, and increased rather less in North and South Carolina.[126] Lawson summarizes the continuing impact of the Voting Rights Act in the South:

> When the statute went into effect in 1965, only 31 percent of the eligible blacks in the seven covered states were enrolled to vote. By 1982, the percentage had soared to nearly 60 (57.7). The most spectacular changes came in Mississippi, the state subject to the most federal supervision and to the extensive organizing efforts of civil rights groups. The Magnolia State came in first among the seven states with 75.8 percent of voting-age blacks registered, up from 6.7 in 1965.[127]

From 1960 to 1980, black turnout in elections lagged behind white turnout, although the patterns differed greatly by region. In the South, black turnout surged after the Voting Rights Act and, despite a subsequent mild decline, remains at a historically high level. Outside the South, turnout declined precipitously (down almost 20 percentage points between 1964 and 1976). Turnout among northern whites also declined, but much less (12 points).[128] In the 1980s, however, black turnout began increasing everywhere, with a total gain of 5.3 percentage points between 1980 and 1984.[129]

Heightened registration and voting, party reforms (especially those preceding the 1972 Democratic National Convention), and the activities of newly formed black political organizations brought about remarkable growth in the numbers, distribution, and visibility of black elected officials. In 1965, there were fewer than five hundred blacks in city, county, state, and national offices; five years later, when the Joint Center for Political Studies began its annual survey to count black officials and analyze their elections, there were close to fifteen hundred; and by the end of the 1970s, over forty-nine hundred. The largest gains occurred in the first five years of the decade. In each of these years, the numbers increased by 14–27 percent. Thereafter the increase leveled off, reaching a low in 1979 of 2.3 percent.[130]

Summary

By 1984, blacks had seen remarkable achievements in the solution of one of their problems in the two-party system—the long-standing problem of participation. Blacks participated in the electoral and party system in numbers unimaginable before the Voting Rights Act of 1965. It was this state action that was primarily responsible for achieving greater political equality by 1984. Black political action had been instrumental in pressing for passage of the original act and in winning extensions for it in 1970 and 1982. As the political climate became less responsive to federal action, including—if not particularly—in racial matters, black leaders and organizations again searched for strategies of independence in order to protect their political gains. They turned again, though briefly, to the idea of a separate black party, but primarily they mobilized to register new voters and to make the black vote an increasingly formidable force in electoral politics. As usual, they used protest and non-electoral mechanisms in the service of electoral politics.

The problem of accountability—how party politics and the electoral system can be used to make government policies responsive to the needs of the black community—was left unresolved. Timing worked against blacks. They succeeded in electoral politics—electing a wide range of black public officials, including members of the House of Representatives—when the political and economic forces of the late 1970s and the 1980s decreased the government's capacity to be responsive. And, as we have seen, the political climate of the 1970s became more conservative. Reaction against an activist, central state increased. Economic slowdown was producing fiscal conservatism and an even more adamantly negative sentiment against redistributive policies. The shift from a high-wage, hard-manufacturing economy to an increasingly bipolar, low-wage service and high-skill technology economy began to jeopardize the economic base of a large sector of the black population.

Under such economic and political circumstances, what could black elected officials deliver to those without a college education or technological skills? Pork-barrel politics requires an expanding economy, something that elected officials could not deliver.[131] So, too, local elected officials could not be accountable to their supporters. Federal, state, and local financial relations changed, reducing the traditional resource base of large cities, where the majority of blacks live.

PARTY INDEPENDENCE AND DEPENDENCE:
THE CONTEXT FOR 1984

Black leaders have continuously worried about party dependency—first with the Republican party, and later with the Democratic party. In repeated elections, they have warned black voters not to allow one party to take their votes for granted. And editorials in the black press have counseled independence. But a strategy of independence is not consistent with United States party traditions, according to which most groups have identified with one party or another. Nor is it congenial with a balance-of-power strategy in which the small but concentrated and consensual black vote can decisively influence the outcome of close elections. It is unlikely that a black bloc vote could be decisive if the black electorate were not committed to a party that it believed best represented its interests. By continually shifting party commitments, how could the black vote function as a bloc? Bloc voting presumes a perception of common interests and party identification so that support for a particular candidate can be easily mobilized in a given election.

Why, then, has there been repeated concern among black leaders and the black press over the "loyalty" of blacks, first to the Republican party and then, after 1936, to the Democratic party? First and most important, the party to which blacks were "loyal" rarely courted them and often shunned their support. Until the northern industrial–southern planter alliance began to dissolve, both parties followed a southern strategy that provided little, if any, opportunity for the participation of blacks in party politics. Thus blacks faced an impossible dilemma. They recognized that even the party that better represented their interests rejected their participation. Talk of independence—supporting the other major party's candidate, forming a separate black party, or endorsing a third-party candidate—increased when the party to which blacks were "loyal" most actively rebuffed them. The history of the black electorate is characterized by blacks' continual commitment to the electoral system and repeated rejection by one or the other party.

Second, even close party competition, which should have given blacks some electoral clout, usually did not help them. In the period when political parties were initially gaining importance in American politics, the Federalist (Whig)–Jeffersonian (Republican) competition should have increased the significance of the small Free Negro vote. Instead, its potential for being the deciding factor in Whig victories usually worked against blacks politically, because the Jeffersonians tried to disfranchise blacks in order to prevent Whig victories. Similarly, when the competition between the Populists and the southern white supremacist Democrats was close enough for the southern black vote to make a difference, both parties wanted only to disfranchise blacks—their way of ensuring that neither party would gain an electoral advantage.

For these reasons, black leaders have always been ambivalent about the major political parties. They did not exhibit unswerving loyalty to the Republican party before the New Deal, nor to the Democratic party afterward. Instead, black electoral politics have involved persistent efforts to make an electoral impact, usually without success and, for most of our political history, simply to be granted the right to vote. Often, the political energy of blacks was devoted to convincing the party they supported that they should be franchised and that the party should speak out on racial violence, accept black support, seat blacks at conventions, and provide them with a role in electoral campaigns. The parties did not politicize blacks as they did other groups;[132] in fact, they treated blacks with ambivalence, and blacks, in turn, responded in kind.

Still, the black vote has nearly always been consensual, whatever the ambivalence of black leaders and whatever the black electorate may have felt. Hamilton says that there has always been a discernible inclination to "go with" one of the two established parties, even among leaders who claimed to prefer an all-black or a clearly Socialist ticket. In terms of laymen, this has meant always having to vote for the "lesser of two evils," never feeling that either party is really in your corner. Thus practicality (defined as voting for candidates and parties that could win and possibly implement a favorable program for blacks) has been a "strong consideration in the electoral judgements of many black Americans."[133] In light of this history, it is not surprising that blacks cast their votes so overwhelmingly for Walter Mondale in 1984, whatever the candidacy of Jesse Jackson and the sentiment for a separate black party meant in that election. The dilemma persists: How can the politics of independence, within or outside the Democratic party, address the problems of participation (no longer one of access, but still one of party influence) and using party politics to make government policy accountable to the black community?

The reactions to this dilemma on the part of black civic leaders and appointed and elected officials have been documented. What is not well-known is how ordinary black citizens react to the options and constraints in two-party politics. The political circumstances of the 1984 presidential campaign offered a special opportunity to study this historic dilemma from the perspective of the black electorate. In Chapters Three, Four, and Five, we address two questions involving party dependency and strategies of independence: How did the black electorate evaluate the Jackson candidacy? and How did blacks feel about the idea of an independent black political voice?

Notes

1. See the following for discussion of the structure and formation of the two-party system: Rosenstone, Behr, and Lazarus 1984; Ranney and Kendall 1951; for discussion of black parties: Walton 1972; Pinderhughes 1986. Rosenstone, Behr, and Lazarus conclude that third parties "are a weapon citizens can use to force the major parties to be more accountable. The threat of exit provides voters and their leaders with an important resource when bargaining with both major parties. Third parties are not aberrations in the American political system; they are in fact necessary voices for the preservation of democracy" (p. 222).
2. Walton 1972, 113–187.
3. Cook, cited in Walton 1972, 1–8.
4. Skowronek 1982, 24.
5. This characterization of the early state and political parties is drawn from Skowronek 1982, 19–30.
6. Walton 1972, 20–22.
7. Franklin 1943, cited in Walton 1972, 22.
8. Skowronek 1982, 25.
9. Ibid.
10. McCormick 1966, cited in Rosenstone, Behr, and Lazarus 1984, 10–11.
11. Examples of the electoral influence of blacks and of party pressure for disfranchisement are found in Walton 1972, 20–22.
12. For an examination of the strength of third parties in these three periods, see Rosenstone, Behr, and Lazarus 1984, 6, 49–63, 79. It should be noted that a 5 percent vote for a third-party candidate is considered unusual, since 1 percent is more typical.
13. Marable 1985, 28.
14. Ibid., 60.
15. Ibid., 60.
16. Walton 1972, 40–44; Flewellen 1981; and Pease and Pease 1971.
17. Holt 1977, 65.
18. Holden 1986, 10.
19. Norton et al. 1982, 422.
20. Ibid., 426.
21. Ibid., 429. Norton et al. describe the process by which Rutherford B. Hayes became president. They also conclude that the negotiations that went on between some of the supporters of Hayes and southerners who were interested in federal aid and patronage and the removal of troops were not decisive in the electoral outcome. The negotiations did convey expectations to southerners, however. In any case, by 1875 there were some four thousand troops outside of Texas. Throughout Reconstruction, the largest units were in Texas and the West, fighting Indians, not white southerners (p. 425).
22. Holden 1986, 13.
23. Skowronek 1982, 288.
24. See the following for discussion of cosmopolitanism: Wiebe 1967; Trachtenberg 1982; for triumph of conservatism: Kolko 1963; for progressivism as purifying a democracy grown corrupt by allowing citizen participation in referenda and pri-

mary elections versus shifting government responsibility to a professional, administrative elite: Skowronek 1982; Cott, 1990; and for growth of interest-group politics: Lebsock, 1990.

25. These figures are given in Lewison (1932) and Woodward (1966), cited respectively in McAdam (1982, 69).

26. Norton et al. 1982, 459.

27. Marable 1985, 141.

28. Edwin G. Walker quoted in Contee 1976.

29. Fishel and Quarles 1970, quoted in Hamilton 1986a, 239.

30. Hamilton 1986a, 239. See also Woods (1982) for the case of Charles H. J. Taylor, editor of the *American Citizen*, a large black newspaper, who urged blacks to split their ticket as a way to influence both parties.

31. Marable 1985, 60.

32. Walton 1972, 63–79.

33. Norton et al. 1982, 461; Jones, 1989. Interracial cooperation was achieved in some areas; the Populist movement in particular benefited blacks by forming schools for black children. Schewel (1981), for example, identifies an effective coalition between blacks and whites in Lynchburg, Virginia, in the mid-1880s. Subsumed by the Knights of Labor, the coalition controlled the city council and built a public school for black children. Racial animosity and competition for jobs in the tobacco industry eventually broke the ranks, however, after which the Democrats returned to power. The Lynchburg case was replicated in many other cities in the South.

34. Franklin 1967, quoted in McAdam 1982, 68.

35. Norton et al. 1982, 504.

36. Katznelson 1973; Hamilton 1981; and Barnett 1982.

37. Holden 1988, 9.

38. Ibid., 9.

39. Weiss 1983, 4–5.

40. Ibid., 5.

41. *Crisis* (November 1912), reprinted in Hamilton 1973, 255–256.

42. Weiss 1983, 5.

43. Lomax 1962, 233, quoted in McAdam 1982, 72.

44. Weiss 1983, 131.

45. Booker T. Washington, quoted in Norton et al. 1982, 591.

46. Holden 1988, 11.

47. Blacks did support third parties at the local level during this period. Wright (1983) describes a situation in Louisville, Kentucky, where a group of young black leaders formed the Lincoln Independent party in 1921 and urged blacks to disavow their loyalty to the Republicans. Although their candidates received few votes, they did exact from city officials greater attention to blacks' concerns.

48. Brooks 1990.

49. A. Philip Randolph, "The Political Situation and the Negro: Coolidge, Davis or La Follette," *Messenger*, VI (October 1924), reprinted in Hamilton 1973, 271–272.

50. See Weiss (1983, 8–11) for discussion of blacks' shift in allegiance from Republican to Democratic candidates from 1924 to 1936.

51. See voting estimates in Weiss (1983, 31). Voters in some cities had already begun shifting their allegiance before 1928. Black voters in Indianapolis, Indiana, began

defecting in 1924 because some Republican leaders were linked to Ku Klux Klan activities. See Griffin 1983.
52. Weiss 1983, 15.
53. W. E. B. Du Bois, "An Indictment Against Herbert Hoover," *Crisis* (November 1932, 362–363) cited in Hamilton 1973, 282–283.
54. Weiss 1983, 15. Weiss points out that there was no massive movement of black voters from the Republican party. Quoting the political analyst Samuel Lubell, she stresses that blacks defected in smaller numbers than did any other group of Republican partisans in the 1932 election. Still, while blacks lagged substantially behind other groups in moving to the Democrats, the black vote had for the first time "broken away from its traditional moorings" (p. 19).
55. Marable 1985, 186; Walton 1972, 51. Also see Flewellen (1981) for discussion of both pressure groups and political parties in this period.
56. Hamilton 1986a, 240.
57. Marable 1985, 63.
58. Ibid., 64. Also see Walton 1972, 48–50; Bracey 1971, 263; and Redkey 1971, 107–192.
59. Marable 1985, 63–65. Marable cites a letter written by C. L. R. James about Trotsky's position urging self-determination for American blacks. James distinguished between the aspirations of blacks in the United States and those of African and West Indian blacks. In Africa and the West Indies, James argued, "the great masses of people look upon self-determination as a restoration of their independence," while in the United States, blacks are looking not for political sovereignty but for incorporation into the American political system.
60. Loyalty to the Republican party even before the demise of Reconstruction in the mid-1870s was apparent in some states. See Howard (1974) for discussion of the defection from the Republicans in Kentucky as early as 1872.
61. McAdam 1982, 67–69.
62. Ibid., 69–73.
63. Ibid., 70.
64. Ibid., 73.
65. Skowronek 1982, 289.
66. McAdam 1982, 73–79.
67. Ibid., 84.
68. Holden 1986, 24.
69. Ibid., 25.
70. Norton et al. 1982, 740.
71. Holden 1986, 14.
72. Emmett J. Scott, *Opportunity* XIV (1936), reprinted in Hamilton 1973, 288.
73. Norton et al. 1982, 741.
74. Editorial, *Crisis* (November 1936, 337), reprinted in Hamilton 1973, 295.
75. Weiss 1983. See Table IX. 2, 206.
76. Kelly Miller, "G.O.P. Would Sacrifice Negro States Rights," *Pittsburgh Courier*, October 10, 1936, reprinted in Hamilton 1973, 292.
77. For various opinions, see Sitkoff 1978, cited in Weiss 1983, xv; Weiss 1983, xiv.
78. Norton et al. 1982, 741.
79. Pollock 1984.
80. Henderson 1982, 7.
81. Weiss 1983, 206–207.

82. Henderson 1982, 7.
83. Walton 1972; Hamilton 1973.
84. Norton et al. 1982, 850.
85. Ibid., 849.
86. This discussion is taken from Holden 1986. See pp. 32 and 33 for a comparison of the committee's and Truman's proposals.
87. Norton et al. 1982, 850.
88. Holden 1986, 35–36.
89. Norton et al. 1982, 847–888. Despite Truman's position on civil rights, a key black newspaper, the *New York Amsterdam News*, came out for the Republican ticket in the 1948 election. This, it said, was "no time for the people of this nation to face the future under a Presidential leadership that is at variance with the Congress, large sections of the population and with a political party in revolt and weakened to a state of impotency . . . with Henry A. Wallace on the left, Strom Thurmond on the right, and Mr. Truman in the middle without sail, compass, rudder, or anchor . . . it is time for a change"—a vote for Thomas E. Dewey and Earl Warren (October 9, 1948, reprinted in Hamilton 1973, 301). Also see Henderson (1982, 8) for election results.
90. Garrow 1986, 98–100. Also see Campbell (1977) for the political implications of feelings about Eisenhower.
91. Henderson 1982, 8.
92. Nonetheless, an important black organization, the National Negro Congress, was formed in 1936. Black leaders, aware that no single organization was dealing with the whole array of problems facing the black population, created the congress to coordinate pressure groups and protest organizations. See Walton 1972, 54–56.
93. Bracey 1971. The quotations are found on pp. 262 and 263, respectively.
94. Morris 1981, 744–767. Also see Morris 1984, 1–7.
95. Weiss 1983, 181–185.
96. Garrow 1986, 93–107.
97. Norton et al. 1982, 856.
98. Garrow 1986, 106–107.
99. Ibid., 117. Garrow notes that while Kennedy staffers made much of the King family's change in attitude, Kennedy's phone calls became neither a major story in the white media nor an issue in the campaign (p. 149).
100. For voting statistics and analysis pertaining to the presidential elections from 1960 to 1976, see Henderson (1982, 10–14). The quotation is on p. 10.
101. Holden 1986, 103.
102. Lyndon B. Johnson, quoted in Norton et al. 1982, 933.
103. See Miller, Miller, and Schneider 1980, Table 6.1, 332. This estimate is based on data from blacks in the 1964 cross-section sample.
104. This material on the Mississippi Freedom Democratic Party is drawn from Walton (1972, 88–130) and Dittmer (1986, 65–95). Walton's analysis depends heavily on McLemore's (1965) research conducted as these events were unfolding.
105. Generally SNCC, CORE, and the NAACP did not compete, since they ran candidates in different localities. In 1967, the MFDP and its former member groups cooperated once again to create nationwide pressure when all the Mississippi bonding companies refused to bond black candidates. Cooperation was further strengthened when Lawrence Guyot, chairman of SNCC, became campaign

manager for Charles Evers, who was running for Congress in 1968. See Dittmer 1986, 84–86.
106. Lawson 1985, Table 1, 297.
107. Coleman and McLemore 1982, 131. These authors detail the continuing tension between black Democrats and the state Democratic party in Mississippi. In 1980, for example, the Democratic governor, William Winter, "suggested to the party that it abolish the four-year co-chairmanship then shared by a white and black male. Black Democrats, who had most often benefited symbolically from party identification, were infuriated by such a suggestion, but William Winter carried the day for his party and subsequently, Aaron Henry, a loyal black Democrat, was no longer chairman of the party" (p. 135). Then, when Henry Jay Kirksey, a long-term black state senator, ran for Congress in the Fourth Congressional District, he bettered his opponent by eleven thousand to seven thousand but lost in the run-off primary. Once again, black Democrats decided to follow an independent strategy, running Leslie McLemore on an Independent ticket (p. 136).
108. See Walton (1972, 131–157) and Frye (1975) for material on the NDPA.
109. Walton 1972, 175–183.
110. Smith 1981, 435–438.
111. For discussion of the expansion of Washington pressure-group activity, see Schlozman 1989; Walker 1983; and Wilson 1981.
112. Only 15 percent put civil rights in even fourth place in 1970. See McAdam 1982, 121, 198.
113. Norton et al. 1982, 936.
114. Ibid., 943.
115. Ibid., 943.
116. Ibid., 946.
117. Miller, Miller, and Schneider 1980, 171.
118. Holden 1986, 47–51.
119. Norton et al. 1982, 952.
120. Shanks and Miller 1985; Shapiro et al. 1987a, 1987b; and Schuman, Steeh, and Bobo 1985. It is important to note that attitudes did not become *increasingly* conservative over the decade. Most polls show that the tilt right had taken place in the late 1960s or early 1970s and thereafter the public's attitudes remained at a fairly stable, preponderantly conservative level until approximately 1983/1984.
121. Norton et al. 1982, 972.
122. Ibid., 978.
123. See Miller, Miller, and Schneider 1980, Table 6.1, 332.
124. Holden 1986; Mack, Coleman, and McLemore 1986.
125. Holden 1986, 105; Norton et al. 1982, 13.
126. Lawson 1985, 296. Lawson also concludes that despite the accomplishments of the Voting Rights Act, the federal government could have gone farther to expand the size of the black electorate and to challenge the remaining obstacles to equal representation if it had taken firm steps to see that southern officials redressed past biases. Instead, the federal government tried to achieve voluntary consent, using federal officials more to encourage and measure than to foster black involvement (p. 298).
127. Ibid., 296.
128. See Coleman and McLemore's analysis of continuing turnout problems as a negative factor in achieving electoral victories in Mississippi (1982, 131–156).

129. Cavanagh 1985a, 12.
130. These statistics are from Williams 1982, 75–76. Although the decline is attrib-
     uted to the fact that early increases were largely in jurisdictions with substantial
     black populations, Williams points out that this explanation is not entirely ade-
     quate, since some counties in which blacks comprise over 50 percent of the
     population have no black elected officials. In 1980, there were none in about one-
     quarter of the counties with a majority of blacks in the states covered under the
     Voting Rights Act. Lawson (1985) argues that had the Justice Department sent
     examiners to areas in which blacks continued to encounter suffrage barriers,
     black participation could have been boosted more than it was: "Had the percent-
     age of registrants been higher, black voters would have had a greater opportunity
     to elect candidates of their own race, especially in counties with a black popula-
     tion majority. . . . In a racially neutral society, such figures (that one-quarter of
     the majority-black counties had no black officials) would have had little mean-
     ing; however, given the long history of southern disfranchisement, if the propor-
     tion of black officeholders falls considerably below the percentage of blacks in
     the population, it is not unreasonable to assume the persistence of racial dis-
     crimination" (p. 298).
131. As a result of all this, black officials, not surprisingly, became exceptionally
     concerned with protecting their offices. It is to these political and economic
     forces that Barnett (1982) attributes the failure of the CBC to deliver or initiate a
     substantial body of legislation that would benefit the total black community.
     Black officials were put in a Catch-22 situation. They were pressured both to
     represent blacks and to protect and promote their own individual political ca-
     reers (when it was increasingly difficult to deliver the goods to their beleaguered
     constituencies). The black Democrats who make up the CBC "can cooperate
     with one another to increase the amount of political resources that are tacitly
     and informally allocated to the black community[;] they must also compete with
     one another for a share of these resources" (p. 36). To stay in power, each must
     deliver resources to his or her own constituency, a political reality that may, at
     times, lessen commitment or the capacity to work for legislation that would
     benefit the entire black population. Barnett analyzes the legislative process be-
     hind the Humphrey-Hawkins-Hatch Bill to show the CBC's difficulties in deliv-
     ering to the black community. While the CBC was successful in getting the
     legislation passed using traditional alliance techniques, the final law was "ut-
     terly meaningless as a vehicle to aid the black unemployed" (p. 45). Some might
     say that the CBC's relationship to this bill shows how blacks can use the political
     system to achieve their legislative priorities, but Barnett views it as an example
     of the CBC's inability to get effective legislation enacted.
132. Hamilton 1973, 249.
133. Ibid., 249.

CHAPTER TWO

The Political Motivation and Resources of the Black Electorate

Bⁿ

B LACK POLITICS ARE INFLUENCED by numerous factors outside the black community: the nation's economy, the mass media, national legislation and judicial decisions, the organization and rules of the two parties and the competition between the parties in various regions and states, and state variations in registration and voting procedures. They are also affected by features within the black community: political, social, and religious organizations; political leadership; and the political motivation and resources of individuals.

A national survey is uniquely suited for giving a broad perspective on the black electorate and for examining the political motivation and resources of the individuals within it. It thus provides comprehensive evidence that may be used to check on the impressions of the relationship between Jesse Jackson and his 1984 supporters that have been widely reported by journalists. As we shall see in Chapter Four, some journalists drew quite misleading conclusions about the bond of racial solidarity between Jackson and his supporters because they depended on anecdotal rather than systematically derived information about the black electorate. A national sample provides both a barometer of average opinion and a portrait of the wider spectrum.

This chapter examines the nature and distribution of the political motivation and resources of the black electorate. We understand that the study of politics demands more than an individual-level approach. Contextual and institutional factors are important for the understanding of political behavior. As noted earlier, however, the approach adopted here is one that has been generally neglected in the study of black politics.

POLITICAL MOTIVATION AND RESOURCES

Two basic concepts, political motivation and political resources, guide our analysis of black politics on the individual level. Political motivation energizes action and defines its aims; political resources provide the means, or tools, for implementing the aims. Although these concepts have proved useful for the study of politics,[1] the distinction between them has not always been clearly drawn.

Political resources derive both from personal qualities of the individual and from the relationship of the individual to the environment. Personal qualities such as interest in politics and political efficacy provide psychological resources. A person's position in the class structure and membership in organizations are the sources of environmentally based resources. These include money, access to the media, information, and contacts with business, government, and potential allies.

There is, of course, some overlap between political motivation and political resources. Psychological resources are part of motivation; environmental resources are not, although they often influence action by increasing motivation. The other component of political motivation is ideology. Ideology is taken here to refer to general beliefs about the appropriate balance between government and individual responsibility and to policy preferences derived from these beliefs.[2]

The distinction between ideology and psychological resources is similar to one drawn in the value-expectancy theory of motivation.[3] A value gives direction to action by defining its aims; expectancy mobilizes it by indicating the likelihood of achieving the aims. Action requires both. The value of equality will not motivate people to demand a reduction in the inequality of income, for example, unless they feel their action will increase the chance that redistributive policies will be enacted. Nor will they work for such policies unless they value a more egalitarian society. In political studies, the value component of motivation is often represented by the individual's political ideology and policy preferences; that of expectancy, by sense of political efficacy.

Blacks bring into their political ideologies ideas and feelings about their group membership and the group's status in society. This ideology, which we describe as group political consciousness, involves three dimensions: evaluation of the group's collective power, evaluation of the legitimacy/illegitimacy of socially defined group differences, and evaluation of collective political strategies. Group political consciousness is likely to be especially influential in the political motivation of those blacks who identify with the racial group. Together group identity and political consciousness form what we call a sense of solidarity.[4]

Owing to complexity in the functions of ideology, the distinction between ideology and psychological resources is sometimes blurred. Ideology gives direction to politics, but it can sometimes serve as a psychological resource by helping individuals filter and organize information about politics.[5] A group-conscious ideology can provide a buffer against the demoralizing impact of social discrimination and economic adversity. A sense of efficacy and a zest for politics can be preserved when blacks or Hispanics or Asians do not blame themselves for problems that are caused primarily by political and economic forces. When ideology filters or buffers experience, it functions as a psychological resource as well as giving direction to political choices.

The psychological resources and ideologies of members are thought of as the collective resources of groups. Even economically deprived groups have influential political resources when their members share a sense of identity and a political ideology, possess psychological resources that help them become engaged in politics, and express their political motivation through membership in organizations. Shared identity, group political consciousness, and organizations—these were the collective resources that provided the base for the Civil Rights and Black Power movements, which reinforced and related them to electoral politics.

STRUCTURAL RESOURCES AND DEMOGRAPHICS

Structural resources, provided by employment and varying levels of education, income, and occupational status, generally affect participation in electoral politics. By supplying economic opportunities, social contacts, and access to government and corporate centers of power, these resources directly affect participation and indirectly foster psychological resources that help people become active in politics. The effect of structural resources is particularly pronounced in the United States. Comparing seven democracies, Verba and Orren demonstrate that socioeconomic status is most closely associated with various indicators of political participation in the United States.[6] In other nations, political activists represent a wider range of income and educational levels.

These structural resources have affected the electoral participation of both blacks and whites, as well as the voting gap between them. Now there is little or no gap when the education and income of blacks and whites are statistically equated.[7] A particularly impressive study, carried out by Sigelman and his colleagues, examined determinants of voting in ten elections between 1978 and 1982. Race was *not* a significant factor when economic status and education were controlled. Education was by far the most important characteristic distinguishing consistent from non-consistent voters. The structural advantages of middle class blacks also help explain their higher voting and campaign-participation rates, although there is some evidence to suggest that since 1978 income and education have affected the participation of blacks less than before.[8]

In many respects, these politically relevant structural resources of the black electorate were more abundant in 1984 than ever before. Nonetheless, black Americans were still structurally disadvantaged relative to whites. Farley, in an analysis of historical trends in racial disparity,[9] and Farley and Allen, in an intensive examination of racial information in the 1980 census,[10] lay out a scorecard that indicates both progress and persisting inequality. The following profile draws heavily on their studies.

With respect to education, time has brought greater racial equality. "On the eve of World War II adult blacks averaged about three fewer years of schooling than whites, but by the early 1980s the racial difference had declined to one and a half years."[11] Despite this obvious progress, the 1980 census shows that of the population aged 16 and older, one and a half times as many blacks as whites had only grammar school education, and whites were twice as likely to have graduated from college. Race differences were, of course, smaller among younger cohorts. In the group aged 26–35, an equal percentage of blacks and whites had graduated from high school and attended college, although twice as many whites had a college degree.[12] Trends in college enrollment from the mid-1960s to the mid-1970s suggested that blacks would soon reach degree parity with whites. In 1976, 33 percent of high school graduates, both black and white, were attending college. By 1984, however, the black rate was back to its 1969 level of 27.2 percent, while after a slight decline the white rate stayed between 33 and 34 percent.[13]

In 1980, 48 percent of the black population of voting age were not high school graduates, 34 percent had high school diplomas, 15 percent had attended college, and 7 percent had a college degree. (See Table 2.1 for the distribution of education, other structural resources, and demographic characteristics of the voting-age black population in 1980.)

Since 1960, racial progress has also taken place with respect to occupations. In 1960, 25 percent more white than black men, and 41 percent more white than black women, held white-collar jobs; by 1982, these differences had declined to 14 and 17 percentage points, respectively.[14] As a consequence of economic growth and civil rights legislation in the 1960s, the percentage of blacks in middle class jobs doubled between 1960 and 1970, growing from about one in eight to one in four black workers. "While this was far below the one in two level of whites in 1970, the gain experienced by the black middle class during the 1960s exceeded their total increase during the previous fifty years. It was a growth shared by both black men and black women in all three strata of the middle class: professionals, managers and small businessmen, and clerical and sales workers."[15] Yet the black middle class continues to be located primarily in the *lower* middle class. "Although blacks won additional jobs in each of the four occupational groups of the middle class, clerical workers accounted for almost 50 percent of the gain. Whites gained most in the professional group."[16] Finally, despite the increase in the size of the black middle class, blacks are still much more concentrated than whites at the bottom of the occupational hierarchy. If the bottom is defined as service workers, operators, and laborers, the 1980 census shows that 54 percent of black and 34 percent of white male workers, and 48 percent of black and 30 percent of white female workers, were located there.[17]

The economic scorecard is more complex. Conclusions depend on whether earnings of workers, personal income (including assets and the transfer of money as well as earnings), or family income is considered. With respect to earnings, there has been racial progress among both men and women. Nonetheless, black men still earn less than similarly categorized white men. Even "among college-educated black and white men who worked the same number of hours and had the same ages and the same regional distribution, blacks still earn 90 percent as much as the whites in 1979."[18] Comparison of the personal income of black men and white men indicates that the racial gap has narrowed little since World War II. The personal income of both groups has increased, but the increase has been greater for whites. As a consequence, the racial difference widened throughout the mid-1960s and has barely contracted since then.[19] The 1984 median personal income of black men was $9,000; that of white men, $15,800.[20] For women, both the earning and the personal-income trends show convergence. The gap in earnings had nearly disappeared by 1979, when black women earned 98 percent as much as white women.[21] And by 1980, the personal income of black women lagged behind that of white women by only $400.[22] Both groups of women, of course, were still far

TABLE 2.1

Demographic and Structural Resources Characteristics of Blacks, Aged 18 and Older

Characteristics and Resources	Men	Women	Total
Education			
0–8 years	23.9%	20.8%	22.1%
9–11 years	23.5	23.9	23.7
High school	30.3	33.0	31.8
Some college	14.9	15.0	15.0
College degree or more	7.4	7.3	7.4
	100.0%	100.0%	100.0%
Household Income[a]			
No income	1.6%	3.3%	1.6%
Less than $10,000	30.9	60.8	35.3
$10,000–19,999	31.6	24.4	29.9
$20,000–29,999	20.8	7.9	18.7
$30,000–39,999	9.4	2.2	8.6
$40,000–49,999	3.4	0.8	3.4
$50,000–59,999	1.2	0.3	1.3
$60,000 and over	1.1	0.3	1.2
	100.0%	100.0%	100.0%
Labor Force Status			
Status at Time of Census Interview			
Working	62.4%	47.9%	54.2%
Temporarily out of work, looking	0.4	0.2	0.3
Temporarily out of work, not looking	1.6	1.6	1.6
Unemployed, looking	6.3	4.9	5.6
Unemployed, not looking	1.1	0.7	0.8
Not in labor force	22.7	37.9	31.3
Not ascertained as to whether looking	5.5	6.8	6.2
	100.0%	100.0%	100.0%
Summary Status, 1979			
Worked	73.3%	57.5%	64.4%
Did not work	26.7	42.5	35.6
	100.0%	100.0%	100.0%
Hours[b]/Weeks[c] Worked			
Hours worked previous week (people currently working)	mean = 37.9	35.6	36.8
Weekly hours usually worked in 1979 (people who had jobs in 1979)	mean = 37.7	35.2	36.4
Number of weeks worked in 1979 (people who had jobs in 1979)	mean = 42.5	40.1	41.4

TABLE 2.1
(continued)

Characteristics and Resources	Men	Women	Total
Marital Status			
Married	51.9%	39.9%	45.2%
Widowed	4.1	13.7	9.5
Divorced	7.1	10.1	8.7
Separated	6.4	9.6	8.2
Never married	30.5	26.7	28.4
	100.0%	100.0%	100.0%
Region			
Northeast	18.1%	19.5%	18.9%
North Central	20.1	19.7	20.0
South	9.3	8.1	52.5
West	52.5	52.7	8.6
	100.0%	100.0%	100.0%
Rural/Urban[d]			
Central cities	46.3%	47.6%	47.1%
SMSAs adjacent to central cities	17.5	16.8	17.1
Either central city or adjacent areas	15.5	15.4	15.4
Mixed SMSAs and non-SMSAs	5.9	5.8	5.8
Non-SMSA	14.8	14.4	14.6
	100.0%	100.0%	100.0%

Source: The data used in this analysis are from the 1980 Census of Population and Housing (5 percent PUS). This sample was reduced to a 1/100 sample of the black population. It consists of the non-institutional black population aged 18 and older living in the continental United States.

[a] While all results presented are based on all persons reporting and thus include multiple reports per household, total household income is based on one report per household.

[b] Average hours are based on grouped data, using the midpoint for each category. For the highest open-ended category (40 plus), the number 41 was used.

[c] Week averages are also based on grouped data. For the highest open-ended category (49 plus), the number 51 was used.

[d] Standard metropolitan statistical area (SMSA): except in New England states, a county or group of contiguous counties that contained at least one city of 50,000 persons or "twin cities" with a combined population of at least 50,000. Other contiguous counties may be included in a particular SMSA if they were socially and economically integrated with the central city or with the twin cities (U.S. Bureau of Census).

behind white men in both earnings and personal income. Comparing full-time workers in 1981, black women earned 53.9 percent and white women 59.8 percent of what white men earned.[23]

The conclusions that are drawn regarding racial trends in family income depend on whether relative or absolute gains are judged to be more important. Because the black family's median income rose an average of 1.3 percent a year during the 1959–1982 period while that of white families rose 1.1 percent a year,

> the incomes of black families became larger relative to those of white families. . . . But the actual, absolute increase in family income in this period was considerably larger for whites than for blacks. Income, or pur- chasing power, went up about $4,200 for the typical white family but only $2,600 for the typical black family. Thus the gap between the races in median family income widened: the average white family had about $6,700 more purchasing power than the average black family in 1959, but $8,300 more in 1982. In this sense blacks fell further behind whites: the absolute racial gap in family income expanded.[24]

This puzzling situation occurred because the somewhat larger growth in family income for blacks was applied to a lower initial level in 1959.

Variation in the 1980 household income of voting-age blacks is shown in Table 2.1. Two-thirds of this segment of the population were living in a household with a total income under $20,000, and slightly over half in this group were living in a household with a total income under $10,000; only 2.5 percent lived in a household with a total in- come of $50,000 or more.

On three indicators of male employment—labor force participation, unemployment rates, and employment-population ratios—there has been little racial progress. The unemployment rate of black men was twice that of white men in the mid-1950s, and the ratio has changed little since then. The gap did decline in the prosperous late 1960s but rose again during the 1970s and 1980s.[25] Racial disparity in labor force participation has actually worsened. A time line from 1970 to 1984 shows that the proportion of adult men outside the labor force has been rising for both groups, but the annual increase is three times greater for black men than for white men. The time line shows a gradual increase in racial disparity until the 1973–1975 recession and a sharper rise thereafter. The drop in employment is especially pronounced among black men younger than 25 but also exists among men aged 25–54. By 1984, only 79 percent of black men aged 25 and older held jobs, as opposed to 90 percent of white men.[26]

Racial differences in the employment of women have changed greatly over time. Historically more black women than white women have participated in the labor market; but owing to a marked increase in employment among white women, this racial difference decreased in the 1970s. In the early 1980s, for the first time, the proportion of employed women aged 15–54 was actually greater among whites than blacks.[27] In contrast, unemployment rates remain higher for black women than for similarly categorized white women. In 1980, the unemployment rate for black women with a college degree was comparable to that of white women with a high school diploma.[28]

Table 2.1 shows that slightly more than four-fifths of black men and slightly less than one-half of black women of voting age were working when interviewed by the 1980 census takers. When people were included who had worked during at least part of 1979 but were not working at the time of the census interview, the employment figure rose 10 percent for both men and women. Nearly 10 percent of the men and 8 percent of the women were temporarily laid off or unemployed, and approximately 70 percent of the unemployed men and women were looking for jobs.

Socioeconomic resources do not exhaust the ways in which social structure can influence politics. Black turnout and the translation of the vote into the election of black officials are affected by customary procedures and structural features of the local political situation. The election of blacks is facilitated by district rather than system-at-large elections and by partisan rather than nonpartisan elections. (The partisan system also has a cost, however, as blacks are less likely to run for office in cities that have partisan elections.) Not surprisingly, blacks are also more likely to be elected in jurisdictions with large black populations. Racial composition is, in fact, the most important predictor of the success or failure of black candidates.[29]

The participation in electoral politics of both blacks and whites is affected by state and regional residency. State variations in registration procedures and laws are especially influential. Wolfinger and Rosenstone estimate that overall turnout in presidential elections would increase 9.1 percent if all states adopted four registration provisions: eliminating the closing date, opening registration offices during the forty-hour work week and during evenings and/or on Saturday, and permitting absentee registration for the sick, disabled, and absent.[30] These changes would have greatest effect in the South, because southern states, even now, have the most restrictive statutes in the country.

The South's more demanding registration laws do not completely account for regional differences in electoral participation. Another reason the southern electorate has not participated in electoral politics as much as other Americans is that the level of education is lower in the South than in non-southern states, and that alone reduces participation. In addition, culture has discouraged the citizenry's active involvement in politics. The presence of a cultural factor is suggested by data showing that fewer poorly educated southerners vote than do comparably educated people outside the South.

Historically the region has had a decisive influence on black politics. Yet since the Voting Rights Act and the activities of southern black political organizations have dramatically increased black registration and turnout, black southerners have been rapidly catching up to the participation rate of blacks elsewhere in the country. Thus, although it was not clear that the long-standing South/non-South distinction was still applicable in 1984, we included it to see whether Jesse Jackson's appeal was greater in the South or outside the South and whether the political motivation and resources of the black electorate differed regionally. In 1980, the black population was nearly evenly split between the South and the non-South: 52.5 percent lived in the South; 18.9 percent in the Northeast; 8.6 percent in the West; and 20 percent in the rest of the country.

Urbanicity has also long been a major factor in black politics. Until the Depression ended the supremacy of cotton in the southern economy, most blacks lived in the rural South. At the turn of the century, when twice as many whites as blacks lived in cities,[31] the use of repressive techniques by southern planters to control black farm laborers, coupled with registration and voting laws passed after Reconstruction, essentially kept southern blacks out of politics. At that time, both electoral and protest politics were almost exclusively a northern, urban phenomenon. When the massive migrations from the rural South began taking blacks to both southern and northern cities in the 1930s, the urban environment became politically important for southern blacks as well. It promoted the growth of political organizations and resourceful black churches, which brought ordinary people together in elaborate communication networks. These proved critical in mobilizing a base for the Civil Rights movement and, some argue, for the Jackson candidacy.[32] Urban concentration also made the black vote politically influential, since bloc voting allows for the election of black officials.

Marital status and gender, though not structural resources, also influence participation in electoral politics. Gender has been studied more than marital status in research on black politics. Most studies have focused on establishing the size of gender differences in turnout, which is now substantial.[33] Figures from a 1984 current population survey conducted by the Census Bureau show that "the turnout of black women was a full 7.5 percentage points higher than that of black men, and among blacks under the age of 21, the gender gap had expanded to a remarkable 11.3 percentage points."[34] These disparities suggest that black men and women might also differ in political motivation and resources. Yet research that has investigated relevant characteristics (political opinions, racial solidarity, and sense of political efficacy) has generally found few gender differences among blacks.[35] We have included gender (and marital status) more in an exploratory mode than in a hypothesis-testing mode.

ORGANIZATIONAL RESOURCES

The new theories of political mobilization emphasize the role of organizational resources in fostering all types of collective action. Critical of the crowd metaphor and of social breakdown and individual frustration as sources of collective movements, these theories stress the importance of previously existing organizations and resources. Organized collectivities are able to marshal participants for specific events and activities, recruit new members, formulate strategies, garner support from potential allies, and sustain action even in the face of failure.[36] Both electoral and protest politics are seen as instrumental and rational modes of pursuing a group's goal, and collective action is the broadest definition of politics. It stands for all occasions in which sets of people commit pooled resources, including their own efforts, to a common end.[37] In this view, mobilization to defeat or elect a candidate, to advance a social policy through party politics, to challenge an appointment through pressure-group activities, and to demonstrate against an unjust law are all forms of political behavior and potentially affected by the same organizations that historically encouraged social protest in the black community.

We focus on two organizations, churches and civil rights groups, both of which have received special attention in recent analyses of the Civil Rights movement. Although blacks have divided opinions regarding the role of the church in partisan politics and, specifically, regarding the church's endorsement of candidates, most congregations accept that the black church has historically had responsibility for mobilizing collective action. The church has had to play a role in ameliorating the social, economic, and political conditions that have impinged on the lives of parishioners. It is the concept of collective activity that makes politics consonant with the historic mission of the black church. In the 1984 election, churches and civil rights organizations once again became the locus of mobilization, this time serving as a bridge to party politics.[38]

From the point of view of the individual, all phases of participation in the electoral process—registering, learning about the campaign issues, deciding whom to support, working for a candidate, influencing others to support a candidate, voting, and pressuring officials once elected—are easier and less costly for the individual when organiza-

tions set up activities, supervise volunteers, and provide opportunities
for participation. Election turnout, therefore, increases in precincts
and counties where voter-registration groups, educational organizations, and political caucuses have mobilized the electorate.[39]

The impact of county-level organization is seen in two examples of
black politics in Mississippi. Salamon and Van Evera asked a panel of
political activists to judge black political caucuses and civil rights
organizations in twenty-nine Mississippi counties.[40] Variation in the
number of these organizations accounted for 20 percent of the variation in turnout among blacks in the 1968 presidential election. St.
Angelo and Puryear used a similar approach.[41] They asked a panel to
nominate four counties in Mississippi: a well-organized rural county
in which blacks were highly united politically, a recently organized
rural county, a poorly organized rural county, and a semi-organized
urban county. In the 1971 election, in which Charles Evers ran for
governor, turnout was 71 percent in the well-organized county, 54
percent in the recently organized one, 18 percent in the poorly organized rural county, and 32 percent in the urban county.

Hamilton highlights the importance of organizations in city politics, especially in mayoralty contests: "In every instance when Blacks
have contested successfully for a top public office like the mayoralty,
there has been an effective, locally-based organization behind the effort
that has included both extensive voter registration and election-day
turnout campaigns with Black voters giving the candidate an overwhelming (usually in the 90 percent range) vote."[42]

In our survey, organizational impact is demonstrated by a correlation between an individual's membership in a church (or in a
civil rights organization) and his or her support for the Jackson candidacy as well as for an independent political voice. We examine such
evidence in Chapters Four and Five. Here we raise three questions
about the extensiveness of organizations: (1) How active in churches
and civil rights organizations was the black electorate in 1984? (2) How
many blacks attended churches that became involved in the election? (3) What sectors of the black community were reached by these
organizations?

Frequent church attendance was widespread. (See Table 2.2.) Three-
quarters went to church at least once or twice a month; a third as often
as once a week. Only 6 percent said they never attended services.
Frequency of attendance was highest among women and blacks who
were older, married, and living in the South. Churches were also a
source of political involvement in the campaign. One-third of the electorate attended a church where they heard announcements or discus-

sions about the campaign, and women and the most highly educated blacks were the most likely to attend such churches. (See Appendix B.2, Table 1.)

Civil rights organizations reached fewer people, although nearly a quarter said they were members of an organization working to improve the status of blacks. Of these, three-quarters were fairly or very active. Membership and activism were highest among the most affluent and highly educated, as well as among older blacks. (See Appendix B.2, Table 1.)

GROUP SOLIDARITY

By providing opportunities, making action easier, and exerting group pressure, structural resources and organizations increase the likelihood that group members will take part in collective action. Group solidarity helps ensure that they will. When members of a deprived social category care about each other, feel themselves bound by a shared culture and common fate, and develop an ideology concerning the group's position in society, they are motivated to take part in collective activities. In categories in which few members identify with the group and few have a sense of group political consciousness, members cannot be readily mobilized. Group solidarity is a powerful resource, especially for social categories lacking access to many of the economic and political channels that normally are used to secure attention to a group's interests.

Traditional accounts of electoral politics have generally not emphasized the importance of solidarity.[43] Notable exceptions are Olsen[44] and Verba and Nie,[45] who in the early 1970s used concepts similar to the components of political consciousness delineated here to explain why blacks participate in electoral politics at rates higher than would be predicted on the basis of their socioeconomic resources alone. Their explanation is that political activism is fostered by the awareness among blacks of their shared status as members of an unjustly deprived category. Previous research shows that among blacks the effects of solidarity are seen in voting as well as in other forms of political activity: electoral campaign activities and traditional non-electoral citizen actions, such as contacting public officials and participating in protest activities.[46]

Drawing from both relative-deprivation and solidarity or resource-mobilization theories of collective action, we distinguish two components of solidarity: group identification—awareness of commonality and acceptance of group membership as important to the self; and

TABLE 2.2
Group Solidarity and Organizational Resources

Resource	Total Sample[a]	Significant Structural or Demographic Predictors[b]
Group Solidarity Resources		
Closeness to Other Blacks		
Respondent feels close to black people in this country in terms of ideas and feelings about things.	93%	
Sense of Common Fate (post-election)		No significant predictors
Summary Index of Components Below		Common fate higher among the more educated, male, and higher income respondents
How much of what happens to black people has something to do with respondent's own life?		
A lot	23%	
Some	10	
Not very much	30	
Not at all	30	
No response	7	
	100%	
Has the movement for black rights affected respondent personally?		
Yes	59%	
No	41	
	100%	
How much does respondent think about being black and what he or she has in common with other blacks?		
A lot	16%	
Fairly often	14	
Once in a while	27	
Hardly ever	41	
Don't know/no response	2	
	100%	
Exclusivist Black Identity (post-election)		Black identity more important among those not working full-time and younger respondents
Which is more important, being		
Black	11%	
Both black and American	72	
American	13	
Neither	4	
	100%	

76

TABLE 2.2
(continued)

Resource	Total Sample[a]	Significant Structural or Demographic Predictors[b]
Group Consciousness (post-election)		
Power Discontent		Discontent greater among more
The amount of influence blacks have in American life and politics is:		educated, higher income, older, and non-southern respondents
Far too little	44%	
Somewhat too little	35	
The right amount	16	
Too much	2	
No response	3	
	100%	
The amount of discontent with influence of subordinate groups (the Rainbow Coalition): blacks, the poor, people on welfare, the old, women, the young (percentage in highest category of discontent, on five-point index)	36%	Discontent greater among non-southern, more educated, higher income, and female respondents
Rejection of Legitimacy of Race Stratification		No significant predictors
If black people don't do well in life, it is because:		
They are kept back because of their race	62%	
They don't work hard enough to get ahead	38	
	100%	
Discrimination against blacks is no longer a problem in this country.		No significant predictors
Disagree strongly	68%	
Disagree somewhat	22	
Agree (somewhat and strongly)	10	
	100%	

77

TABLE 2.2
(continued)

Resource	Total Sample[a]	Significant Structural or Demographic Predictors[b]
Collective Political Strategies		No significant predictors
To have power and improve their position in the United States:		
Black people should be more active in black organizations	62%	
or		
Each black person should work hard to improve his or her own personal situation	33	
No response	5	
	100%	
Nationalism		Nationalism higher among more educated and male respondents
Respondent strongly agrees or agrees that:		
Black people should shop in black-owned stores whenever they can	57%	
Black children should learn an African language	37%	
Blacks should not have anything to do with whites	4%	
Organizational Resources		
Church-Based		
Frequency of church attendance (pre-election)		More frequent among women, older, southern, and married respondents
Every week	32%	
Almost every week	15	
1–2 times a month	27	
Few times a year	19	
Never	6	
No response	1	
	100%	

78

TABLE 2.2
(continued)

Resource	Total Sample[a]	Significant Structural or Demographic Predictors[b]
A church encouraged political involvement (post-election)		Church encouragement greater among female and more educated respondents
Summary index of components below (the percentage in highest category, on three-point index)	31%	
Respondent attends a church where announcements or talks about the campaign were made.	35%	
Respondent attends a church that encouraged members to vote in 1984 election.	36%	
Civil Rights Organization		Membership in civil rights organization greater among more educated, older, and higher income respondents
Respondent is a member of an organization working to improve the status of blacks. (post-election)	23%	
How active is respondent in these organizations? (Asked only of those who are members.)		
Very	40%	
Fairly	32	
Not very	24	
Not at all	4	
	100%	

[a] Percentages are based on a weighted N of 1,293, which represents an unweighted N of 871 respondents who participated in both the pre- and post-election surveys.

[b] Results summarized are based on multiple regressions in which group solidarity and organizational resources are regressed on age, education, family income, employment status, Social Security and receipt of other government assistance, gender, region, and urbanicity. Race of interviewer was controlled in each regression.

group political consciousness—a political ideology about the group's position in society.[47]

Group identification transforms a social category into a collectivity[48] and leads to political consciousness. Most relative deprivation theories, however, do not explicitly address how group identification affects awareness of collective deprivation or gives it a political interpretation. In contrast, resource-mobilization theories do offer a motivational interpretation of members' awareness of common feelings.[49] Recruitment, mobilization, and organization are more easily achieved when members feel a strong group identity and have bonds with others who share the same feelings. Action, in turn, strengthens identification and helps members grasp the politics in intergroup relations. Even without group action, identification has cognitive effects that foster political consciousness.[50] By sharpening the salience of groups and the likelihood that members will draw intergroup comparisons, identification encourages group members to recognize the collective bases of deprivation and deny its legitimacy. When perceived as a common rather than an individual condition, deprivation is more easily interpreted in political terms.

Group political consciousness, a multidimensional ideology, involves three components. The first, discontent with the group's power and share of societal resources, reflects the central concern of relative-deprivation theories. To develop a sense of collective discontent, members must make comparisons between their group and others. Yet the social psychological literature on social comparison suggests that people usually focus less on groups than on other individuals in making social comparisons.[51] Thus a central question is: What structural and psychological forces might encourage members to focus on groups and to compare their group with relevant outgroups, so as to become collectively discontented?

One structural condition that either facilitates or blocks outward comparisons is the legitimacy of the prevailing social structure.[52] When societal arrangements are widely accepted as legitimate, members of deprived groups usually accept the normative view. Not questioning the dominant ideology, they tend to look inward at members of their own group. This suggests the second component of political consciousness, how group members appraise the legitimacy of disparities between their group and other groups. Disparity will not be experienced as unjust deprivation unless members perceive illegitimate forces as its source. If disparity is believed to develop from the inadequacies of individuals in one group and the talents of individuals in another, it will be judged legitimate. The same disparity will be judged illegitimate if it is believed to result from structural barriers that hold back the members of a group through little fault of their own.

The third component of group political consciousness, commitment to collective political strategies, is common to relative-deprivation and resource-mobilization theories in that each seeks to explain how and why change-oriented action emerges in a constituency. Group political consciousness requires that group members believe that they should work together to attack obstacles that affect the group as a whole.

To test this conception of group solidarity, responses to sixteen questions intended to measure group identification and consciousness were factor-analyzed. (One question, which measured closeness to other blacks, was not included in the factor analysis because virtually everyone answered it showing a high level of group identification. Of the sample, 93 percent said they felt close to other blacks in terms of shared ideas and feelings. This widespread sense of closeness simultaneously verifies the solidarity of the black community and makes this measure unusable in statistical analysis.)

The factor-analysis results support the differentiation between identification and political consciousness as well as the distinctions within political consciousness. They also demonstrated an unexpected distinction within identification.

Group Identification

Two of the factors measured group identification. One was based on a sense of common fate; the other, on a sense of being black rather than American. The distinction between these two types of group identities is supported by their separation in the factor analysis as well as by other criteria (see pages 85–86).

Group identification based on common fate[53] involves two elements: awareness of interdependence (recognition that what happens to blacks generally also affects one's own life and that the black rights movement affects one personally), and centrality of group membership (following Converse, measured by asking how much individuals think about a particular issue[54]—in this instance, about being black and what they have in common with other blacks). The survey indicates that more blacks felt that the black rights movement had had personal impact than recognized a general interdependence between themselves and the group. Three-fifths believed the movement had affected them, but the same proportion also said that there was either "no" or "not very much" connection between the outcome of their own life and what happens to blacks generally. On the centrality question, one-third said that they think "a lot" or "fairly often" about being black and their commonality with other blacks, while 44 percent said they "hardly ever" did. (See Table 2.2.)

The level at which blacks maintain a sense of common fate can be put in broader perspective by comparing it with results of a 1983 national study of women's gender identity. That study used the same three indicators of common fate, substituting the label "women" for "blacks." Not unexpectedly, the comparison demonstrated that the sense of common fate was more widespread among blacks than among women.[55] Compared with women, 15 percent more of the nation's blacks believe there is a general contingency between personal and group outcomes, 28 percent more feel that the group's movement for equal rights has affected them personally, and 10 percent more say they think "a lot" or "fairly often" about their group membership.

On the summary index formed from responses to the three indicators, the sense of common fate was particularly widespread among the most highly educated and affluent blacks and among men. Structural advantage rather than deprivation undergirds this aspect of group identification. (See Appendix B.2, Table 2.)

The exclusivist black identity was measured by responses to a question asking, "Which would you say is more important to you—being black or being American, or are both equally important to you?" A large majority reported feeling a dual identity as both black and American. The remainder were equally split between feeling exclusively American and exclusively black.[56] For the analyses in this book, this measure was scored dichotomously, as having an exclusivist black identity or not. Younger blacks and those not working full-time were the most likely to have such an identity. (See Appendix B.2, Table 2.)

Group Political Consciousness

Collective discontent was measured in two ways—in reference to the political power of blacks and in reference to groups Jackson included in the Rainbow Coalition: the poor, the elderly, women, people on welfare, and the young.[57] Respondents were asked whether they thought each of these groups had "too much," "the right amount," "somewhat too little," or "far too little" influence in American life and politics. In a factor analysis, evaluations of the power of blacks clustered with evaluations of other Rainbow Coalition groups. The black electorate judged poor people the most powerless (65 percent thought they have "far too little" power), then people on welfare (50 percent) and blacks

(44 percent), followed by the elderly (38 percent), young people (33 percent), and women (26 percent). (See Table 2.2.)

Blacks living outside the South and having the most education and highest family income expressed the most discontent with the limited collective power of blacks and of other groups within the Rainbow Coalition. Older blacks also were especially discontented, but specifically with the powerlessness of blacks. Again, the structurally advantaged, not the deprived, displayed most solidarity. (See Appendix B.2, Table 3.)

Rejection of legitimacy was measured by two questions. One asked respondents to choose between two alternatives: "if black people don't do well in life, it is because they don't work hard enough to get ahead" (the personal attribution), and "they are kept back because of their race" (the structural attribution). Choosing the personal attribution indicates a belief that racial disparities are legitimate in that the rules by which rewards are allocated are fair—blacks just need to work harder. Choosing the structural attribution indicates a belief that discrimination makes racial disparities illegitimate. People can subscribe to both beliefs, of course, and a question forcing them to choose between the two may not represent the subtlety of their beliefs. Nonetheless, forced-choice questions are useful in pressing people to decide which of two accepted beliefs is dominant. The other question asked how strongly respondents agreed or disagreed with the statement that "discrimination against blacks is no longer a problem in the United States."

To measure collective action, respondents were asked to choose between two political strategies blacks might use "to have power and improve their position in the United States." One was a collective, organizational strategy; the other, an individual mobility strategy. Respondents were asked whether "black people should be more active in black organizations" or "each black person should work hard to improve his or her own personal situation."

The structural and collective perspectives were broadly based in the black electorate. Approximately 60 percent in all sectors preferred the structural over the personal explanation for blacks "not doing well in life" and the collective over the individual political strategy. And all but 10 percent thought that discrimination was still a serious societal problem.

A final component of solidarity, black nationalism, bridges the distinction between identification and consciousness by referring to both group bonds and action strategies. Respondents were asked their level of agreement with three statements: "black people should shop in black-owned stores whenever possible"; "blacks should not have anything to do with whites if they can help it"; and "black children should learn an African language." Although very few "strongly agreed" with any of these statements, combining those who did with those who just "agreed" indicates that a majority thought blacks should support black businesses, and over one-third believed that black children should learn an African language. Interpersonal separatism of blacks and whites was resoundingly rejected: only 4 percent thought that blacks should have nothing to do with whites. Like most other elements of solidarity, support for nationalism on the summary index proved strongest among the most highly educated and the older members of the black electorate.

The statistically reliable effects of structural and demographic influences consistently indicated that solidarity was heightened by the same structural resources that generally promote participation in politics. (See Appendix B.2, Table 3.) Education and economic resources strengthened racial solidarity and its organizational expression through membership in groups working to improve the status of blacks. These results consistently demonstrate that middle class blacks were not unconcerned about the collective fate of the group or disassociated from the least privileged in the black community. The positive effects of structural advantages should not be exaggerated, however, since education and income accounted for only 2–11 percent of the variation in solidarity. Thus, while solidarity was somewhat more prevalent among the structurally advantaged, it was also present throughout the black community.

Two Types of Solidarity

Two types of identity, that based on a sense of common fate and that based on feeling black but not American, define two types of solidarity. One was politicized, the other was not.

The political distinction is revealed by different patterns of associations between the two identity measures and measures of group political consciousness, policy preferences, and political participation. (See Table 2.3 and Appendix B.2, Table 4.) Blacks whose group identity was based on a sense of common fate were more discontented with the group's political influence and economic status than were other blacks; they more frequently said that racial discrimination is still a serious problem, attributed racial disparities in status and resources to systemic causes, and advocated collective political strategies to deal

TABLE 2.3
Two Types of Solidarity

	Common-Fate Identity	Exclusivist Black Identity
Politicalization		
Group political consciousness	Discontented with limited power of blacks Believes discrimination is still a problem Rejects legitimacy of racial disparities Discontented with economic status of blacks	Discontented with economic status of blacks
Policy preferences	Approves greater spending on social welfare and community needs Believes in pressuring Congress to change toward South African policy Favors government assurance of standard of living Favors government aid to minorities	Favors government assurance of standard of living Favors government aid to minorities
Political participation	Member of black organization Involved in church-based campaigning Involved in traditional campaigning Involved in petitioning Involved in direct action Voted for a black candidate in 1984 Voted in the 1980 and the 1984 presidential races	
Intergroup Context		
Pro-black (nationalism)	Feels close to Africans and West Indians Believes black children should learn an African language Believes blacks should patronize black-owned stores	Believes black children should learn an African language Believes blacks should patronize black-owned stores
Feelings toward whites		Doesn't feel close to whites Believes blacks should have nothing to do with whites

TABLE 2.3
(continued)

	Common-Fate Identity	Exclusivist Black Identity
Political judgments of superordinates	Believes whites have too much political power Believes whites want to keep blacks down Believes businessmen have too much political power Believes men have too much political power	Believes whites have too much political power Believes whites want to keep blacks down
Political judgments of subordinates	Believes people on welfare have too little political power Believes women have too little political power Believes poor people have too little political power Believes older people have too little political power	
Structural Location	Higher education Higher income	Not employed full-time Younger

with these problems. They were also more active than others in a wide range of protest and electoral political activities, and they more strongly favored an activist role for the government in both racial and non-racial matters. This type of solidarity had a consistent political underpinning. In contrast, few of these political measures were related to the other type of solidarity. Solidarity based on an exclusivist black identity was naturally pro-black, but sentiments were more cultural and economic than political.

Associations with measures of intergroup attitudes further validate the distinctiveness of the two types of solidarity. Common-fate solidarity was pro-black yet inclusive. Blacks who claimed this kind of solidarity evaluated whites as positively as other blacks did, and they were more, rather than less, bothered about the limited power of older people, poor people, people on welfare, and women. In contrast, the solidarity based on an exclusivist black identity showed an exclusivity in identity itself and in a narrow preoccupation with black-white relationships. Blacks who thought of themselves as black but not American did not feel close to whites and, more than other blacks, believed that blacks should have nothing to do with whites and that whites want to keep blacks down. Moreover, they were not broadly concerned with power differences between the haves and have-nots but were aggrieved in particular about the excessive amount of power held by whites.

The distinction between these two types of solidarity is used in Chapters Four and Five to clarify the two expressions of independence found in support for Jackson and a separate black party.

IDEOLOGY AND POLICY PREFERENCES

The political beliefs comprising group consciousness are not the only beliefs that influence the engagement of citizens in politics. In choosing additional beliefs and policy preferences for this large-scale national survey, we were guided by research on the determinants of candidate choice and participation in electoral politics.

According to political scientists, some of these political orientations are basic and have persistent influence, while others are more immediate and have transitory impact on an individual's judgments and decisions. Among the former, great stress is placed on liberal/conservative ideology and party identification. Roughly two-thirds of the American public claim to be either liberal or conservative, and their positions are associated with beliefs about the appropriate balance between government and individual responsibility—the aspect of political ideology that is emphasized in this book.[58] Shanks and Miller make a case for considering ideological identification as the most distal of all political influences, preceding the effect of party identification on the individual.[59] Recent evidence supports their view in that ideological position is more stable than party identification. The political literature, however, says little about the importance of either liberal/conservative ideology or party identification among blacks, since national samples have not yielded a large enough number of blacks to explore their meaning among different groups of blacks.

Party identification varies so little among blacks as compared with whites that the evaluation of candidates by blacks cannot be distinguished by party identification. In 1984, the vast majority (86 percent) of the black electorate considered themselves Democrats. Degree of partisanship varied more. Slightly over half of these black Democrats considered themselves strong Democrats; nearly three-tenths, weak Democrats; and the remainder, independent Democrats. Older people and women were the most partisan; social class was not a significant factor. (See Table 2.4 for the distributions on these and

TABLE 2.4
General Political Orientations

Orientation	All Respondents[a]	Respondents with Opinion[b]	Significant Structural/ Demographic Predictors[c]
Basic Political Dispositions			
Liberal/Conservative Identification (post-election)			Liberal: older, more educated, urban
Strong liberal	16%	—	
Not very strong/slightly liberal	23		
Moderate	6		
Not very strong/slightly conservative	23		
Strong conservative	11		
Don't know/no response	21		
	100%		
Party Identification (pre-election)			Democratic: older, female
Strong Democrat	47%	—	
Weak Democrat	24		
Independent/leaning Democrat	15		
Independent	6		
Republican—all strengths	8		
	100%		
Domestic Policy Issues (post-election)			
Spending on Community Needs *Summary index of components below*			Favoring increased spending: urban, more educated
Increase spending on dealing with crime	58%	—	
Public schools	81%		
Government jobs for unemployed	80%		
Spending on Social Welfare *Summary index of components below*			Favoring increased spending: non-southern, less educated
Increase spending on Medicare	79%	—	
Food stamps	50%		

TABLE 2.4
(continued)

Orientation	All Respondents[a]	Respondents with Opinion[b]	Significant Structural/ Demographic Predictors[c]
Government Assurance of Jobs and Standard of Living (percentage advocating government involvement, on a seven-point scale)			Favoring government involvement: not working full-time
Extensive (1–3)	43%	—	
Moderate (4)	24		
Minimal (5–7)	33		
	100%		
Pro-government Action to Help Blacks			No significant predictors
Summary index of components below			
Because of past discrimination, minorities should be given special consideration in hiring.			
Strongly/somewhat agree	58%	—	
Government should make every possible effort to improve the social and economic position of blacks and other minorities.			
Strongly/somewhat agree	86%	—	
School integration			Favoring integration: male
Summary index of components below			
Racial integration is so important that it justifies busing children to schools outside their neighborhood.			
Strongly/somewhat agree	48%	—	
Improving schools in black neighborhoods is more important than busing children to achieve racial integration.			
Strongly/somewhat agree	79%	—	

89

TABLE 2.4
(continued)

Orientation	All Respondents[a]	Respondents with Opinion[b]	Significant Structural/ Demographic Predictors[c]
Foreign Policy Issues (post-election)			
Central America (percentage responding to U.S. involvement, on a seven-point scale)			Favoring more involvement: male, southern
U.S. should become			
More involved in internal affairs of Central American countries (1–3)	11%	18%	
Neither more nor less involved (4)	10	14	
Less involved (5–7)	50	68	
Haven't thought about it.	29	—	
	100%	100%	
South Africa			Strongly favoring pressure to change U.S.– South Africa policy: older, non-southern
How important is it that black people should bring pressure on Congress to change U.S. policies toward South Africa?			
Very important	39%	63%	
Somewhat important	16	25	
Not too important	7	12	
Haven't thought about it.	38	—	
	100%	100%	
Defense Spending (percentage responding, on a seven-point scale)			Favoring increased spending: less educated, lower income, southern
Federal spending on military should be	—		
Increased (1–3)		25%	
Kept the same (4)		37	
Decreased (5–7)		38	
		100%	
Evaluations of Economic Conditions (pre-election)			
Personal Evaluations			
Compared to a year ago, your and your family's economic situation is		—	Worse economic situation: older, not working full-time, lower income, not receiving Social Security

90

TABLE 2.4
(continued)

Orientation	All Respondents[a]	Respondents with Opinion[b]	Significant Structural/ Demographic Predictors[c]
Much better	12%		
Better	33		
The same	21		
Worse	23		
Much worse	10		
Don't know/no response	1		
	100%		
Compared to four years ago, your and your family's economic situation is		—	Worse economic situation: older, not working full-time, lower income, not receiving Social Security, receiving other welfare
Much better	22%		
Better	29		
The same	11		
Worse	19		
Much worse	17		
Don't know/no response	2		
	100%		
Group Evaluations			
Contemporary			Worse economic position of blacks: non-southern, older, married
Summary index of components below			
The economic position of blacks relative to whites is		—	
Much better	3%		
Better	4		
The same	26		
Worse	28		
Much worse	33		
Don't know/no response	6		
	100%		
As a group blacks are getting along economically		—	
Very well	11%		
Fairly well	44		
Not too well	30		
Not well at all	10		
Don't know/no response	5		
	100%		

TABLE 2.4
(continued)

Orientation	All Respondents[a]	Respondents with Opinion[b]	Significant Structural/ Demographic Predictors[c]
Historical			
Compared to a year ago, the economic situation of blacks is			Worse economic situation of blacks: non-southern, older, more educated
Much better	6%	—	
Better	21		
The same	35		
Worse	18		
Much worse	16		
Don't know/no response	4		
	100%		
Compared to four years ago, the economic situation of blacks is			Worse economic situation of blacks: non-southern, older, more educated, married
Much better	9%	—	
Better	27		
The same	12		
Worse	22		
Much worse	24		
Don't know/no response	6		
	100%		
Economic Circumstances of the Nation			
Over the past year, the nation's economy has gotten			Worse national economy: older, receiving welfare
Much better	4%	—	
Better	16		
The same	31		
Worse	20		
Much worse	27		
Don't know/no response	2		
	100%		

[a] Responses on policy questions in which respondents were asked explicitly whether they had thought about the issue. If they said no, they were not asked the attitude question.
[b] Post-election percentages are based on a weighted N of 1,293 (unweighted 871); pre-election percentages, on a weighted N of 1,700 (unweighted 1,150).
[c] Results summarized are based on multiple regressions in which political orientations are regressed on age, education, family income, employment status, Social Security and receipt of other government assistance, gender, region, and urbanicity. Race of interviewer was controlled in each regression.

other political orientations and Appendix B.2, Tables 5–10, for their structural correlates.)

Ideological position varied more. Of those who placed themselves on a liberal-conservative scale (one-fifth declined to do so), about half considered themselves liberals; a few, moderates; and slightly less than half, conservatives. Yet since most blacks favor an activist federal government and redistributive social and economic policies, perspectives indicating a liberal ideology, the self-definition scale appeared invalid as a measure of political ideology and not likely to distinguish reactions to the 1984 election.[60]

Two other sets of political orientations, usually treated as having short-term influence on electoral politics, were included: preferences on policy issues, and evaluations of economic conditions (including personal and family economic situations, the economic position of blacks as a group, and the general health of the economy).

Controversy surrounds both. With respect to policy issues, the controversy concerns the relative importance of issues and party identification in accounting for voters' choices. For a long time, the claim asserted by Campbell and colleagues in *The American Voter*[61]—that party identification is more influential than issues—dominated the view of political scientists. Now, however, it is clear that voters also make candidate choices based on their policy preferences, especially when parties and candidates define clear alternatives.[62]

With respect to economic judgments, the controversy concerns the extent to which voters are motivated by economic self-interest. Although it is widely believed that people "vote their pocketbooks," systematic empirical tests provide only weak support for this assumption. Reviewing the evidence, Kinder and Sears conclude that "neither losing a job, nor deteriorating family conditions, nor pessimism about the family's economic future has much to do with support for policies designed to alleviate personal economic distress. Economic self-interest influences policy beliefs only when the stakes are especially clear and large and even then the effects tend to be highly circumscribed."[63]

Kinder, Sears, and their colleagues have also demonstrated that the decisions of voters are shaped by what they call sociotropic economic evaluations (judgments of the nation's economic health) often more than by personal economic circumstances. In addition, candidate preferences sometimes reflect concern with the economic condition of one's social group, although as the relevant group narrows, group interest becomes difficult to distinguish from self-interest, and as it widens, it becomes difficult to distinguish from national interest.[64]

Because employment and low-wage scales affect the lives of many blacks, economic issues at all three levels—personal, group, and national—might have great political significance for the black electorate. We emphasized group-level economic judgments as another way of tapping collective discontent and determining whether political and economic bases of discontent have similar political implications. Our analyses showed that discontent with the group's economic status was part of group political consciousness (see Appendix B.2, Table 4) but was not related as strongly to support for Jackson or for a black political voice as was political discontent. (See Chapters Four and Five.)

The black electorate expressed much greater concern for the economic situation of the racial group and the nation than for its personal circumstances. Only one-third felt their personal and family economic status was worse than it had been a year earlier, whereas nearly half thought the nation's economy had deteriorated in that period. Even more striking, 57 percent felt that the economic situation of blacks was worse than a year earlier; 63 percent felt that it was worse than the economic situation of whites; and 41 percent felt that blacks were not getting along very well in an absolute sense. (See Table 2.4.)

Did these appraisals measure a generalized perspective on economic problems? The average correlation among them (.255) was statistically significant, but differences in their relationships to demographic factors showed that they did not all mean the same thing. Material self-interest fueled judgments of personal circumstances but not judgments of the economic status of blacks as a group. Blacks who felt themselves and their families worse off than they were a year or four years earlier were poorer than other blacks. They had a lower income; fewer of them were employed full-time; and more were receiving Social Security and various forms of welfare.

In marked contrast, judgments of the group's economic situation were unrelated to personal financial circumstances. Middle income blacks were as concerned as those with lower incomes about the economic problems experienced by the group as a whole. This finding demonstrates that the relatively greater affluence of middle class blacks does not make them insensitive to the collective problems of the black population. Moreover, the more negative appraisal of the group's economic situation among the most highly educated shows that education promotes collective economic discontent as well as political discontent and other elements of political consciousness. (See Appendix B.2, Tables 8 and 9, for these effects.)

To examine policy preferences, evaluations of thirteen policies (ten concerning domestic issues and three concerning foreign policy or military issues) were measured and factor-analyzed. Four multiple-item factors emerged, all involving domestic policies.

Two factors gauged whether federal spending should be increased, decreased, or kept the same in two policy areas: social welfare (spending on food stamps and Medicare) and community needs (spending on crime-related programs, public schools, and jobs for the unemployed). The majority believed that spending should be increased in all these programs, and three-quarters or more supported an increase for public schools, jobs, and Medicare. Slightly less than the majority favored an increase for food stamps. (See Table 2.4.)

A question traditionally asked in the Michigan election surveys— whether or not government should ensure jobs and a decent standard of living—clustered together with the items on the community-spending factor, but only slightly. We decided to treat the standard-of-living question as a separate policy indicator. It states: "Some people feel the government in Washington should see to it that every person has a job and a good standard of living; others think the government should let each person get ahead on his/her own. Where would you place yourself?" Respondents were given a seven-point scale, with these statements representing the extremes. Favoring government involvement (positions 1–3) were 43 percent; nearly one-quarter placed themselves in the middle (position 4); and one-third were opposed (positions 5–7).

Another factor, comprised of two items, focused on government intervention in racial matters. The vast majority agreed that "government should make every possible effort to improve the social and economic position of blacks and other minorities." Fewer (slightly over half) agreed with affirmative action as we identified it: "Because of past discrimination, minorities should be given special consideration in hiring."

Attitudes toward school integration involved considerable ambivalence. There was greater support for improving schools in black neighborhoods than for busing children to non-neighborhood schools, but half also agreed that racial integration is important enough to justify busing.

The survey included only a few questions on foreign and military policies, and the factor analysis showed that they did not cluster together. On one question concerning South Africa—"How important is it for black people to bring pressure on Congress to change U.S. policies on South Africa?"—slightly over one-third had no opinion. Of those who did have an opinion, two-thirds considered it very important (38 percent had not thought about it). Two-thirds of those who had thought about policy in Central America were opposed to greater United States involvement in the affairs of Central American countries (29 percent had not thought about it). Virtually all respondents had thought about, and had opinions on, military spending, as they did on spending for social welfare and community needs. Support for increased military spending paled in comparison to support for social programs: only one-quarter favored increasing the military or defense budget, and the remainder split evenly between keeping expenditures at the 1984 level and lowering them.

The positions blacks took on these policy issues were only weakly affected by their age, gender, structural position, or geographic location. (See Appendix B.2, Table 6.) Of these, region had the most consistent—though small—effects. Support for government spending on crime and on food stamps and for a change in United States policy toward South Africa was greater outside the South, while support for greater involvement in Central America and for increases in the military budget was greater within the South. Education had three significant effects: the highly educated favored greater spending on schools and less spending on Medicare and the military. The electorate's positions on policy were only weakly tied to personal economic self-interests. Income, for example, had only two reliable effects: people with a lower income more frequently supported increases for the military budget and job programs for the unemployed. On other material bases of self-interest, the results were mixed. Support for Medicare was greater among people receiving Social Security, and approval of food stamps and government assurance of a decent standard of living was greater among people not working full-time. No other policy attitudes were motivated by personal circumstances, however.

PERSONAL PSYCHOLOGICAL RESOURCES

Individual citizens bring many personal resources to the political world. Some are interested in politics; others are bored by it. Some feel politically efficacious, capable of understanding political events and confident they can influence government officials and agencies; others do not. Apathy, political disaffection, and feelings of powerlessness may keep people from acquiring the habit of voting.

Younger people usually are less interested in politics and participate less than their elders.[65] In 1984, however, young people seemed more interested than usual, possibly because voter-registration groups had targeted the young. Throughout the campaign, the media highlighted Jackson's appeal to young audiences, both black and white, and emphasized his attractiveness to black yuppies—young urban professionals. Since it was not clear whether Jackson appealed broadly to young blacks, we paid special attention to the location of Jackson's support among the young, especially to the possibility that age and social class might be mutually reinforcing and that low-income youths would be unusually apolitical.

Scholars have long believed that interest and apathy explain individual differences in political participation as well as group differences between blacks and whites, although the idea that apathy reduces the participation of blacks has also been criticized. Some analysts argued that fear was far more serious until voting rights were ensured by practice as well as law. In Mississippi, Salamon and Van Evera found that fear, measured by the proportion of a county's occupations in which blacks were most subjected to white control, accounted for 20 percent of county variation in turnout in the presidential election.[66] When St. Angelo and Puryear reexamined the impact of fear and apathy in Mississippi across three elections (the 1968 and 1972 presidential and the 1971 gubernatorial races), they found that both feelings were consequential. These researchers collected survey measures of fear and apathy in four Mississippi counties. Fear was indicated by agreement that their voting might bring blacks personal harm and that their voting might lead whites to make trouble for black people in general. Apathy was indicated by admission of not talking about politics, de-emphasizing the importance of voting, and paying little attention to campaigns. Both sets of measures influenced turnout, although individual differences in voting were explained better by apathy than by fear.[67]

Whatever its role earlier, interest in politics was considered a likely resource in 1984. Surveys administered between 1980 and 1984 indicated that over half the black population had become more interested in politics since 1980.[68] We measured political interest in several ways. Three diagnostic questions, traditionally asked in the Michigan election surveys, were included. One was asked in both the pre- and post-election surveys: "Some people don't pay much attention to political campaigns. How about you? Would you say you have been very much interested, somewhat interested, or not much interested in the political campaigns so far this year?" The two others were asked in the pre-election survey: "Generally speaking, would you say you care a good deal which party wins the presidential election this fall, or that you don't care very much which party wins?" and "Some people seem to follow government and public affairs most of the time whether there's an election going on or not. Others are not that interested. Would you

TABLE 2.5
Psychological Resources

Psychological Resources	Pre-election[a]	Post-election[b]	Significant Structural/ Demographic Predictors[c]
Age (in years)			
17–24	19%	—	
25–34	29		
35–54	30		
55 or older	22		
	100%		
General Political Interest			
How much attention paid to political campaigns?			Both pre- and post-election, interest greater: older, more educated; pre-election only: female, not receiving Social Security
Very much interested	42%	48%	
Somewhat interested	41	37	
Not much interested	16	14	
Don't know/no response	1	1	
	100%	100%	
How much do you follow what's going on in government and public affairs?			Follows what's going on: more educated, older, female, urban
Most of the time	38%	—	
Some of the time	35		
Only now and then	17		
Hardly at all	9		
Don't know/no response	1		
	100%		
How much do you care which party wins the 1984 presidential election?			Cares about party: more educated, southern, urban
Care a great deal	75%	—	
Don't care very much	22		
Don't know/no response	3		
	100%		
Interest Aroused by Black Politics			
How has success of black candidates for mayor in some of the big cities affected interest in the 1984 election?			Interest greater: urban

TABLE 2.5
(continued)

Psychological Resources	Pre-election[a]	Post-election[b]	Significant Structural/ Demographic Predictors[c]
More interested	44%	—	
Same	53		
Less interested	1		
Don't know/no response	2		
	100%		
How much has the candidacy of Jesse Jackson affected interest in the 1984 election?			Interest greater: southern
More interested	46%	—	
Same	51		
Less interested	2		
Don't know/no response	1		
	100%		
Belief in Group Political Efficacy			
If enough blacks vote, they can make a difference in who gets elected president.			Pre-election, no significant predictors; post-election, greater efficacy: younger; younger changed less
Agree strongly	72%	48%	
Agree somewhat	17	26	
Disagree somewhat, disagree strongly	11	26	
	100%	100%	
Black people can make a difference in who gets elected in *local* elections.			Pre- and post-election, greater efficacy: more educated; post-election only: married; better educated changed less
Agree strongly	74%	59%	
Agree somewhat	18	29	
Disagree somewhat, disagree strongly	8	12	
	100%	100%	
If blacks, other minorities, the poor, and women pulled together, they could decide how this country is run.			Pre-election, no significant predictors; post-election, more efficacy: better educated; better educated changed less
Agree strongly	53%	43%	
Agree somewhat	27	28	
Disagree	20	29	
	100%	100%	

TABLE 2.5
(continued)

Psychological Resources	Pre-election[a]	Post-election[b]	Significant Structural/ Demographic Predictors[c]
Sense of Personal Political Competence			
Sometimes politics and government seem so complicated that a person like me can't really understand what's going on.	—	39%	Greater feelings of competence: higher income, more educated, younger
Evaluations of the Political System			
System Responsiveness *Summary index of components below*			Both pre- and post-election, perception that system is responsive: more educated, younger, higher income; pre-election only: southern, non-urban
People like me don't have any say about what government does.			
Agree	36%	51%	
Disagree	64	49	
	100%	100%	
I don't think government officials care much about what people like me think.			
Agree	51%	53%	
Disagree	49	47	
	100%	100%	
Trust in Government *Summary index of components below*			Both pre- and post-election, greater distrust: northern, urban; post-election only: full-time workers, female
How much of the time can you trust the government in Washington to do what is right?			
Just about always	5%	4%	
Most of the time	20	19	
Only some of the time	71	73	
None of the time	2	2	
Don't know/no response	2	2	
	100%	100%	

100

TABLE 2.5
(continued)

Psychological Resources	*Pre-election[a]*	*Post-election[b]*	*Significant Structural/ Demographic Predictors[c]*
Would you say that government is:			
Run by a few big interests out for themselves	70%	70%	
or			
Run for the benefit of all the people	30	30	
	100%	100%	

[a] Percentages are based on a weighted N of 1,700 (unweighted 1,150).
[b] Percentages are based on a weighted N of 1,293 (unweighted 871).
[c] Results summarized are based on multiple regressions in which psychological resources are regressed on age, education, family income, employment status, Social Security and receipt of other government assistance, gender, region, and urbanicity. Race of interviewer was controlled in each regression.

say you follow what's going on in government and public affairs most of the time, some of the time, only now and then, or hardly at all?" Both before and after the election, four-fifths were at least somewhat interested in the campaign; over two-fifths were very interested. Three-quarters reported caring about the election outcome and following politics at least some of the time. (See Table 2.5.)

Two new questions referring specifically to black politics were asked in the pre-election survey: "Recently, blacks have been elected mayors in some of the nation's large cities. Would you say that the success of these black candidates has made you more interested in this year's presidential election, less interested, or has your interest stayed pretty much the same?" and "How about the candidacy of Jesse Jackson? Would you say you are now more interested in the presidential election, less interested, or has your interest stayed pretty much the same?" Nearly half said these black candidates had increased their interest. (See Table 2.5.)

The social origins of interest in politics demonstrate a clear distinction between politics generally and black politics in particular. Interest aroused by Jackson's candidacy and the electoral successes of black mayoralty candidates was equally apparent in all social and economic sectors of the black population: the well educated and the less educated, higher and lower income, married and unmarried, male and female, young and old. In contrast, interest in general politics was greatest among the oldest and most highly educated, a social pattern like that found in the white electorate. The two kinds of interest did have similar geographic roots, however: interest in black mayoralty elections was greater in urban settings, and urban dwellers also followed public affairs and cared more about the outcome of the 1984 election. Finally, the Jackson candidacy aroused more interest in the South than elsewhere in the country. (See Appendix B.2, Tables 11–15, for demographic and structural influences on psychological resources.)

Another psychological resource that energizes action is the sense of political efficacy. According to political scientists, citizens participate in politics and remain committed to the basic ideas of democracy and to the electoral process when they believe that they can influence the electoral outcome and the actions of elected officials. When citizens feel incapable of affecting political authorities and institutions, they are far less likely to take part in politics. Hamilton puts it succinctly: "People participate where, when, and how they think it matters."[69]

The existing literature on political efficacy, which primarily treats efficacy as a self-judgment, has limited utility for understanding its impact on participation and political commitment among blacks. Blacks are treated categorically and are discriminated against as a group. Their consciousness of collective treatment and of the power of collective action has been raised by the Civil Rights movement. They have learned that they can have electoral impact by voting as a bloc. Not surprisingly, their sense of political efficacy depends on their perceptions of the collective power of blacks as well as on their individual capacities to affect the political process.

Perceptions of the group's political efficacy were measured in both the pre- and post-election surveys. Respondents were asked the extent of their agreement or disagreement with the following statements: "If enough blacks vote, they can make a difference in who gets elected president"; "Black people can make a difference in who gets elected in local elections"; and "If blacks, other minorities, the poor, and women pulled together, they could decide how the country is run." Although the term *Rainbow Coalition* was not given to respondents, the third statement refers in substance to that theme put forward by the Jackson campaign.

Before the election, the black electorate as a group had a strong sense of political efficacy, for both presidential and local elections. Nearly all agreed (three-quarters strongly) that blacks could make a difference in both types of elections. Four-fifths also agreed (over half strongly) that the Rainbow Coalition could be politically powerful. (See Table 2.5.)

The election dramatically dampened the sense of group efficacy. The figures show a marked decline for the category indicating greatest efficacy (people strongly agreeing with the efficacy statements). Judgments of the group's electoral impact dropped somewhat more for presidential than for local races (24 versus 15 points). This was a realistically assessed difference, since black voters did have more influence in local races than in the presidential outcome. Their views of the Rainbow Coalition's effectiveness were less influenced by the election.

The sense of group political efficacy was spread broadly across the black electorate—in both rural and urban regions, in the South and elsewhere, among the more and less affluent, among men and women. Before the election, only one structural effect was found: education fostered the belief that blacks could influence local elections. Education also buffered the impact of the election: the most highly educated lost less of a sense of group efficacy than others did. (The election also reduced the sense of group efficacy in presidential elections less among younger blacks than among others.)

The distinction between personal and group efficacy is not the only one that must be drawn in order to understand feelings of political effectiveness among blacks. Another pertains to personal efficacy itself, which has an internal dimension involving judgment of the self (the extent to which one can understand politics and act effectively) and an external dimension involving the political system (the extent to which political institutions and authorities are seen as generally responsive to citizens). Lane, a major contributor to the literature on political efficacy, noted this distinction between the self and the system in the late 1950s. He commented that efficacy includes both "the image of the self and the image of democratic government—and contains the tacit assumption that an image of self as effective is intimately related to the image of democratic government as responsive to the people."[70]

These dual images were recognized, but their intimate relationship was not questioned in the quiet political environment of the 1950s. It took activism and confrontational politics to demonstrate that there is no inevitable link between feeling personally competent and believing that authorities and institutions will respond. Outsiders and challengers understand this and are especially likely to distinguish between judgments of the self and those of the system. Belief in the system's responsiveness also affects their participation differently than it does that of conservatives. Perception of unresponsiveness fosters action by challengers; perception of responsiveness fosters action by conservatives. Some research also concludes that a particular combination of beliefs about the self and the system—that oneself is effective while the system is unresponsive—motivates political action among challengers. During the turbulent 1960s and 1970s, this combination fostered participation in protest, and for blacks it also motivated participation in electoral politics.[71]

The measures of political efficacy introduced in the Michigan election surveys in 1952 alluded to both the self and the system. Noting that the items on the original efficacy index did not change the same way over time, Converse suggested that efficacy was not unidimensional.[72] The self component of efficacy is represented by the statement "Sometimes politics and government seem so complicated that a person like me can't really understand what's going on." Competence was identified by disagreement with this item (39 percent of the sample). The system component is represented by two statements: "I don't think public officials care about what people like me think" and "People like me don't have any say about what government does." Both before and after the election, half of those surveyed said that public officials don't care. The election affected responses to the second statement. Before the election, only 36 percent felt that people like them have no say in government; this perception rose 15 percent over the course of the election. (See Table 2.5.)

Some analysts use the term *trust* rather than *system responsiveness* in discussing the system aspect of efficacy. Studying efficacy as the counterpart of political alienation, Gamson and Paige contrast trust (the perception that political institutions and authorities will do what they are supposed to) with competence (the perception that one is personally able to act effectively).[73] Two questions measuring trust introduced in the 1964 Michigan election surveys were included in both our pre- and post-election surveys.[74] Distrust was widespread. Both before and after the election, 70–75 percent thought that only some (or none) of the time can "the government in Washington be trusted to do what is right" and that "the government is pretty much run by a few big interests looking out for themselves instead of for the benefit of all people."

Why was there broader criticism of government on these statements than on those measuring government responsiveness? A thorough analysis of the historical trends, demographic correlates, and internal structure of these system evaluations, carried out by Mason and his colleagues,[75] confirms that there is a persisting, meaningful difference between the trust and the responsiveness items. We suspect that the difference derives from the phrasing of the target being evaluated in the two sets of statements. In the trust statements, the target is simple and straightforward—the government itself. In the responsiveness statements, the target is complex—the relationship between government and citizens.

The social roots of personal political competence, system responsiveness, and trust in government verify differences among them. (See Appendix B.2, Tables 14 and 15). Not surprisingly, the sense of personal competence was most marked among the most educated, affluent, and younger blacks. Like interest in politics, it strongly reflected certain structural advantages but was not influenced by geographic or urban residence. Judgments of the system's responsiveness reflected the same structural origins, although the effects of education and income were weaker.[76] In sharp contrast, distrust was found in all socioeconomic strata and age groups. Even the most highly educated and affluent believed the government cannot be trusted to do what is right or to operate for the benefit of all people. Geographic location was a factor, however: distrust was significantly higher in urban areas and outside the South.

AN OVERVIEW OF MOTIVATION AND RESOURCES

A summary of the wide range of attitudes, judgments, and behaviors that we have covered in this chapter is in order, to highlight the diversity and the social and demographic roots of the black electorate's political motivation and resources.

Our analysis yielded evidence of broad agreement, but not unanimity. If unanimity is taken to require agreement of 95 percent or more of the sample, then the black electorate was unanimous on only one issue—rejecting the idea that blacks should have nothing to do with whites.

Diversity was greatest in five areas: a sense of common fate, self-definition as liberal or conservative, attitudes toward the few foreign policy issues that were included in the survey, evaluations of the responsiveness of the political system, and judgments of one's own and the group's economic circumstances. In one area—the controversial issue of school integration—the electorate's views were characterized by social ambivalence. On the one hand, most agreed that improving black schools is more important than busing; on the other hand, however, a majority said that busing is justified by the importance of racial integration.

On other issues, the black electorate held remarkably similar views. (In Chapter Three we will also show that a sizable majority habitually voted and had common judgments regarding the parties and the 1984 candidates.) Approximately two-thirds or more

- felt close to other blacks, viewed themselves as both black and American, and said that the equal rights movement had affected them personally
- believed that blacks (as well as other subordinate groups) have too little influence in American life and politics
- identified with the Democratic party
- were interested in politics: paid attention to the 1984 election campaign, cared about the election's outcome, and followed government and public affairs even when an election was not underway
- believed that blacks as a group could make a difference in presidential and local elections
- approved liberal social policies: favored increased spending on public schools, government jobs for the unemployed, and Medicare
- favored federal action to improve the social and economic position of blacks and other minorities
- thought that structural forces were more important than personal deficiencies of individuals in explaining why some blacks don't do well in life
- believed that racial discrimination is still a serious problem in the United States and that blacks are worse off economically than whites
- approved collective political strategies for dealing with these problems

In brief, the survey revealed a structurally diverse black electorate that had strong political motivation and resources—namely, group solidarity, support for liberal policies, interest in politics, and a sense of group political efficacy.

Patterns of Variation

To some extent, the variation that existed in the electorate's political motivation and resources was systematically related to structural and demographic factors. The impact of age, structural advantages, and living in an urban or non-urban location are taken up below, in our discussion of class in the black community. We found marital status inconsequential and gender nearly so. Men and women differed on only ten of the sixty-three measures of political motivation and resources, and there was no systematic pattern to these few differences. Region was somewhat more influential, although comparisons of southerners and non-southerners did not support a view of a southern political culture uncongenial to citizen involvement. Southerners participated as frequently as others in all modes of politics except protest and voting for a black candidate. (See Appendix B.3, Table 7.) And, with two exceptions, solidarity and organizational resources were as strong in the South as elsewhere. (The exceptions—group economic discontent and discontent with the limited power of blacks and other subordinate groups—were more pronounced outside the South.)

The Impact of Social Class

Up to this point, we have not used the term *social class*. Instead, we have referred to structural resources that are provided by an individual's employment status, schooling, or family economic status. In order to discuss our results in the context of social class, it is helpful to compare our conceptualization and measures with other social science treatments of class.

Social scientists disagree about the meaning of social class. For some, class denotes conflict groups defined by their location in authority structures. For others, class is determined by a group's relationship to the means of production. For still others, it denotes a group's common chances in the market.

Weber's emphasis on market chances has dominated American studies of social class. Weber did not deny the importance that Marx attributed to a group's relationship to the means of production, but he stressed different implications of owning property. For Weber, property gives owners a privileged position for acquiring valued goods; for Marx, property gives owners control over labor. Weber, like Marx, thought that the basic class division is between capitalists and workers, between owners of property and the propertyless. Property and lack of property are, according to Weber, the "basic categories of all class situations."[77] But Weber drew additional distinctions as well: first, among the propertied, according to the kinds of property they can use for returns in the market; and second, among the propertyless, according to the kinds of skills and services they can offer in the market.

These variations influence life chances and command of the market's rewards.

American social scientists have been drawn to Weber's conception of class because it captures differences in education and skills (represented by the terms *manual* and *nonmanual, blue collar* and *white collar, skilled* and *unskilled*) that have emerged among workers in industrial economies. Moreover, as an individual mode of analysis in which a worker's command of the market's rewards (wages in particular) is determined by the worker's skills and services, the Weberian theory of class fits the characteristic of individualism that prevails in popular theories of income determination in America.

Not surprisingly, most studies of the black class structure have also followed a Weberian approach, typically emphasizing common chances in the market and especially the manual/nonmanual distinction.[78] Two contemporary analysts of black class structure are good examples. Landry, author of *The New Black Middle Class*, defines classes as "groups differing from each other by the average market situation."[79] Wilson, author of *The Declining Significance of Race* and *The Truly Disadvantaged*, defines them as groups of people "who have more or less similar goods, services, or skills to offer for income . . . and who therefore receive similar financial remuneration in the marketplace."[80]

We also define social class in Weberian terms, although instead of emphasizing occupation as the indicator of position in the market, we stress education and economic position. Economic position is represented primarily by family income and secondarily by having a job and enough income from family members' exchange of services in the market to manage without welfare. (Receiving Social Security is not considered part of social class, since it is an age-defined substitution for employment-based income.) We do not treat occupation as the prime criterion of class for two reasons. First, the survey did not collect sufficiently detailed occupational information to make politically relevant distinctions between those whose services and products are used mostly by blacks and those whose services and products are aimed at a white market. (See Chapter Six.) Second, economic rather than occupational inequality is at the heart of current controversies about growing class disparities in the black community.[81]

The conclusions presented in the tables in this chapter (and in Appendix B.2) are based on two sets of multivariate analyses. In the first, single indicators of class (family income, for example) are examined to probe how much each one influences politics when other indicators of class (as well as age and other demographic factors) are equated. This mode of analysis determines whether each indicator of social class has unique effects. In the second set of analyses, we probed the combined effects of education and family income by forming an index on which a standardized measure of each was equally weighted. Analyses using this index show the total effect of education and income and were used to check whether the first mode of analysis produced misleading conclusions about the impact of class. We might have missed a reliable joint effect of education and income when each had small, non-statistically significant effects.

The electorate's policy preferences were largely unaffected by the various indicators of social class. Education and family income rarely influenced attitudes toward the role of government or evaluation of specific policies (holding other indicators of class constant). On nine of the thirteen policy items, education and income were neither separately nor jointly significant. Moreover, there was no policy on which the joint effect of education and income was statistically significant when neither independent effect was reliable. Receipt of welfare and employment status were also largely inconsequential. Receiving welfare had no independent effect on policy attitudes, and, with two exceptions, neither did unemployment.

Social class was a factor in group solidarity, but, contrary to some popular views, middle class blacks were more rather than less group-identified and group-conscious. Compared with other blacks, middle class blacks had a stronger sense of common fate; they were more discontented with the economic position and political power of blacks and with the powerlessness of other subordinate groups; and they were more approving of buy-black campaigns and of black children learning an African language. Education was the primary source of their heightened solidarity, although family income also fostered some elements of solidarity. Moreover, when we assessed the joint effects of education and income, we found another reliable influence on solidarity: approval of collective political strategies was greater among blacks who had both higher education and a higher family income.[82]

In brief, if the black community is polarized by class, that is not apparent in its evaluations of candidates or parties, its stance on policy issues, its group identification, or its awareness and explanations of racial disparity and its solutions for it. The major class division reflected realistic assessments of personal and family economic circumstances among the most and the least affluent respondents. Blacks with a low income, not fully employed, and receiving welfare most frequently believed that their circumstances had deteriorated during the Reagan years.

Social class is an important factor in black politics, however, because it affects the psychological and organizational resources of the
black electorate. Interest in politics was widespread, but the most
highly educated were nonetheless the most interested and the most
involved in black organizations. They felt unusually efficacious personally and especially believed in the group's potential effectiveness.
With one exception, family income had much weaker effects than
education on these psychological and organizational resources. (Income was as influential as education in heightening the sense of personal political efficacy.) Of course, the joint effects of education and
income were larger than their separate effects.

Chapter Three will show that the advantages provided by higher
education and income also enhanced all types of political participation: voting, electoral-campaign activities, and non-electoral and protest activities. (In Chapter Five, we shall also see that class exerts a
determining influence on attitudes about a separate black party and a
vote-black strategy.) Social class is thus a decisive factor in black politics because lack of structural resources reduces interest and participation and because class position affects matters of strategy. But class
does not divide the black community's commitment to electoral politics, appraisal of candidates, or policy preferences (including those not
explicitly concerned with race), and class stratification is definitely not
a threat to group solidarity.

A Locked-Out Youth?

Social class might be a more significant factor among young blacks,
who, as a group, have been especially affected by recent economic
trends. Was social class a more significant factor among the young
than among other blacks? Were the least privileged black youths especially apolitical? Were their psychological resources unusually low?

First, let us summarize the overall effects of age. Lacking trend data,
we can only infer that the 1984 election and voter-registration drives
led young blacks to exhibit higher levels of interest than they (or other
youths) usually exhibit. The survey showed that people below age 25
cared as much as their elders about the outcome of the election, and
their interest in politics had been just as often aroused by the Jackson
candidacy and by the electoral successes of black mayoralty candidates. On personal political efficacy, they scored higher than their
elders. And, as Chapters Three–Five collectively show, they were
more supportive of the Jackson candidacy and of an independent political voice. They were also less positive toward the Democratic party

and its 1984 ticket, more positive toward the Republican party and President Reagan, and less critical than older blacks of the Republican party's responsiveness to the concerns of blacks. These reactions indicate a young electorate that was especially independent.

In some ways, however, young people engaged less in politics than did their elders. They followed the 1984 campaign and general public affairs less, voted less frequently, and were less active in campaign activities (although, as expected, their youth was not a disadvantage in protest politics). Moreover, because they generally did not belong to civil rights organizations or attend church as frequently as older blacks, they had access to fewer organizational resources. In other respects, age was simply irrelevant. It did not influence policy preferences or group solidarity.[83]

Of especial interest are the young blacks who were structurally disadvantaged by both low income and little education. Were they unusually apolitical—locked out of politics as well as out of good jobs and material success? Do the data show, as is widely assumed, that low income and little education lowered political efficacy, interest, and participation more among young than among older blacks?

Four age cohorts were categorized: (1) people born between 1893 and 1915, who reached voting age before the Great Depression and before blacks shifted allegiance from the Republican to the Democratic party (aged 69 and older in 1984); (2) those born between 1916 and 1943, who became old enough to vote during and after the Depression but before the height of the Civil Rights movement (aged 41–68); (3) the civil rights generation, those born between 1944 and 1959, who reached age 18 during the Civil Rights and Black Nationalist movements of the mid-1960s to early 1970s (aged 25–40); and (4) the post–civil rights generation, those born in or after 1960 (aged 24 and younger in 1984). Three categories of social class were also distinguished: the most disadvantaged lived in a family earning no more than $10,000 a year and had no more than a high school education; those in the middle category surpassed one or the other of these criteria; and the most advantaged surpassed both.

On most measures of the psychological resources for politics, social class had the same effect in all age groups.[84] It affected the sense of competence for dealing with politics and interest in electoral politics evenly in all age groups. Most significantly, when its effect was uneven, as it was with respect to participation, younger blacks were affected less by social class background than were older blacks. The most disadvantaged youths took part in electoral campaign activities and protest politics and voted in the 1984 presidential, congressional, and

state or local races at about the same rate as their more advantaged
peers. Young, disadvantaged blacks were not unusually apolitical. In
contrast, the most disadvantaged of the older groups participated less
than the most advantaged. (See Figure 2.1, which gives predicted participation scores for the various categories of socioeconomic status
(SES) and age.)

The Urban Poor

Theories regarding the impact of the social organization of the city on
its citizens' involvement in politics generally follow one of two different approaches. One casts the city as anomic, unorganized, and a de-
pressant of citizens' interest in politics and their capacity to influence
public policy. The other casts it as a complexly structured set of organized, communalist neighborhoods that foster citizenship.[85] As noted
in Chapter One, the history of black political participation supports
the latter view—that the urban environment has fostered the development of strong black churches and community and political organizations and through these several types of organizations has increased
participation in both electoral and protest politics. Community organizations have provided finances, leadership, communication networks,
and reinforced group solidarity.

Many now worry that the positive effect of an urban environment
on black life has declined. It is argued that once highly organized and
culturally rich black communities in the large cities are now deci-
mated by the loss of industrial jobs and the migration of middle class
blacks to the suburbs, and that these communities no longer provide a
politically resourceful environment.[86] According to Allen and Farley,

> The concentration of problems in the ranks of the black urban poor results
> from shifts in the country's economic and social organization since World
> War II. Thousands of jobs in the black community were eliminated as
> the economy moved from a labor-intensive industrial base to a capital-
> intensive, service industry base. As the black community itself became
> more diverse and dispersed in social terms, a deterioration in community
> cohesion, stability, and cultural identification resulted.[87]

Our studies looked into this matter of significant differences in the
political resources of people living in urban and non-urban environments. Church attendance, exposure to a church involved in the 1984
election, and membership in civil rights organizations were not affected by urban/non-urban residency. Nor were racial solidarity and
political participation more evident among urban than non-urban

blacks. If an urban environment once promoted solidarity and opportunities for citizen action by means of community organizations more than life in other environments did, our survey data showed that, on average, this is no longer the case. Some would argue, however, and we agree, that a national survey, one not drawn to represent particular cities, is ill-suited to discovering the organizational features of specific urban environments. Failure to find a significant urban factor in the aggregate may result from positive effects in some cities being canceled out by negative effects in others.

Of course, the insignificance of an urban factor contradicts a now widely held view of life in the urban black community as socially isolated and politically alienated. We found no evidence of unusual isolation from churches or community organizations or of political alienation among urban residents. They attended church as frequently and were as involved in organizations aimed at improving life in the black community as other blacks were. They participated in all kinds of politics and felt as much group solidarity as other blacks. And, in fact, they had more psychological resources than people living outside the large cities. Urban residents were more interested in politics, more attentive to government and public affairs, and cared more about the outcome of the 1984 election. Their interest in politics had been aroused by a distinctly urban phenomenon: the electoral successes of black mayoral candidates. At the same time, urban dwellers were more critical of the responsiveness of the political system and less likely to regard government officials as trustworthy—perspectives usually associated with political engagement, not alienation, among liberal and challenging constituencies. In brief, we found the urban factor to be more psychological than organizational or collective.

Were these psychological resources of urban residents restricted to blacks with structural advantages? Were there two urban electorates, one affluent, well educated, and politically aware and the other an alienated class living in poverty?[88] To answer this question, the same three education-income categories used in the analysis of a locked-out youth were combined with residency. Urban residency was defined for these analyses as living in a large city; non-urban, as living anywhere else (the suburbs, a small city, a small town, or in a rural or country area).

The most disadvantaged blacks living in large cities were not unusually apathetic. Indeed, when educational and economic disadvantages were especially influential in a particular environment, as they were on five measures of psychological resources, their effects were stronger in non-urban areas.[89] It was the non-urban poor who were the

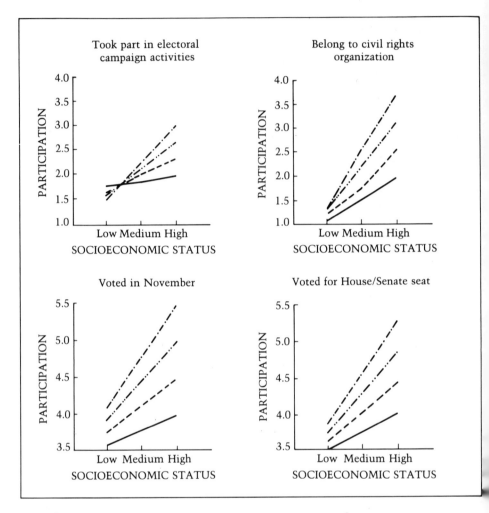

FIGURE 2.1
Predicted Participation Scores for Four Age Groups and Three Socioeconomic Status (SES) Groups

most uninterested in the election campaign, cared least about its outcome, and least frequently followed government affairs. They were also the most trusting of government officials. (See Figure 2.2.) In contrast, socioeconomic status mattered little, or not at all, in the urban environment. The urban residents with the lowest income and the least education were as interested in politics and as distrustful of government officials as were the most advantaged urban residents.

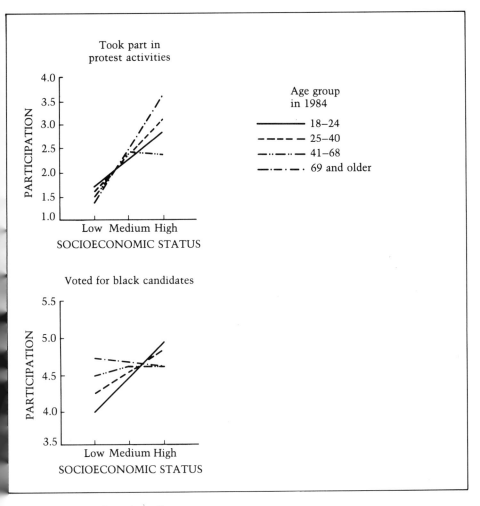

FIGURE 2.1 *(continued)*

Conclusions

In brief, social class affected three areas of motivation and behavior. First, not surprisingly, we found that blacks with more socioeconomic resources also had stronger psychological resources for politics. They were more interested in politics, thought blacks as a group more efficacious, and believed more in their own personal political competence. Yet there was no evidence that the negative effect of low socioeconomic status was greater in urban than in non-urban areas or

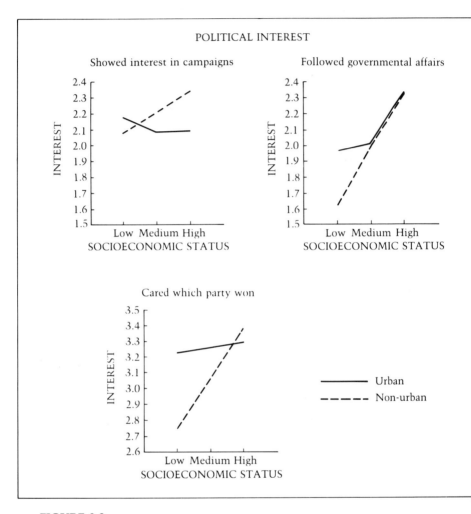

FIGURE 2.2
Predicted Psychological Resources of Urban and Non-urban Residents and Three Socioeconomic Status (SES) Groups

among younger than older blacks. The effect of low education and income on these psychological resources was comparable in all age groups and actually greater in non-urban than in urban settings. Second, of course, blacks who had more socioeconomic resources also had greater access to organizational resources, and this effect held equally in all age groups and in all environments. Third, as would be expected from their more abundant psychological and organizational resources,

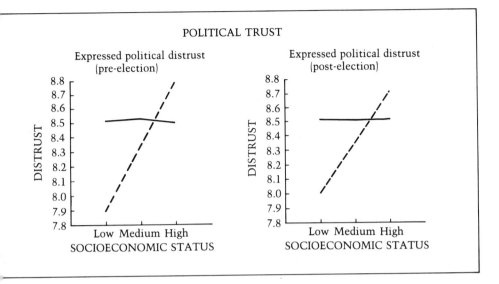

POLITICAL TRUST

Expressed political distrust (pre-election)

Expressed political distrust (post-election)

FIGURE 2.2 *(continued)*

middle class blacks participated in both electoral and protest politics more frequently than lower class blacks did. Contrary to what is widely assumed, however, the impact that being poor and not well educated had on participation was similar in urban and non-urban areas and was actually greater among older than younger people. We found no evidence of an uninterested, apolitical group of locked-out youths or of unusual political demoralization among the urban poor.

In our view, the most important conclusion to be drawn from our analyses is that this was a solidary electorate in two senses: blacks from all walks of life had similar political goals and policy preferences and also felt a sense of racial solidarity. There was certainly no evidence that middle class blacks were dissociated from the problems of the black community.

SUMMARY

In this chapter, we have used our survey's measures of political motivation and resources to paint a picture of an electorate that had been rendered nearly invisible by previous research on the mass public. Surveys sampling the general electorate on a nationwide basis do not yield enough blacks to provide a valid political portrait of them. Therefore, one of our purposes was to present basic descriptive information about the black electorate. Another, to which we turn in the next three chapters, was to see whether the political motivation and resources of blacks would clarify their reactions to two-party politics. We did this by relating the measures comprising the political portrait covered in this chapter to the measures of support for Jesse Jackson (Chapter Four) and to the measures of support for a black political voice (Chapter Five). The following three chapters will show that each of these political phenomena was reliably associated with political motivation and resources, but with subtle distinctions that help clarify these two forms of political independence.

Notes

1. See the following for a resource account of political participation: Dahl 1961; Lane 1959; Milbrath and Goel 1977; Verba and Nie 1972; and Verba, Nie, and Kim 1978. Verba, Nie, and Kim include civic attitudes and personal problems, neither of which gives direction to policy preferences, as the elements of individual motivation and suggest that motivation involving identification with groups provides the issue basis for political motivation. They also distinguish among individual and group bases of resources. Personal resources of individuals include money and other material assets, time, prestige, and political skill; organizational resources derive from group membership.

2. The term *ideology* implies an organization of beliefs about human life and humanity's relation to the social order. For beliefs to be called an ideology, at the very least they should have some internal consistency (Converse 1964). This internal consistency was ensured here by including as part of ideology only those beliefs that refer to the theme of individual and government responsibility and that clustered together in a factor analysis. We focused on individual and government responsibility because it evolved over time as a critical dimension of individualism. In the eighteenth century, individualism was crystallized in the philosophy of Immanuel Kant, who asserted a claim of moral autonomy for each individual and for the individual's freedom from the constraints of estate, guild, and church. As strong central states emerged in the nineteenth century, more slowly and less completely in the United States than elsewhere, the meaning of individualism expanded to incorporate opposition to state power as a threat to individual autonomy. The political culture of the United States has always included a preference for limited government and for individuals to be responsible for their own welfare as fully as possible.

   The political culture of black Americans, however, has dealt somewhat differently with government and individual responsibility. Blacks have historically been less opposed to strong government, especially a strong central government. Government at the federal level was the only political institution that responded to the grievances of blacks during most of their political history. Blacks are still far more favorable than whites to a strong, activist federal government. (See the discussion in Chapter Six.)

3. See Atkinson 1964; Atkinson and Feather 1966; and Atkinson and Birch 1978.

4. Our definition of solidarity has much in common with Tilly's concept of solidarity as involving "catness" and "netness," the former representing shared identity and awareness of ingroup/outgroup boundaries and the latter representing the density of networks within a constituency. Group identification and consciousness overlap the idea of catness, although we emphasize individual beliefs and feelings about group membership, while Tilly stresses the constituency level. Fireman and Gamson (1979) reserve the term *solidarity* for the social relationships that link group members to each other, which in turn may "generate a sense of common identity, shared fate, and general commitment to defend the group" (p. 21). Solidarity can develop among members of superordinate social categories, especially when their power or privilege is threatened. In most Western liberal democracies, however, the ideology of individualism so permeates the political thinking of the privileged that they reject the idea that group membership can affect the individual's life chances or that it is a legitimate aspect of politics and a basis for determining the extent to which equality is achieved in society. Members of subordinate groups more easily recognize that the freedom of the individual and equality of opportunity have in reality not prevented enormous inequalities between groups. Not surprisingly, the political ideologies of subordinate groups therefore emphasize group disparities and group-based equality.

5. As a psychological resource, ideology is similar to other knowledge structures, or schemata. These mental structures are representations of interrelated cognitions and feelings. For the most part, social psychologists who have used the term *schemata* "have viewed them as subjective 'theories' about how the social world operates. These 'theories' are derived from generalizing across one's experiences with the social world" (Markus and Zajonc 1985, 145). Once formed, schemata lend organization to experience. They shape expectations, determine how a situation is framed and which stimuli are selected for attention, guide the processing of new information and the retrieval of stored information, and constitute a basis for inference, or going beyond the information given. Whatever term is used to signify these internal structures (ideology, knowledge structure, schema), they are psychological resources in the sense that they help the individual deal efficiently with information and experience.

6. Verba and Orren 1985, 18.

7. A summary of the research on race differences, given by Wolfinger and Rosenstone (1980), supports our conclusions. There is still some controversy, however, about the extent to which race merely reflects socioeconomic status (SES). Abramson and Claggett (1984) contend that when voting is validated by election records, instead of being measured only by self-reports, there is a racial difference that withstands SES controls. Of course, they, too, show that controlling SES sharply reduces racial disparities in turnout. The controversy centers on the question, "Are racial disparities in political participation entirely explained by differences in the structural resources of blacks and whites?"

8. Sigelman et al. 1985. Electoral participation in specific situations is not always heavily influenced by education and income. Explaining the voter turnout of blacks from Jackson, Mississippi, and from three rural Mississippi counties in the 1968 presidential, the 1971 gubernatorial, and the 1972 presidential elections, St.

Angelo and Puryear (1982) show that education was not a significant influence and that income, a reliable effect in the latter two elections, explained less than 1 percent of the variance in voting.

9. Farley 1984.
10. Farley and Allen 1987.
11. Farley 1984, 194.
12. Farley and Allen 1987, Table 7.1.
13. Landry 1987, 205.
14. Farley and Allen 1987, 47.
15. Landry 1987, 70.
16. Ibid., 197–198.
17. Farley and Allen 1987, Table 9.1.
18. Farley 1984, 197.
19. Farley and Allen 1987, Chap. 10, 14.
20. Ibid., Figure 10.1.
21. Farley 1984, 195.
22. Farley and Allen 1987, Chap. 10, 14.
23. U.S. Department of Labor 1983, Table III.15.
24. Farley 1984, 14.
25. Ibid., 198.
26. Farley and Allen 1987, Chap. 8, 14–15.
27. Farley 1984, 198.
28. Farley and Allen 1987, Chap. 8, 26.
29. Karnig and Welch 1980; Engstrom and McDonald 1981.
30. Wolfinger and Rosenstone 1980, 73.
31. Farley and Allen 1987, Chap. 5, 33.
32. Reed (1986) contends that the role of the black church in protest politics was mainly to provide institutional support for activities initiated and led by other non-church leaders and that its political significance for protest and electoral politics has been greatly overstated. Morris (1984) presents a different view, showing that the black church was not only the center of movements but also that ministers played influential roles as leaders. See also Mays and Nicholson 1933; Olsen 1970; Brown and Jackson 1986; and Morris, Hatchett, and Brown 1987.
33. Baxter and Lansing (1983) refer to the earlier disappearance in the voting gap between black men and women (favoring men) as an "enigma," a phenomenon well documented but little analyzed or understood. See also Brown and Lansing 1985; Lansing 1985b.
34. Cavanagh 1985a, 16.
35. Survey studies have never shown large gender differences in the political views of blacks, with the exception of attitudes toward militancy and behavior in riots. Marx (1967) found men more militant and more frequent riot participants. The riot-behavior difference was still found in later surveys, but the militancy-attitude difference had nearly disappeared by 1970 and was gone by 1976. See Schuman and Hatchett 1974; Hatchett 1982.
36. Fireman and Gamson 1979; Tilly 1978.
37. Tilly 1981.
38. Whatever their historic role in black politics, black churches were involved in the 1984 election. Although Reed (1986) discounts the general political importance of black churches, he agrees that "the Jackson campaign seems to have encouraged ministerial inclinations toward direct involvement in politics in black com-

munities. . . . In the District of Columbia and Maryland—as elsewhere—ministerial alliances constituted the most energetic organizational support base for the campaign . . ." (p. 43).

39. Kinder and Sears 1985, 703.

40. Salamon and Van Evera 1973a, 1973b.

41. St. Angelo and Puryear 1982.

42. Hamilton 1978, 25.

43. In an extensive review of the social and psychological influences on electoral politics, Kinder and Sears (1985) discuss group identification but primarily cover evidence on racial membership, not racial self-identification. They conclude that membership is the preeminent predictor of policy evaluations. Not surprisingly, this is especially true of issues that bear directly and unambiguously on the fortunes of racial groups. Yet being black or white does not mean that one feels solidarity with other blacks or whites. Kinder and Sears have little to say about the political implications of what we are designating solidarity. But studies of electoral behavior are beginning to take note of group identification and consciousness. The work of Conover (1984) and Conover and Feldman (1984) promises to give a truly political cast to group identification.

44. Olsen 1970.

45. Verba and Nie 1972. See also Verba, Ahmed, and Bhatt 1971.

46. Shingles 1981; Aberbach and Walker 1970; Klobus-Edwards, and Klemmack 1978; Gurin and Epps 1975; Gurin, Gurin, and Morrison 1978; Gurin, Miller, and Gurin 1980; Miller et al. 1981; Morris, Hatchett, and Brown 1987; Brown 1986; Brown, Jackson, and Bowman 1981; Broman, Neighbors, and Jackson 1988.

47. The emergence of identification and consciousness has been discussed by writers from a variety of perspectives, with terminology unique to each; for example, as the processes of decolonization (Memmi 1968; Fanon 1963), identity transformation (Hall, Cross, and Freedle 1972; Tajfel 1974), disassimilation (Hayes-Bautista 1974), the shift from generation to generation unit (Mannheim [1952] 1972), class consciousness (Morris and Murphy 1966), and the growth of feminism (Carden 1974). Despite their concerns with different target groups, these writers nonetheless suggest nearly identical concepts as comprising identification and consciousness. All have been heavily influenced by Marx's concept of class consciousness, the transformation of a class in itself to a class for itself.

48. Merton [1957] 1968.

49. Oberschall 1978; Tilly 1978; Fireman and Gamson 1979.

50. Solidarity theories have had little to say about the perceptual and cognitive consequences of identification. In the sense that awareness of group boundaries is considered an aspect of solidarity itself, they, of course, do deal with intergroup perception. But they pay little attention to the ways in which solidarity, once present, influences perceptions of the membership and non-membership groups. Overt conflict is generally credited with sharpening boundaries and exaggerating perceptions of difference (Coser 1956). Current research on social cognition, however, suggests that solidarity itself could help group members sharpen their perception of boundaries, even without conflict. See especially Tajfel 1978; Stephan 1985.

51. Stephan 1985; Brewer and Kramer 1985.

52. Merton and Kitt (Rossi) 1950; Tajfel and Turner 1986.

53. Lewin (1948) was an early proponent of the view that common fate is more important than actual or perceived similarities of members. ". . . It is not similarity or

dissimilarity of individuals that constitute a group, but interdependence of fate. Any normal group, and certainly any developed and organized one, contains and should contain individuals of very different character" (p. 165). Of course, members may also perceive various kinds of similarities among themselves—traits, preferences, values, culture. The critical notion behind common fate, however, is that members recognize that they are often treated categorically despite variability in their personal characteristics.

54. Converse 1964.
55. Gurin and Townsend 1986; Gurin 1987.
56. See Broman, Neighbors, and Jackson (1988) and Jackson, McCullough, and Gurin (1981) for analyses of another national sample of blacks. They also show that three-quarters accepted the dual identity, and the remainder were divided equally between an exclusively black and an exclusively American identity.
57. Unfortunately, labels for ethnic minorities, also part of the Rainbow Coalition, were not included.
58. Kinder and Sears 1985.
59. Shanks and Miller 1985, 33–36. Identification as a liberal or a conservative sometimes triggers strong reactions to particular issues or candidates, although party identification usually determines a voter's choice. The vast empirical literature on voting demonstrates repeatedly that party identification and degree of partisanship are the central and causally decisive elements in candidate choice (Kinder and Sears 1985).
60. Tate (1985) shows that liberal/conservative self-placement does correlate with the policy preferences of college-educated blacks but not with those of blacks with less education. But because 20 percent of even the college-educated group (and 35 percent of those with less education) declined to answer a question asking what they meant by the labels "liberal" and "conservative," Tate concludes that these concepts may not be meaningful in accounting for the black electorate's reactions to politics.
61. Campbell et al. 1960.
62. Kinder and Sears (1985) note that a voter's clarity about policy depends on the clarity provided by candidates. The effects of policy preferences also depend on the centrality of the particular policy to the voter's view of the world and sense of self.
63. Kinder and Sears 1985, 671. A recent analysis of NES data shows, however, that personal economic circumstances are more consequential than was previously thought. When account is taken of measurement unreliability in economic self-assessments, personal economic situations do influence evaluations of presidential performance choice in voting and assessment of the nation's economy. See Rosenstone, Hansen, and Kinder 1986.
64. Kinder and Sears 1985, 672.
65. In contrast, youth does not inhibit participation in protest activities. Young people were leaders in the 1960s' Civil Rights movement and in the 1970s' Black Nationalist movement. In addition, they were readily mobilized to demonstrate and protest in specific campaigns.
66. Salamon and Van Evera 1973a, 1973b.
67. St. Angelo and Puryear 1982. Despite this evidence, these analysts discount the significance of individual apathy in explaining aggregate voting levels because very high apathy (answering six or more questions apathetically) was required to reduce voting, and only 11 percent of the blacks surveyed were that apathetic.
68. Cavanagh 1985a.

69. Hamilton 1982a, xi.
70. Lane 1959, 149.
71. Shingles 1981; Gurin, Gurin, and Morrison 1978.
72. Converse 1972.
73. Gamson 1968; Paige 1971.
74. Mason, House, and Martin (1981) have thoroughly analyzed the items generally used to measure trust. Using factor and canonical analyses, they confirm Gamson's distinction between an input and an output dimension to trust: the input concerns the actor's own sense of competence in dealing with politics; the output concerns the evaluation of the likelihood that authorities and institutions will respond to ordinary citizens.
75. Ibid.
76. Belief that the system is unresponsive was also affected by demography: urban dwellers saw it as less responsive.
77. Weber [1922] 1946, 182.
78. Marxists criticize this approach on a number of grounds. First, they view it as descriptive and static rather than a dynamic analysis of group relationships. Second, they question why a concept of social class is needed if an individual's occupation or income entirely captures hypothesized effects. And finally, as applied to the black class structure, they suggest that the Weberian approach has encouraged analysts to merge the black capitalist with the middle class instead of analyzing it separately, however small and embryonic it is. See Boston 1985, 48–49.
79. Landry 1980, 3.
80. Wilson 1978, ix.
81. Of course, it is generally conceded that growing income inequality among blacks partially reflects their increasing occupational differentiation.
82. The other two indicators of class did not influence solidarity. Receiving welfare had no significant effects and unemployment only one: the unemployed more frequently thought of themselves as black rather than as Americans or both.
83. There are two exceptions to this conclusion. Older blacks were more discontented with the limited power of blacks and felt more negatively about their personal economic circumstances, the national economy, and the economic condition of blacks as a group.
84. We tested multiplicative effects of age and socioeconomic status on all measures of political motivation and resources. The multiplicative effect was statistically significant on only six of the sixty-three tests. These six involved measures of participation.
85. Merton (1987) uses controversy over urbanization to illustrate the important role of sociological inquiry in establishing social facts: ". . . It would seem premature to ask why 'urbanization is accompanied by destruction of the social and moral order' inasmuch as evidence accumulates to suggest that the connection is rather more an assumption than a repeatedly demonstrated fact" (p. 3). He cites the work of Fischer (1977) on social networks in urban settings, which generally discredits the assumption of demoralization brought about by urban conditions.
86. Wilson 1986, 1987; Lemann 1986.
87. Allen and Farley 1986, 303.
88. We approached this question as we did the question of a locked-out youth, testing statistical interactions among socioeconomic status, urbanicity, and political resources. On only eight of the sixty-three tests was the multiplicative effect of SES

and the urban/non-urban environment statistically significant. Five of the eight significant interactions involved psychological resources. The other three concerned attitudes toward United States policy in Central America, spending on defense, and nationalism. Socioeconomic status was again more influential in non-urban settings.

89. The geographic distribution of non-urban blacks means that there is no way to test the relative importance of urbanicity and region. Most of the non-urban black population lives in the South, leaving too few blacks elsewhere for comparing rural-urban effects in various regions. In any case, since region did not critically distinguish the level of psychological resources, the unusually low interest levels of the non-urban poor cannot be explained by their southern origins. It is worth noting in Figure 2.2 that on several measures the highest socioeconomic group in non-urban areas shows an unusually high level of interest in politics. To ensure that this did not result from the degree of urbanicity *within* the non-urban category, we compared proportions of the three SES groups in suburbs, small cities, small towns, and country areas. As expected, there were some differences—13 percent more of the highest SES groups lived in the suburbs; 11 percent fewer, in country areas. Yet these differences were not large enough to explain the impact of socioeconomic status within the non-urban category.

CHAPTER THREE

Separate Themes:
Support for Jesse Jackson
and Advocacy of
a Black Political Voice

In LIGHT OF THE history of rejection and disfranchisement of blacks by the major parties, Jesse Jackson's 1984 candidacy may be considered a watershed in black electoral politics. In some ways, it was such a watershed. In 1984, blacks participated in the presidential election by taking part in Democratic party politics at the local, state, and national levels in higher positions in the party hierarchy than ever before.

The closeness of most elected black officials and party regulars to the Democratic party can be seen most dramatically in their initial rejection of the outsider, Jesse Jackson. Nonetheless, the dilemma blacks had faced before was raised again by the Jackson candidacy: Could their support for him lessen their dependency on an unresponsive party? Should they back him instead of a presidential candidate who was more likely to win and who would, in turn, feel indebted to the black electorate? Should they vote for Jackson if he eventually decided to run as an independent? Would widespread support for Jackson lead the Democratic party to take the black vote less for granted, earn Jackson greater influence at the nominating convention and with the party's leadership, and focus the party's attention on policies of concern to them?

This chapter explores the reactions of the black electorate to Jackson's candidacy and to the idea of a separate black party. It also considers how these reactions were related. The core question is: What do the

political views of the Jackson supporters and advocates of a black political voice reveal about the electorate's thinking on party politics?

SEPARATE OR RELATED VIEWPOINTS?

Although Jackson made his bid as a Democrat, political commentary
posed the possibility that he might run independently and take a portion of the black vote from the Democratic ticket. This alternative
was, of course, one of Jackson's bargaining chips, since it might have
allowed him greater influence in the writing of the Democratic party
platform and with the choice of appointments to the party leadership
positions. Voters watched and read about the dynamics among Jackson, Gary Hart, and Walter Mondale for clues to the party's response to
the black challenge and the path Jackson might follow during the convention and afterward. As the campaign progressed, Jackson's candidacy could be viewed strictly as an internal party phenomenon or as a
move to go outside the party.

A bid outside the Democratic party would have been consistent
with the meaning of third parties in twentieth century America. Unlike third parties in the nineteenth century, which usually encompassed a genuine party organization, ran candidates at local, state, and
national levels, and lasted beyond a single election, contemporary
third parties are not stable organizations; rather, they are represented
by the independent candidacy of a charismatic figure who fades or
returns to a major party after one presidential race.[1] Thus blacks who
approved of a separate party could have easily construed the Jackson
candidacy as a step toward a separate party in its current meaning:
Jackson could mount an independent challenge to the two major parties in a specific contest.

The political context in which Jackson decided to run for the nomination in 1984 also suggested that his strongest supporters in the black
electorate might see his candidacy as an expression of an independent
black political voice. Jackson announced his candidacy on November
3, 1983, after spending nearly a year campaigning to boost the idea of a
black candidacy and finding many sectors of the black community
divided over that idea and him as a possible candidate. Even the black
left and black nationalists, who were reasonably united behind the
strategy of a bid by a black candidate, were not urging Jackson to run.
Marable writes that

> when Jackson's name first surfaced in early January 1983 as that of a
> potential presidential candidate, most Black leftists, radical Black

nationalists, community organizers and elected officials did not relish the idea at all. But . . . by the summer of 1983 it became apparent to Black progressives that the only Black "presidential hopeful" we had was the "country preacher," and that it was going to be either him or no one in 1984.[2]

Black elected officials and heads of national organizations were divided not only over Jackson but over any kind of black challenge in the Democratic primaries. Opposed were most members of the Congressional Black Caucus; such mayors as Coleman Young of Detroit, Andrew Young of Atlanta, and Harold Washington of Chicago; Clarence Mitchell, president of the National Black Caucus of State Elected Officials; John Jacob, president of the Urban League; Benjamin Hooks, director of the NAACP, and Joseph Madison, head of the NAACP's division of voter education; Coretta Scott King; and black labor spokesman Bayard Rustin. In favor were Joseph E. Lowery, president of the SCLC, who gave qualified support to the idea of a black candidate; M. Carl Holman, president of the National Urban Coalition, who strongly endorsed it; and three members of the CBC, John Conyers of Detroit, Gus Savage of Chicago, and Ron Dellums of Oakland-Berkeley, who pushed the strategy throughout 1983. Once Jackson announced his candidacy, few well-known black leaders backed him and several, including Richard Arrington, mayor of Birmingham; Charles Rangel, congressman from Harlem; Coleman Young; and Coretta Scott King, threw their support to Mondale. Thus, as Jackson took his campaign to ordinary citizens, generally reaching them through television coverage and personal appearances in black churches and with the assistance of endorsements of over 90 percent of the black clergy, he was a political outsider who could easily be viewed as an independent force in electoral politics—a newcomer ready to challenge the party regulars and traditional political leadership in the black community, perhaps even to mount an independent bid outside the Democratic party.

Jackson's candidacy appeared poised to test what Walters calls independent as distinguished from dependent leverage.[3] Both strategies are predicated on a stable two-party system and on the black vote providing the margin of victory in close contests—the balance of power. In theory, dependent leverage comes when blacks are integrated into the party organization and the black leadership can deliver the black vote. It represents a hope that the concerns of blacks will influence government policy when their votes are critical to the victory of the party's presidential candidate. As discussed in Chapter One, however, this potential influence through electoral and party politics has historically been weak because of the tendency of the sympathetic party to take the black vote for granted. In 1984 the ingredients for independent leverage seemed to be in place. Jackson's campaign had mobilized an autonomous organization of the black electorate. If he won enough delegates, Jackson could be the "king maker" at the convention or threaten to take his candidacy outside of the party.

For these reasons, it seemed plausible to expect a close relationship between support for Jackson and advocacy of a black political voice. We turn now to what we found in the views of the black electorate during the primaries and pre-election period of the 1984 campaign.

Support for Jackson was measured by responses to three questions in the pre-election survey. In states with a presidential primary election or party caucus, respondents were asked whether they had voted; and if they had, they were asked, "Which presidential candidate did you support?" People who had not voted or who lived in states without primaries or caucuses were asked, "If you had voted, which presidential candidate would you have supported?" All respondents were asked, "If Jesse Jackson ran as an independent presidential candidate, would you vote for him, Walter Mondale, or Ronald Reagan?" They also evaluated Jackson's decision to mount a campaign in 1984. The interviewer said, "Some people feel it was a good idea for Jesse Jackson to run for the Democratic nomination for president. Others disagree and think he should not have run. What do you think? Was it a good or bad idea for Jesse Jackson to have run for president?" Respondents indicated the extent of their positive or negative feeling on a scale ranging from "very good," "somewhat good," and "somewhat bad" to "very bad."

Advocacy of a black political voice was measured according to responses to three questions in the post-election survey. Two focused on the advisability of a separate black party. Respondents first answered the question "Do you think that blacks should form their own political party?" Intensity of opinion was then measured: "How strongly do you feel that way?" Response categories ranged from "very strongly," "fairly strongly," and "not too strongly" to "not strongly at all." A third question gauged the extent of agreement with a strategy of voting for black candidates: "Blacks should always vote for black candidates when they run." Response categories were "strongly agree," "agree," "disagree," and "strongly disagree."

The distribution of opinions on these questions is presented in Chapters Four and Five, which take up support for Jackson and support for an independent political voice, respectively. At this point, the issue is their relationship to each other. Correlations among the responses to

TABLE 3.1
Support for the Jackson Candidacy and Advocacy of a Black Political Voice: Separate Themes

Attitude Measures	Support for Jackson Candidacy (Factor 1)	Advocacy of a Black Political Voice (Factor 2)
Voted for or preferred Jackson in primary	.769	.045
Thought it was a good idea for Jackson to run	.719	.044
Would vote for Jackson if he ran	.666	.334
Strong approval of blacks forming their own political party	−.046	.759
Agree blacks should always vote for black candidates	−.012	.786
Percentage of total variance explained	31%	26%

Note: Principal-component factor analysis was used. The Kaiser criterion was applied to determine how many factors would be rotated. The factor loadings are based on varimax rotation. The analysis was performed on the 871 respondents who participated in both the pre- and post-election surveys.

these questions were factor-analyzed to test how the black electorate viewed the Jackson candidacy, a black party, and a vote-black strategy—as a single issue, as entirely separate matters, or as different expressions of the same underlying theme of independence. As Table 3.1 shows, two separate factors emerged in the analysis. The only question overlapping the two referred to intention to vote for Jackson were he to run as an independent presidential candidate. The reference to both Jackson and independence doubtless explains the overlap. Since responses to this question were related more highly to support for Jackson (.666 compared with .334 on the factor measuring independent voice), it was included only on the Jackson-support index when two unit-weighted indexes were formed, each ranging from 1 to 4.

In brief, the black electorate did not think of the Jackson candidacy as a step toward a separate black party. Although both support for Jackson and advocacy of a black voice may reflect concern with party dependency, they are not viewed as a single strategy for handling that problem. The separation found in the factor analysis suggested that they might represent "insider" and "outsider" strategies. But evaluations of the candidates and parties, to which we now turn, will demonstrate that such a distinction is overly simplified.

TABLE 3.2
Political Positions Taken in the 1984 Election by Jackson Supporters and Advocates of a Black Political Voice

Political Position	Support for the Jackson Candidacy		Advocacy of a Black Political Voice		Total Sample
	High (297)	*Low* (71)	*High* (62)	*Low* (165)	(871)
Pre-election					
Voted in primary for (N = 594 who had a primary and voted)					
Mondale	0%	89%	46%	31%	30%
Jackson	100	—	39	53	65
Hart	0	2	—	7	2
Reagan	0	9	6	8	3
Other	—	—	9	1	—
	100%	100%	100%	100%	100%
Pre-election judgment that the election will be won by					
Reagan, by quite a bit	26%	47%**	19%	45%****	31%
Reagan, a close call	35	16	25	23	28
Mondale, a close race	30	30	41	29	32
Mondale, by quite a bit	9	7	15	3	9
	100%	100%	100%	100%	100%

Mean Thermometer Ratings
(Thermometer degrees on scale 0–100)

Jackson	84.9	56.8**·**·	83.8	67.1**·**·	74.2
Black officials who supported Jackson	82.0	61.2**·**·	80.8	69.6**·**··	74.3
Reagan	25.4	34.9**·**·	24.2	33.1**	30.2
Republican party	32.8	36.9	33.6	36.5	35.1
Black people who voted for					
Reagan	26.9	30.0**	37.6	33.1	33.6
Mondale	58.5	70.5**·**·	66.7	59.7*	63.7
Ferraro	59.8	63.4*	67.5	58.9**	61.4
Black officials who supported Mondale in primaries	64.5	70.0**	72.5	62.6**··	66.8
Democratic party	76.8	75.8	80.6	70.8**	75.0

Judgment of Party Responsiveness

Democratic party					
Treated Jackson worse than other candidates	34%	9%**·**·	19%	22%	24%
Works very hard on issues black people care about	26%	28%	46%	22%	28%
Republican party does not work hard at all on issues black people care about	41%	26%	30%	40%	37%

Post-election
Candidate Choice

Voted in November for					
Reagan	6%	8%	2%	13%	9%
Mondale	92	92	95	86	89
Other	2	—	3	1	2
	100%	100%	100%	100%	100%

TABLE 3.2
(continued)

Political Position	Support for the Jackson Candidacy		Advocacy of a Black Political Voice		Total Sample
	High (297)	Low (71)	High (62)	Low (165)	(871)
Strength of Voting Preference					
Reagan strong	3%	4%	2%	9%****	5%
Reagan weak	3	4	—	4	4
Mondale weak	31	27	30	37	26
Mondale strong	61	65	65	49	64
Other	2	—	3	1	1
	100%	100%	100%	100%	100%
Voted straight ticket	65%	70%	75%	51%**	67%
Among people who didn't vote straight ticket, voted					
Mostly Republican	0%	0%	*N too small*	*N too small*	2
Half and half	36	31	"	"	35
Mostly Democratic	64	69	"	"	63
	100%	100%			100%
Voting History					
Voted in 1984 primary [primary states]	60%	65%	64%	60%	61%
Usually vote in primaries	77%	79%	77%	80%	78%

Political Position	Pre-election	Post-election	Pre-election	Post-election	Pre-election	Post-election	Pre-election	Post-election	Pre-election	Post-election
Voted in 1980 presidential election	66%		69%		65%		69%		68%	
Voted in November 1984	78%		75%		74%		79%		76%	
Among people who voted for										
House/Senate seat	77%		77%		65%		84%**		77%	
Local/state races										
Black candidate	81%		81%		74%		86%****		82%	
Party identification[a]										
Strong Democrat	50%	56%	56%	60%	53%	61%	41%	45%	46%	52%
Weak Democrat	22	17	21	11	20	11	28	25	24	23
Independent/leaning Democratic	15	13	8	10	7	10	15	14	12	14
Independent	4	5	1	4	5	7	6	4	7	5
Republican, all strengths	6	8	10	12	9	8	9	9	7	8
Other	—	—	1	—	—	—	—	—	—	8
Apolitical	3	1	3	3	6	3	1	6	4	4
	100%	100%	100%	100%	100%	100%	100%	100%	100%	100%

Note: Percentages of the extreme groups, highs and lows, illustrate relationships. Asterisks indicating significance level reflect the relationship using the entire range of support for Jackson and advocacy of a black political voice, with demographic influences controlled. Total percentages are based on the weighted N of 1,293 in the post-election survey. This represents an unweighted N of 871 who participated in both the pre- and post-election surveys. Unweighted Ns for each category and for the total sample are shown in parentheses at the top of the table.

[a] Jackson support is not related to party identification; advocacy of a black political voice is related in both the pre- and post-election surveys at .05.

*$p < .05.$ **$p < .01.$ ***$p < .001.$ ****$p < .0001.$

CANDIDATE AND PARTY EVALUATIONS

How did the Jackson supporters and non-supporters evaluate the 1984 candidates and party symbols? It hardly needs telling that during the primary phase the supporters of course preferred Jackson over other candidates. By the time the Democratic convention had been held and respondents were asked about the final candidates, the Jackson supporters felt less warmly toward Ronald Reagan and blacks who supported him and toward Mondale, Geraldine Ferraro, and black officials who supported Mondale in the primaries than non-supporters did. And, as one would also expect, Jackson supporters were more negative about the Democratic party's treatment of Jesse Jackson. (See Table 3.2 for a summary of similarities and differences between supporters and non-supporters. Also see Appendix B.3, Tables 1–3, for demographic effects, and Table 4, for relationships between Jackson support and candidate and party evaluations with controls for demographic influences.)

Critical of the Democrats as they were, Jackson supporters were not ready to move outside the party. They identified themselves as Democrats as frequently as non-supporters did, and their overall warmth toward the party, as measured by a thermometer rating of warmth and coldness, did not differ from that of non-supporters. Nor were they more negative about how hard the party works on issues of concern to blacks. The Republican party certainly was not viewed as an alternative. On the thermometer scale, the Republican party was rated 40 degrees lower than the Democratic party, and the Republicans received significantly lower ratings by the Jackson supporters than did non-supporters. Furthermore, 15 percent more of the supporters thought the Republicans "do not work at all hard on issues of interest to blacks." In short, the Jackson supporters of course wanted their Democratic candidate to win the nomination and understandably felt less warmly toward the final Democratic ticket. Before the election, most said they would vote for Jackson even if he were to run for president as an independent, perhaps partly because they were less impressed with the likelihood of a Reagan landslide. (Compared with non-supporters, 21 percent fewer of the Jackson supporters thought Reagan would win reelection by "quite a lot.") They seemed ready to act independently within the party but not to defect.

Their voting behavior confirmed their loyalty. Jackson supporters voted a straight ticket as often as others; and when they split votes, two-thirds of them (just like the non-supporters) voted mostly Democratic. By the November election, approximately two-thirds of both groups strongly favored Mondale, and 92 percent actually voted for him. Their voting histories also show that both groups were equally reliable voters. Virtually the same proportions said they usually vote in primary elections, that they did vote in a 1984 primary, and that they also voted in the November election for House and Senate seats, candidates in local and state races, and the president. When given the opportunity, the Jackson supporters did vote more frequently for black candidates.

What does the comparison of advocates and non-advocates of a black political voice disclose about party politics? Were the advocates likely to defect from the Democratic party? Or was their approval of a separate black party largely an effort—as black satellite parties historically have been—to gain some voice in a major party?

In their evaluations of the Republicans, the advocates were decidedly more negative toward Reagan than the non-advocates, but not toward blacks who supported him, nor toward the Republican party itself. Nor were they unusually critical of the party's response to black concerns. These results might suggest that the Republicans could have appealed to this group, but other findings negate this possibility.

The advocates were surprisingly positive toward the Democrats. Contrary to the way one might suppose separatists would feel, and unlike the Jackson supporters, the advocates were not unusually critical of the Democratic party's treatment of Jackson; they were much more positive than non-advocates about how hard the party worked on issues black people care about; and they felt more warmly than non-advocates toward black officials who voted for Mondale. They also evaluated the party's ticket and the party itself slightly more positively than non-advocates did and identified somewhat more strongly with the party. (The slight Democratic edge among the advocates resulted primarily, however, from the views of people favoring a vote-black strategy. The party identification and candidate evaluations of people favoring a separate party closely resembled those expressed by people opposed to it. These subtle differences show that even highly related measures can produce different shades of meaning.) The overall picture of the advocates is not of a group of separatists but of Democrats who would like the party to respond to them.

Their voting behavior substantiated their support of the Democratic party, as well as their commitment to electoral politics. More advocates than non-advocates voted for Mondale in the primaries, nearly all voted for him in November, and their preferences for him were stronger. More also voted a straight Democratic ticket. In general, they were reliable voters. They voted in the 1984 primaries and in both the 1980 and 1984 presidential elections as frequently as non-advocates, though not in the 1984 congressional races or state and local elections. (The advocates of a black party accounted for the lower voting rates in these types of elections, showing that they were less involved in electoral politics at levels where an independent party can sometimes be successful.) In brief, the independence of the advocates appears to be a strategy for incorporation into rather than separation from the politics of the major parties.

POLITICAL PARTICIPATION

Partisanship and voting are only two forms of electoral politics, and electoral activities comprise only one form of politics. In their classic work, *Participation in America,* Verba and Nie delineate three modes of citizen action, all intended to produce a collective outcome but distinguished along three dimensions: (1) level of initiative required to engage in the act, (2) whether the issue targeted by the act, or its timing, is controlled by individuals or by political institutions, and, (3) level of conflict likely to ensue from the act.[4] According to this scheme, voting is a low-demand activity: it requires little individual initiative and lies outside the individual's control of issues and timing. Campaign activities (such as working for or against a candidate, influencing others to vote, attending political meetings, and contributing money to campaigns) require more personal effort but are not much more controllable by individuals. Communal activities (such as working with others to solve a community problem or contacting public officials about a particular group's interests) demand considerably more individual assertion and also allow individuals to have more personal control. Verba and Nie suggest that since voting and campaign activities press people to make choices between partisan positions, more conflict is associated with them than with communal activities. This may not be true, however, since American political parties have never been strongly ideological.[5] Moreover, when a community lacks ideological consensus or when the action that is taken challenges political and economic relations between divided groups, communal activities may become highly conflictual.

No mode delineated by Verba and Nie taps the protest activities that blacks as political outsiders have undertaken historically to pressure the parties and branches of government to allow them to participate in party politics, give them the vote, and enact policies reflecting the interests of their community. For blacks, protest and electoral politics have always been complementary.[6] Even when denied the vote, they tried to influence electoral outcome through protest politics, the only mode available to them. Nelson describes how in 1864 black leaders used abolitionist meetings, informal gatherings, and the press to express their opinions of presidential candidates and election issues.[7] During and after Reconstruction, blacks used the entire repertoire of political actions that characterized nineteenth-century politics. They organized their own political conventions and factions in the Republican party; they formed race-advancement groups; and they launched protests and demonstrations to curb terrorism against blacks and to protect or regain the vote.

After the 1965 Voting Rights Act expanded opportunities for blacks in the electoral system, some political commentators began to argue that protest is a less modern form of politics. Taking this position, Reed asserts that formally elected officials provide a more advanced form of leadership since, according to him, protest leaders claim to represent the black community through an organic relationship that cannot be tested at the polls; the accountability provided by elections makes elected officials the appropriate political leaders and electoral politics more mature than protest politics.[8]

Others dissent from this interpretation, for two reasons. In the first place, exercising the right to vote "does not, ipso facto, lead to the public goods and services needed or sought" by the black community,[9] especially now that the economy is no longer expanding at the rates that were achieved in the 1960s and the majority of Americans want less, not more, involvement of the federal government in social welfare.[10] Elected officials may be unable to enact social and economic policies of benefit to blacks. Thus protest may be as necessary today as in the past, not to gain the right to vote, but to force public and private decision makers to confront and do something about growing inequality, deteriorating public schools and services, and the changing job structure in which industrial, high-wage jobs are being replaced by temporary, part-time, low-paying jobs in the service sector. And, in the second place, protest is a lasting feature of all democracies, a form of action as modern and necessary as elections to ensure the state's accountability to the will of the people.[11]

Whatever ambivalence both black leaders and white leaders might have felt about protest, the black electorate approached the election of 1984 with a particular historical perspective on the congruence of protest and electoral politics. For that reason, we predicted that its pattern of participation would demonstrate the complementarity of these two modes. Beyond the general picture, we also examined the political activities of the Jackson supporters and the advocates of an independent voice to determine whether they revealed distinctive patterns and whether the Jackson supporters were more active across the board.

Modes of Participation

The survey included questions on voting as well as on participation in political campaigns. Four campaign questions were adapted from Verba and Nie:

- During the campaign, did you talk to any people and try to show them why they should vote for or against one of the parties or candidates?
- Did you go to any political meetings, rallies, speeches, dinners, or things like that in support of a particular candidate?
- Did you give any money to or help raise money for any of the candidates?
- In your lifetime, have you ever worked for a political party or campaigned for a political candidate?

Questions that related specifically to the 1984 campaign and to participation through the church were also asked:

- Did you help with a voter-registration drive or get people to the polls on election day?
- During this election year, did you help campaign for a black candidate?
- Did you attend anything at a church or place of worship in support of a black candidate?
- Did you do any work for one of the candidates through your church or place of worship?
- Did your church or place of worship take up a collection for any candidate during this election year?

To measure non-electoral activities, additional questions were included. One was taken from the Verba and Nie indicators of communal activities ("Have you ever written to a public official about a concern or a problem?"),[12] and several focused on protest. Respondents were given the following definition of protest acts: "things people may do to protest something they feel needs to be changed in the nation, their neighborhoods, schools, or communities." Then they were asked whether in the last five years they had:

- signed a petition in support of or against something
- attended a protest meeting or demonstration
- picketed, taken part in a sit-in, or boycotted a business or government agency

Factor analyses of the answers given to these and the questions on voting (see Appendix B.3, Table 5) show how political activities clustered together. They also allowed us to determine whether the patterns differed for blacks who did or did not support the Jackson candidacy and did or did not advocate an independent political voice. Separate analyses were run for these four subgroups and for the total sample. Five conclusions can be drawn from these analyses.

First, the acts undertaken by individuals in all subgroups, except the strong Jackson supporters, clustered in five modes of participation: voting, taking part in traditional campaign activities, campaigning through the church, and engaging in two forms of non-electoral politics—petitioning and direct protest action.

Second, there was some unreliability between the two forms of non-electoral political action. Although petitioning and direct action were separate factors (in all analyses except those of the strong Jackson supporters), they were merged in the analysis of the total sample. In that analysis, four instead of five factors were found. When we specified that five factors should be extracted for the total sample, the distinction between petitioning and direct action was replicated.[13]

The activities that comprised the five modes are (1) traditional campaigning—influencing other people to vote for or against a party or candidate, going to a political meeting in support of a candidate, giving money for a candidate, campaigning for a black candidate, helping with voter registration or getting people to the polls, and working for a party; (2) church campaigning—attending a church activity to support a black candidate, working for a candidate through the church, and contributing to a church collection taken for a candidate; (3) voting—for a black candidate, in the 1984 congressional races and in state or local elections, and in the 1980 presidential race;[14] (4) petitioning—contacting a public official and signing a petition; and (5) protesting through direct action—attending a protest meeting or demonstration and picketing or boycotting.

Third, voting was the most distinct mode of participation, and protest through petitioning the least. (See Appendix B.3, Table 5, which shows that the items defining the other four participation modes have only minimal loadings on the voting factor, while several items from other factors have sizable loadings on the petitioning factor.)

Fourth, as predicted, protest and electoral politics were not alternative forms. Of the thirteen voting and campaign activities, eleven were positively related to petitioning, and ten were positively related to protest through direct action. Conversely, all four protest activities loaded positively on the voting and campaign factors.

TABLE 3.3
Level of Political Participation of the Jackson Supporters and Advocates of a Black Political Voice

Political Participation Measure	Support for the Jackson Candidacy		Advocacy of a Black Political Voice		Total Sample
	High (297)	Low (71)	High (62)	Low (165)	(871)
Traditional Campaign Activities					
Influenced people to vote for/against party/candidate	43%	46%	29%	40%*	39%
Went to political meetings in support of candidate	25%	16%	12%	21%*	21%
Gave money for candidate	23%	15%*	13%	24%*	19%
Campaigned for a black candidate	22%	11%****	13%	17%	17%
Helped with voter registration; got people to polls	18%	15%	17%	15%	17%
Worked for a party	31%	23%*	18%	31%*	27%

Church Campaign Activities

Attended church in support of a black candidate	30%	18%*	25%	20%	22%
Worked for a candidate through church	14%	4%**	12%	10%	10%
Contributed to a collection for a candidate taken at church	25%	13%*	27%	16%	21%
Petitioning					
Contacted a public official	33%	23%*	16%	40%****	29%
Signed a petition	54%	38%*	36%	66%*****	50%
Direct Action					
Attended a protest meeting or demonstration	21%	7%****	13%	20%*	15%
Picketed; boycotted	12%	2%****	5%	12%**	9%

Note: Percentages are respondents saying yes when asked whether they took part in each activity. As in Table 3.2, percentages of the extreme groups illustrate significance level reflect the relationship using the entire range of support for Jackson and advocacy of a black political voice, with demographic influences controlled. Total percentages are based on the weighted N of 1,293 in the post-election survey. This represents an unweighted N of 871 who participated in both the pre- and post-election surveys. Unweighted Ns for each category and for the total sample are shown in parentheses at the top of the table.

* *p* < .05. ** *p* < .01. **** *p* < .0001.

Fifth, the political activities of the strong Jackson supporters were patterned somewhat differently from the activities of other blacks. Among the Jackson supporters, traditional and church-based campaign acts formed a single, strong factor, showing that Jackson brought the church *into*, not merely *alongside*, electoral politics. Petitioning and direct action were also combined in a single protest factor.[15] That factor was related to electoral campaigning more among the Jackson supporters than among other blacks—a result that confirms the fusion of protest and electoral politics in the Jackson campaign. Three acts in particular were common to both protest and campaigning: talking to people to influence their vote; attending political meetings, dinners, or speeches in behalf of a candidate; and giving money to a candidate. (See Appendix B.3, Table 6, for the factor structure of the strong Jackson supporters.)

Levels of Participation

The complementarity of electoral and protest politics is also demonstrated by comparing the levels of participation of Jackson's supporters and non-supporters. The strong supporters were more active in both modes. Differences between them and the non-supporters were statistically reliable on three of the six traditional campaign activities, on all three church campaign activities, and on all four protest acts. (See Table 3.3 below, which summarizes the differences between strong supporters and non-supporters on all modes except voting. See Table 3.2 for the voting comparisons.) The group differences were approximately the same size on all participation modes (ranging from 8 to 16 percent on the various acts). The differences on five indexes summarizing the separate acts were reliable even when structural and demographic factors were held constant. (See Appendix B.3, Table 7, for the demographic and structural effects on participation, and Table 8, for relationships between Jackson support and participation.)

Those advocating and those not advocating a black political voice also showed different levels of political participation. (Separate analyses of the two components of the independent-voice measure—a black party and a vote-black strategy—supported this conclusion.) Advocates less often than non-advocates raised money for candidates, attended political meetings, tried to influence the vote of others, and worked for a political party, the differences being around 10 percent. They also took part less often in direct-action and petitioning activities. The differences on contacting a public official, 24 percent, and on signing a petition, 30 percent, were especially dramatic. The advocates were active, however, through their churches; they participated as often as non-advocates in all three church campaign activities. (The differences between advocates and non-advocates withstood structural and demographic controls, which are critical to these comparisons, since the advocates had fewer politically relevant resources. See Chapter Five.)

CONCLUSIONS

Two preliminary conclusions may be drawn from comparisons of the supporters and non-supporters of Jackson and of the advocates and non-advocates of an independent voice.

First, support for Jackson and advocacy of a black political voice represented separate viewpoints, although our original expectation of them as "insider" and "outsider" strategies proved false. Both the Jackson supporters and the black-voice advocates were Democrats, expressing some kind of independence within the context of the party. Neither was ready to defect; both were loyal voters for Democratic candidates. As internal critics, the strong Jackson supporters, in fact, found more fault with the party than did the advocates of an independent black voice.

Second, voting and other forms of political participation show that neither group was alienated from the electoral process, nor from politics in general.

These conclusions provide a backdrop for Chapters Four and Five, which take up in depth the political motivation and resources of the Jackson supporters and the advocates of a black political voice. Our objective in these chapters is to depict the structural and social psychological bases of these two expressions of what appears to be an underlying independent posture in the relationship to the Democratic party and the electoral system.

Notes

1. Rosenstone, Behr, and Lazarus 1984, 79.
2. Marable 1985, 266–267.
3. Walters 1988.
4. Verba and Nie 1972. See Jackson, Hatchett, and Brown (1985) for further analysis

of participation using this survey. Verba and Nie have a fourth mode involving interaction with the state to solve personal needs. See note 12 below.

5. Skowronek 1982.

6. Morris 1984; Nelson 1982; Brown 1986.

7. Nelson, cited in Henderson 1982.

8. Reed 1986, 4–7, 33–36.

9. Hamilton 1982a, xx.

10. According to Shanks and Miller (1985), criticism of the power of the federal government has been growing ever since it was first measured in 1964 by the NES at the University of Michigan. By 1980, the opinion that the government had become too powerful outweighed contrary views three to one. By 1984, however, the trend turned. Shanks and Miller suggest that "many Americans appear to have concluded that the federal government should return to a more active role in domestic policy" (p. 34). Even so, the dominant opinion in 1984 still favored the conservative position on this and other issues concerning poverty and race: that government should play only a minimal role in providing jobs, a good standard of living, and aid to minorities and that school integration should be achieved through busing.

11. Barnes et al. 1979.

12. No distinction was made between contacts concerning community problems and those concerning personal problems. Interacting with the state apparatus over personal needs and problems is the fourth major form of political action in the Verba and Nie typology. As we see from our factor analyses, in which contacting a public official was part of protest through petitioning, the respondents interpreted the question collectively, not personally.

13. A maximum number can be specified if fewer than the desired number of factors exceed eigenvalues of at least one. In the analysis of the total sample, only four factors met this criterion. In the second analysis, we set the maximum at five.

14. Whether the respondent voted at all in the 1984 election was excluded since, in some subgroups, the response to that question was perfectly correlated with voting for a congressional seat and/or for a state or local office.

15. Verba and Nie do not consider petitioning a form of protest action. Various acts of petitioning have long been ways in which ordinary people have expressed their discontent and made claims on authorities, however. According to Tilly (1981, 19–20), petitioning was part of the eighteenth-century repertoire of collective action and continued to be used in both the nineteenth and twentieth centuries. In the eighteenth century, individuals directed petitions and other recurrent forms of politics (such as food riots, resistance to conscription, invasions of fields and forests, and rebellions against tax collectors) immediately toward the object of their claims. In the nineteenth century, petitions (along with demonstrations, protest meetings, strikes, and electoral rallies) began to be addressed to the public as well as to immediate objects and to be organized by special-interest associations. The Jackson supporters, seeing closer relationships among petitioning, picketing, boycotting, protest meetings and demonstrations, reflect this underlying connection between petitioning and other modes of making claims on authorities.

CHAPTER FOUR

Supporters of Jesse Jackson: Their Solidarity and Their Political Outlooks

J ESSE JACKSON APPEALED TO a large majority of the black electorate in 1984. Exit-poll figures for the primaries showed that after the first Super Tuesday, March 6, 1984, when 50 percent of voting blacks in Alabama, 61 percent in Georgia, and 30 percent in Massachusetts voted for him, Jackson consistently won at least 70 percent and usually more of the black vote.[1] There was less support for him, however, among blacks who did not vote and those residing in states without primaries. To understand the political meaning of the black elector- ate's evaluation of Jackson, we must therefore examine the entire black electorate, not merely those who voted in the primaries.[2]

A nationally representative sample of blacks makes it possible to estimate the breadth of support for Jackson and to analyze its sources. This chapter addresses five sets of questions about that support: (1) Who were his strongest supporters? What were their social and demo- graphic origins? (2) Was support for Jackson an expression of black identity and political consciousness? Were his strongest supporters anti-white as well as pro-black, as some commentators have claimed? (3) What was the organizational base of his support? What role was played by membership in black organizations and black churches? (4) Was his appeal primarily symbolic or also related to the policy prefer- ences of the black electorate? (5) As internal critics of the Democratic party, were his strongest supporters critical of government generally? As Democrats taking an independent stance in the party, were they

unusually optimistic in thinking that blacks could be politically influential by acting as a group?

Underlying these questions is a broader aim—to examine support
for Jackson as an expression of both commitment to the political system and independence within the parties.

THE BREADTH OF SUPPORT

As is more fully described in Chapter Three, the measure of support
for Jackson is an average of responses to three questions: preference for
Jackson over other candidates in the primaries; evaluation of whether
Jackson's candidacy was a good or bad idea; and willingness to vote
for Jackson had he run as an independent presidential candidate. These
attitudes and evaluations, though clustered together in a factor analysis, provided somewhat different pictures of the breadth of his support.
His candidacy was thought a good idea by 88 percent (68 percent said
"very good"); 53 percent said they would vote for him if he were to
make a presidential bid outside the Democratic party; and 66 percent
of those who voted in a primary cast ballots for him (an average figure
somewhat below the exit-poll average), although only 22 percent who
lived in states without primaries said they would have voted for him.

Estimates of the extent of black support for Jackson varied somewhat across the polls taken during the campaign. At the time our pre-
election survey was in the field, the *New York Times* reported that
"Black Democrats prefer Mondale to Jackson as a nominee."[3] That
conclusion was based on a telephone poll of black Democrats, conducted jointly with CBS. Respondents were asked, "Who would you
like to see the Democrats nominate for President in 1984—Walter
Mondale, Jesse Jackson, or Gary Hart?" Favoring Mondale were 53
percent; 31 percent said Jackson; and the remainder split between
favoring Hart and being undecided. Rather than favoring Mondale, we
found that 53 percent of our national sample of blacks were ready to
vote for Jackson as an independent candidate. The differences largely
reflect context and wording of questions.

Our survey question asked, "If Jesse Jackson ran as an independent
presidential candidate, would you vote for him, Walter Mondale, or
Ronald Reagan?" It presented a hypothetical situation that few people
expected would materialize and allowed expression of preference despite language of intention ("would you vote?"). The *Times* question,
asking about the candidates shortly before the Democratic National
Convention, presented a real situation. It encouraged realism despite
language of preference ("would you like?"). Throughout the campaign

blacks were realistic about Jackson's chances: responding to our pre-election survey, none thought Jackson would be elected president; nearly three-fifths believed Reagan would be reelected. As the Democratic convention approached, blacks doubtless knew that Mondale would be nominated. David N. Dinkins, then clerk of New York City and Jackson's campaign coordinator in Manhattan, interpreted the poll in terms of the reality it presented: "The people in your poll were responding to reality. . . . Many people felt it was vital that Jesse get votes to give legitimacy to the issues and causes he discussed, but I believe most people who voted for him understood that he would not be the nominee."[4]

Did the *Times*/CBS finding of 53 percent in favor of Mondale mean that "Mondale commanded considerably larger support than Jackson among blacks," as Woodward concludes in a review of Reed's book *The Jesse Jackson Phenomenon?*[5] The answer depends on the context in which support is gauged. The primary votes of blacks showed greater support for Jackson. So, too, did their reaction to the idea of Jackson's making an independent presidential bid. Anticipating Jackson's failure to win the nomination, they then expressed preference for Mondale. These subtleties should be remembered as we analyze support for Jackson based on the black electorate's responses to three specific questions drawn from the pre-election survey.

THE SOCIAL ORIGINS OF THE JACKSON SUPPORTERS

The extent of Jackson's support among "black elites" and "black masses" is a contentious point in the debate over his political significance. According to Reed, who has written a widely cited book on the Jackson candidacy, his campaign forces asserted that his support came from " 'grass roots' rather than elite elements in the black community."[6] Were they claiming greater support from low income blacks than from the more privileged, or were they merely stating that those with a low income were more responsive to Jackson than they usually are to presidential candidates? If the latter, exit-poll figures showing that Jackson "received impressive majorities from all income groups"[7] confirm that he was able to reach groups who usually do not have strong candidate preferences or vote in large numbers. Equal support across income groups is damaging evidence only if Jackson or his campaign managers held out that his support was actually *stronger* among "grass roots blacks."

Reed uses figures from nine of the thirteen primaries covered by the *Times*/CBS polls to argue that Jackson in fact "ran better among the highest-earning income groups than he did among the lowest."[8] Close examination of the data demonstrates, however, that the elite edge was as sizable as 10 percent in only three primaries—those in Washington, D.C., Illinois, and Indiana. (In Washington, D.C. and Illinois, a difference of that size is found only when the small group of blacks earning $35,000 or more annually are compared with all other blacks.) Income differences were smaller than 10 percent in Alabama, Texas, Ohio, and Pennsylvania and followed no particular pattern in Maryland and Tennessee, all states that Reed said showed an elite edge. There were no differences in New Jersey and a slightly lower vote for Jackson among the highest income groups in Georgia, New York, and North Carolina.

Reed also concludes that a CBS survey of delegates to the Democratic convention shows that those favoring Jackson "scored roughly equal in income and substantially higher in educational attainment relative to Mondale and Hart delegates."[9] Jackson delegates were impressively elite when compared with the black electorate but not when compared with Hart delegates.[10] Furthermore, the educational edge of Jackson delegates over Mondale delegates was nearly offset by the latter's income advantage. (The percentage of Mondale delegates earning $35,000 or more was 63; of Hart delegates, 56; and of Jackson delegates, 58; the percentage of Mondale delegates with professional or postgraduate academic degrees was 40; of Hart delegates, 52; and of Jackson delegates, 54.)[11] Neither the income nor the education comparisons confirm Reed's conclusions.

Two other sources of information on the background of Jackson's supporters provide somewhat stronger evidence of a social class effect. The Joint Center for Political Studies, which sponsored a pre-election survey of nine hundred blacks conducted by the Gallup Organization, reported an effect of education but not of income. Blacks with at least a high school education preferred Jackson to other candidates.[12] The New York Times/CBS telephone surveys conducted from January to April 1984 (and including a total of some four hundred blacks) showed both an education and an income effect.[13] Blacks earning $25,000 and more or with some college education were the most favorable to Jackson.

The conclusions of the Gallup and Times/CBS surveys may not be valid, however, since their figures are not adjusted for age, which consistently influenced Jackson support. Exit polls showed that a larger proportion of blacks younger than age 45 voted for Jackson in the primaries.[14] The Gallup and Times/CBS surveys also revealed weaker preferences for and less favorable ratings of Jackson among blacks age 55 and older. Since younger cohorts in the black population also have more education and a higher income, survey results showing greater support among elite blacks may be spurious, attributable largely to age.

Table 4.1 presents our survey's results, showing the structural and demographic influences on support for Jackson. It substantiates that the marginally significant uncontrolled-income effect is not statistically reliable when age and other demographic characteristics are held constant. Nor are the effects of working full-time and receiving Social Security and other welfare. Thus, economic status was inconsequential as an independent influence in explaining who supported Jackson.

All the surveys that were conducted in the months preceding the 1984 election show, however, that support for Jackson was influenced by education and age. On our measure, age influenced that support more than education. As in other surveys, we found approximately equal support for Jackson up to age 45 and a lower level after that.[15] But there was no evidence of unusually high support among black yuppies. A regression analysis, testing the significance of a possible interaction among age, urbanicity, and socioeconomic status, revealed no unusual combined effect of being young, urban, and affluent.

The only other significant demographic effect is that Jackson received greater support in rural areas, small towns, and small cities. Half of those who lived in these sites but only one-third in the large cities were among his strongest supporters.

Except for lower support among older, less educated blacks and those living in large cities, Jackson reached many sectors of the black population. Men and women, the married and the unmarried, those with lower and higher incomes, those on and off welfare, and those living in and outside the South all supported him to about the same extent. The geographic, economic, and social breadth of Jackson's appeal affirms the political significance of his campaign.

SOLIDARITY:
GROUP IDENTIFICATION AND CONSCIOUSNESS

The feelings of a 69-year-old black man, a retired Pennsylvania forklift operator, captures an aspect of Jesse Jackson's appeal. As noted in the *New York Times*, William T. Hayes believed Jackson would lose. Nevertheless, he voted for Jackson because he thought he would never have another chance to vote for a black presidential candidate. There have been other black candidates—Shirley Chisholm in 1972 and Eldridge Cleaver and Dick Gregory in 1968—but for Hayes and many other blacks, Jackson was the first to be taken seriously. "There's such a thing as a righteous minority," Hayes explained. "Even if he doesn't

TABLE 4.1
Demographic and Structural Sources of Support for Jackson

Characteristics and Resources	r	B^a
Age: older	−.178****	−.139*** (.039)
Education	.160****	.129*** (.040)
Family income	.088*	−.010 (.033)
Employment status: full-time	.087*	−.025 (.040)
Receiving Social Security	−.108**	−.027 (.039)
Receiving other welfare	−.035	−.018 (.035)
Marital status: married	.067	.057 (.036)
Gender: female	−.002	−.010 (.033)
Region: non-South	−.034	.036 (.036)
Urbanicity	−.129***	−.144**** (.037)
R^2		8.2%****

Note: Regressions are based on the 1,150 respondents in the pre-election survey. Standard errors are shown in parentheses.
[a] These effects were also estimated with a multiple classification analysis (MCA), a technique designed to handle categorical predictors like gender and southern/nonsouthern. The MCA and regression betas were highly similar. Although the coefficient is not shown, race of interviewer was included as a control in the regression.
*$p < .05$.
**$p < .01$.
***$p < .001$.
****$p < .0001$.

win, there's a chance for someone else of his caliber next time. He's doing better than I thought he would. In my opinion, he's already a winner."[16]

Some support for Jackson was based on group identification and pride, sentiments his critics dismiss as emotional and symbolic,[17] rather than strictly political. But much of politics is symbolic, and by no means trivial. Reagan, for instance, represents traditional values and a simpler America.

The bond of solidarity connecting Jackson and the black community in 1984 was criticized on three grounds: that voting for Jackson was just an emotional response and not hardheaded, realistic politics; that voting to express racial solidarity was inherently racist and anti-white; and that voting for him would polarize the black and white electorates. The evidence for this characterization, provided principally by journalists, comes from interviews with political commentators, elected black officials, other national leaders, and an occasional ordinary citizen. Journalists' quotations, however vivid, cannot provide a substitute for careful estimates of political reality. Our survey data allow us to question widely believed criticisms of Jackson's support in the black electorate. First we may ask: What proportion of the black electorate mentioned themes relating to solidarity when asked whether "it was a good idea or a bad idea for Jesse Jackson to have run for president"? Second, we may consider to what extent group identity and political consciousness accounted for variation in support for Jackson. And, third, we may consider to what extent the solidarity base of Jackson's appeal was anti-white.

The Jackson Candidacy: A Good or a Bad Idea?

The 88 percent of the sample who believed it was good that Jackson ran gave positive reasons, of course.[18] Of this large approving majority, nearly nine in ten referred to solidarity or to Jackson's being a black candidate. Very few gave emotional reasons (such as allusions to primordial ties, hope, or pride), however, to describe this sense of solidarity. Instead, they spoke of political reasons. One-third thought that Jackson's candidacy was positive because it set an important political example: "he showed everyone—blacks and whites both—that it's possible for a black candidate to make a good showing"; "Jackson was an example"; "he opened doors for blacks to run in the future"; "Jackson made it easier for others to follow"; and "he proved that a black candidate can have an impact—another first for us." Two in ten of this approving majority thought the campaign reflected determination, that running is trying, and trying is winning: "Jackson was right to try because it is his constitutional right to run—our right to run even if a black can't win"; "he couldn't win the nomination but he should have tried, just like anyone else"; and "just by running he won a victory for black people—it wasn't the nomination or even winning a primary but running well—that was winning." Another two in ten emphasized Jackson's mobilizing effect on the black electorate. They believed "his candidacy was good first and foremost because it increased registration and voting—people who never vote in primaries came out"; "he got blacks interested in the political system, even those who usually badmouth politics and politicians sat up and took notice of this campaign"; and "he educated a lot of blacks who usually pay no mind to politics." A few (one in ten) referred specifically to the political interests of the black community: "we need a President who has a black perspective"; and "Jackson understands and will act on the social and economic needs of the black community." Finally, a bare 2 percent felt that his candidacy would enhance black influence in the Democratic party.

Some of these comments admittedly represent feelings as well as beliefs and judgments. Setting a political example, symbolizing the importance of trying, and mobilizing interest in politics all imply pride but do not convey emotionality—for example, that Jackson offered an emotional catharsis or made his supporters feel better about themselves. They spoke in terms of rational politics. Jackson appealed to them because he stood for their interests and because they believed he could mobilize black power to benefit the black community.

The divergent interpretations of Jackson's meaning to the black electorate found in our interviews and in many journalistic accounts doubtless result from different approaches. We used sampling techniques designed to give a representative picture of the black population; journalists relied on selective interviews. Social science data and journalistic information are also collected in different contexts. Some of our respondents may have emphasized rational political themes because they were talking on the phone to a person from a university-based research center. The journalistic quotations were generally gathered in emotion-charged contexts, such as political rallies, meetings, or other campaign settings. And, of course, context has profound effects on style of discourse.

Some blacks who thought Jackson's candidacy was a good idea did not mention solidarity. Their comments could refer to any presidential candidate. One-tenth of those approving Jackson's candidacy emphasized his personal qualifications: "he's intelligent"; "he would make a good President because he's knowledgeable about politics at home and abroad"; "Jackson is a good speaker who is able to express himself and state his ideas"; and "he's religious and we need a moral man as a leader." (Since these comments about Jackson's personal qualifications were volunteered, they clearly underestimate the proportion of the black electorate who, if explicitly asked, would have attributed positive qualities to him. A Gallup poll did ask blacks to evaluate the major candidates on the basis of several personal traits. It found that 80–90 percent described Jackson as caring about people like them; as hardworking, fair, knowledgeable, compassionate, and a strong leader; as representing a new way of thinking, able to get things done, and clear on issues.)[19]

Another one-tenth of the approving majority discussed Jackson's stance on policy issues without referring to race or to the black community. They approved of Jackson's running because "he would insist on government help for the poor and on a strong employment policy"; "Jackson's policies provided a real choice in a slate of candidates who outdid each other in not talking about jobs, housing, the homeless or poverty in America"; "Jackson was the only one not afraid to question American anti-communist foreign policy"; "I liked his willingness to try new approaches internationally, like in Cuba and Syria, to get political prisoners and [captured Navy Lieutenant Robert] Goodman back [from Syria]"; "Jackson forced discussion of issues the Democrats, and certainly Reagan, would have avoided"; "he had a positive effect on the Democratic party by raising unpopular policies"; and "bringing up problems and policies for debate—that's what candidates who know they can't actually get nominated do best, and Jackson did it."

Of the 12 percent who thought the Jackson candidacy a bad idea, the dominant concern, expressed by four-fifths of this small minority, was that it was not realistic and thus not hardheaded politics. The stated reasons: "a black can't win, so it's a waste of your vote"; "a black candidate just splits the black vote and allows the white nominee not to feel indebted to blacks as a whole"; and "if blacks support a black candidate as a bloc, it's just symbolic; if they don't, it shows weakness; either way a black candidate dilutes the political clout blacks realistically can have—being the pivotal vote for the nominee who makes it." The next most frequent criticism concerned Jackson's personal qualities. One-third of the critics (4 percent of the total sample) either didn't "like him" or judged him "not knowledgeable," "too inexperienced," or "too religious." One-tenth of the critics (less than 1 percent of the total sample) mentioned worry about polarization of blacks and whites. They said, "whites won't let a black go that far, running just brings out white racism"; and "I feared for his life—no black leader has been able to stand up like that without being shot or cut down." These comments, rare though they were, focused exclusively on the polarization created by the reactions of whites to the Jackson candidacy. No one suggested that mounting a campaign pushed blacks into an anti-white or racially hostile posture. Only one person in the survey worried that the campaign was racist in that it created the expectation that blacks would support Jackson only because he was black.

The Solidarity Bases of Jackson's Support

Further evidence indicates that support for Jackson was related to racial solidarity. A pre-election Gallup survey mounted by the Joint Center for Political Studies found that preference for Jackson over other Democratic candidates in the primaries was significantly influenced by racial consciousness, indicated in that survey by three beliefs: (1) racial progress is too slow; (2) blacks should be given preference in hiring to overcome past discrimination; and (3) a separate black party is a positive move.[20]

As noted in Chapter Three, we made a considerable effort to measure a theoretically derived conception of solidarity, defined as the beliefs and feelings members have about their group membership and the group's position in society. It is comprised of two components: group identity and group political consciousness. The former refers to feelings about group membership and is measured by two indicators. The first, called common-fate identity, is a two-item index of the centrality of being black to one's sense of self and of the acceptance of a common fate with other blacks. The second, called an exclusivist black identity, is a feeling that being black is more important than being American or both black and American. Group political consciousness involves an ideology about the societal position of the group. For blacks, it encompasses discontent with the comparative powerlessness of blacks as a group, rejection of the legitimacy of racial disparities in economic status, and advocacy of collective political strategies. Approval of nationalism bridged identification and consciousness.

How do group identity and group political consciousness clarify the bases of support for Jackson? Three conclusions may be drawn. First, the support was related to both indicators of identity and all but one indicator of political consciousness.[21] Second, the relationships partly reflected the greater structural advantages of the blacks with stronger solidarity. Third, the relationships between support for Jackson and both identity and consciousness were still statistically reliable when education, income, and other demographic factors were held constant. The effect of the identity measures was even reliable when the group-consciousness measures were controlled. This means that support was greater among blacks who felt a sense of common fate over and beyond their higher education and stronger political consciousness, both of which fostered support for Jackson's candidacy. (See Table 4.2.)

Was Jackson's Solidarity Base Anti-white?

As Jackson entered the race, he believed that most whites would not support a black candidate. And, in a crunch, white politicians would turn to their own.[22] As the campaign wore on and Jackson won no

Table 4.2
Group Solidarity and Support for Jackson

Group Solidarity Measure	r	B^a	B^b
Group Identity			
Identity based on sense of common fate	.197****	.152****	.128***
		(.031)	(.032)
Exclusivist identity: being black is more important than being American or both black and American	.163****	.128***	.114***
		(.032)	(.033)
Group Political Consciousness			
Collective discontent: blacks have too little political influence	.148****	.130****	.105**
		(.034)	(.033)
Rejection of the legitimacy of racial disparities	.096**	.061*	.035
		(.030)	(.033)
Approval of collective political strategies	.050	.006	−.016
		(.033)	(.032)
Black nationalism	.206****	.218****	.116***
		(.033)	(.033)

Note: Regressions are based on the 871 respondents who participated in both the pre- and post-election surveys. Standard errors are shown in parentheses.
[a] Coefficients are based on six regressions in which each identity or consciousness measure was used separately and all structural or demographic and race-of-interviewer measures were included as controls.
[b] Coefficients are based on a regression in which all identity and consciousness measures were used as predictors simultaneously and all structural or demographic and race-of-interviewer measures were included as controls.
*$p < .05$.
**$p < .01$.
***$p < .001$.
****$p < .0001$.

more than one-tenth of the white primary vote, experience substantiated his initial beliefs. He turned increasingly to the black constituency that supported him. In the words of the black speaker of the California assembly, Willie Brown, he was forced to be "unabashedly black."[23] But did his appeal to black solidarity necessarily mean that the relationship between him and his supporters was racist? Even the few blacks who thought his candidacy a bad idea did not worry about the campaign arousing anti-white feelings among blacks. Nonetheless, some political analysts discerned a racist theme in the campaign and in the comments of some of its supporters.

While conceding that one can be unabashedly black and still be able to build bridges between blacks and whites, some feel that Jackson crossed the dangerously thin line between black pride and racism. Harvard law professor Alan Dershowitz argued that it wasn't running black but "running black *that way*"—"being unwilling to broaden the base of his coalition at the expense of losing some votes within the black community"—that made the campaign racist.[24] The charge is clear. Since a broader appeal would alienate some presumably racist supporters, was Jackson playing a brand of racial politics that was anti-white and exclusionary?

Did our survey results substantiate the racist charge? Was the solidarity base of Jackson's support anti-white as well as pro-black? And is it possible for a political candidate to appeal to ingroup bonds, such as are found among blacks, without creating, arousing, or reinforcing hostility and exclusionary behavior toward whites as an outgroup?

This is a persistent question in the social psychology of intergroup relations. In 1906, when Sumner invented the terms "the we-group, or in-group, and everybody else, or other-groups, out-groups," he observed that conditions of amity usually exist within the ingroup, while hostility characterizes relations with outgroups.[25] To Sumner, positive feelings within the ingroup depended on negative feelings toward members of the outgroup. Merton later argued that in adopting a descriptive, rather than an analytic, outlook on ingroup-outgroup relations, Sumner inevitably "blurred and obscured the otherwise conspicuous fact that, under certain conditions, the outgroup becomes a basis of *positive*, not merely hostile, reference and that the science of sociology is thereby committed to determine the conditions under which one or the other orientation to outgroups obtained."[26]

After much study, social psychologists now know something about these conditions. Ingroup favoritism is more closely related to outgroup bias when group boundaries are made especially salient, when groups are pitted against one another in competition over scarce resources, and when their goals are opposed, with this supplemented by a history of conflict. There is, however, no inevitable connection between ingroup and outgroup sentiments. American race relations, of course, have been characterized by the very conditions in which outgroup hostility tends to go along with ingroup bonds. Since blacks have had to compete with whites to gain employment, housing, and other resources and have tried to achieve full political equality with whites who have historically wanted or tolerated their disfranchisement, political commentators have believed that the ingroup bonds of blacks must be closely tied to anti-white feelings.

Two types of solidarity can be used to gauge whether Jackson supporters were anti-white and exclusionary. Black identity is at the core of each. Both were related to support for Jackson, but, as noted in Chapter Two, the two types were not significantly correlated and did not have the same social origins; and only one was consistently associated with the various elements of group political consciousness. We took advantage of this statistical independence to form two distinct groups of strong Jackson supporters.[27] One group's solidarity was based on a politicized sense of common fate. These strong supporters scored extremely high on the common-fate identity measure, attributed racial disparities to structural obstacles, and agreed that blacks have too little political influence. The other group's solidarity was based on an exclusivist black identity, though these strong supporters indicated no strong political consciousness. Each group comprised about 20 percent of Jackson's strong supporters.

Table 4.3 shows comparisons of the intergroup attitudes of these two extreme groups. It also compares them with the remaining three-fifths of Jackson's strong supporters and with non-supporters. (The residual group of strong supporters contained some who exhibited solidarity based on a politicized sense of common fate but at a level below that required for inclusion in the extreme group, as well as a smaller set who had little or no group solidarity. The residual group did not include any supporters with an exclusivist identity, since all of them were, by definition, members of an extreme group.)

What do intergroup attitudes reveal about support for Jackson? His supporters were demonstrably pro-black. All three groups of strong supporters felt closer to black people in Africa than non-supporters (although not to West Indians). All three groups more often believed that black children should learn an African language and that black people should shop in black-owned stores whenever possible. Not surprisingly, supporters with strong solidarity were even more pro-black than other strong supporters.

Were the strong supporters of Jackson who were pro-black also anti-white? The answer depends on whether solidarity was politicized or not. Supporters whose solidarity was based on a politicized sense of common fate were definitely not anti-white. (Note the comparisons in the first two columns in Table 4.3) Compared with the group with a non-politicized, exclusivist identity, 40 percent fewer of them indicated that they did not feel close to whites. Significantly fewer also agreed that "blacks should have nothing to do with whites if they can help it." In their feelings toward whites, those with a politicized identity resembled the non-supporters. This shows that ingroup solidarity

TABLE 4.3
Intergroup Attitudes of Jackson's Supporters with Strong Solidarity

	Strong Supporters			
Intergroup Attitudes	Politicized Identity Based on Sense of Common Fate (68)	Non-politicized Exclusivist Identity (82)	All Other Strong Supporters[a] (288)	Non-supporters (89)
Pro-black: Nationalism				
Feel very or fairly close to				
Black people in Africa	76%	74%	57%	46%
West Indians	50%	59%	45%	43%
Agree that black children should study an African language	55%	53%	37%	13%****
Black people should shop in black-owned stores whenever possible	88%	74%	56%	32%****
Feelings toward Whites				
Don't feel close to whites	28%	68%	35%	21%*
Agree that blacks should have nothing to do with whites if they can help it	1%	10%	5%	1%*

158

Political Judgments of Superordinates

Believe that the following groups have "too much" power in American life and politics

Whites	67%	85%	62%	49%****
Business executives	86%	65%	56%	45%***
Men	73%	60%	60%	42%***
Believe that, on the whole, white people want to keep blacks down	43%	60%	48%	33%

Political Judgments of Subordinates

Believe that the following groups have "too little" power in American life and politics

Poor people	78%	73%	65%	65%
People on welfare	70%	54%	48%	52%
Women	52%	26%	23%	37%**
Older people	52%	47%	35%	31%
Young people	33%	30%	27%	39%**

Note: This table excludes respondents who had scores of 2 or 3 on the four-point Jackson support scale. The probability level is based on an F-test for the full range, showing the reliability of a relationship between the full range of support for Jackson and intergroup feelings. The analysis was conducted on data from the 871 respondents who participated in both the pre- and post-election surveys. The numbers in parentheses show how many were in each of three Jackson support groups that had strong solidarity, and how many were in the group of non-supporters.

[a] This category deletes the 12 respondents who met the criteria for both types of solidarity. The analysis was conducted on data from the 871 respondents who participated in both the pre- and post-election surveys.

   $*p < .05.$
  $**p < .01.$
 $***p < .001.$
$****p < .0001.$

can motivate members to support "one of their own" without inter-group hostility or even emotional distance from the outgroup.

The only group of strong supporters with negative feelings toward whites was the one whose members had a non-politicized, exclusivist identity; even so, their negative feelings should not be overstated. While two-thirds of them said they did not feel close to whites, only one-tenth advocated having nothing to do with whites. (These senti-ments were found among only 2 percent of Jackson's most supportive group, since supporters with an exclusivist identity comprised just under 20 percent of the strong supporters.)

Other intergroup attitudes shown in Table 4.3 address a second important question—Did Jackson's strongest supporters show concern for the life circumstances of blacks but not of other deprived groups?

The survey asked for opinions of the power of several social catego-ries: whites, business executives, men (who have relatively strong in-fluence), poor people, people on welfare, older people, women, and young people (who have less). Three conclusions can be reached by comparing the opinions of supporters and non-supporters of Jackson.

First, all the strong supporters were more critical than the non-supporters of the political power of whites, business executives, and men.

Second, discontent with the excessive power of superordinate groups was especially marked among Jackson supporters with a politicized sense of common fate (a finding that further substantiates the political nature of this type of identity). In contrast, Jackson sup-porters with a non-politicized, exclusivist identity were aggrieved by whites in particular. More than other supporters (and, of course, the non-supporters), they thought that white people, on the whole, want to "keep blacks down." Their political analysis centered on race itself and was not a broad critique of discrepancies between "haves" and "have-nots."

Third, in general the strong supporters were broadly concerned about the political influence of people in other subordinate social cate-gories. Moreover, the supporters whose solidarity was based on a politicized sense of common fate were actually more dis-contented than were other blacks with the powerlessness of people on welfare, women, and older people. (Note that blacks in every group were critical of the limited power of poor people.) Group solidarity thus does not necessarily limit empathy with other groups. The Jack-son supporters whose identity was based on a sense of common fate definitely felt ingroup bonds but recognized that other groups also have negligible political influence.

In short, the racial solidarity behind support for Jackson did not necessarily imply racial hostility or insensitivity to the plight of other deprived groups. Supporters whose solidarity was based on a politicized sense of common fate were simultaneously pro-black and inclusive; they were not anti-white. The rainbow metaphor was especially apt for them. It is true that there were a few among the strong supporters whose identity was both less politicized and more tied to race per se. It was important to them that they were black instead of both black and American, and their exclusive involvement with being black was reflected in an exclusive focus on black-white relations rather than on power itself. Even among them, however, only a few wanted nothing to do with whites.

The Jackson Candidacy and Racial Polarization

Our data do not bear directly on the charge that the Jackson candidacy polarized the black and white electorates. To measure polarization, data must be collected from both blacks and whites. Fortunately, the ongoing election surveys at Michigan do provide relevant data, which other analysts have used to examine racial trends in the vote and in party identification. The evidence for *growing* racial polarization is at best mixed.

Blacks and whites were no more polarized when they voted in 1984 than in previous years. Measuring polarization by differences between the percentages of whites and blacks voting for the Democratic presidential candidate, Miller concludes that it has remained fairly constant since the Democratic Congress passed the 1965 Voting Rights Act and the Johnson administration implemented it.[28] In 1984, the racial voting difference for the Democratic candidate was 54 percentage points; in 1980, 56 points; in 1976, when Carter brought some blue-collar and southern whites back to the Democratic majority, it was down to 48 points; and in both 1968 and 1972, when the Wallace vote made inroads into the white Democratic vote, it was 57 points. The greatest voting disparities (61 points) occurred in the South in 1964, but even this is characteristic. In all these elections, racial polarization has been most pronounced in the South. Miller writes that "it is quite incorrect, therefore, to characterize the election results in terms of a sudden white flight from the Democratic party . . . the context is a society with a decades-long history of extreme polarization along racial lines. The Democratic leadership must deal with this situation, but should not interpret the 1984 election results as a new directive to ignore black America in exchange for white support."[29]

The Joint Center for Political Studies, which has monitored racial trends in national and local politics since 1970, concurs with Miller, pointing out that it would be a mistake to conclude that Jackson had much of a role in the growing vote for the Republican presidential candidate among southern whites.[30] Reagan was enormously popular in both 1980 and 1984, hardly testifying to a special impact of the Jackson candidacy.

Trends in party identification do indicate that something special was happening in 1984. Party identification had been fairly constant from 1972 to 1982: the Democratic edge was usually around 20 points. In 1984, it was only 9. The shift toward the Republicans was greatest among (1) the oldest and youngest cohorts—people who cast their first votes before 1936 and after 1963; (2) the least educated, especially voters with no more than a grade school education who were also elderly; (3) self-designated conservatives; and (4) southerners. Shanks and Miller believe that these facts fit the

> thesis that the consistent articulation of conservative ideas by a successful and remarkably popular president may have persuaded many lifelong Democrats, who have also been lifelong Conservatives, that the time has come to reject their partisan roots and declare allegiance to the conservative Republican party of Ronald Reagan. As a consequence, their party identifications have changed with no change in their ideological orientations or their issue preferences. At this juncture, it is impossible to tell whether 1984 marked the early phase of a tide that will continue to sweep the Democratic party, thereby achieving a transformation of American politics comparable to that of 50 years ago.[31]

The question is, did Jackson's candidacy influence this partisan shift? A comparison of party identification surveyed in the primary phase of the campaign (January through June) and in the post-convention phase (late August to election day) shows a 10 percent nationwide shift favoring the Republicans.[32] Many commentators attributed this Republican increase to the increasingly negative reactions to Jackson among white Democrats in the South. Using data collected monthly throughout the campaign by the Michigan NES, Sears and his colleagues have tried to isolate the impact of Jackson's candidacy. They argue that "if the greater centrality of race, and especially Jackson, in presidential decisions among white Southerners was responsible for this shift of party identification toward the Republicans, then it should be detected in a greater centrality of racial attitudes over time as determinants of Southerners' party identification."[33] Over the course of the campaign, racial attitudes, and especially evaluations of Jackson, did show increasingly high correlations with party identification. Regression coefficients indicating the effect of evaluations of Jackson on party identification increased from .12 to .30 in the South, although they barely budged in the North (.08 to .11).

Do these results provide conclusive evidence that Jackson influenced the shift? Sears and his associates point out that the enlarged correlations between southerners' reactions to Jackson and their party identification were found in data collected after Jackson was no longer a major contender and was not receiving much media attention. If feelings toward Jackson had motivated party realignment, the effect should have been greatest in the months when Jackson was a highly visible candidate closely associated with the Democratic party. According to these political analysts, the large effect as late as October suggests that feelings about race did become increasingly important determinants of the party identification of southerners as the election approached, but this was not necessarily a result of the Jackson candidacy.

THE ORGANIZATIONAL RESOURCES OF JACKSON'S SUPPORTERS

Parties and campaign organizations have traditionally influenced the electoral process by mobilizing support for particular candidates and by increasing turnout. People contacted during a campaign are more likely to vote.[34] The positive impact of organizations on turnout among blacks is especially clear from analyses of the 1965 and 1967 mayoral elections in Cleveland, the 1968 and 1972 presidential elections, the 1971 gubernatorial election in Mississippi, and the 1979 mayoral primary and the 1983 mayoral election in Chicago.[35]

In 1984, organizations of many kinds—voter-registration and voter-education groups; civil rights, social, and fraternal organizations; black churches; and the Democratic party organization—worked to mobilize the black vote for the primaries. A few states experienced increases in turnout of as much as 80–100 percent. Political organizations also had a demonstrable effect on support for Jackson. It was much higher in states where local Jackson groups and the national campaign forces organized for the primary election. This evidence is, of course, largely inferential and does not substantiate the question of whether individuals contacted by organizations actually supported Jackson or voted more than those who weren't contacted.

By measuring the relationship between support for Jackson and membership in black organizations and churches, the political impact of organizations can be determined. Although frequency of church attendance did not affect support for Jackson, frequent attenders more often voted in the presidential primaries. (See Table 4.4.) Membership in politically active churches had broad political effects: it increased support for Jackson, voting in the primary, and voting in November for president, although not for state, local, or congressional seats.[36]

Membership in black organizations had still broader effects on participation in the 1984 election. Blacks who belonged to organizations working to improve the lives of blacks were stronger supporters of Jackson and more frequent voters in both the primaries and all contests in the November election. Moreover, except for congressional and state or local races, the positive effect of membership persisted after education, income, and age were controlled. The organizational effect on voting in a primary was especially strong.

POLICY PREFERENCES AND POLITICAL DISPOSITIONS

Above all else, dispute about Jackson's level of interest in policy fueled the controversy over his political significance in 1984. His critics contended that he offered few suggestions. In Reston's view, "most of his policies could be expressed on a bumper sticker."[37] Reed, less gratuitously but in the same vein, charges that Jackson was so uninterested in social and economic policy that he ignored the advice of his own political advisers, Joseph McCormick and Robert Smith, who developed a liberal-progressive agenda to guide his convention platform.[38] This agenda included national economic reconstruction aimed at full employment, welfare reform targeted at the unemployed and the underemployed, comprehensive health insurance, educational programs (especially for child care and higher education), a national industrial policy, reorientation of military budgets and priorities, and more affirmative action. Of these, Jackson's platform incorporated only the last two. His emphasis on affirmative action especially troubled his critics, who saw it as serving primarily the interests of middle class blacks.[39]

Some commentators argue to the contrary, that Jackson more than any other 1984 candidate raised unpopular policy issues and pressed for discussion of national priorities. Faw and Skelton saw this as his major accomplishment.

> Easier to pin down than his effect on voter registration and turn-out was his impact on issues in the campaign. He cornered a few the other candidates couldn't afford to touch: trade with South Africa, the rights of Pales-

TABLE 4.4

Organizational Resources and Support for Jackson and Participation in the 1984 Election

Organizational Resources	Support for Jackson		Voted in Primary		Voted in November Presidential Race		Voted in House/Senate Race		Voted in Local/State Race	
	r	B†	r	B†	r	B†	r	B†	r	B†
Attended church frequently	.019	.026 (.034)	.104	.073* (.033)	.079	.054 (.036)	−.005	−.005 (.034)	.062	.056 (.036)
Attended a church that encouraged political involvement	.106**	.095*** (.034)	.139***	.094*** (.033)	.189****	.153**** (.033)	.055	.030 (.033)	.007	−.031 (.034)
Was a member of an organization working to improve the status of blacks	.095**	.085** (.036)	.258****	.178**** (.034)	.170****	.091*** (.035)	.124***	.051 (.034)	.111**	.025 (.036)

Note: These fifteen regressions are based on the 871 respondents who participated in both the pre- and post-election surveys. Standard errors are shown in parentheses.

† Coefficients in these columns are based on three regressions in which each organizational resource measure was used separately and all structural or demographic and race-of-interviewer measures were included as controls.

* $p < .05$.
** $p < .01$.
*** $p < .001$.
**** $p < .0001$.

tinians, an "evenhanded" policy in the Middle East, famine in Africa. Repeatedly he brought them onto the agenda. On South Africa, he challenged Mondale directly, admonished him for being on the board of directors of a company, Control Data, that conducted business with the apartheid nation and forced Mondale to propose tougher sanctions against South Africa than he had suggested before.[40]

Commoner went further, asserting that Jackson managed to win about one-fifth of the popular primary vote and victories in four states, the District of Columbia, sixty congressional districts, and most of the large cities in the Northwest and Midwest while "giving powerful voice to a comprehensive program—a rousing return to old-fashioned, issue-oriented politics not seen in the Democratic Party since Franklin D. Roosevelt."[41] Marable credited the policy issues that Jackson emphasized in his 1984 campaign to Jackson's autonomy in the realm of elected black officials and to the influence that black nationalists and the white and black left had on his staff.[42] To his mind, Jackson in particular stimulated constructive discussion of foreign policy, and his campaign found a popular base because of its progressive political program.

Some critics maintain that Jackson did not press national policy positions that were in line with a progressive Rainbow Coalition because he had contradictory aims—to reach a black constituency by emotional appeals to group identity and to offer a programmatic agenda. The implication is obvious: blacks who responded to Jackson because of racial solidarity could not be motivated by policy preferences as well.

Are symbolic and programmatic politics as antithetical to each other as some analysts believe? Is it true that Jackson's supporters were uninterested in industrial, employment, welfare, educational, and health policies? Were his group-identified supporters particularly unconcerned with policy issues? Our survey is well suited to answer these questions, owing to its coverage of solidarity as well as racial and other policies. The role of policy preferences in support for Jackson and the relation between solidarity and policy involvement can be directly assessed. Four conclusions may be drawn about the relationship between solidarity and policy preferences.

First, of the two indicators of group identity, the sense of common fate was more closely associated with policy preferences. It was significantly related to all the issues we measured, except school integration and United States policy in Central America. Blacks who felt a sense of shared fate with other blacks naturally took a stronger position on racial policy. They more than other blacks wanted the federal government to play an active role in improving the economic and social circumstances of minorities. They supported affirmative action. They also believed blacks should pressure Congress to change this country's policy toward South Africa. Their concerns, however, were not restricted to racial matters. They were more liberal on other issues as well. They favored increased spending on community programs such as public schools, crime prevention and control, and jobs for the unemployed; and, to a lesser extent, they favored increased spending on social welfare programs such as Medicare and food stamps. They more frequently wanted government intervention to ensure a decent standing of living for all Americans. They favored decreased spending on defense.

Second, the other measure of black identity—perception of the self as black but not as American or both black and American—was related to government policy on race but not to broader issues (again demonstrating the lesser politicalization of this identity type). The only non-racial policy favored more by blacks with this kind of identity was government assurance of a reasonable standard of living.

Third, with one exception,[43] measures of group consciousness were correlated with both racial and other policies.

Fourth, blacks with an identity based on their awareness of common fate had thought about policies more than other blacks had. On five questions, respondents were allowed to say that they did not have an opinion since they had not thought much about the topic. These questions concerned the government's role in ensuring a standard of living and aiding minorities; spending on defense; and policies toward South Africa and Central America.[44] Blacks whose identity was based on a sense of common fate had opinions on significantly more of these questions. This was true even after adjusting for level of education.

Examination of the policy preferences of the strong Jackson supporters confirmed the absence of conflict between symbolic and programmatic policies. Had Jackson's appeal been only symbolic, as critics claim, and if symbolic and programmatic policies were actually antithetical, his supporters would not have had definite policy preferences. But, as Table 4.5 demonstrates, they did.[45] Unquestionably, there was a special connection between support for Jackson and opinions on policies that directly affect blacks. Nevertheless, Jackson's supporters had preferences on broader policy issues and had opinions on more policy questions as well.

The survey probed the political significance of the judgments of

TABLE 4.5
Policy Preferences, Economic Assessments, Liberal/Conservative Ideology, and Support for Jackson

Policies	r	B
Domestic Policies		
Approved increased spending on		
Social welfare (Medicare, food stamps)	.110*	.071*
		(.034)
Community needs (public schools, jobs for the un-employed, crime)	.091**	.086*
		(.036)
Favored federal government action in order to ensure a decent standard of living	.083	.099**
		(.034)
Favored improving position of blacks and minorities and affirmative action	.125***	.133****
		(.039)
Opposed federal action to assist blacks	−.118**	−.091**
		(.032)
Favored school integration	−.021	−.037
		(.036)
Thought given to policy issues		
How many of five issues has the respondent thought about and has a position on?	.112***	.082*
		(.034)
Liberal/Conservative Ideology		
(Higher points on a seven-point scale scored liberal)	.006	.012
		(.034)

Note: Regressions are based on the 871 respondents who participated in both the pre- and post-election surveys. Standard errors are shown in parentheses.
*$p < .05$.
**$p < .01$.
***$p < .001$.
****$p < .0001$.

blacks on economic problems. Respondents were asked to evaluate their personal or family circumstances, those of blacks as a group, and those of the nation as a whole. The goal was to examine two questions: Were evaluations of the group and the nation more politically meaningful than evaluations of the respondents' own personal situations? Was economic discontent a critical feature of racial solidarity?

To answer the first, respondents were asked whether their personal or family economic conditions had improved, remained the same, or worsened during the past year and over the previous four years. Support for Jackson was somewhat stronger among the blacks whose cir-

TABLE 4.5
(*continued*)

Policies	r	B
Foreign Policies		
Favored		
Decreased spending on defense	.062	.075*
		(.032)
Greater U.S. involvement in Central America	.036	.039
		(.036)
Increased black pressure to alter U.S. policies toward South Africa	.110***	.092**
		(.032)
Economic Assessments		
Personal Economic Assessments		
Respondent and family are worse off than a year earlier	−.077*	−.019
		(.035)
Worse off than four years earlier	−.088**	−.040
		(.035)
Economic Assessments of Blacks as a Group	.011	.034
		(.033)
Blacks are worse off than whites were four years earlier.	.023	.037
		(.033)
Blacks are doing less well than whites and not well in an absolute sense.	.071*	.069*
		(.034)
Economic Assessment of the Nation		
The economy is worse off than it was a year earlier.	.045	(.075)*
		.033

cumstances were stable or had improved, with this largely attributable to the relative youthfulness of the supporters. When age was held constant, the respondents' judgments of their personal situations had no bearing on their support for Jackson. In contrast, judgments of the nation's economy and of blacks as a group reliably influenced his support. It was higher among respondents who thought the economy had worsened and that blacks were not doing as well as whites and not well in an absolute sense. These relationships were small, however. (See Table 4.5.)

Turning to the second question, we found that the economic assessments of the group were significantly correlated with all the identification and consciousness measures and that the average intercorrelations were as large as those among the solidarity indicators

themselves. Nevertheless, economic discontent was not as important
as political discontent in explaining support for Jackson. (See Tables
4.2 and 4.5.) This is possibly due to perceptions of the major alternative
in 1984. Walter Mondale, with his long-time association with New
Deal policies, was heir to an image of the Democrats as a party dedi-
cated to alleviating economic distress. Mondale could therefore be expected to receive support from blacks discontented with the group's
economic situation. In contrast, political discontent, which more decisively distinguished Jackson supporters from Mondale supporters,
could not be expressed through support for Mondale.

THE PSYCHOLOGICAL RESOURCES
OF JACKSON'S SUPPORTERS

It will be recalled that Chapter Two dealt with the black electorate's
interest in the campaign. On average, blacks were quite interested and
believed that their vote could matter. Political scientists have found,
not surprisingly, that interest in politics and a sense of political efficacy make for political participation. Was this the case in the support
of Jackson? How did efficacy operate as a motivating force? Was it an
independent influence? An enhancer of other psychological resources?
What effect did the election have on these motivational resources?

Interest, Efficacy, and System Evaluations

Support for Jackson was related to interest in politics and to a sense of
political efficacy, but only in specific reference to black or group-based
politics. This is seen in two ways in Table 4.6. Interest in mayoral
elections involving black candidates and in Jackson's campaign distinguished supporters from non-supporters. In contrast, general interest
in political campaigns had no such influence. Supporters expressed no
greater interest in the general presidential campaign than non-
supporters, nor did they care more about the election's outcome. Since
interest was high overall, it is not surprising that interest was nearly
the same among Jackson and Mondale supporters. That group efficacy
was more important than personal efficacy also demonstrates a specific tie between support for Jackson and group-based politics. The
three beliefs comprising perceived group efficacy—that blacks can affect local and presidential elections and that the Rainbow Coalition
can be politically influential—distinguished Jackson supporters from
non-supporters. Belief in their own political efficacy did not. Jackson
disproportionately appealed to people who thought the black vote potentially influential.

Our analyses of psychological resources also confirm the importance of distinguishing judgments of self from judgments of the political system. Judgments of personal political competence did not influence support for Jackson but judgments of the system did. Supporters criticized the system more than non-supporters.

Democratic theorists usually argue that citizenship is threatened when people believe that political institutions are not responsive or cannot be trusted to represent all people equally. A certain kind of distrust can actually mobilize rather than depress political engagement, however, insofar as it reflects a realistic criticism by a comparatively powerless group that the system does not represent them. Blacks in the 1960s who perceived flaws in the system participated in protest politics and even in electoral politics more than those who were not as critical.

What kind of distrust did the supporters exhibit? They were critical of the system's unrepresentativeness—that "government is run to benefit a few big interests rather than all the people." Jackson's candidacy was viewed as a way to make government more accountable to underrepresented groups. The supporters, however, did not feel unusually ignored by political authorities. No relationship existed between the level of support for Jackson and the feeling that public officials "don't care what people think" or cannot be trusted to "do what is right" and that individuals have "no say about what government does." (Chapter Five reports a markedly different pattern of system evaluations among advocates of an independent voice—not criticism of government's representativeness, but an appeal to be heard.)

The Role of Efficacy

In the expectancy-value theory of motivation, the value placed on a goal motivates action more when the person believes there is a reasonable, though not certain, chance of reaching it. There is controversy over the level of expectancy that is maximally motivating, but most variants of the theory hold that a value (or motive) has greater significance when it is expected that personal initiative will bring a payoff.

Much the same reasoning can be applied to politics. Nonetheless, political analysts who emphasize the role of expectancy (usually cast as a sense of political efficacy) generally have not explicitly defined the exact nature of that role. Does efficacy motivate people independently of the value they place on politics? Does it depend on their level of interest? Does it enhance the effects of interest and other psychological resources?

TABLE 4.6
Psychological Resources and Support for Jackson

Psychological Resources	r	B^a
Interest in Politics		
General Political Interest		
Paid attention to the political campaign	.008	.000
		(.033)
Cared which party won the 1984 election	.019	.016
		(.034)
Interest Aroused by Black Politics		
Success of black mayoral candidates aroused interest	.143	.152****
		(.034)
Jackson candidacy aroused interest	.310	.312****
		(.033)
Political Efficacy and System Evaluation		
Believed in personal political competence	.066	.016
		(.035)
Group Efficacy		
Believed blacks can		
Affect local elections	.135	.121***
		(.034)
Affect the presidential election	.104	.093**
		(.034)
Believed the Rainbow Coalition can affect how the country is run	.094	.101***
		(.034)
Believed political system unresponsive	.005	.029
		(.034)
Was distrustful of government	.091	.087**
		(.035)

Note: With the exception of personal political competence, these ten regressions are based on the 1,150 respondents in the pre-election survey. Personal political competence analyses are based on the 871 respondents in the post-election survey. Standard errors are shown in parentheses.
[a] Coefficients are based on ten regressions in which each psychological resource measure was used separately and all structural or demographic and race-of-interviewer measures were included as controls.
**$p < .01$.
***$p < .001$.
****$p < .0001$.

The analyses presented in Table 4.6 treat group efficacy, interest, and system evaluations as independent influences on support for Jackson. We assumed that they combined additively to increase that support. Yet we did not find a significant effect of general interest in the campaign, and this may result from misspecifying how interest in politics affects candidate choice. Perhaps general interest in electoral

politics motivated support for Jackson only among those feeling politically efficacious.

Analyses of political mobilization in the 1960s were implicitly based
on a multiplicative theory of motivation. Mobilization was thought to
result from a mutually reinforcing combination of beliefs: I am effective (or my group is effective), but the system is flawed. Distrust, it was
argued, mobilized people who believed they could be effective individually or collectively but not people who felt inefficacious.

What do our data show? Did group or personal efficacy exaggerate
the influence of interest in politics or distrust of the system? Regression analyses were run using a multiplicative measure of efficacy and
interest (or efficacy and system evaluations). As usual, structural and
demographic factors as well as the perceived race of the interviewer
were held constant. Two conclusions can be drawn. The sense of personal efficacy did not enhance other psychological resources, nor did it
independently motivate support for Jackson. Nor did the sense of group
efficacy greatly increase the impact of interest in black politics or
criticism of the system's unrepresentativeness. Both influenced support for Jackson, but no more for blacks who believed in the group's
political efficacy than for those who did not.

Scant research attention has been directed to a different question
about group efficacy, whether it magnifies the political significance of
group solidarity. We explored this issue by using the same regression
approach outlined above: a series of multiplicative terms were formed,
each comprised of the group-efficacy measure and one identity or
group-consciousness measure. We found that identity and consciousness influenced support for Jackson more when people believed in the
group's political effectiveness. These results can be summarized by
comparing relationships between solidarity and Jackson support for
those who believed most and least in the group's efficacy. The effect of
common fate was three times greater for the high- than for the low-
efficacy group; self-labeling as black, five times greater; power discontent, five and a half times greater; system blame, four and a half times
greater; nationalism, eight times greater. Having both a belief in the
group's potential power and a sense of group solidarity boosted support
for Jackson; lacking both greatly inhibited it.

The Change in Psychological Resources

Some black leaders worried that in the long run Jackson's candidacy
might demoralize the black electorate. They feared that his inevitable
failure to win the nomination would create disillusionment with electoral politics. The fact that blacks were one of few demographic groups

voting in larger numbers in 1984 than in 1980 shows indirectly that the Jackson candidacy had no such depressing effect. Moreover, as we have seen in Chapter Two, blacks were no less interested in political campaigns after the election than before, nor did they change their judgments of the political system or feelings of solidarity as a function of the election. (Only two elements of solidarity—centrality of being black to one's sense of self and discontent with power—were assessed in both surveys. On these there was practically no change.) The very high sense of group efficacy expressed by respondents before the election, however, was much lower afterward, dampened no doubt by various aspects of the campaign and its outcome, though not necessarily by Jackson's candidacy.

We can test Jackson's possible negative effect on the efficacy of black electorate by noting whether his supporters lowered their sense of group efficacy more than others. We ran a regression analysis that treated change as that part of the post-election efficacy scores not accounted for by the same pre-election scores. The measure of Jackson support along with the usual demographic or structural measures and perceived race of interviewer were entered as predictors of change. (See Appendix B.4, Table 1.) A nonsignificant regression coefficient for the measure of Jackson support means that supporters and non-supporters evenly reduced their sense of group efficacy; a negative coefficient, that the supporters lost efficacy more than others; a positive coefficient, that they lost it less. The results indicated that, with one exception, change in group efficacy was independent of support for Jackson. The exception showed that Jackson's effect was positive: his supporters' beliefs in the potential impact of the Rainbow Coalition were less affected by the election than was the same belief held by non-supporters. Nor did the election dampen the supporters' interest in politics or feelings of their own political competence. In fact, they became more interested in political campaigns, while non-supporters became less interested. (See Appendix B.4, Table 1.)

CONCLUSIONS

As internal critics of the Democratic party, Jackson's strong supporters possessed resources that help individuals become politically active and give a constituency collective power. Spread across regions and most sectors of the electorate, the strong supporters had more education and organizational experience than non-supporters. They more frequently belonged to organizations working to improve life in the black community; they were affiliated with politically active churches and participated more than non-supporters in a wide range of political actions—church-related campaign events, traditional campaign activities, voting, and protest. Their strong solidarity, a major motivation for supporting a black candidate, was a resource that Jackson could and did draw upon. For most, solidarity did not entail racial hostility or exclusive concern with problems facing blacks. This was especially true of supporters whose solidarity was based on a sense of common fate with other blacks.

The solidarity that prompted support for Jackson did not mean that his appeal was merely symbolic. Supporters were also motivated by policy concerns, which extended beyond racial matters, and had opinions on more issues than non-supporters did. They favored an activist national government, were exceptionally bothered about United States policy in South Africa, and favored spending less on defense.

Judgments of the political system and of the potential effectiveness of blacks as a group gave them added motivational resources. In particular, they were critical of the unrepresentativeness of government and receptive to Jackson's efforts to make it more accountable to underrepresented groups. They believed more than others that blacks acting collectively could affect the outcome of elections and that groups with limited power could be influential by working in a coalition. The sense of group efficacy itself fostered support for Jackson and also strengthened the impact of solidarity. Having both solidarity and group efficacy boosted Jackson's support greatly. The relationship between Jackson and his strongest constituency was decidedly a group phenomenon, but it was an example of identity politics that did not preclude coalition or concern for other groups.

Notes

1. The *New York Times*/CBS polls indicated that Jackson received 79 percent in Illinois, 77 percent in Pennsylvania, 73 percent in Ohio, 83 percent in North Carolina, 78 percent in California, and 86 percent in New Jersey. (See *New York Times*, March 6, 21, and 22, April 4 and 13, and May 8, 1984).
2. Exit polls for primary elections cannot give an accurate estimate of the breadth of support for Jackson, since they do not record sentiments of non-voters. Although black turnout in the primaries was the highest ever (up 103 percent in New York, 82 percent in Alabama, 43 percent in Florida, 38 percent in Pennsylvania, 19 percent in Illinois, and 10 percent in Georgia [see *New York Times*, April 13, 1984]), our data show that voter support for Jackson was not necessarily representative of the black electorate at large. Support for him might have risen among the non-voting blacks had they confronted the real choice in the voting booth or had they been mobilized by the Jackson forces as much in non-primary as in primary

states. At the very least, these differences between voting and non-voting blacks and primary and non-primary states demonstrate the importance of considering the entire black electorate.

3. *New York Times*, July 10, 1984.
4. Ibid.
5. Woodward 1986, 32–34.
6. Reed 1986, 13.
7. Ibid., 13.
8. Ibid., 13.
9. Ibid., 15.
10. The comparison of the education of delegates who supported Hart with that of the delegates who supported Jackson confirms Reed's argument only if professional degrees are excluded. Among Hart delegates, 10 percent fewer had nonprofessional postgraduate degrees, but 8 percent more held law degrees. Woodward (1986) accepts Reed's interpretation of the figures in Tables 1 and 2, stating that "in the 1984 primaries Jackson usually ran better among the higher black income-earning groups than among lower-income groups. A larger percentage of Jackson's delegates to the nominating convention than of Gary Hart's delegates reported annual incomes of $35,000 or more, and also a higher percentage reported postgraduate education than did either the delegates of Hart or Fritz Mondale" (p. 33).
11. See Reed 1986, Table 2.
12. Cavanagh 1985a, 32.
13. *New York Times*, April 29, 1984.
14. *New York Times*, March 15 and April 4, 1984.
15. Of those aged 18–24, 41 percent strongly supported Jackson; of those aged 25–34, 44 percent strongly supported Jackson; and of those aged 35–44, 43 percent did. Of those aged 45–54, however, only 33 percent supported him; and of those aged 55 and older, only 28 percent did.
16. *New York Times*, April 13, 1984.
17. Reed (1986) is not entirely clear in his views on group identification. On the one hand, he asserts that "mobilization of emotional commitment and collective vision are required to maintain concerted action, especially among people whose principal political resource is political energy" (p. 39). On the other hand, he accuses Jackson of "pandering to catharsis" and "securing identification with his effort" by "tapping reservoirs of emotion in the black community" (p. 38). His critique is primarily leveled against Jackson, not the black community, whose collective vision can be mobilized for "purposive, rational political action" under the right leadership (p. 38). That leadership would be rational, programmatic, and democratic rather than authoritarian and demagogic, as he claims Jackson's leadership was.
18. Although as many as three reasons were coded, this procedure proved to be unnecessary; only 4 percent gave more than one. The first reason was taken to indicate how it was thought the Jackson candidacy was good or bad.
19. Cavanagh 1985a.
20. Ibid. Our analyses showed that approval of a separate black party and support for Jackson were different political issues. The two were separate in factor analyses and had different demographic and social psychological correlates.
21. The exception was approval of collective strategies. Since the Jackson campaign became a demonstrably collective phenomenon, this anomalous exception may stem from the phrasing of our question on collective strategy. It stated that "to

have power and improve their position in society, black people should be more active in black organizations." But, as we note later, membership in civil rights organizations was only moderately related to Jackson support.

22. Faw and Skelton 1986, 12.
23. Ibid., 39.
24. Dershowitz, cited ibid., 134.
25. Sumner 1906, 12.
26. Merton [1957] 1968, 331.
27. There was some overlap between the two groups even though the two types of identities were not statistically related. For that reason, we deleted twelve respondents who met the criteria for both groups in order to achieve their complete separation.
28. Miller 1984, 6.
29. Ibid., 8.
30. Cavanagh 1985a, 63.
31. Shanks and Miller 1985, 20.
32. Sears, Citrin, and Kosterman 1985, 37.
33. Ibid., 39.
34. Kramer 1971; Andersen 1990; Kinder and Sears 1985.
35. See St. Angelo and Puryear (1982), Coleman and McLemore (1982), Preston (1982), and Nelson (1982) for analyses of these elections.
36. See Brown and Jackson (1986) for further analysis of the role of the church in the political participation of blacks.
37. J. Reston, "Jackson's Arrogant Pride," *New York Times*, September 2, 1984, E15.
38. Reed 1986, 74.
39. Some commentators have criticized Jackson's emphasis on such policies as biased toward middle class blacks and oblivious to the concerns of the less advantaged. But our data do not show a class bias in the level of support for affirmative-action policies. Even if less-educated blacks do not benefit as much from such policies, they support them as strongly as the more advantaged do.
40. Faw and Skelton 1986, 208.
41. B. Commoner, "Jackson's Historic Campaign," *New York Times*, July 10, 1984, 23.
42. Marable 1985, 269, 272–276.
43. The exception, advocacy of collective strategies, was related only to spending increases on community needs and to pressuring Congress on policy toward South Africa.
44. The black electorate varied greatly in the number of policy issues that had been thought about: one-third had thought about all five; another one-fourth, about four; one-fifth, only three; and another fifth, even fewer.
45. An apparent contradiction was that blacks who described themselves as liberal did not have stronger racial solidarity or show greater support for Jackson. The definitions that blacks assign to the terms *liberal* and *conservative* probably account for this. In our survey, identification as a liberal and position on policies were only weakly related. The correlations between defining oneself as a liberal and agreeing that government should ensure a decent standard of living, supporting increased spending for social welfare, and advocating government aid to minorities averaged .10. For whites in the general NES, the correlations between ideological identification and the same three policies averaged .28.

CHAPTER FIVE

Advocates
of a Black Political Voice:
The Powerless
Seeking to Be Heard

SEPARATE BLACK PARTIES HAVE come into existence historically when politically involved blacks have concluded, nearly always reluctantly, that the major parties were not allowing them to participate, exercise leadership, or have influence commensurate with the votes they delivered or were not representing the interests of blacks as they once had. In these circumstances, some leaders have reasoned that forming a black party and mobilizing the black vote behind its candidate is better than voting for the lesser of two evils. In general, however, black voters have not heeded the counsel of the leaders who support independence. Even in 1972, when support for a black party was greatest, poll data show that only one-quarter to one-third of the black population (depending on which poll is cited) approved of a separate political party for blacks.[1]

This chapter examines attitudes toward a separate black party and the strategy of always voting for black candidates. These two indicators of a black political voice are consistent with plural nationalism as defined by Hamilton. Plural nationalism is the advocacy of a separate black political organization that tries to create new forms of decision making, new structures, and new relationships between parties. But it falls short of separation. ". . . it is not accurate to label this view as separatist . . . because its ultimate goal is not black legal sovereignty. It is more precisely exclusivist."[2]

Three sets of questions require attention in the discussion of this topic: (1) How widespread was approval of a black political voice in 1984? Was a vote-black strategy more acceptable than a separate black party? (2) Who supported a black voice most strongly? How did the advocates differ from non-advocates in their structural positions, organizational experiences, solidarity, political preferences, and psychological resources for politics? (3) How did potential leaders of a black voice differ from other strong advocates? Were the potential leaders a unified group? How might their internal differences and differences from their constituency affect its mobilization?

A RARE POINT OF VIEW

Most of the black electorate opposed a black political voice. Three-quarters or more disapproved of both aspects of this kind of independence—that blacks should form a separate political party and that they should always vote for black candidates. (See Table 5.1.) Intensity of opinion was somewhat more divided on a separate black party—respondents more strongly approved or disapproved. On the index that represents both strategies, strong disapproval was four times greater than strong approval. Only one-quarter of those surveyed can be called advocates, and only one-third of them (altogether 8 percent of the sample) were strong advocates.

In Chapter Three, we learned that advocacy of a black political voice and support for Jesse Jackson's candidacy were statistically separate issues. The two components of a black voice were not related to whether it was thought good or bad that Jackson was running in 1984 or to whether the voters preferred Jackson over other candidates in the primary. (See Table 3.1.) Nevertheless, the indexes of support for Jackson and advocacy of a black political voice were slightly correlated, since the intention of voting for Jackson as an independent candidate was related to both.[3]

Chapter Three also demonstrated that the Jackson supporters and black-voice advocates did not react to the Democratic party in the same way. The advocates of a black voice were surprisingly positive about the party. They rated the party ticket, the party itself, and blacks who voted for Walter Mondale in the primaries more positively than did Jackson supporters. More of the advocates than non-advocates thought that the Democratic party worked hard on issues affecting blacks, that it treated Jackson the same as other candidates, and that Mondale would defeat Ronald Reagan. The advocates of a black voice

TABLE 5.1
The Black Electorate's Opinions of a Black Party and of a Vote-Black Strategy

Should Blacks Form Their Own Political Party?	Total Sample	Should Blacks Always Vote for Black Candidates?	Total Sample	Index of a Black Political Voice	Total Sample
Yes, and feel strongly about it	16%	Strongly agree	6%	Strong approval	8%
Yes, but feel less strongly about it	8	Agree	13	Approval	17
No, but don't feel very strongly about it	32	Disagree	53	Disapproval	41
No, and feel strongly about it	44	Strongly disagree	28	Strong disapproval	34
	100%		100%		100%

Note: Percentages are based on a weighted N of 1,293, which represents an unweighted N of 871 respondents who participated in both the pre- and post-election surveys.

appeared to be Democrats seeking to be heard by a party not likely to pay attention to them.

We know that they are a rare few. But who *are* these blacks whose independence appears to be a way of finding a voice rather than expressing an ideology of separatism or alienation from the party system?

THE ADVOCATES:
STRUCTURALLY AND ORGANIZATIONALLY
DISADVANTAGED

An analysis of third-party voting, spanning the elections from 1952 to 1980, shows that among the general American electorate social class has not influenced voting for a third party's candidate.

> Voters' social and economic class has no bearing on the likelihood that they will abandon the major parties. Those at the bottom rungs of the socio-economic ladder are no more disloyal to the major parties than are other citizens. The very poor are no more likely to defect to third parties than the very rich; those with the least prestigious occupations are no more prone to defect than people with the most enviable jobs; the less well-educated are no more apt to abandon the major parties than the well-educated.[4]

But this strong conclusion does not necessarily apply to the black electorate. Disagreement among blacks over political strategies has always had a class basis. The constituencies of satellite parties formed in the 1960s in Mississippi and Alabama were almost exclusively blacks living in rural poverty. In these states, the middle classes had already created civic associations and voter leagues that worked as closely with the regular Democratic party as was allowed. Class conflict also emerged within the Mississippi Freedom Democratic party when SNCC, one of its founders, withdrew because its leaders believed that other founders, especially the NAACP, could not or would not reach out to impoverished blacks in rural Mississippi. At times, even blacks who normally adhere to an insider strategy become disillusioned and embrace a pluralist nationalist position. When the 1972 National Black Political Convention received broad class-based support, this unity was recognized as unusual and therefore newsworthy.

Chapter Two reported a remarkable lack of class cleavage in the black electorate's policy preferences, evaluations of the major parties, and solidarity. Nor was there class division in support for Jackson. Nonetheless, historical evidence suggested that there would be class-based disagreement regarding a separate black party and a vote-black strategy. And indeed there was.

Apart from age (younger blacks were more approving), social class was the only significant structural or demographic predictor of reactions to a black political voice. The least educated and, especially, the least affluent most strongly supported a separate black party and a vote-black strategy. Family income affected advocacy of a black voice more than education did. (See Table 5.2.) Education and income differences between the strongest advocates and the strongest non-advocates were quite dramatic: over half of the former but only one-fifth of the latter had a family income of $10,000 or less and no education beyond high school.

Was the effect of social class especially marked among youths or

TABLE 5.2
Demographic and Structural Sources of Support for a Black Political Voice

Characteristics and Resources	r	B^a
Age: older	− .041	− .141*** (.038)
Education	− .189	− .097** (.039)
Family income	− .276	− .216**** (.042)
Employment status: full-time	− .141	− .050 (.039)
Receiving Social Security	.090	.042 (.038)
Receiving other welfare	.116	.000 (.035)
Marital status: married	− .107	.005 (.035)
Gender: female	− .065	.019 (.033)
Region: non-South	.069	− .023 (.036)
Urbanicity	− .106	− .047 (.036)
R^2		11.8%****

Note: Regressions are based on the 871 respondents who participated in both the pre- and in the post-election surveys. Standard errors are shown in parentheses.
[a] These effects were also estimated with a multiple classification analysis (MCA), a technique designed to handle categorical predictors like gender and southern/nonsouthern. The MCA analyses were highly similar.
  $**p < .01$. $***p < .001$. $****p < .0001$.

urban dwellers? We used the same procedures described in Chapter Three to answer this question. There was no evidence that the class effect was exaggerated in the urban environment, though the mutually reinforcing effect of class and age was significant. It was not the young who were most divided by class, however. As Figure 5.1 reveals, class division was most pronounced among older people. The class effect was nearly three times larger among blacks aged 69 and older than among those 25 and younger. The strongest opposition to a separate black party and a vote-black strategy came from the oldest, most privileged blacks.

The social origins of the black-voice advocates were quite different from those of Jackson's strong supporters. Younger age was the only common factor. Support for Jackson was not bound to economic circumstances, whereas living in a lower income family best predicted approval of a black voice. Education had opposite effects. Support for Jackson was strongest among college graduates; advocacy of a

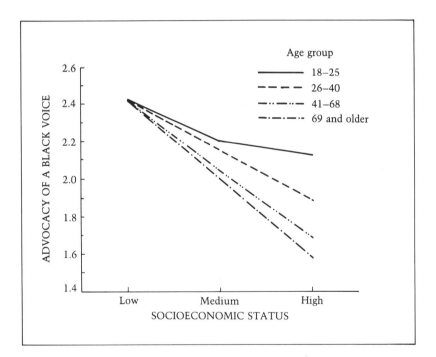

FIGURE 5.1
Predicted Support for a Black Political Voice for Four Age Groups and Three Socioeconomic Status (SES) Groups

black political voice, among blacks without a high school degree. Jackson's candidacy was popular and received equal support from many sectors of the black electorate; a separate black party and a vote-black strategy were generally unpopular and appealed to the structurally disadvantaged.

Their structural positions explain why the advocates also lacked organizational resources. If they had had the same economic advantages as the non-advocates, they would also have had equal organizational resources. And indeed, among blacks of comparable income and education as many advocates as non-advocates belonged to organizations working to improve life in the black community.[5] The lower level of education among the advocates also explains why fewer of them belonged to politically active churches. Since membership in such churches was higher among people with more schooling (see Chapter Two), the advocates' education level masked the underlying relationship.[6] Unveiling the effect that organizational resources would have had if the advocates had not been structurally disadvantaged does not minimize the actual facts. After all, the advocates did lack the structural and organizational resources that usually help people become politically engaged. These resources are as necessary for making a separate party effective as for fostering participation in the traditional two-party system of electoral politics.

RACIAL SOLIDARITY:
A SPECIFIC FOCUS ON BLACK-WHITE ISSUES

Solidarity equally influenced support for Jackson and advocacy of a black political voice, but the type of solidarity differed markedly. Supporters of Jackson were exceedingly group-oriented: they were identified with other blacks; they were discontented with the group's limited political power; and they were pro-black (although their nationalism did not outweigh other aspects of solidarity). Above all, however, they were not anti-white. Moreover, the Jackson supporters with a politicized indentity were more concerned with power relationships than with race per se. In contrast, it is race—black-white relations—that defines the solidarity of the advocates of a black political voice.

This can be seen in several ways. Nationalism was by far the most important dimension of solidarity in accounting for the advocacy of a black voice. The measure of nationalism included the desire to have black children learn an African language and approval of interpersonal racial separation and a buy-black strategy. Its effects were more than twice as large as those of any other solidarity measure. The second most important element of the advocates' solidarity was their sense of being black rather than American. The other type of identity—that based on a politicized sense of common fate—was not a significant predictor of advocacy of a black political voice. (See Table 5.3.)

Feelings toward whites among advocates of a black political voice further corroborate the importance of race for this sector of the electorate. Compared with non-advocates, 16 percent more advocates thought that whites want to keep blacks down, and 26 percent more indicated that they did not feel close to whites. And most striking, one-fifth of the advocates but none of the non-advocates believed that blacks should have nothing to do with whites.

Advocates' views of high- and low-power groups further confirm

TABLE 5.3
Group Solidarity and Advocacy of a Black Political Voice

Group Solidarity Measures	r	B^a	B^b
Group Identity			
Felt a sense of common fate	−.039	.024	.014
		(.033)	(.035)
Exclusivist identity: felt being black is more important than being American or both black and American	.156	.145***	.139***
		(.032)	(.033)
Political Consciousness			
Collective discontent: felt that blacks have too little political influence	−.059	−.012	.000
		(.034)	(.032)
Rejected the legitimacy of racial disparities	.082	.087**	.074*
		(.032)	(.032)
Approved of collective strategies	.067	.086**	.070*
		(.032)	(.033)
Black nationalism	.342	.353***	.296***
		(.038)	(.037)

Note: Regressions are based on the 871 respondents who participated in both the pre- and post-election surveys. Standard errors are shown in parentheses.
[a] Coefficients are based on six regressions in which each identity or consciousness measure was used separately and all structural or demographic and race-of-interviewer measures were included as controls.
[b] Coefficients are based on a regression in which all identity and consciousness measures were used as predictors simultaneously and all structural or demographic and race-of-interviewer measures were included as controls.
   *$p < .05$.   **$p < .01$.   ***$p < .0001$.

their focus on race. Although advocates and non-advocates were equally critical of the excessive power of whites, advocates were less discontented with the power of men and business executives and with the limited power of poor people and people on welfare. Their appraisals showed an exclusivity not found among the strong supporters of Jackson.

These findings fit Hamilton's characterization of plural nationalists as collectivist, group-oriented, and exclusivist. They believe that race discrimination is the preeminent determinant of the subordination of blacks, and, though willing to work with existing decision-making institutions, they doubt that these institutions can and will bring about changes that would benefit blacks. The solidarity of the advocates is a political resource, but their preoccupation with race raises a question about their capacity to work in a coalition.

RACIAL POLICY: THE CENTRAL CONCERN

Although economic problems often foster the rise of third parties,[7] economic factors did not significantly influence advocacy of a black political voice. Advocates and non-advocates judged their personal circumstances alike and also agreed in evaluating the group's economic status. They differed only in their judgments of the national economy. Blacks who thought it had deteriorated during the previous year were stronger advocates of a black voice (as well as stronger supporters of Jackson). Both types of independence reflected concern with the health of the nation rather than with personal hardships or group adversity.[8]

It was racial policy, not economics or social welfare or foreign policy, that best distinguished advocates from non-advocates. (See Table 5.4.) The advocates especially wanted the government to enact policies that would improve the position of minorities and extend affirmative action. They also felt it important that the federal government follow the racial policies they espoused, an indication of how central racial matters were to them.

To understand disenchantment with the major parties and support for a third party, we must consider both the voters' own policy positions and those of the major candidates. When voters believe that the views of the major candidates differ greatly from their own positions, they generally become more responsive to third parties and to independent candidates.[9] Voters' distance from Reagan and Mondale on matters of racial policy proved to be a distinct factor in the black electorate's advocacy of a black political voice.

Respondents gave their own positions and their perceptions of

TABLE 5.4
Policy Preferences, Economic Assessments, Liberal/Conservative Ideology, and Advocacy of a Black Political Voice

Policies	r	B^a
Domestic Policies		
Approved increased spending on		
Social welfare (Medicare, food stamps)	.067	.017
		(.034)
Community needs (public schools,		
jobs for the unemployed, crime)	.048	.028
		(.035)
Favored federal government action in order		
to ensure a decent standard of living	.122	.077*
		(.033)
Improve the position of blacks and minorities		
and approve affirmative action	.224	.204****
		(.034)
Considered government racial policy		
important to self	.068	.086**
		(.033)
Perceived major party candidate to be		
less favorable than self toward government		
action in matters of race		
Reagan	.071	.066*
		(.033)
Mondale	.109	.090***
		(.032)
Thought Given to Policy Issues		
How many of five issues has the respondent		
thought about and has a position on?	−.139	−.028
		(.035)
Liberal/Conservative Ideology		
(Higher points on seven-point scale		
scored liberal)	−.028	.024
		(.035)

Note: Regressions are based on the 871 respondents who participated in both the pre- and post-election surveys. Standard errors are shown in parentheses.

^{a} Coefficients are based on nineteen separate regressions in which each policy preference, economic assessment, or liberal/conservative ideology was included as a separate predictor and all structural or demographic and race-of-interviewer measures were included as controls.

*$p < .05$.
**$p < .01$.
***$p < .001$.
****$p < .0001$.

TABLE 5.4
(continued)

Policies	r	B^a
Foreign Policies		
Favored		
Decreased spending on defense	.060	.001
		(.034)
Greater U.S. involvement in Central America	.009	.012
		(.034)
Increased black pressure to alter U.S.		
policies toward South Africa	.007	.037
		(.035)
Economic Assessments		
Personal Economic Assessments		
Respondent and family are		
Worse off than a year earlier	.066	.043
		(.034)
Worse off than four years earlier	.033	−.055
		(.034)
Economic Assessments of		
Blacks as a Group		
Blacks are worse off than they were		
a year earlier	−.041	.001
		(.033)
Blacks are worse off than they were		
four years earlier	−.063	−.005
		(.034)
Blacks are doing less well than whites		
and not well in an absolute sense	−.064	−.039
		(.035)
Economic Assessment of the Nation		
The economy is worse off than it was		
a year earlier	.109	.086**
		(.034)

Reagan's and Mondale's positions on racial policy by placing themselves and both candidates on a scale defined at one end by the statement "the government in Washington should make every possible effort to improve the social and economic positions of blacks and other minority groups" and at the other end by "the government should not make any special effort to help minorities because they should help themselves."

Not surprisingly, the black electorate believed that Mondale's position was much closer to their own than was Reagan's. On a discrepancy scale where zero indicates that the candidate is thought to have the same position as the respondent and minus six indicates that the candidate is far less favorable toward government action, Mondale was judged to be quite close (on average, $-.49$) and Reagan much farther away (-2.33). Advocates and non-advocates both believed that Reagan's position was far from their own policy preferences, but the discrepancy was larger for advocates (-2.77) than for non-advocates (-1.90). Advocates also perceived a larger discrepancy in judging the liberal, Mondale. Non-advocates thought that Mondale had virtually the same position as they ($-.07$), while advocates thought he was somewhat less favorable to government action than they were ($-.85$). The turn by some blacks to a black party and vote-black strategy reflected a sense that neither candidate wanted as much government action in the racial area as they did.

The policy picture is clear. The advocates were not uninterested in public policy. Policy issues mattered a great deal to them, but their interest was narrowly focused on race. They favored government action to help minorities, wanted government to adopt the policies they preferred, had given more thought to racial policy, and felt the candidates did not represent their positions. In all these ways, their independence reflected racial discontent. In contrast, supporters of Jackson were concerned with a broader range of policy issues. His supporters wanted larger expenditures for programs that would advance social welfare and solve community needs and a smaller budget for defense. They believed Congress should be pressured to alter policy toward South Africa. They had also given thought to a wider range of policy issues than had the advocates of a black voice.

THE ADVOCATES' PSYCHOLOGICAL RESOURCES

Third-party voting is viewed by some as an instrumental act by efficacious citizens who are trying to advance policy goals previously thwarted by a major party. It is considered by others an alienated expression of inefficacious citizens. The two conceptions are not necessarily contradictory if a distinction is drawn between two components of political efficacy—personal political competence and evaluation of the political system. Efficacious individuals, or group members who believe they can be effective collectively, may express their sense of efficacy by going outside the parties they believe ignore their interests. To what extent was support for a black political voice an expression of alienation or an efficacious reaction to a flawed system?

The strong policy preferences of the advocates demonstrate that they were not personally alienated from politics, as does their level of interest in electoral politics. (See Table 5.5.) Advocates were no less interested than non-advocates in the 1984 campaign and its outcome; they felt as competent in the political arena; and they were especially interested in mayoral contests involving black candidates and in the Jackson campaign. In these ways, they resembled Jackson's supporters, though the advocates did not share their sense of group efficacy.[10]

Though not personally alienated, the advocates were more critical of the political system. Their complaints included agreement with the statements that "people like me don't have any say about what government does," "public officials don't care much about what people like me think," and "white officials always get their way." Feeling ignored by government officials, they turned to a group-based political strategy.[11] But to do what?

Recall that the advocates did not especially believe that blacks could affect electoral outcomes; they were not as active as non-advocates in most political activities; they lacked organizational and structural resources; and they felt positive about the Democratic party and its 1984 candidates. Characteristics such as these plainly inhibit independent action. The advocates' endorsement of a group-based political strategy thus suggests a hope that it would make the major parties respond to an otherwise powerless element within the black community.

POTENTIAL LEADERS OF A BLACK POLITICAL VOICE

How might advocates of a black voice accomplish the aim of obtaining the attention of and responsiveness from the Democratic party? Who could mobilize their racial discontent to create a political party that would bring pressure on the regular parties? To address this question, we must depart from the broad sweep of national-survey data to look more closely at small subgroups among the advocates that did not fit the general statistical profile. These exceptions, who did have structural and organizational resources, are theoretically and politically important as potential leaders—people with an income above $10,000, an education beyond the high school level, and/or the organizational experience and skills needed to mobilize a constituency.[12]

The advocates of a black voice comprised one-quarter of the total sample, altogether 220 people. By our definition, fifty-one of them were atypical as potential leaders: twenty-five by virtue of having both structural and organizational resources; thirteen by virtue of having a college education and a family income over $10,000 but no organiza-

TABLE 5.5
Psychological Resources and Advocacy of a Black Political Voice

Psychological Resources	r	B^a
Interest in Politics		
General Political Interest		
Paid attention to the political campaign	−.095	.041
		(.034)
Cared which party won the 1984 election	−.006	.019
		(.035)
Interest Aroused by Black Politics		
Success of black mayoral candidates aroused interest	.088	.071*
		(.035)
Jackson candidacy aroused interest	.149	.142**
		(.035)
Political Efficacy and System Evaluation		
Believed in personal political competence	−.059	.036
		(.031)
Group Efficacy		
Believed blacks can		
Affect local elections	−.091	−.043
		(.035)
Affect presidential elections	−.037	−.014
		(.035)
Believed the Rainbow Coalition can affect how		
the country is run	.055	.069
		(.035)
Political system believed unresponsive		
Felt there was no say in what government does	.120	.091**
		(.035)
Felt public officials don't care	.077	.061*
		(.034)
Felt white officials always get their way	.196	.135***
		(.034)
Was distrustful of government	−.028	−.000
		(.035)

Note: With the exception of personal political competence, regressions are based on the 1,150 respondents in the pre-election survey. Personal political competence analyses are based on the 871 respondents in the post-election survey. Standard errors are shown in parentheses.

[a] Coefficients are based on twelve regressions in which each psychological resource measure was used separately and all structural or demographic and race-of-interviewer measures were included as controls.

*$p < .01$.

**$p < .001$.

***$p < .0001$.

192

tional experience; and thirteen by virtue of having participated in black organizations but having a low income and no more than a high school education. By examining these three atypical subgroups and how they compared with the other 169 advocates (who had neither structural nor organizational resources), we may learn how these potential leaders might work together and relate to the population they would have to mobilize.

We adopt two methods for that purpose: one, quantitative, comparing the three types of potential leaders using standard statistical techniques (see Appendix B.5, Tables 2–6, for the tabular comparisons and tests of statistical significance), and the other qualitative, in which we describe individuals who typify the profile of each subgroup. With these joint procedures, we may learn something about a small but important sector of the black electorate—atypical advocates of a black voice who have the economic and educational resources and/or organizational resources to provide leadership in a black party.

The most obvious difference between the potential leaders and the other advocates is in their evaluation of Jackson's candidacy. Seven in ten of the atypical, potential leaders were among Jackson's strongest supporters, but only three in ten of the other advocates and four in ten of the non-advocates were. Like the strong Jackson supporters, the atypical advocates were less exclusively focused on race than were other advocates. The atypical groups had broader policy concerns and were discontented with the limited power of women, people on welfare, and poor people as well as blacks and with the excessive power of business executives and men as well as whites. They felt a stronger sense of group efficacy. These potential leaders resembled Jackson's strong supporters, and for good reason—they were.

The major distinction between the atypical advocates of a black voice and Jackson's strong supporters was in their intergroup attitudes. The advocates of a black voice felt more negatively toward whites. They more frequently agreed that blacks should have nothing to do with whites and that whites want to keep blacks down. They also felt less close to them. Heightened misgivings about whites motivated the leadership cadre, though this did not cause them to focus exclusively on racial policy or on race rather than on power more broadly.

The three groups of potential leaders differed among themselves in ways that would affect their capacity to work together. For example, there were marked age differences, although on average these atypical black-voice advocates were four years younger than other advocates. As one might expect, the potential leaders with only organizational resources were older—in fact, on average twenty years older—than members of the other two groups. These older, less privileged potential leaders more frequently lived in the South. All of them were active in organizations with a strong local orientation. They were local community leaders for whom a separate black party was a natural extension of experience in other black organizations. The younger, more privileged advocates belonged to organizations with a national scope—the NAACP, fraternities and sororities, professional groups, and politically active service organizations. These nationally oriented advocates had more in common politically with the local community leaders, however, than with the individualistic advocates, who shared their middle class status. The individualistic advocates favored government action less and self-help strategies more than did the other two groups. All of these political differences remind us that many individuals can endorse apparently identical strategies for dissimilar reasons.

Potential Leaders with a Focus on the Local Community

The thirteen potential leaders with a local community focus were on average 48 years old and had not graduated from high school (six in ten). They generally lived in the South (six in ten) and had a family income below $10,000 annually. They were unusually active in various local black organizations and in local churches. Eight in ten attended church weekly (only three in ten in the general electorate went as often). Five in ten belonged to a church that encouraged voting and collected money for a 1984 candidate. While their participation in the campaign and their history of participation in protest activities did not equal the more privileged, nationally oriented potential leaders, they were extremely active compared with other blacks with a comparable economic and educational background. Five in ten worked for a candidate, and six in ten tried to influence other voters' choices. Whereas advocates of a black voice generally voted less than non-advocates in local and state elections, eight in ten of these potential leaders showed their commitment to local affairs by voting in the very elections in which independence can be most effective.

The local community black-voice advocates had strong psychological resources. Their lack of structural advantages had not destroyed their interest in politics (as it had not restrained their involvement with organizations working to improve the lives of people in their communities). They were interested in electoral politics, cared which party won the election, and were critical of the system's unrepresentativeness. Their organizational experience apparently had given them a sense that political authorities can be made to respond, since they felt less ignored by officials than non-leaders did. Their lack of structural resources appears to have affected them primarily by leaving them with a feeling of being less personally efficacious, although they were confident about the group's political efficacy. They were activists who worked in black organizations, believed blacks as a group could be politically effective, and, as a consequence of their organizational experience, embraced a black party and a vote-black strategy.

Loyalty to the Democratic party is the most distinctive characteristic of these potential leaders who were oriented toward the local community. All of them rated themselves as strong Democrats, whereas only half of the others did. They were much less critical of the party's relationship to blacks. Only three in ten thought the party treated Jackson worse than it did other candidates, and eight in ten thought that it was committed to black issues. Their ratings of Mondale further showed them to be old-line Democrats: they rated him 20–30 degrees more warmly than they did other leaders. Three portraits are illustrative of this group of potential leaders.

A 36-year-old truck driver for a school system in a large New Jersey city provides the first example. In his words, a black party "just makes sense when whites in the two parties don't take the black vote seriously enough." Raised in the same city where he is now working, his political involvement began at age 13, when he joined a local drill squad. He continued to take part in the squad throughout adolescence and then, as an adult, became its leader. In the meantime, the group had become politically active in the community, and he became a leader of a committee that patrols the neighborhood to protect it against crime.

This community leader has been married for several years (his wife does not work outside the home), is educated through the eleventh grade, earns $10,000 a year working full-time, and is an active Baptist. Religion is important to both him and his wife. A lifelong, strongly identified Democrat, he has always been politically active. Loyal to the party, he gave Mondale the highest possible rating and voted for him in the final election even though he considered Jackson's position on racial policy much closer to his own than either Mondale's or Reagan's. He wanted defense spending lowered and viewed the situation in South Africa as "very, very, very important." He did not vote for Jackson in the New Jersey primaries because he thought Jackson's timing was poor. When reinterviewed after the election, he had changed his opinion of Jackson's candidacy, saying that it was a "good thing, because Jesse got a lot of blacks registered and interested in politics." He saw this as a coup of sorts on Jackson's part. He wished

Jackson had made an independent bid for the presidency because it "might have made the Democrats take stock."

The second example is a 67-year-old, eighth-grade graduate who lives far below the poverty level (earning considerably less than $10,000 a year). She baby-sits sometimes to supplement the money she draws from Social Security. An old hand at protest, she is active in her small-town Baptist church in Virginia and in a community group that provides services to local blacks. She campaigned for Jackson through the church, though she is typically not active in electoral politics and believes that blacks cannot affect the outcome of presidential elections. But she does believe in local activism, group effectiveness, and the power of blacks to influence local elections.

"A black party would show blacks they can get things done when white people in power don't care at all what happens to black people." She is a believer in the power of blacks as a united force (even within a coalition of other minorities, women, and the poor). Still, her advocacy of a black political voice does not include anti-white feelings. On the contrary, she reports feeling that "blacks and whites have to learn to live together. But they can do that better when whites realize that blacks can't be pushed around, that we can take things into our own hands."

The third example of a potential leader working at the community level is a 63-year-old North Carolinian who did not complete grammar school. She, too, depends financially almost entirely on Social Security. An active Baptist, she sees herself as a woman "doing for others," "spending a lot of time assisting her neighbors," and "bringing love, one for another." She is not inclined to protest, but her attitude toward helping others is translated into membership in a neighborhood committee that "acts as a trouble-shooting group, trying to draw the community together to make our streets and lives safer."

A strong Jackson supporter, she voted for him in the North Carolina primary, saying that she would have cast her ballot for him had he become an independent presidential candidate. Her backing "wasn't of him as a black; he would be good for the whole United States. He made a lot of Americans think about what we are doing in the world." She, like Jackson, favored a reduction in defense spending and opposed greater United States involvement in Central America.

How does support for a black party and a vote-black strategy fit with this woman's humanitarian concerns? Her approval of independence certainly is not disavowal of the Democratic party. She voted a straight Democratic ticket, rated Mondale as highly as Jackson and the Democratic party at 100, and believed that Mondale, quite as much as Jackson, shared her point of view on defense spending and her desire for the government to aid minorities. Instead, it is an outgrowth of local activism and long-term experience in black organizations—an expression of the idea that blacks should be drawn together.

Potential Leaders with a National Orientation

The twenty-five nationally oriented advocates with both structural and organizational resources were mostly college graduates (seven in ten), employed in professional or technical jobs, and on average earned $30,000 or more a year (four in ten earned $40,000 or more). They averaged 32 years of age and lived in both the North and the South.

By definition, all of them belonged to organizations working to improve the status of black Americans, and in every case the organizations included at least one operating on the national level. In keeping with their resources, they had an unusually high sense of personal political competence. At the same time, they were critical of the political system as unrepresentative and believed strongly that blacks could collectively affect electoral politics and thereby make the system more representative. They were very active in their black organizations, believing that a stronger commitment to organizational methods was the best way for blacks to increase their power and improve their position.

The nationally oriented potential leaders were the most active in politics. Twice as many of them as those in the other two groups of potential leaders reported having contacted a public official and having attended protest meetings or demonstrations; three times as many had signed petitions; and four times as many had picketed or taken part in a sit-in or a boycott. With the exception of working for candidates and convincing others to support a particular candidate, which local leaders did in significant numbers as well, these nationally oriented leaders were also more active in electoral politics. Twice as many of them as members of the other two groups had attended political meetings, dinners, or speeches during the 1984 campaign; six times as many had donated money to raise funds for a candidate; and, in accordance with their strong nationalism, twice as many as the locally oriented advocates and four times as many as the individualistic advocates had worked for a black candidate during the 1984 campaign.

Usually the black candidate was Jackson. All of them were his strong supporters, and most worked in his campaign. Resembling other Jackson supporters, they criticized the Democratic party's treatment of him and its commitment to black issues. They rated Mondale lower by 11 degrees than the individualistic leaders did and by a full 30 degrees lower than the local leaders did. Yet they all identified themselves as Democrats (more than half, as strong Democrats). They, like other Jackson supporters, were internal critics of the party; but unlike Jackson's other supporters, they believed a separate party was the most effective way in which to pressure the Democrats to support policies reflecting their views of what is in the best interest of blacks.

They were adamant in their belief that the government should adopt their perspective on racial policy—that affirmative action and government aid to minorities are essential components of government policy. They felt that Reagan's position on racial policy was poles apart from their own. Racial policy was central to them, although they had other policy concerns as well. Like the potential leaders active in local communities, they thought blacks should pressure Congress to alter United States policy toward South Africa, and they favored spending less on defense.

While their concern with race did not swamp their interest in other issues, they were more keenly discontented with the disparities in power between blacks and whites than with those between other groups. Furthermore, compared with the other groups of potential leaders, their group identities were especially based on a sense of common fate. Positive regard for nationalism follows naturally. Three young professionals illustrate the background and organizational involvement of these nationally oriented atypical advocates.

One is a laboratory technician in Manhattan. He is 33 years old, a New York native, and a college graduate. He earns a high income (over $30,000 a year). No longer married, he helps support his two children. He is a Baptist, and religion is very important to him, although he attends church only once or twice a month. He is active in an organization of black Vietnam veterans and participates in protest and electoral politics. He was dedicated to Jackson, voted for him in the New York primary, and until Jackson "threw his support" to Mondale, planned to write in Jackson's name in November. Like other Jackson supporters, he had little regard for the 1984 ticket and for blacks who voted for Mondale in the primaries. When he voted for Mondale, he was in essence voting against Reagan and the Republican party, to both of which he gave extremely low ratings (only 5 degrees).

The second nationally oriented atypical advocate is a 28-year-old man who works as a stockbroker on Wall Street and earns well over our top-income category of $40,000 a year. He was born in New Jersey and still lives there. A bachelor, he works sixty to eighty hours a week, like others in his profession; but unlike many of them, he finds time for organizational work. He is a member of the NAACP, is associated with the Urban League, and is a participant in an organization devoted to development and education in a local black neighborhood. Raised a Baptist, he is not as religious as other leaders, but he does identify as strongly with the Democrats. He has an extremely low regard for Reagan, blacks who supported him, and the Republican party. His vote for Jackson in the New Jersey primary was merely one indication of his strong support. He also admired Jackson's effect on mobilizing the electorate—getting a lot of people registered and involved in the 1984 campaign.

For the third nationally oriented potential leader, the Jackson campaign was a way of proving to the Democratic party that blacks should be taken more seriously. This 27-year-old woman considered herself "an exceptionally strong Democrat" and was not prepared to defect to a separate party. She wanted to exert pressure within the party. Formerly a financial officer in a credit organization, at the time of our pre-election interview she was preparing to enter law school. She has wide political and organizational experience, being active in the NAACP and involved in both electoral and protest politics. Closely associated with the Jackson campaign, she also had worked for Jackson's organization, PUSH.

The opinions on matters of policy held by these three young people are best exemplified by the 33-year-old lab technician. For him, race was the most important issue, although he was concerned with other matters as well. He believed his views on racial policy should be followed more closely by the federal government. Discrimination was for him the most pressing problem facing blacks, one that could be partially handled by strong government commitment to affirmative action. He emphasized the unresponsiveness of the candidates and parties by stating that "neither Mondale nor Reagan has the slightest interest in or understanding of what black people in this country are up against or need the government to do." He wanted spending increased for social welfare programs and community needs and the defense budget decreased. He favored government intervention to ensure a decent standard of living and employment for all Americans.

In many ways, these nationally oriented advocates are indistinguishable from Jackson's other strong supporters. As their profiles indicate, however, the importance of black-white relations and the belief that blacks must join together independently of whites set them apart from supporters of Jackson who did not advocate a black political voice.

Not all of the potential leaders with a national orientation were young or advantaged occupationally and economically. Three others demonstrate the variation. One is a 44-year-old man living in a small Virginia town who attended but did not finish college. He works as a repairman for a gas company, earning slightly more than $20,000 a year. A 47-year-old legal secretary in Memphis provides another example. She is active in the NAACP and worked for Jackson through her Baptist church. She has been married just over twenty years, and her husband works in a mill. She and her husband both attended but did not complete college, and together they earn $20,000–30,000 a year. The third is an elementary school teacher in Tennessee. Between her husband's and her own teaching job, they have a family income somewhat over $30,000 annually. A college graduate, she is active in a sorority as well as in the NAACP, whose annual national convention she regularly attends. She is also involved in educational activities in the local black community and regularly attends a Baptist church.

Though somewhat less advantaged and older than the first three examples, the policy views of these three are similar: black-white relations and racial policy figure prominently among their concerns but do not submerge others; discontent with the power differentials between blacks and whites is great; and the feelings of shared fate and solidarity among blacks are paramount.

Although they are more critical of the Democrats than are potential leaders active in local affairs, would the nationally oriented potential leaders defect from the Democratic party to mobilize others in a separate black party? Under the right circumstances they might. If Jackson or an equally attractive black candidate mounts an independent challenge for the presidency at a time when the Democratic party proves unwilling to make race a policy priority, or if local political factors make electoral victories easier to achieve through an independent party, these are the kinds of blacks who would most likely lead an independent party. But since they are strongly allied with the Democrats, they are more likely to rally behind a candidate such as Jackson, who pushes a progressive agenda within the party. Why, then, did they support a black political voice? Our statistical analysis and individual cases suggest an answer: they were predisposed to a wide variety of strategies that would bring blacks together to act without the controlling influence of whites. Forming a black party and voting for black candidates are just two examples of the same undercurrent.

Individualistic Advocates of a Black Political Voice

How did the thirteen individualistic advocates differ from the other two atypical groups of advocates? They approved of individualism and disapproved of government action more than others. They were much less discontented with power differences between groups in America. They were more accepting of the Republicans. The comparative statistical analyses and examination of particular cases show that this group consisted largely of people who have achieved middle class status through great personal effort. They believe, far more than the other two atypical groups and most of the black electorate, that group advancement can be achieved best through individual action and mobility. To be sure, this view is not unanimous, though quite striking compared with the beliefs of the other two groups.

Their individualism is evident in their greater opposition to action by the federal government. Compared with the other atypical advocates, three times as many believed that the government should not "see to it that everyone has a job and good standard of living" but should "let each person get ahead on his or her own." Twice as many thought that the government should not "make any special effort to help minorities because they should help themselves." Specifically on affirmative action, half as many agreed that "minorities should be given special consideration when decisions are made about hiring for jobs," and twice as many agreed that "job applicants should be judged solely on the basis of test scores and other individual qualities." Six times as many endorsed the idea that "if black people don't do well in life, it is because they don't work hard to get ahead." They maintained that to improve their status "each black person should work hard to improve his or her own personal situation." Compared with the other two groups of atypical advocates, they did not consider the power disparity between blacks and whites as large, nor did they as frequently judge business executives "too powerful" or people on welfare and older people as having "too little power."

Since their attitudes and values were congenial to a conservative ideology, it is not surprising that they rated Reagan, the Republican party, and blacks who voted for him more positively than other potential leaders did (though still 30–50 degrees lower than they rated Democratic candidates and the Democratic party). Nonetheless, only one of the thirteen identified as a Republican; 60 percent strongly identified as Democrats; and they all rated the Democratic party no less warmly than other leaders. Hence, though they were more receptive to a conservative agenda than either the general black electorate or the other two groups of atypical advocates of a black political voice, they were not likely to convert to the Republican party.

Why did they advocate an independent voice? A black party and vote-black strategy are both consistent with their commitment to self-help. Rather than pressuring government for greater responsibility and action, they believe blacks should depend on themselves individually or on each other when collective approaches are needed. An independent political voice is not as much a strategy for action as an expression of "blacks going it alone," as one of the advocates put it. Indeed, these individualistic advocates were not political activists. They did not belong to black organizations, this distinguishing them from the other atypical advocates who had structural advantages. They were less active in campaigns as voters and, compared with the nationally oriented leaders who shared their structural advantages, in protest politics.

Although these individualistic advocates met the income and educational criteria we set for potential leaders, they were by no means as advantaged as those with a national orientation. Only four in ten had a college degree. All had escaped from occupations commonly held by blacks, having held positions as operatives, laborers, providers of service, and the like, but most were in only middle status clerical and skilled crafts jobs. Only one was a manager (of a small enterprise), and only three in ten had professional jobs. They all had an income over $10,000, but three in ten fell below $20,000, and nine in ten below $30,000. They were solid middle class citizens working hard to improve their lives. Three vignettes depict their life situations and political beliefs.

The first example, a 23-year-old father of three, is separated from his wife and trying to raise their children alone. He attended college for one year and now works forty to fifty hours a week as a carpenter for a general contracting company in Florida. In 1983, he was laid off for almost a month but didn't seem concerned, explaining that he was very good at what he does. When we reinterviewed him after the November election, he had received a raise and was earning about $20,000 a year. His mother helps him with the family, but being a parent "takes all the time I have," he says. He is interested in politics, but does not have time to get involved. He attends church once or twice a month. A strong Democrat, he voted for Mondale in both the Florida primary and the November election.

For this young, hard-working father, a black party and vote-black strategy were not so much strategies to get the Democratic party's attention as extensions of his self-help ideology. He placed himself at the extreme end of our government–self-help scale, indicating that he believed minority groups should help themselves. Responding to the question of whether he thought whites want to keep blacks down, he said, "whites think it is up to us to pick ourselves up, and I agree. I'm working hard, everyone has to." Though favoring black nationalism, he didn't have anti-white feelings. In fact, he felt close to whites and strongly disagreed that blacks should not have anything to do with them. Booker T. Washington's philosophy captures this man's beliefs perfectly: he wants blacks to depend on their own resources.

The second example has slightly different opinions of whites. Acutely aware of discrimination, she says, "when blacks strive for something, whites secretly discriminate behind our backs. Blacks often don't figure out that whites are discriminating. No one admits it, but if you're wise, you know." She is 37 years old and single and does not have any children. She works as a data-entry clerk in a large manufacturing firm in Chicago, where she earns approximately $15,000 a year. She trained for her current job after working as a domestic for ten years. At one time, she received help from her family; now, after her successful struggle for upward mobility, she helps them.

A strong advocate of a black political voice, she thought Jackson's candidacy a very good idea and would have voted for him had he run as an independent. She volunteered that she was glad he didn't, however, because "it didn't make sense to split the black vote when Mondale was running." She considers herself a strong Democrat, voted for Mondale in November, and voted a straight Democratic ticket in congressional, state, and local elections. Apart from voting, she took no part in the 1984 campaign, nor did she participate in other political activities.

Her nationalism, it can be argued, emanates from her racial experience. Saying that she did not feel close to whites, she added, "I would be close to them if they would be close to me." Her advocacy of a black political strategy is less a political statement than a reflection of her appraisal of whites and her belief in the necessity of handling situations herself. She would not agree with black conservatives that discrimination is no longer a major hindrance for blacks but would concur that individuals should be held responsible for themselves. She says, "You have to be on the lookout for discrimination and handle it yourself."

The third example, a 30-year-old married mother of two, works fifty hours a week managing a restaurant in a small southern town. Her husband and she are high school graduates. He works in a mill, and together they earn $20,000–30,000 a year. Married at age 21, they grew up in the same town where they now live. "We both work so hard that sometimes we don't see each other much. But the kids are taken care of; I work evenings, he works days. We make sure the kids have one of us." She described her work as managing the restaurant as well as "doing everything, depending on who shows up. I cook, cashier, the whole bit." By the time we reinterviewed her after the election, she had received both a raise and an award from the state restaurant association.

Regular churchgoers but with little time for other activities outside of work and family, she and her husband, though strong Democrats, did nothing political in 1984 except vote. She voted for Mondale but would have voted for Jackson had he run as an independent. For a strong Democrat, she rated Reagan and the Republican party surprisingly high, 20 degrees more positively than the black electorate on average.

In line with other individualistic advocates, her support for an independent political voice came out of her commitment to self-help. She repeatedly extolled hard work and individualism. She talked disparagingly of people she and her husband had known in high school who had dropped out, hung out, leeched onto their families, or did nothing with their lives. "They're still around, still doing nothing." She disapproved of government "handouts that people get used to—except for old people, of course. They need every bit of help they can get, and I for one, don't mind paying lots of taxes for that." Jackson's appeal to her was his insistence on individual responsibility: she believed that Jackson shared her extremely negative evaluation of government programs to aid blacks and minorities.

These individualistic advocates expressed the ideas that the new black conservatives have brought to public debate. They believed in hard work, a minimal role for the state, and a maximal level of choice and responsibility for the individual. Their nationalism also included an important theme of black conservatism that is usually not cast in nationalist language—distrust of well-intentioned whites, whether in government or not, making decisions for blacks.

POTENTIAL LEADERS AND A BLACK PARTY CONSTITUENCY

Were these potential leaders of an independent party similar to blacks who actually have been leaders of a black party? A survey taken of the fifteen hundred delegates to the 1980 National Founding Convention for a Black Independent Political Party provides a profile of such leaders.[13] Nine in ten were between the ages of 18 and 40, and seven in ten had both a college degree and a professional job.[14] In contrast, only seven in ten of the atypical advocates we identified as potential leaders were as young as 40, only three in ten had a college degree, and four in ten held a professional job (none of the local community leaders did).

Moreover, the convention delegates were not partisans of the major parties: nearly seven in ten did not identify with either party, and five in ten did not vote in the 1980 presidential election. In striking contrast, nine in ten of our potential leaders identified with a major party—nearly all with the Democratic party—and virtually all of them were regular voters. In short, our potential leaders had fewer political resources and greater loyalty to the Democrats. They would not as easily go outside the two-party system. The formation process would have to be set in motion by others.

How effective would they be as leaders of a black party? Since they approved of a black political voice for various reasons, they were not a unified cadre. Two major beliefs bound them: blacks need to control their own destiny, and whites, too powerful in any case, cannot be trusted to make political decisions that affect blacks. Beyond these shared perspectives, cleavages existed between the individualistic advocates and the other two groups of atypical advocates identified as potential leaders. They did not agree on the role of government or on the importance of organizations relative to individual action, and they did not perceive power relations in the same light. They were hardly a cohesive group that could work together effectively to mobilize support for a black party or a black political organization.

The nationally and locally oriented potential leaders were united ideologically and should be able to collaborate. They basically agreed on public policy and on a broad set of issues pertaining to the distribution of power in the United States. Both favored a strong, activist federal government. Moreover, their respective skills and experience at different levels of politics ought to strengthen the effectiveness of their leadership despite differences in age and status.

What constituency would they have to mobilize? The rest of the advocates by definition had a low socioeconomic status and were not members of black organizations. Given their lack of resources, it is not surprising that they were less interested in politics, felt less politically competent, were much less convinced that blacks could be collectively efficacious, and participated much less in all kinds of politics. (See Appendix B.5, Tables 2–6.) Identified as Democrats (though inactive in electoral politics), they had not given up on the established electoral mechanisms of democracy. For these reasons, they would not be easily mobilized, although they did have resources that could be drawn on. They felt a strong sense of racial solidarity; they were discontented with the comparative power of blacks and whites; and they wanted an active government concerned with racial matters.

This constituency among the advocates of a black political voice seemed to have adopted their position almost entirely because they had had negative racial experiences and were acutely aware of racial division. A 76-year-old South Carolina woman who has "spent a lifetime cleaning private homes" said, "over and over, I've seen what happens. At best, whites don't care what happens to black babies and black families. At worst, they want to keep us down because they want people who can't do anything but clean their houses and take care of their families." A 32-year-old Chicago woman essentially agrees: "Whites and blacks are completely divided in this society. Some things are better now—we have better jobs and more of us have gone to college. But the society is just as divided; we still can't move where we want without trouble. Whites want it the way it is. They don't have to think about problems they don't see from their homes in the suburbs." A 25-year-old man who works as a cook in a North Carolina nursing home sums it up: "Blacks do better than they used to—that's true. But we're a long way from catching up, after all we have given to this country. I don't see whites caring about it or wanting to deal with that. Many of them believe there's no problem. That's what's different from twenty years ago. The problems we know are all around us aren't even admitted anymore."

The actual leadership of a black political voice would have to harness this singular focus on race. Single issues can provide a basis for mobilizing a group, and in this group awareness of racial division and feelings of outrage are widespread and ever smoldering. What is the likelihood that these sentiments could be mobilized for political ends?

In the past, black parties have failed for many of the same reasons other third parties have failed. Failure can mean two things: inability to survive or—even as a short-lived party—inability to affect the policy agendas of the major parties. Rosenstone and his colleagues list several reasons for failure.[15] The single-member district plurality system that governs most American elections discourages third parties, as does the electoral college system. The major parties have constructed a maze of cumbersome regulations making it difficult for minor parties and independent candidates to get on the general election ballot. Since the separate states determine their own ballot-access laws, minor parties have to overcome fifty-one different sets of hurdles. Campaign finance laws, which make candidates eligible for public funds only after an election and only if they had appeared on the ballot in at least ten states and won at least 5 percent of the national popular vote, usually freeze third-party challengers out of national races. Minor parties also face various resource constraints. They have fewer financial resources, receive poorer press coverage, are less capable of mounting a campaign nationwide, and generally run less experienced candidates.

The resource constraints on black parties are especially severe. Potential wealthy contributors are both few in number and typically opposed to a separate black party. This means, of course, that the needed financial resources are difficult to obtain in the black community. Building coalitions with white progressives is a formidable task subject to misinterpretations on both sides. Racial discontent, the very issue around which blacks favoring a black strategy can be mobilized, may be construed by white allies as prejudice and hostility on the part of the black community. White progressives may bring their own form of prejudice, hostility, and arrogance to a predominantly black third party.

Efforts to form a black party have also suffered from organizational and programmatic failures.[16] An organizational infrastructure is needed to connect the party with ongoing social and political groups at the local and state levels and to handle divergent points of view without suppressing them or allowing irreconcilable splits. A political program must be able to work with geopolitical and international economic forces and with structural features of the United States political and economic systems.

Even if there were adequate structural and organizational resources and if racial factors did not preclude coalitional politics (in our survey, neither the typical nor the atypical advocates opposed coalition, although the negative racial experiences of the typical advocates raise doubt as to the success of an interracial coalition), certain political conditions would have to exist before the potential supporters of a black party would go outside the two-party system. The faith of blacks in the two-party system, their commitment to the electoral mechanisms of democracy, and their loyalty to the Democratic party are major deterrents. What political conditions would allow these constraints to be overcome?

Both parties would have to be perceived as unresponsive to black interests. As long as one party is considered much more receptive to policies desired by the black electorate, even if it does not follow the black electorate's preferred racial policies as closely as they would like, not even the independent-voice advocates are likely to vote for a black-party candidate. The more responsive party may be seen as the lesser of two evils. But as long as a substantial difference is perceived between the two parties, this black-party constituency will not abandon the two-party system.

The evidence summarized in Figure 5.2 demonstrates that the necessary political conditions did not exist in 1984. The solid black bar indicates how distant Reagan's stance was perceived to be from our respondents' preferred racial policies; the bar marked with horizontal

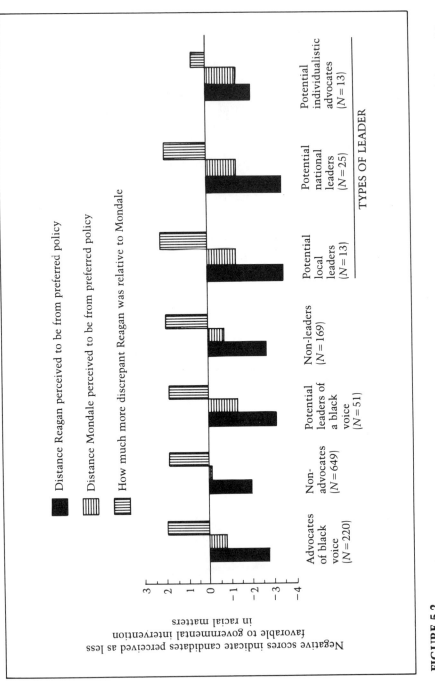

FIGURE 5.2
The Discrepancy between Respondents' Preferred Racial Policy and Their Perceptions of Reagan's and Mondale's Positions

lines indicates how distant Mondale's stance was perceived to be; and the bar marked with vertical lines shows how much more discrepant Reagan was than Mondale. Advocates of a black voice and the potential leaders thought both candidates were farther from their own preferences than non-advocates and non-leaders, respectively. Nonetheless, the advocates and the potential leaders believed Mondale was considerably closer than Reagan. Advocates and non-advocates, potential leaders and non-leaders, and the different types of potential leaders on average all thought Reagan was approximately 2 points farther away from their own policy preferences than Mondale was. The only exception, the individualistic advocates, thought Reagan had a position somewhat more congenial to their own.

The bottom line is clear: in 1984, the political conditions did not exist for this constituency to leave the Democratic party. They voted as often as non-advocates, and they voted for Mondale. Some would have voted for Jackson had he mounted an independent campaign, but Jackson himself judged the situation not conducive to an independent candidacy. Unless differences between the two parties disappear or become markedly smaller, blacks are not apt to support a candidate outside the Democratic party. Dependency on a major party will endure as long as one party even approximately represents the interests of the black electorate—and that is the black electorate's continuing dilemma.

Notes

1. See Rosenstone, Behr, and Lazarus (1984, 179) for the 1952–1980 trends and Brown, Jackson, and Bowman (1981) and Marable (1985) for the 1972 poll data.
2. Hamilton 1973, 68.
3. There were 12 percent more advocates than non-advocates among Jackson's strongest supporters.
4. Rosenstone, Behr, and Lazarus 1984, 179.
5. The uncontrolled relationship between belonging to a black organization and advocacy of a black political voice was $-.153$ $(p < .001)$. When income and education were controlled, there is virtually no relationship: $-.039$.
6. When education was not controlled, there was no relationship between membership in a politically involved church and advocacy of a black political voice: .015; but when adjustments were made for the advocates' lower level of education, the relationship was statistically significant: .062 $(p < .05)$.
7. There are exceptions: minor parties won less than 3 percent of the vote in the 1932 election in the middle of the Great Depression. Yet in prosperous years they have

sometimes done well (for example, they gathered 13.9 percent of the vote in 1968, when real per capita income was up 2.8 percent). In the elections between 1968 and 1980, economic considerations poorly accounted for third-party voting. "The unemployed were about 13 percent more prone than other citizens to vote for an independent; those who felt personally worse off financially were about 3 percent more likely to abandon the major parties. . . . Citizens who saw a deteriorating national economy were about 10 percent more likely to vote for an independent challenger than their counterparts who thought the country was in good shape." See Rosenstone, Behr, and Lazarus 1984, 134–138, 167–168.

8. See Brown and Tate (1985) for further discussion of economic factors in support of a black party.

9. See Rosenstone, Behr, and Lazarus 1984, 127–132.

10. Our analysis of change from before to after the 1984 election reveals a positive feature of the advocates' perspectives on strategy. (See Appendix B.5, Table 1.) The election's negative impact on a sense of the group's possible political effectiveness was less pronounced among advocates than among non-advocates. Yet the buffer provided by their orientation to strategy did not protect them from feeling the election's dampening effect on a sense of efficacy in local elections. The advocates also ended the election period even more convinced that the system was unresponsive and that being black was central to their sense of self; the non-advocates changed less. Neither of these psychological characteristics was affected generally by the election, but advocates came through the events of 1984 with an even stronger sense of blackness and being left out of the governmental process.

11. By comparing how much advocates and non-advocates changed on measures in both the pre- and the post-election interviews, we were able to consider whether the strong advocates of an independent black voice became especially disillusioned during the course of the election. (See Appendix B.5, Table 1.) The results of this analysis show that being an advocate had no effect on interest in the campaign or on political distrust and that disillusionment is too simple an explanation of the effects that were found. The advocates more than other blacks did show an increase in their sense that the system is unresponsive to people like themselves; but at the same time, they held onto a belief in collective efficacy more than others did. They also became more involved in identity issues. The election can thus be thought of as a consciousness-raising experience for these advocates of a black voice. As they became more aware of the system's unresponsiveness, a black identity became more central to them.

12. Atypical case analysis, a sociological technique that refines and amplifies typical patterns, is not uncongenial to statistical analysis, although survey analysts rarely utilize it. Since the numbers involved in atypical case analysis are often quite small and samples are not originally drawn to represent them, error is likely to be a serious factor. For this reason, survey analysts are often wary of examining people or subgroups that do not confirm the general pattern.

13. Flewellen 1981.

14. These black party delegates were very similar in education and occupation to the delegates supporting Jackson at the 1984 Democratic National Convention. Both groups are composed of elites in the black community.

15. Rosenstone, Behr, and Lazarus 1984, 16–47.

16. See the following for discussion of problems facing a black political party: Flewellen 1981; Walton 1972; Pinderhughes 1986; Marable 1984, 1985; Walters 1975; Holden 1972; and Brown and Tate 1985.

CHAPTER SIX

Social Class, Black Solidarity, and Politics

H AVING PRESENTED DATA CONCERNING the role played by social class in the formation of group solidarity and the influence that both social class and group solidarity had on support for Jesse Jackson and the advocacy of an independent black political voice, we turn now to an interpretation of our findings. We shall consider here the meaning of our survey results from the perspectives of both history and social psychology.

CLASS AND BLACK POLITICS

To understand the impact of social class in black politics, it is necessary to view the distinctive history of class formation in the black community and the way in which internal class differentiation has influenced various modes of black politics.

Class Formation among Blacks

Class formation and the current class structure differ between the black segment of the population and the white segment in two respects. First, since historically blacks have not been able to participate in the full range of economic activities in the United States, class differentiation has occurred more slowly among blacks than among whites. Second, despite a growing convergence in the class distributions within each group, the class structures remain markedly different: the black population is still primarily working or lower middle class; the white population, predominantly middle class. (See Table 2.1, p. 68.) Landry describes these phenomena:

> Historically, the pattern followed within the white class structure has been a steady growth of the middle class with a corresponding decline in the other classes. . . . Because of a faster increase in white-collar compared to blue-collar jobs, the white middle class grew from 24 percent in 1910 to 54 percent in 1980. . . . Unlike whites, black upward mobility into the middle class progressed at a snail's pace until the late 1960s.[1]

> . . . The black middle class lagged behind the white middle class not only in total size but in their *distribution* over different strata. . . . Blacks were overrepresented at the lower-middle-class level and underrepresented at the upper.[2] . . .

> [However,] it is as much the overconcentration of black workers in the unskilled working class as the slow growth of the black middle class that has distinguished the black class structure from that of whites. While the white unskilled working class declined steadily as the white middle class grew, the black unskilled working class remained the single largest group of black workers until about 1978.[3]

Scholars usually delineate four phases in the development of black class structure.[4] The first phase took place before the Civil War, when all but a few blacks were enslaved and thus were living in a homogeneous economic situation. The second phase, lasting from Emancipation until sometime between 1910 and 1920, was a period of black land tenancy in which the major distinctions were among farmers (landowners, cash renters, share tenants, and sharecroppers).[5] As of 1910, half the black population but only one-quarter of the white population was still employed in the farm economy. Another 39 percent of the blacks, as opposed to 19 percent of the whites, were unskilled laborers and service workers. And as more blacks remained unskilled, more whites were climbing the socioeconomic class ladder. Nearly 25 percent of the whites but only 3 percent of the blacks were already in middle class occupations.[6]

During this same period, an elite group emerged in the black community with the defining characteristics of light skin color and a close relationship to whites. Because membership in this elite depended less on one's relationship to the market than on status distinctions, Landry calls this mulatto elite a status group rather than a true social class.[7] In addition to skin color and white patronage, prerequisites for membership included having been freed from slavery before the Civil War, having a leadership role in the black church or local black school, owning property, and behaving according to the conventional standards of the time.

> What especially bound this group together . . . was its unique relationship with whites and its life style. The service nature of most of their occupations placed them in daily close contact with wealthy whites, which, even more than the monetary rewards, gave these occupations (craftsmen, caterers, barbers, tailors, shoemakers and other small businesses) a high status in the black community. . . . [However, this emphasis on] the various occupational elements within the black elite should not be construed to mean that membership in the elite was correlated with occupation. The very occupational diversity of black elites . . . underscores the fact that other characteristics unified the group.[8]

Changes in the structure of race relations and in the political economy ushered in the third period of black class formation, beginning around 1920 and continuing into the 1960s. After Reconstruction, segregation, racism, and violence against blacks increased, destroying the close contact between the black elite and whites. Subsequently, the drastic reduction in European immigration following passage of the restrictive quota law of 1924 and the economic demands of two world wars provided industrial opportunities for blacks at a time when the mechanization of agriculture and the collapse of cotton tenancy were forcing blacks off the land. These pull and push factors sent waves of rural southern blacks into urban areas, especially to cities in the North. In both northern and southern cities, many blacks found employment as unskilled laborers; fewer, as skilled workers. Their ever-growing numbers created a demand for professionals who could provide services—such as realtors, insurance agents, funeral-parlor operators, journalists to work on the newly created black newspapers, doctors, dentists, and bankers. Whites were unwilling to provide such services in black communities, and so a black middle class of professionals, owners of small businesses, and manufacturers (largely of cosmetics and caskets)[9] developed. As a consequence of these changes in race relations, the political economy, and demography, both an industrial wage-labor force and a middle class formed in the black segment of the population.

The fourth phase of class formation, beginning in the 1960s, produced a much larger black middle class and a larger underclass. Analysts are by no means in agreement, however, on the causes of these two developments or their future trajectories.

With respect to the black middle class, the growth between 1960 and 1970 was dramatic. Analyzing long-term trends in the occupations of black workers, Freeman concludes that in the 1960s blacks for the first time competed successfully for middle class jobs: "In the new market of the 1960s, the historic pattern of little or no occupational progress was broken. Blacks moved up the occupational hierarchy rapidly, with the highly-educated breaking into previously 'closed' managerial and professional occupations."[10] The percentage of middle class blacks doubled during that decade, from approximately one in eight to one in four.[11]

The growth of the black middle class continued between 1970 and 1980. Now, however, some analysts anticipate a markedly smaller rate of growth in the 1980s, due to the decline of black students enrolled in college (see Chapter Two) and to the Justice Department's challenge, beginning in 1982, of affirmative-action agreements and court rulings.[12] Although the full story cannot be told until the end of the decade, there is some evidence that supports these fears. Using the new occupational categories developed for the 1980 census, Farley and Allen show that the black middle class growth rate slowed between 1980 and 1986, the last point for which they had occupational data.[13] (The data for 1986 were collected by the Census Bureau and are basically comparable to those of 1980, although the sample size is much smaller.) Since the Census Bureau had recoded a sample from the 1970 census using the new occupational codes, Farley and Allen were able to compare trends for the five categories of occupations usually considered middle class. The growth rate for these five sets of occupations was 41 percent between 1970 and 1980 but only 8 percent between 1980 and 1986.[14]

Analysts also disagree about the causes of class polarization in the black community and, in particular, about the growth of a black underclass. The idea that economic inequality has been growing larger in the black population was first suggested by Moynihan in 1965: "There is considerable evidence that the Negro community is, in fact, dividing between a stable middle class group that is steadily growing stronger and more successful and an increasingly disorganized and disadvantaged lower class group."[15] Since the 1960s, class polarization has become more extreme. Of course, the size of the black underclass depends on definition—whether it is to be considered strictly in economic terms, as a group persistently falling below poverty standards, or more broadly in behavioral terms, as a heterogeneous grouping of "families and individuals who are outside the mainstream of the American occupational system . . . who lack training and skills and either experience long-term unemployment or are not members of the labor force, . . . who are engaged in street crime and other forms of aberrant behavior, and . . . [who] experience long-term spells of poverty and/or welfare dependency."[16]

A careful examination of various trends from 1960 through 1980 shows that the extensiveness of class polarization among blacks depends on what indicator of social class is used to measure polarization. According to Farley, "it is an oversimplification to claim that the black community is now split into an elite and an underclass. Some trends point toward such polarization, but others point in the opposite direction."[17] Trends in educational attainment do not show increasing polarization. In fact, the level of educational attainment has become more equal since 1960. In contrast, economic trends show greater inequality. The gap in occupational prestige among employed blacks has grown larger. And since there has been a sharp increase in the percentage of adult black men who neither work nor look for a job, the separation in occupational prestige would be greater if these nonworking men who are not counted were placed, as surely they should be, at the bottom of the prestige distribution. The gap in purchasing power between the families with the lowest and those with the highest incomes also increased, and economic polarization by family is now certainly more pronounced.[18]

The causes of the increasing marginalization of unskilled black workers are also debated. Everyone agrees that macroeconomic factors are influential. Slower productivity in the nation and slowed wage-rate growth have left the most vulnerable more so. Some analysts further stress the importance of structural changes in the economy: (1) the internationalization of capital and the loss of manufacturing jobs to countries with lower wage rates, both of which have caused a major shift from a manufacturing, goods-producing economy to one based increasingly on provision of services, where often part-time or temporary employees earn low wages; (2) the expansion of the technological part of the service sector outside the central cities of major metropolitan areas, leaving impoverished inner-city minorities unemployed; and (3) the weakening of labor unions.[19] Others do not consider these structural and institutional factors important.[20]

Scholars also disagree about the role of racial barriers in creating a larger underclass among blacks. These macroeconomic and structural forces are not just a racial matter. They impinge on both black and white workers who lack education and skills. Landry points out, however, that blacks have found themselves increasingly shut out of the new unskilled working class jobs in the service sector even though these jobs do not require much education or training and are primarily located in the central cities. Between 1973 and 1981, the number of black workers declined 31 percent among unskilled laborers and 37 percent among domestic workers. Compensating for this drop-off in employment was an increase of only 19 percent in the number of unskilled service workers. The increase for white unskilled service workers for the same period was 26 percent. Landry concludes that

> the recent high unemployment rates of blacks, therefore, is partly due to the difficulty of securing sufficient jobs in the unskilled service area to offset losses among laborers and domestic workers. . . . In the face of a declining skilled working class, white workers are turning to jobs in the unskilled working class and winning out in the competition with blacks, largely because of discrimination. . . . Thus, it appears that occupational discrimination continues to be at least as important as economic change in maintaining a large black underclass and a large black unskilled working class.[21]

Although the future of the enlarged black middle class and black underclass is not certain, the sharper class differentiation that has taken place in the black community since the 1960s has raised an obvious political question: Will the widening class division produce corresponding class-based political divisions?

The Historical Role of Class in Black Politics

There is disagreement also about the political importance of class divisions in the black population. The debate is often waged on theoretical or ideological grounds without benefit of empirical evidence. In general, Marxists more than others believe that class has been influential in black politics. Boston, whose definition of class follows the conceptualization of Lenin, asserts that the political consciousness of blacks has always been strongly correlated with economic position and that "[the black masses have] been at the forefront of every major social transformation, from the Civil War to the Civil Rights era. . . . [This class has been] the most progressive stratum of black society, . . . the foundation of every great social change affecting black society."[22]

Marxists are not of one mind on this matter, however. Marable, a leading black Marxist, distinguishes among various modes of politics, suggesting that class differentiation has been a significant factor in electoral politics but not in social-movement politics: ". . . Within the Black Diaspora, given the ideological and political weight of both white racism and national oppression, almost all Black social movements have a multiclass constituency."[23] He argues that there are two reasons for this: "in pre-capitalist environments, distinctly proletarian movements seldom develop, and, . . . within advanced capitalist social formations with a racial division of labour, oppressed Blacks frequently express their 'class' outrage in distinctly 'racial' terms."[24]

Scholars of various persuasions generally concur on two points: (1) that the racial division of labor and the slower class differentiation in the black community historically provided little possibility of social class becoming a strong influence in black politics, and (2) that its influence, although quite minor, has been greater in electoral politics than in other forms. Social class has also distinguished leaders from participants and defined attitudes toward separatism and defensive violence as political strategies.

Holt's study of leaders in South Carolina during Reconstruction is helpful in understanding the impact of class on political leadership. This leadership was disproportionately comprised of the old mulatto elite, antebellum free blacks, and former slaves whose trades and skills had allowed them to acquire property and economic resources after Emancipation. Although the free blacks and mulattos and the enslaved mulattos together made up less than one-tenth of the state's nonwhite population, 44 percent of the black delegates to the 1868 constitutional convention had been free before the Civil War. Holt argues that this class pattern persisted throughout Reconstruction: "Out of a total of 255 Negroes elected to state and federal offices between 1868 and 1876, approximately one in four had been free before the war, and one of every three was a mulatto. Almost one in three owned some real estate, and 46 per cent possessed some form of wealth, real or personal."[25]

On the question of strategy, these mulatto antebellum free blacks were less likely than other blacks drawn into electoral and party politics during Reconstruction to push for land redistribution and for material compensation for ex-slaves. The elite accommodated the growing alliance between the planter aristocracy and northern industrialists.[26]

At the other end of the class distribution, separatist and emigrationist movements have always appealed disproportionately to economically deprived blacks. Disagreement about the use of defensive violence has likewise reflected class divisions, although at no time has any of these strategies—emigration, separatism, or defensive violence—drawn more than narrow support in the black community. Marable notes a heated disagreement among Communists in the 1930s on exactly this point.[27] Trotsky held to a dogmatic belief that the overwhelming majority of black workers and farmers supported the right to self-determination. James, the West Indian Marxist theoretician, thought Trotsky completely wrong in his view of the political aspirations of blacks in the United States. In correspondence to Trotsky, James contrasted African and West Indian blacks who look upon self-determination as a restoration of their independence with United States blacks who desperately want to be American citizens.

Some scholars argue that class differentiation became more influential politically in later stages of class formation, between 1920 and 1960, when both an industrial working class and a middle class developed and when economic divisions became more salient. The classic statement of class relations during this period is found in Frazier's *Black Bourgeoisie*.[28] Frazier depicted the black middle class as a group politically and psychologically dissociated from the black masses and shallowly preoccupied with society and conspicuous consumption. However, Drake and Cayton, who published a study of black life in Chicago up to World War II, stressed that the middle class was itself variable and self-critical.[29] This internal criticism

> accused some of "frivolity," referring to them as the "butterfly group." . . .
> To be sure, there was considerable preoccupation within the black middle class with maintaining the correct "front" and with "respectability," but there were also the civic-minded, or "Race Women" and "Race Men," as they were called. . . . They were the men and women who formed and led such organizations as the NAACP, the Urban League, and other local groups whose primary interest was civic rather than social. They attempted, and often succeeded, in goading the more frivolous to participate in civil activities. . . . These were the men and women who developed parallel institutions in the black community to serve the needs of black people denied access to white institutions.[30]

The racial prejudice experienced by the "old" middle class and its dependency on black patronage are credited with minimizing class divisions in black politics during this period of class formation. Blacks of all classes were categorically discriminated against because of their race. Since the old middle class lived among, served, and marketed their products to other blacks, they were an intimate part of the black community.

During the most recent period of class formation, since the 1960s, the question is whether the sharper class differentiation has produced a sense of class interests that supersedes racial interests in politics. The idea that class is likely to have become a basis of political division among blacks arose not only from the larger size of the new middle class but also from other differences between it and the old middle class.

Landry argues that the new middle class is different in four ways that theoretically should increase its sense of class interests.[31] First, its proportion is twice that of the old middle class. Second, middle class blacks now work in a much wider variety of occupations and in settings that relate them more closely to whites—as staff in white-owned corporations, as owners of small businesses linked to white businesses through government contracts, as professionals serving an increasingly interracial clientele, and as manufacturers or entertainers who market their products or talents to an audience comprised of whites as well as blacks. In addition, more middle class blacks now live in racially integrated neighborhoods.

The third difference in the new middle class is that due to laws prohibiting discrimination in public accommodations and housing, the new professionals, managers, and businesspeople can now legally consume the same kinds and quality of goods and services as middle class whites of the same economic means. For the first time, there is the possibility that the life chances of middle class blacks will be more fully determined by the size of their pocketbooks than by the color of their skin.

The fourth difference is that the members of the black middle class are now more able to pass on their class privilege to their children. Between 1962 and 1973, the proportion of black males inheriting their middle class positions more than doubled, so that almost one out of every two blacks with middle class parents remained in the middle class.[32] The new black middle class is thus less dependent on black patronage and more able to use its class position to benefit itself and its families than was the old middle class that emerged as blacks became more concentrated in urban settings between 1920 and 1960.[33] Not surprisingly, many suspected that the new black middle class would begin to act politically on its class interests rather than on racial interests as part of a solidary, discriminated-against population.

The Impact of Class in 1984

As noted in Chapter Two, social class has a number of meanings in social science. In this book, it refers to the relative number of society's valued resources—primarily income and education but also a job and welfare support—that a group possesses. In most of our analyses, these indicators of class were examined separately to see whether each affects politics differently. According to these analyses, two overall conclusions may be drawn.

First, education is generally more influential than family income. Education had a stronger impact on organizational resources, most of the psychological resources measured in the survey, and on all but one type of political participation (traditional campaign activities were affected equally by income and education).[34] The only aspect of black politics that was governed more by income than by education was approval of a black party and a vote-black strategy.

Second, neither unemployment nor receipt of welfare was consequential, and the little impact they had was through their contribution to the family's economic condition. When family income was controlled, unemployment and receipt of welfare had virtually no independent effects on political motivation, resources, or participation.[35]

We also investigated the joint effects of education and income so as not to miss a possible impact of class by emphasizing the separate influences of these factors. Only rarely, when neither education nor income was separately related to political outcome, did we find their combined impact statistically significant.

In the "Conclusion" below, we pay special attention to the debate about class polarization and its possible effects on black politics by highlighting the areas of politics for which class was influential and the areas for which it was not. We also compare our results on the political impact of social class with those reported in other recent studies of blacks and with studies of its effect generally in American politics.

Social class: A factor in political resources and participation. Consistent with the resource theory of politics, we found that blacks who had the highest family income and the most education were the most active in politics. Middle class blacks voted more frequently than other blacks in all kinds of elections. In 1984, they were also more active in campaign activities. Moreover, it was not only electoral politics that were facilitated by advantages that derive from higher income and more education: the positive impact of a middle class status was in fact two to three times greater on participation in protest than on electoral politics.

The participation effect of social class resulted partly from class-based political motivation and organizational resources. Compared with poorer blacks, middle class blacks were more interested in electoral politics, felt more competent in their understanding of politics, and believed more in the group's political efficacy. Education was the critical influence here. Middle class blacks also had the strongest sense of group solidarity and belonged most frequently to black organizations that provided a link to politics. Family income as well as education fostered these resources. When these politically relevant characteristics were taken into account, the impact of social class on participation was much smaller. This shows that social class was influential partly by promoting psychological resources, group solidarity, and organizational resources. And these factors in turn fostered participation.[36] (See Appendix B.6, Table 5.)

Social class is thus an important issue in black politics, as it is in American politics generally, because it influences participation and therefore threatens the democratic ideal. The democratic ideal

> condemns gross disparities of political power among individuals and groups, and hence approaches equality of result. The ideal implies both a floor and a ceiling: No preferences ought to be totally ignored in the political system, nor should the preferences of any one individual or group predominate. The floor under political influence is established by institutions such as universal suffrage. . . . The ceiling is manifested in the one-vote limit, periodic attempts to curb the "big interests," and the recent campaign finance laws.[37]

In the United States, the ideal of political equality is vitiated by the correlation between political participation and social class (a correlation higher than in nearly all other democracies). "This correlation, together with the one anomaly in social policy, the fact that the United States exceeds other nations in spending on education, produces a vicious cycle of inequality. Education fosters increasing disparities in income and occupational status. In turn, people who are better educated, more affluent, and higher in occupational status are more likely to participate in politics."[38] Our results make clear that this problem is not restricted to whites: social class also reduces political equality among blacks.

The impact of class was restricted, however, to particular sectors of the black electorate. Its effect on participation was primarily confined to those who reached voting age before the height of the Civil Rights movement. Among these older blacks, less education and a low family income severely depressed political participation. The impact of class was much smaller among the two youngest cohorts: the civil rights–black power generation, which reached voting age between 1962 and 1977, and the post–civil rights generation, which reached voting age in 1978 or later. Among these younger blacks (aged 40 or younger in 1984), the most disadvantaged took part in electoral campaign activities, protest politics, and voted in various elections at about the same rate as the most advantaged. The Civil Rights and Black Power movements involved a broad spectrum of the black population and may have permanently reduced the political importance of social class for those who attained voting age during and after these movements achieved their impressive political victories and strengthened organization in the black community. Of course, only time will tell whether this is a permanent effect or whether social class will assume greater significance as younger blacks grow older. What the survey does demonstrate is that social class limits political equality among the middle-aged and older sectors of the black electorate.

The effect of class on psychological resources was also restricted to a particular sector of the black electorate—not to an age group, but to residents of certain geographic locations. For blacks living outside large cities (in suburbs, small cities, towns, or rural areas), social class had a decided effect on psychological resources for politics. In these locations, blacks most disadvantaged by a low family income and low level of education were much less interested in politics and, at the same time, much more trusting of political authorities than those who were least structurally disadvantaged. This pattern—feeling personally alienated but trusting authorities—has historically depressed the involvement of blacks in both electoral and protest politics. Thus it was outside the large cities that social class was especially influential. Contrary to popular depictions of the psychological state of poor urban black communities, we did not find an apathetic lower class in the large cities. Instead, social class was largely irrelevant for the psychological resources of urban blacks.

Social class: Not a basis of policy division.   Social class was not a major basis of ideological cleavage. Blacks from all walks of life were in remarkable agreement about the candidates, parties, issues, and appropriate role of government. Even the 8 percent who identified themselves as Republicans were not disproportionately middle class. Nor did social class affect how warmly blacks felt toward the parties or toward the 1984 presidential candidates (Ronald Reagan and Walter Mondale as well as Jackson) or toward blacks who supported them. Moreover, when class had a small effect, it was middle class blacks who felt more negatively toward the parties—both parties, not one in particular. The most highly educated blacks were most critical of the responsiveness of both parties to issues of concern to blacks and of the Democratic party's treatment of Jackson. Not surprisingly, they were also stronger supporters of Jackson. Income, however, did not distinguish Jackson's supporters from non-supporters. Furthermore, the idea that the Republicans might find a potential constituency among affluent blacks was not verified.

Policy preferences were also affected very little by class-based interests. A racial policy in which the government takes an active role in aiding minorities and uses affirmative action to compensate for past discrimination was approved of equally by blacks of all class backgrounds, and class had only a minor impact on opinions of social programs not targeted specifically at blacks. It was not at all related to spending preferences for community programs to deal with crime and only weakly related to approval of programs to provide jobs for the unemployed and for public schools. The less affluent wanted more expenditures for jobs; the more educated, for public schools. The two social welfare programs evaluated in the survey were also only weakly related to social class. Medicare was supported most by people receiving Social Security or other forms of welfare as well as by people not working full-time. Blacks who were unemployed were also the strongest supporters of government assurance of a decent standard of living for all Americans. Income itself, however, was not a factor in attitudes toward either social welfare programs or the government's role in individual economic security.

With these few exceptions, our survey found a solidary black electorate not divided by class. Its solidarity was further evident on our measures of group identity and political consciousness. Blacks from all class backgrounds believed that blacks are economically deprived relative to whites, rejected an individualistic explanation in favor of a structural theory of racial disparity, and supported collective political strategies. Moreover, when class was a factor, it was the middle class that was the most group-identified and politically conscious. Middle class blacks felt a greater sense of common fate with other blacks and said that being black was more central to their sense of self; they were more discontented with the collective power of blacks as well as with the power of other groups included in Jackson's metaphor, the Rainbow Coalition. There was certainly no evidence that middle class blacks were dissociated from the collective needs and political interests of the least privileged in the black community.

Were there no sectors of the black electorate where class more strongly divided policy preferences and threatened group solidarity? We systematically investigated the possible impact of class in cohorts of varying ages and in urban and non-urban environments and found no evidence that family income and education had stronger effects on policy preferences, evaluations of the candidates and parties, or group identification and group consciousness in particular subgroups.

Our survey is not alone in finding little or no effect of social class on blacks' policy preferences and racial solidarity. Three other national

surveys conducted in the 1980s interviewed enough blacks to test reliably for class differences.[39] None found evidence of class division in
opinions about government expenditures on social programs (crime,
housing, drugs, education, environment, and health), in party identification, or in confidence in the executive, legislative, and judicial
branches of the national government.[40] The policy views of middle-
class blacks do not reflect a simple notion of class interest, as they support programs primarily benefiting other class groups. Other studies
also show that middle class blacks feel at least as much racial solidarity, usually more, than lower class blacks.[41]

Do these survey results mean that the black middle class views a
class-stratified society as unfair? Studies that have measured beliefs
about stratification show that blacks of all class backgrounds recognize
the existence of a class system, believe that some occupations deserve
higher pay, and generally accept the fairness of some degree of class
stratification,[42] although they also believe that income inequality
should be reduced and that poverty is caused more by structural problems in the economy than by personal deficiencies of the poor.[43] The
beliefs about stratification and social justice that distinguish blacks
from whites are as characteristic of middle class blacks as of lower
class blacks.

Is there no evidence of class division in any area of policy or strategy? As noted above and in Chapters One and Five, social class has
historically been a factor in attitudes toward strategy. With few exceptions, however, this class-based division has not been about separatism
as a political end but about independence as a strategy by which to
achieve incorporation. In our survey, too, the class division over a
black political voice was, on close examination, not about separatism.
Instead, lower income blacks who supported an independent black
political voice seemed to do so to make the Democratic party, to which
they were loyal, more responsive to the concerns of blacks.

Thus, although middle class blacks understand that racial inequality has an economic base and, like other blacks, want more equality
between (class as well as racial) groups, they are perhaps too integrated
into mainstream organizations to fight for economic and structural
changes. The only class-based political disagreements we were able to
find in recent surveys support this idea. In one study, black elites
drawn from the political and civil rights worlds were compared with a
national sample of blacks. The elites much more frequently agreed
that the capitalist system is fair and denied opposition between the
interests of workers and management.[44] In another study, blacks living
in poverty were compared with those not in poverty.[45] Despite near

consensus that poverty is structurally caused, the non-poor as compared with the poor were more critical of the welfare system, more frequently believed that antipoverty programs have not worked because money was wasted on ineffective interventions, and more frequently believed that poverty is best alleviated by job-training programs. Blacks living in poverty disagreed. Overall, they were more positive about antipoverty programs, and when critical they emphasized the failure of these programs to get funds to the poor and their inapplicability to the most serious problem facing the poor: the need for jobs paying above-poverty-level wages.

The Political Significance of the Widening Economic Division Among Blacks

We have reviewed evidence demonstrating that economic division among blacks has increased in recent years. Economic polarization has been increasing in the white population as well, though to a smaller extent. This can be shown using the index of family-income concentration (a statistical measure of income inequality ranging from 0, which indicates perfect equality, to 1, which reveals perfect inequality). Family-income inequality was already greater for black families than for white families in 1966, but between then and 1981 inequality increased more for blacks than for whites (from .377 to .481 for black families and from .346 to .359 for white families).[46]

Why hasn't this widening of economic disparity resulted in a major class cleavage in black politics? The evidence from our survey and other national surveys shows that the widening economic rift between middle and lower class blacks has not destroyed policy agreement or racial solidarity within the black community. Isn't this contradictory to the claim made by Wilson that class is becoming increasingly significant in the black community?[47]

Wilson's original contention that class is becoming more important as race declines in significance did not concern politics but rather the life chances of blacks. Although his work is often cited as a source for the expectation that class is increasingly dividing the black community politically, he did not focus on politics or deny racial antagonism in the sociopolitical order.[48] Wilson claims that structural changes in the economy and the exodus of middle class blacks from previously segregated black central-city communities have produced a serious gulf in the resources for survival available to middle and lower class blacks. His primary concern in his current work is with the urban underclass, whose life chances, he argues, worsened when the structure of the economy shifted from goods-producing to service-producing industries, the labor market became increasingly divided into low-wage and high-wage sectors, and manufacturing industries relocated outside the central cities. Poor inner-city minorities have been especially vulnerable because occupations in the growth sectors usually require levels of education and training beyond the attainments of poor inner-city residents.[49] Wilson does not focus on the implications of these structural changes for the political perspectives or mobilization of poor urban blacks or for class cleavage in black politics. The insignificance of class in the black electorate's political opinions is thus not so contradictory to his widely known arguments.[50]

Nonetheless, there is some incongruity between the growing economic inequality and the minimal influence of social class on the black electorate's policy preferences and feelings of racial solidarity. Why did class matter so little among the young, whose life chances have been especially affected by the economic and political forces of the past two decades? Well-educated youths in particular have been helped by affirmative-action policies; poorly educated youths have been hard hit by structural changes in the economy. One would expect a larger political division between them. Yet when class was more influential in certain age groups, it divided middle-aged and older blacks and was immaterial among the young. Why did class matter so little in the large cities, where economic and population shifts have contributed to the growth of an urban underclass? We found that class was more influential outside than inside the large cities.

Five factors may explain why recent surveys have not found a class cleavage in black politics. The first is methodological. As we have already pointed out, no household survey reaches the most downtrodden of the urban black community. Since the low income urban residents in our sample probably are not representative of the most deprived in the central cities of the large metropolitan areas, we have deliberately not used the term *underclass* in discussing our results. There are also problems at the other end of the income-distribution scale. According to the 1980 census, only 6 percent of the nation's black population lived in a family earning $40,000 or more annually. Even a national survey the size of ours does not yield enough such families to study their politics intensively. For these reasons, we may have missed a political cleavage between the economic extremes of the black community. Nor did we ask questions that would have distinguished the old from the new middle classes on the dimension presumed to be critical to their class and racial consciousness, namely, how closely their occupational settings link them to the white corporate structure rather than keep them dependent on the black community's use of their services and purchase of their products. We might have found more evidence of class-based policy preferences had we compared prototypes of the new black middle class with low income blacks. Another methodological point is that we may not have covered the issues for which class cleavage is most pronounced. For example, there may be class-based disagreement about dispersed public housing in the suburbs to solve the housing problems of the homeless, the deinstitutionalized, abandoned babies, and even intact poor families. Doubtless, there are other issues that might also divide the black community.

Our failure to find a serious class-based political cleavage is not wholly attributable to these methodological issues, however. Our survey covered a wide range of issues, as have other national surveys. Ours may have missed the most deprived, but, as previously indicated, it achieved an income distribution that approximately matches the estimates given by the Census Bureau. Across respondents living in very poor and much more affluent families and with wide differences in education, there was impressive agreement about policies, the parties, and candidates. And there was no evidence that the widening economic inequality in the black community has destroyed racial solidarity.

The second is a substantive explanation, that racial solidarity creates political agreement cutting across social classes. We have argued throughout this book that group solidarity, historically developed and maintained by a racial division of labor and by economic and social discrimination against blacks of all social classes, is still broadly present in the black community and provides a basis for political unity. One type of solidarity—that based on a sense of common fate and a political analysis of the power and economic status of blacks as a group—was in fact more widespread among middle class blacks than among other blacks. We argue that if these middle class blacks had not felt such strong group solidarity, they would not have supported redistributive government policies as much as they did or as much as less-privileged blacks did. If we are correct, reliable class differences in policy preferences should emerge (or become larger) when we statistically control the effect of racial solidarity.

Statistical evidence supports our argument. We carried out an analysis in which a measure of the common-fate type of solidarity was used as a control and then estimated the effect of social class on the thirteen policy measures. Of the nine policies for which class was originally not a significant factor, six then showed reliable class differences. The three exceptions—foreign policy attitudes toward South Africa and Central America and approval of expenditures to control crime—remained unaffected by class. As expected, class differences were also larger on all four of the policies for which class was originally a significant factor. These analyses show that the middle class would have been less positive about increased expenditures for social welfare and jobs programs, about government assurance of a reasonable standard of living for all Americans, and about government aid for minorities had they not had such strong group solidarity. Of course, this statistical support for our argument should not be interpreted to mean that policy preferences are in fact closely tied to class position. That is not the case. The middle class does have heightened racial solidarity, and for this reason (and doubtless others), class differences in policy preferences are minimal.

The third explanation of the lack of class cleavage in black politics involves the patterns of social interaction characteristic of middle class blacks. One of the reasons given by some commentators for expecting a unique political perspective among the new middle class is that the blacks in this group presumably are losing connections to blacks of other social classes. But are middle class blacks isolated from the larger black community when they move out of the central cities? Landry in *The New Black Middle Class* shows that most black migrants to the suburbs have had to settle in expanding black enclaves or areas from which whites were fleeing. His 1976 survey found that in the neighborhoods in which the majority of middle class blacks lived, the average probability that whites would live there too was 20 percent. "In some areas," he wrote, "the probability was as low as 8 or 9 percent . . . [and] in only two metropolitan areas was the probability . . . as high as 40 percent."[51] Their black neighbors, moreover, were frequently not middle class. In the Northeast, the average percentage of middle class blacks in any neighborhood was only 38 percent; other residents in neighborhoods where the black middle class lived were about as likely to be from the unskilled as from the skilled working class. In the South, the probability of middle class blacks having middle class neighbors was 31 percent, and in the North Central region black middle class neighborhoods hardly existed at all. Only in Washington, D.C., did the proportion of the black middle class living in neighborhoods where the majority of residents were middle class reach 50 percent. Thus, while few among the black middle class live in inner-city ghettos, the vast majority share neighborhoods with large numbers of both skilled and unskilled working class blacks. Landry concludes that "the idea of a black middle class living in social isolation from other classes is largely a myth."[52]

Most black middle class families in the suburbs thus have cross-class contact in predominantly black areas, and many of them work in public schools, hospitals, and other public institutions serving the urban underclass. Many have relatives still living in the central cities. The black middle class is not so isolated from the economically deprived as to be unaware of their needs and problems or so isolated from other blacks as to lose a sense of racial solidarity.

The fourth factor, pertaining especially to the strong racial solidarity of blacks with a college education and a comfortable family income, also concerns the structure of social life. Group identity and group consciousness tend to flourish when members have frequent and intimate contact with each other and also interact a good deal with non-members, especially when the outgroup interactions involve some conflict or unpleasantness.[53] This pattern fosters outward comparisons, recognition of group disparity, and awareness of categorical treatment on the basis of group membership. Sensitivity to categorical treatment is further enhanced when members are subjected to prejudice and discrimination despite having followed societal norms for achievement and success. Many middle class blacks have these consciousness-raising experiences. They have more contact with whites than do many lower class blacks and through discourtesy and mistreatment are reminded that no one completely escapes categorical treatment, whatever his or her individual achievements.

Long ago, Park observed that the racial consciousness of blacks would inevitably increase if their educational and occupational achievements were not accompanied by reliable social acceptance.[54] We are not claiming that middle class blacks experience as much racial discrimination in the 1980s as was typical before the legislative and judicial victories in the 1960s. Much has changed. Many, if not most, of their contacts with whites may now be positive. Yet middle class blacks do not have to encounter discrimination every day or as severely as they did twenty or even ten years ago to feel it as a constant reality. Taxis refuse to stop; the police flag down one's car for no apparent reason, strangers sling racial slurs, and service personnel in restaurants, hotels, and shops behave rudely. Such racial incidents need not be trivialized as mere self-interest or as a narrow form of race consciousness that is preoccupied with status to the exclusion of concern for the problems of survival faced by the lower classes. These reminders of categorical treatment usually extend far beyond protection of status and personal dignity. They arouse feelings of common fate and solidarity that, for the middle class, encompass the most deprived of the black community.

A fifth, related factor is that as children, black adults of all classes were socialized in black churches and family units that emphasized communal values alongside the importance of individual achievement. Denominations whose members are the most advantaged in the black community have long been at the forefront of black protest and electoral politics. The term *the black church* does not refer as much to common religious practices across denominations as to general acceptance of the fusing of religious and sociopolitical ends.[55] This theology continues to be a critical psychological resource, as it was in the times of slavery. The black church has been instrumental in developing and supporting traditionally black colleges, which have generated most black leaders and professionals. Before public schools were integrated, these two institutions—education and religion—were also connected at the primary school level. Research on the political socialization of blacks notes the importance of these institutions and the family in helping youngsters become aware of the flaws in the system as they relate to blacks.[56] These institutions have repeatedly given black youngsters of all class backgrounds a common message: Do not take racial insults and discrimination personally; see them for what they are—a societal problem, not something wrong with you. These institutions have also fostered in youngsters a sense of obligation to the group.

Finally, we must also put the lack of class division among blacks in the broader context of policy in the United States. On only a few policy issues is there a significant class effect. Shapiro and his colleagues, who have gone back to the 1930s in their investigations of the role of social class in polls, show that while there has been a stable economic cleavage on issues concerning the role of government in welfare, income redistribution, and urban problems, disagreement between income groups has always been smaller than disagreement between racial groups and between Democrats and Republicans.[57] Moreover, there has never been an economic division in attitudes toward Social Security, medical and health care, and education. Cook and her colleagues also find only a weak effect of class on the attitudes of whites toward three welfare programs (Aid to Families with Dependent Children, Medicaid, and Social Security). They further point out that people of different class backgrounds have strikingly similar opinions about which groups in America deserve government assistance.[58] Other surveys have examined the possible impact of class on Ameri-

cans' beliefs about the stratification system and have discovered that
the correlation between class background and beliefs about the causes
of poverty and the causes of race and gender disparities is exceedingly
weak.[59] Belief in individualism is so widespread that even the poor
subscribe to the dominant ideology.[60] And lastly, we are reminded that
economic self-interest rarely determines the vote or the policy stance
of individuals unless the personal impact is both powerful and immediate and made extremely clear.[61]

The catalog of only weak effects of class has led social scientists to
suggest cultural, historical, and sociological mechanisms that in the
United States have blocked the formation of a class vote and the translation of simple dissatisfaction into a politically oriented class consciousness.[62] This is not the place to review the major explanations. It
is important, however, to remember that while class is more influential in the policy preferences of whites than it is in the preferences of
blacks, in general it is not a powerful force in the American policy
debate. In America, social class pales in comparison with the political
significance of race.

THE SOCIAL PSYCHOLOGY OF GROUP SOLIDARITY

Black Solidarity: Divisive or Not?

The lack of policy division by class is but one indicator of the black
electorate's solidarity. Another is its commitment to a social psychological form of solidarity. In political sociology, the term *solidarity*
usually denotes the social relationships that link group members to
one another. A solidary group is composed of people who frequently
interact with each other, usually live in proximity, and share life experiences, including being treated similarly by outsiders. Though it is
recognized that these relationships "generate a sense of common identity, shared fate, and general commitment to defend the group,"[63]
solidarity and resource-mobilization theories rarely emphasize or
measure these social psychological dimensions of solidarity. Our
study has attempted to do that. We distinguished two social psychological aspects of solidarity, group identification and group political
consciousness.

In brief, we found an electorate in which group political consciousness was widespread. Collective discontent with the group's limited
power and share of societal resources was felt by the vast majority:
eight in ten thought blacks have too little influence in American life
and politics; six in ten thought that the economic position of blacks is

worse than that of whites. Most believed that the economic and political systems are largely responsible for these inequalities. Nine in ten denied that racial discrimination is no longer a serious problem for blacks; and two-thirds said that when blacks do not do well in life, discrimination is a more important cause than lack of individual motivation. This does not mean that discrimination was seen as the only structural cause, or even the most critical one. In fact, among the structural problems facing blacks, unemployment was judged important by three times as many as mentioned discrimination. The major point is that this electorate did not subscribe to an exclusively individualistic ideology. Instead, its dominant view was sociological and structural—that the position of blacks in the stratification system is a consequence of both discrimination and economic forces that impinge especially heavily on the black population. The majority also believed that collective political solutions are required to attack these systemic problems and were optimistic about the capacity of blacks to have a collective impact in electoral politics.

Group identity was more variable. On the one hand, virtually everyone felt close to other blacks; approximately one-half also felt close to blacks outside the United States—in Africa and in the West Indies. On the other hand, a sense of common fate was less widespread. Only one-third said that what happens generally to black people would affect their lives, though nearly twice as many thought the movement for black rights had affected them personally. Nor did the issue of group identity preoccupy most of the electorate. Only one-third said that they think often or a lot about being black and about their commonalities with other blacks. The other type of identity—a race-centered sense of self as black rather than as American or as having a dual identity—was extremely rare; only one in ten had this kind of identity. Most saw themselves as having a dual identity, as being both black and American.

Our analysis of the origins and political consequences of group identity and group consciousness revealed a subtlety that these overall percentages hide. It turns out that there were two distinct types of solidarity. Both were related to support for Jackson, and one was related to the advocacy of a black political voice. They were located in different sectors of the black electorate and had different implications for politics and intergroup relations. One is defined by identity based on common fate; the other, by an exclusivist black identity.

The common-fate identity, found most frequently among those with structural advantages, was politicized. It entailed discontent with the economic and political powerlessness of blacks as compared to whites and with the belief that racial disparities are largely illegitimate, the result of structural barriers. Blacks with this kind of group identity were unequivocally pro-black: being black was central to their sense of self; they recognized the interdependence of blacks as a group; and they approved of black children learning an African language and of blacks patronizing black businesses. Furthermore, they had a political analysis of racial stratification as it operates in both the political and the economic arenas. This kind of solidarity was also associated with a wide range of policy preferences. Blacks who felt a sense of shared fate with other blacks naturally took a stronger position on racial policy. Their concerns were not restricted to racial matters however. They were more liberal on other issues as well—increased spending on community programs and social welfare, an active government role in providing individual economic security, and decreased spending on defense. People showing this kind of solidarity were the strongest supporters of Jackson in the 1984 campaign.

The exclusivist identity—based on a perception of one's self as black but not as American or as both black and American—was most frequent among the young and less-than-fully employed. This kind of identity, also pro-black, was not broadly politicized. It was not part of a group-conscious ideology or related to policy issues other than government policy on race. Still, it had political significance, seen in this study by its association with advocacy of an independent black political voice and with support for Jackson.

The intergroup contexts associated with the two independent kinds of identity show that black solidarity does not necessarily result in hostility toward whites or limit empathy with other groups. It depends on the kind of solidarity. The most prevalent, a politicized sense of common fate, was not related, either positively or negatively, to feelings toward whites. Blacks with a strong sense of common fate and group political consciousness were no more positive or negative toward whites than were blacks with less of this kind of solidarity. Nor were their political concerns restricted just to blacks. They were more discontented than other blacks with the limited power of poor people, people on welfare, women, and older people. This is a group identity that was neither anti-white nor exclusive. In contrast, blacks who thought of themselves as black rather than as having a dual black-American identity did not feel close to whites and, more than others, believed that blacks should have nothing to do with whites and that whites want to keep blacks down. Moreover, they were not concerned broadly about power relationships in American society but were aggrieved in particular about the excessive power of whites. Race itself was the distinctive issue for blacks with this kind of solidarity.

In general, our results on solidarity support a basic generalization drawn from extensive social psychological research on intergroup relations—that there is no inevitable connection between ingroup and outgroup sentiments. Reviewing a host of these studies for the latest edition of *The Handbook of Social Psychology*, Stephan concludes that "it is the ingroup that is evaluated and treated more positively as a result of categorization, not the outgroup that is treated more negatively. The motive typically is to create positive social comparisons, a result which can be achieved by evaluating the ingroup positively without it being necessary to negatively evaluate the outgroup."[64] This was clearly the case in the solidarity based on a politicized sense of common fate. Ingroup bonds were strong without hostility toward whites. It is primarily when intergroup relations have been historically conflictual or currently involve strong competition that ingroup bonds entail outgroup antagonism. This was evident in the vignettes of the advocates of a black political voice whose politics reflected their sense of self within a black-white framework. Their personal histories of rejection by whites and their current negative racial experiences lay behind the anti-white feelings that were associated with their exclusivist black identities.

Black Solidarity: Illustrative of a Broader Political Phenomenon

Group solidarity is not unique to black politics. Other groups have achieved political incorporation through group processes—bloc voting, a symbolic tie between candidate and constituency, group claims on patronage, and representation of group interests in legislatures at all levels of government.[65] In national politics, there was the historic midwestern ethnic vote for William Jennings Bryan in 1896[66] and the Catholic votes for Alfred E. Smith in 1928 and for John F. Kennedy in 1960. In local politics, the ethnic factor has been the dominant feature of political organization.

Many commentators who characterized the bond between Jackson and his constituency as racist or as "merely symbolic" failed to see the solidarity basis of his appeal as an instance of a broader political phenomenon—the historic significance of ethnicity in American politics and the heightened importance worldwide of identity politics since World War II (not least in the Western, industrial democracies). As

Isaacs describes the modern ethnic revival, the "soft facts of life—race, language, history, origin, and religion—are the stuff of which group identities are made and group identities have become, more than ever before, the stuff of which politics is made, world politics everywhere in the world."[67]

Race is one of many elements defining an ethnic group. Following Yinger, we define an ethnic group as "a segment of a larger society whose members are thought, by themselves and/or others, to have a common origin and to share important segments of a common culture and who, in addition, participate in shared activities in which the common origin and culture are significant ingredients."[68] Some mixture of language, religion, race, and ancestral homeland with its related culture are defining elements. No one element by itself demarcates an ethnic group.

Most Marxists as well as liberals believed that the importance of ethnicity would recede after World War II.[69] They assumed that ethnicity would be overcome by class as capitalism advanced or that ethnic groups would be bound together as technology progressed, as communication capablities grew and state centers and bureaucracies expanded and became more centralized, and as industrial capitalism demanded production and trade on regional, continental, and global scales. Instead, an ethnic revival took place in newly formed as well as old states[70] and is now attributed to the very same economic and political forces that were once thought to erode ethnicity. Ethnic politics, legitimated by the ideology of nationalism, have actually been fostered rather than destroyed by modernization.[71]

Black solidarity and Jackson's appeal to the black electorate on the basis of group bonds can thus be located within the broader context of the ethnic factor in politics. Of course, political analysts are quite divided in the views they take on the role of ethnicity in contemporary politics. Some applaud the current resurgence of ethnicity: "Ethnic attachments are variously seen as ways to preserve a precious cultural heritage; to soften class lines; to protect or to win economic and political advantages for disadvantaged groups; to furnish a more intimate and flavorful connection with large, impersonal societies; and to retard the shift of overwhelming power to the state."[72] Others abhor the current stress on ethnicity, arguing that it is divisive and inegalitarian and that it obscures more serious structural causes of inequality by leading people to focus on cultural issues rather than economic forces and the structures of discrimination.[73] Patterson, for example, insists that ethnic politics are inherently conservative politics; at worst, "vulgar chauvinistic polemics"; at best, "a sophisticated attack on modern industrial civilization."[4] Yet whether embraced or detested, the ethnic factor in politics is strong. It cannot be willed away, neither in the United States with its urban concentration of blacks and regional concentrations of Latinos, nor in Europe with its remarkable flowering of ethnic movements.[5]

Applying the ethnic analogy to black politics in the United States can be misunderstood, however, even as it broadens a frequently parochial discourse. The problem is that the idea of playing the political game as other ethinc groups have done is sometimes used invidiously to define a standard blacks have failed to meet, as if their political history could have mirrored that of the Irish, Italians, or Jews. Scholars of black politics argue that it could not have. They have carefully delineated critical differences between the political experiences of blacks and those of European immigrants.

The Europeans arrived in the large, industrial cities in the North a half-century or more before the southern blacks did, at a time when the United States was undergoing economic growth and could absorb them as unskilled laborers. Southern blacks arrived when the economy could incorporate them only sporadically, mostly in war-related cycles. They became a reserve work force, hired when labor was scarce and laid off when labor was plentiful.[76] The European immigration occurred when urban party machines were especially strong. The large black migrations took place after the reforms of the Progressive era had weakened the power of the machines in most cities (Chicago is a notable exception). Nor did the machines treat blacks as they had the white ethnic immigrants. White political elites were fearful of disrupting the racial status quo. As Katznelson argues, instead of entering the politics of ethnic collaboration and conflict as equals, blacks were linked to the polity through "buffer institutions with uni-directional power capabilities . . . appendages to be used when convenient and to which power could be conferred when necessary. . . . Almost inevitably, blacks, largely excluded from decision-making positions and to whom local political elites were largely unaccountable, were denied an equitable share of the cities' political resources and rewards: patronage, governmental services, and contracts."[77]

Barnett points out that the use of the ethnic model to analyze black politics also conceals an important political reality—that the American political system is designed for and encourages incremental change. Because the European immigrants came under favorable economic conditions and were courted by party machines, they "did not demand basic or far-reaching economic and/or political change . . . and certainly did not wrench substantial collective benefits from the national political system."[78] The demands of the European immigrants—help in getting naturalizational papers and pushcart licenses; patronage jobs; and protection from the most overt discrimination—could be easily met by parties and local government.[79] In their continuing struggle, blacks have had to stress fundamental issues of redistribution that are not at all congenial to incremental politics. It is only under crisis that questions of redistribution tend to receive widespread public attention, and in any case actual change requires action by the federal government.[80]

These differences between the politics of blacks and those of other ethnic groups in the United States should not be discounted. Nonetheless, the Jackson phenomenon and black solidarity must be seen in a broad context. Jackson's oft-repeated slogan, ensconced on the button identifying his 1984 supporters—"Our Time Has Come"—echoes the aspirations of other groups in earlier times and in other places.[81]

In our view, the political significance of black solidarity will long outlive the Jackson phenomenon. This solidarity is grounded in black political history and in communal experience that was originally fostered by enforced segregation and then institutionalized in churches, social groups, and political organizations that have survived the demise of legal segregation. Both the solidarity based on a politicized sense of common fate and that based on an exclusivist black identity were aroused by the 1984 Jackson campaign. But they will be there for other candidates as well. Both types of solidarity will persist as long as racial discrimination exists and as long as a large portion of the black population is economically vulnerable and its chances for decent housing, health care, and quality education remain problematic. We have seen that the middle class has not cut itself off from the most disadvantaged sectors of the black electorate. Improving the quality of life among deprived blacks is one of the political interests of middle class blacks. The middle class feels as much solidarity as other blacks, and usually a good deal more.

The political significance of black solidarity must not be misunderstood as merely an aspect of the Jackson phenomenon or as a theme restricted to politics in the 1980s. It is a vital and long-lasting feature of blacks' struggle for political incorporation, one that has been expressed differently in different historical contexts, sometimes in protest, but also in electoral politics; sometimes in nationalist movements, but also in traditional party politics. In the late twentieth century, it is an indubitable feature of national electoral politics.

Notes

1. Landry 1987, 221–222.
2. Ibid., 197.
3. Ibid., 12.
4. Various scholars define periods of black politics slightly differently. Wilson (1978) lays out three economic periods that resulted in three stages of race relations: (1) antebellum slavery and the early post-bellum era, which were characterized by a pre-industrial plantation economy and racial-caste oppression; (2) the last quarter of the nineteenth century to the New Deal, the modern industrial period, during which both race and class conflict were present; and (3) the modern industrial post–World War II era, in which there has been a progressive transition from racial inequalities to class inequalities. Baron (1985) identifies three racial formations corresponding to three modes of production: plantation racism, agrarian paternalism, and advanced racism. Boston (1985) identifies only two major periods (slavery and post-slavery), with three stages within the latter period: black land tenancy, the development of a black urbanized wage-labor force, and the increased differentiation within black social classes as a result of black workers' becoming progressively marginal and the evolution of a new black middle class. The four stages delineated by Landry (1987), used here, basically conform to those outlined by Boston, although Landry ends the second period around 1915; Boston, closer to 1930.
5. Boston 1985, 52.
6. Landry 1987, 21.
7. Ibid., 25. Marxist analysts argue that this elite was a true social class, however small and embryonic it was, because it owned property and acted on its class interests. See Marable 1985; Boston 1985.
8. Landry 1987, 32–33.
9. A national survey of black-owned businesses conducted in 1946 showed that of the nineteen engaged in manufacturing, thirteen made either cosmetics or caskets. The majority of black businesses, furthermore, were small establishments in the areas of personal service; 85 percent were owned by one person, and 81 percent located in black neighborhoods. See Landry 1987, 45.
10. Freeman 1976, 2.
11. Landry 1987, 70.
12. Analysts also disagree on the importance of economic expansion (and other aspects of macroeconomic activity) relative to non-discrimination laws and affirmative action in producing the growth of the black middle class. Some attribute the growth largely to macroeconomic factors; others, to action by the courts and to the successes of the Civil Rights movement and black lobbies in convincing Congress to act against employment discrimination.
13. Farley and Allen 1987, 271–272.
14. The five categories include executive, administrative, and managerial (a 97 percent increase between 1970 and 1980; 18 percent between 1980 and 1986); professional specialties (a 37 percent versus a 7 percent increase); technicians and related supports (an 82 percent increase versus a 15 percent decrease); sales (a 34 percent versus a 33 percent increase); and administrative support (a 19 percent increase versus a 2 percent decrease). Ibid., Table 9.2, 272–273.
15. D. P. Moynihan, cited in U.S. Department of Labor 1965, 5–6.

16. Wilson 1987, 8.
17. Farley 1984, 190.
18. Farley (1984) notes that "income levels have gone up much more rapidly in hus-
    band-wife families than in those headed by women. As a result, families headed by
    black women are falling further behind husband-wife families in both absolute
    and relative terms. This is particularly important because a large and increasing
    proportion of all blacks live in families headed by women" (p. 191).
19. See Wilson 1978, 1987; Bowles et al., 1989; Boston 1985; and Landry 1987.
20. See Welch and Smith 1986.
21. Landry 1987, 226.
22. Boston 1985, 62, 65.
23. Marable 1985, 13.
24. Ibid., 19–20.
25. Holt 1977, 36–38; quotation from p. 37.
26. Marable 1985, 150–151.
27. Ibid., 53.
28. Frazier 1962.
29. Drake and Cayton 1945.
30. Landry 1987, 62.
31. Ibid., 85.
32. Ibid., 87.
33. A heated debate, stimulated by Wilson's 1978 book, *The Declining Significance of
    Race,* has centered on how secure the new black middle class is and whether it
    still experiences economic discrimination because of race. Wilson argues that the
    life chances of blacks now have less to do with race than with economic class
    affiliation and that racial conflict and competition in the economic sector have
    been substantially reduced. Many of his critics accuse him of insensitivity to the
    role that discrimination still plays and to the fragile economic condition of the
    new middle class. Landry's 1987 analysis is a good example of the controversy
    involving the state of the black middle class. He claims that the black and white
    middle class experiences remain different because (1) black middle class males are
    still far more likely to find a job in government service than in the private sector;
    (2) the absolute gap in median family income has actually widened; (3) the distri-
    bution of blacks and whites within the middle class remains quite different, with
    blacks disproportionately in the lower middle class and whites in the upper mid-
    dle class; (4) the black middle class is three times as likely to depend on the
    income of both spouses to maintain a middle class standard of living; (5) the
    average black middle class family is approximately $2,000 short of the highest
    criterion of a middle class standard of living given by the Bureau of Labor Stan-
    dards, while the average white family falls right at that level; and (6) middle class
    blacks have less in savings than middle class whites, who also have two and a half
    times the total assets of middle class blacks (see pp. 193–233). Wilson argues,
    however, that his primary focus has always been on the growing class polarization
    in the black community that is due to the worsening condition of the underclass
    rather than to the improving condition of the middle class. He says in an epilogue
    to *The Declining Significance of Race* and in the preface of his 1987 book, *The
    Truly Disadvantaged,* that his critics have been so preoccupied with what he had
    to say about the improving conditions of the black middle class that they virtually
    ignored his "more important arguments about the deteriorating conditions of the
    black underclass" (p. vii).
34. Danigelis (1982) examined the relative importance of income, occupation, and

education in explaining voting and campaign participation of blacks and whites from 1952 to 1976. In general, the analysis shows that income was a stronger determinant of participation for blacks than for whites, especially when political climate is intolerant, as it was earlier in the South. This discrepancy in the effect of income for blacks and whites decreased greatly by the mid-1970s. Occupation was unimportant for both groups, and education was relatively more important for whites than for blacks. The effect of education was comparable for the two groups by the mid-1970s, however. Our data show that both aspects of social class influenced many kinds of participation in 1984, and education was somewhat more important.

35. Unemployment was correlated with only three of more than sixty measures of political motivation and resources; welfare, with none.

36. These analyses show that when psychological resources, a sense of group solidarity, and organizational resources are controlled, the original effects of education were reduced by 46 percent in explaining protest participation, 57 percent in explaining participation in campaign activities, and 31 percent in explaining voting in the 1980 election. Nonetheless, the effect of education was still statistically significant for all three of these types of political involvement. Social class had an effect on participation beyond creating greater interest in politics and a stronger sense of group efficacy and group solidarity and beyond providing organizational resources that help individuals become politically active.

37. Verba and Orren 1985, 8.

38. Ibid., 17.

39. In 1982, the National Opinion Research Corporation's General Social Survey (GSS) oversampled blacks and achieved a sample of five hundred. In 1984, the Gallup Organization carried out a survey for the Joint Center for Political Studies that reached some nine hundred blacks. In 1986, an ABC/*Washington Post* poll interviewed one thousand blacks.

40. Gilliam 1986, 54–57; Daniels 1981.

41. Dillingham 1981, 438.

42. *Public Opinion* 1985, 7–8.

43. Gurin and Epps 1975; Shingles 1981; and Dillingham 1981.

44. Dawson 1986.

45. *Public Opinion* 1985, 7–8.

46. Wilson 1987, 111.

47. Wilson 1980, 1986, 1987.

48. Wilson 1980.

49. Wilson 1987.

50. Wilson's thesis has stimulated much of the recent work on class and black politics. Other writers go further than Wilson in drawing out political implications of class division in the black community. In 1963, for example, Banfield and Wilson argued that urban black communities are handicapped in city politics by a lack of identification on the part of the middle class with lower class blacks: "The relatively small Negro middle class is separated from the lower class by differences of ethos and interest" (p. 429). They cast these differences in terms of "status" and "welfare." Middle class blacks were presented as favoring status goals (destruction of discrimination and support of equal rights); the lower class, as favoring welfare goals (concrete social and economic benefits). (See Smith [1981] for a discussion of this contrast.) We find equal support across the social classes for status goals (affirmative action, for example) and for most welfare goals.

51. Landry 1987, 180.
52. Ibid., 185.
53. See Merton and Kitt (Rossi) 1950; Williams 1975.
54. Park 1913.
55. Cone 1970; Paris 1985.
56. Morris, Hatchett, and Brown 1987.
57. Shapiro and Patterson 1986.
58. Cook, Barrett, and Popkin 1987.
59. Huber and Form 1973; Feagin 1975; Williamson 1974a, 1974b.
60. Kluegel and Smith 1981.
61. Sears et al., 1980.
62. For a review of some of the mechanisms that account for what is called American exceptionalism, see Kluegel and Smith 1981; Benson 1973; Skowronek 1982.
63. Fireman and Gamson 1979, 21.
64. Stephan 1985, 615.
65. See Glazer and Moynihan 1975; Katznelson 1973; Greeley 1974; and Yinger 1985.
66. Kleppner 1970.
67. Isaacs 1975, 1979.
68. Yinger 1985, 159.
69. For discussion of nationalism in Marxist theory, see Connor 1984; for evidence of ethnic attachments in China, Dreyer 1976; and for evidence in the Soviet Union, King 1973; Azrael 1978; and Allworth 1977. A. D. Smith (1981) claims that "liberals have generally taken the view that, as mankind moved from a primitive, tribal stage of social organization toward large-scale industrial societies, the various primordial ties of religion, language, ethnicity, and race which divided it would gradually but inexorably lose their hold and disappear" (p. 2). Marxists expected that ethnicity would recede as proletarian internationalism was achieved. But "neither visionary beliefs, nor large-scale industrialization and urbanization, nor the passage of generations, nor concentrated centralized power, nor massive repression, nor elaborate theories, nor structural schemes have been able to check the survival and the persistence of the distinctive separateness of the many nationalities or tribes of people who live under the Communist system" (Isaacs 1975, 19).
70. Glazer (1975) has observed the erosion of the close tie between state (a bureaucratic administrative unit over a geographic territory) and nation (a collection of individuals sharing a conscious identity and loyalty) that had dominated the state-making efforts between the two world wars. He explains that most of the new states, formed out of colonial empires whose boundaries were not coincident with nations, were not nation-states. Furthermore, many of the old ethnically homogeneous states became heterogeneous as labor migrations occurred. And, of course, the United States was never a nation-state. Few states are. According to Connor (1978), of the 132 independent states in 1971, only 12 were ethnically homogeneous, and another 25 had a single ethnic community comprising over 90 percent of the population. In 39 states the largest ethnic group comprised less than 50 percent, however; and in 53, the largest ethnic group comprised only 40 percent of the population.
71. Olzak (1983) reviews four major structural explanations of ethnic mobilization: (1) developmental theories, which emphasize the transient quality of ethnicity activated during the process of development; (2) theories focused on internal colonialism and the cultural division of labor, which argue that ethnicity is

mobilized when a rich, culturally dominant core exploits an ethnically iden-
tifiable periphery, especially when class converges with and reinforces it; (3) explanations in terms of segregated labor markets, which also attribute the mobilization of ethnicity to ethnically segregated occupations but do not assume the
primacy of class (these theories, instead, emphasize specialized economic institutions and networks, such as credit institutions, that produce and maintain solidarity); and (4) competitive models, in which two or more ethnic groups are pitted
against one another in the labor market or for housing, education, and other scarce
resources. Political factors are also said to foster ethnicity and its political mobilization. Among them are increasing world pressure for geographic units to organize
themselves as states; growth of bureaucracies with civil rights laws and constitutional guarantees of regional and ethnic equality; state policies that target specific
groups for housing, welfare, taxation, and quota recruitment systems to fill official
representative bodies; regime tolerance for cultural diversity, regime repression,
and homogenization policies; the relationship of state boundaries to tribal boundaries, especially the division of subunits that converge with tribal or ethnic differences; uneven regional development and ethnic inequality; and party structures
that institutionalize ethnically identified subunits in party representation. While
agreeing that these economic and political forces are causally significant, A.D.
Smith (1981) stresses that there are also psychological and cultural sources of
ethnic mobilization, which suggests that ethnicity will persist as an important
political factor regardless of the economic and political changes that take place.
Also see Glazer (1975) for discussion of factors that help explain the mobilization
of ethnicity since World War II.

72. Yinger 1985, 152.
73. Ibid., 153.
74. Patterson 1977, 152.
75. A. D. Smith (1981) lists among the European movements the Protestants and
    Catholics of Northern Ireland; the Scots and Welsh; Bretons and Corsicans;
    Basques and Catalonians; Serbs and Croatians; Flemings and Walloons; the Juras-
    siens in Switzerland; the Tatars, Lithuanians, Slovaks, and Ukranians; the Greeks
    and Turks (especially on Cyprus); and smaller movements on the behalf of
    the Manx, Cornish, Faeroese, Shetlanders, Channel Islanders, Alsatians, French
    Basques, Galicians, Andalusians, Frisians, Valle D'Aostans, Sardinians, Sicilians,
    Tyrolese, Slovenes, Lapps, Estonians, Latvians, and Canary Islanders.
76. Barnett 1982; Hamilton 1981.
77. Katznelson 1973, 110.
78. Barnett 1982, 50.
79. Hamilton 1981.
80. Barnett 1982, 50.
81. See Glazer (1971) for a position stressing both similarities in and differences be-
    tween blacks and white ethnic groups in their experiences and politics.

CHAPTER SEVEN

Basic Themes in Black Politics

Lift every voice and sing
Till earth and heaven ring
Ring with the harmony of liberty
Let our rejoicing rise
High as the lis--t'ning skies
Let it resound loud as the rolling sea.

Sing a song full of the faith that the dark past has taught us
Sing a song full of the hope that the present has brought us
Faith in the rising sun
Of our new day begun
Let us march on till victory is won. *

A s WE HAVE SEEN by now, hope, always a prominent theme in black politics, was kindled first by the Declaration of Independence and the American Revolution, which demonstrated to blacks, as it did to all the world, that freedom was a realistic aspiration. It was nurtured by the Abolitionist movement, by the amendments to the Constitution and the legislation enacted after Emancipation, and, most recently, by the dramatic political achievements won by the Civil Rights movement.

Betrayal has been the shadow of hope. In the new American democracy, blacks were excluded from the basic rights conferred on "all men"; they were deserted by white abolitionists when blacks insisted that the Abolitionist movement fight for the full citizenship of blacks

---

* National Negro anthem, "Lift Every Voice and Sing" (first verse and refrain), by James Weldon Johnson and R. Rosamond Johnson.

and not merely for their freedom from slavery; they were abandoned by the major political parties when those parties agreed to control electoral competition by silencing the black vote through disfranchisement; they were terrorized and totally disfranchised in the South when the alliance of northern industrialists and southern planters brought Reconstruction to an end; and they were shunned and rebuffed when the parties pursued a strategy of trying to win the southern vote (the Republicans always unsuccessfully until the 1970s). After enfranchisement by the Voting Rights Act of 1965 and after extraordinary electoral successes were achieved by the vastly enlarged black electorate, blacks again felt betrayed, this time by the Reagan administration's assault on civil rights and by a political economy inhospitable to the translation of political successes into economic gains.

Discouraged, disappointed, sometimes in despair, blacks never gave up on the political system. To say they had no choice—that politics was the only game in town—is to minimize the remarkable fact of their perseverance. With the exception of a few nineteenth-century efforts to emigrate, the even earlier establishment of maroons (separate black communities), and, in the twentieth century, the Garvey movement and the Nation of Islam, blacks have steadfastly tried to participate in the American democracy: to vote, to influence the parties, and to affect public policy. They recurrently turned to independence, not as an end but as a means to gain access to political institutions and make them accountable to black interests. Independence was not as much a choice as a necessity—a strategy embraced when other tactics failed to achieve the goal of incorporation. In 1984, Black Americans reacted to the candidacy of Jesse Jackson and to the idea of a separate black party in light of their political history of hope and betrayal.

HOPE AND BETRAYAL

On the whole, the 1984 black electorate was highly motivated and committed to electoral politics. A distinctive element of its motivation was the ideological unity in favor of a strong, activist national government. These voters were broadly supportive of liberal public policies and were not at all alienated from electoral and party politics. Of course, the fact that they were united does not mean that they were in total agreement. A small group, approximately 10 percent, consistently espoused an individualistic, anti-government ideology across various policy questions asked in our survey. Apart from this small sector, there was a great deal of political agreement in the black electorate, demonstrated in the survey by a two-thirds or greater majority favoring an activist government in response to all questions that focused on the role of government.

In 1984, the black electorate's support for an activist government and redistributive social and economic policies was far greater than that of the white electorate. Comparisons of responses to identical questions asked in the 1984 University of Michigan surveys of the general electorate (the NES) and the black electorate (the NBES) show that nearly twice as many blacks as whites wanted the government in Washington to ensure that every person have a job and a decent standard of living, over twice as many specifically wanted the government to make every possible effort to improve the social and economic position of blacks and other minority groups, and, except for spending on crime prevention, which both groups supported equally, many more blacks than whites wanted spending on community and social welfare programs increased. Approximately 30 percent more blacks than whites wanted increases for public schools, jobs for the unemployed, Medicare, and food stamps. These racial differences were robust and persisted when we compared blacks and whites of the same age, the same income, and the same education and living in the same geographic areas. (See Appendix B.6, Tables 1 and 2.)

These discrepancies reflect long-standing differences between the political philosophies of blacks and other Americans who have historically wanted limited government and preferred local to national government action. Hamilton stresses that

> Black Americans have always had to look to the national government for a more responsive hearing of their grievances. This began, of course, with the Civil War and has continued until now. . . . It was the national Congress (under the Radical Republicans) that instituted Reconstruction in 1867. The national government—particularly the United States Supreme Court after the turn of the century—was more sympathetic to demands of black Americans than the local or state governments. For several decades, from 1915 to long after World War II, only the Supreme Court could be looked to for reforms. . . . States' rights became synonymous with black oppression. . . . This has caused black political thought to be influenced heavily by reliance on the federal government and very pessimistic about the ultimate willingness or ability of local governments to deal with black problems.[1]

Analysis of racial trends in opinion polls over a fifty-year period shows large and persisting differences in the policy preferences of blacks and whites. Examining surveys conducted by thirteen polling organizations from the 1930s on, Shapiro and his colleagues find racial differences of 20–25 percentage points on questions about welfare and redistributive policies.[2] Differences were extremely large even when whites became more supportive of spending on social welfare during the 1960s and again after 1982, seemingly in reaction to the recession and the cutback in social spending during the first two years of the Reagan administration.

Blacks are not alone, of course, in wanting government to do more. Surveys of various ethnic groups conducted in 1982, 1983, and 1984 by the National Opinion Research Center indicate that a fault line in American society now divides Americans of European origin from blacks and Latinos.[3] Nearly as many Latinos as blacks favored a strong national government. Compared with ethnic groups of European background, even those most favorable to government (Americans of Italian and eastern European ancestry), 15–20 percent more of the blacks and Latinos agreed with statements asserting that the government in Washington should "do more to solve our country's problems," "do everything possible to improve the standard of living of all poor Americans," and "reduce the income differences between the rich and the poor." (The least supportive European groups were 30–40 percent less likely than blacks to agree with these statements.)[4]

Racial differences in policy preferences reflect a more basic ideological cleavage. Huber and Form argue that there is a dominant American ideology that includes the following beliefs: the opportunity to get ahead is available to all; therefore, the position of individuals in the stratification system is determined by their personal efforts, traits, and abilities, not by economic and social circumstances. And since people are personally responsible for the rewards they receive, an unequal distribution of rewards across individuals and groups is fair rather than unjust.[5]

Studies that have measured adherence to this ideology show large racial differences.[6] More blacks than whites believe that inequality is influenced by structural features of the economic system and by racial, ethnic, and gender discrimination. Studies conducted in the 1970s show racial differences of 20–30 percentage points in causal interpretations of why some Americans are poor and why there are economic disparities between blacks and whites and between men and women. Blacks more than whites consistently considered social and economic circumstances influential.[7] Their causal attributions for individual and group disparities still differ greatly. Polls conducted in the 1980s, summarized in the magazine *Public Opinion,* show that nearly 40 percent more blacks than whites believe that circumstances beyond a person's control are a more important cause of poverty than lack of effort on the poor person's part; nearly 20 percent more deny that there are jobs available for anyone willing to work and claim instead that poor people have great difficulty finding jobs. More blacks than whites also understand, correctly, that most of the poverty in America is transitory. Twice as many blacks as whites endorsed a statement saying that most poor people move in and out of poverty in a relatively brief period of time.[8]

Unemployment is also explained differently by blacks and whites. A 1986 survey found that 20–30 percent more blacks than whites (depending on the specific question) believe that unavailability of jobs and problems in the economy are more responsible for unemployment than are personal deficiencies of the unemployed themselves.[9] (Of course, with racial differences ranging from 15 to 40 percent across these many measures of ideology, there are many blacks and many whites who agree with each other and form the solid ideological center of America. That fact should not be lost in emphasizing the large racial differences that reliably emerge in opinion polls.)

Psychologists suggest that people are generally biased in favor of individual, dispositional attributions and have difficulty perceiving causes lying in the environment and in social circumstances. They call this a fundamental-attribution bias. Whatever its origin—likely in the different experiences of various groups with constraints in the social structure and in their varying levels of education[10]—this difference in the causal attributions of blacks and whites reflects a basic disagreement about the meaning of individualism and equality.

Blacks, like whites, believe in the importance of the individual, individual rights, and equality of opportunity. They question, however, more than whites do if a theory of justice can be based solely on individualism. In discussions of distributive justice, a distinction is frequently drawn between principles of micro- and macro-justice.[11] Principles of micro-justice define fairness according to a fit between what individuals contribute to a social system and what they obtain from it. The distribution of resources is supposed to be determined entirely by the attributes of individuals. Principles of macro-justice go beyond the individual to an independent concern with the shape of the distribution of resources. They specify a priori constraints on the allowable form or pattern for the overall distribution. Fairness, according to principles of macro-justice, could legitimately include limitations on the range between the highest and lowest incomes or on the size of subgroup differences in income.[12] Most Americans use principles of micro-justice more than principles of macro-justice in deciding what is fair in the economic arena, although a large majority does endorse the idea of an economic floor below which no individual should be allowed to fall.[13]

Completely consistent with individualism and principles of micro-justice, there is widespread agreement among blacks with equality of opportunity—that rewards should be determined by the attributes of individuals, provided everyone starts from a position of equality. The demands of the Civil Rights movement were largely couched in the language of equality of opportunity and were basically in line with individualism.[14] But historically blacks have not had equality of opportunity, and most are convinced that such equality is not yet a reality. Most Americans have yet to recognize that the legal guarantees of equal opportunity cannot easily be taken advantage of by many individuals in groups that have long been denied the very skills and resources needed to compete. Believing that group disparities are produced largely by these historical, structural, and political forces, most blacks want the idea of justice to include a recognition that a just society must be concerned with results as well as opportunity, with the economic as well as political arena, and with group as well as individual equality.

Blacks' awareness of structural and group issues was shown in our survey by their widespread views that discrimination is a powerful force in the lives of black Americans and that collective solutions must be adopted to deal with systemic sources of inequality. This was one component of what we have called group political consciousness. It was also seen in our respondents' concern about group inequalities in political influence. They were nearly united in the view that blacks have too little influence in American life and politics. Their concern, however, was not restricted to blacks. Nine in ten thought poor people too powerless, and seven in ten thought that older people and people on welfare ought to have more power. On the other side of the equation, six in ten said that whites and business executives have too much power in American life. Though the electorate was not of one mind on these matters, one of its unifying strengths was a broadly based adherence to an ideology stressing social determination and greater group equality. This ideology may not have a realistic chance of guiding social policy in America. Nevertheless, the black electorate's sizable agreement on political goals is one of its political strengths. Another is its racial solidarity.

The black electorate's strong political motivation was also evident on measures of psychological resources: interest in politics, sense of political efficacy, and evaluations of the political system. To review briefly, over three-quarters expressed interest in the campaign and in the outcome of the election and also said that they follow public affairs at least some of the time when an election is not under way. Nearly one-half said that the recent victories of black mayoralty candidates as well as the Jackson campaign had aroused their interest in electoral politics. Before the election, nearly all believed that blacks as a group could influence the outcome of both the presidential and local elections, and four-fifths further believed that a coalition comprised of blacks, women, poor people, and other minorities had the potential to be influential. This electorate was incontestably engaged, not alienated.

The impact of the history of betrayal was apparent, however, in respondents' evaluations of the degree to which political institutions can be trusted. Though interested in politics and confident that blacks can influence electoral politics, three-quarters thought that the government cannot be trusted to do what is right and is more likely to represent a few big interests than the interests of all the people. We noted in Chapter Two that a particular combination of beliefs about oneself and the political system—that one or one's group is politically effective but the system is flawed—has been a powerful psychological resource for political outsiders and challengers. The challenge faced by blacks, and other underrepresented groups, is to make the democratic, pluralist ideal a reality. To do that, they need a certain wariness about political institutions as they depend on the power of their personal and collective resources to make political parties and legislative bodies accessible and accountable.

The psychological resources of blacks are impressive when compared with those of whites. On identical questions asked of whites in the NES and of blacks in the NBES, more blacks than whites reported being interested in the campaign and its outcome as well as in public affairs in general. More blacks felt competent to understand politics. Since education and income affect these psychological states, the higher level of interest and personal political efficacy among blacks is even more impressive when comparisons are drawn between blacks and whites with the same family income and the same level of schooling. (See Appendix B.6, Table 3, for comparisons of eight groups— blacks and whites with a family income of less than $10,000, those with a family income of $40,000 and above, those with less than a high school education, and those with at least some college. Also see Appendix B.6, Table 4.)[15] Evaluating the system, blacks were slightly more likely to say that government officials are unresponsive to people like them and considerably more likely to question how much government can be trusted to represent all interests and to do what is right. In brief, these profiles show whites somewhat less interested in politics but more trusting of political institutions and blacks more engaged in politics but also more wary of institutions.

Blacks want an activist national government, although they do not believe that government, unless carefully monitored, will represent the interests of the entire populace. What most Americans take for granted blacks feel cannot be left to chance. Their political history has taught them that they themselves must hold institutions accountable. Needing the intervention of government, they base their hopefulness on shared political goals, racial solidarity, and belief in their collective political influence, not on the benign intentions of political authorities.

This portrait shows a politically engaged, liberal, and policy-oriented electorate that is remarkably involved in politics given its structural disadvantages. Have we painted too vibrant a picture? Is there not more political alienation than what is found in our survey? We have been very careful to adjust for possible biases that may derive from non-coverage of the black population and from response-rate problems. No household survey manages to reach the most deprived and alienated of the society, however. By design, a household survey excludes people living in prisons, mental hospitals, and other residential institutions. Of the non-institutionalized population, some of the most deprived are homeless; others move about, living temporarily with friends and relatives who, not considering them part of their household, fail to include them when asked by survey interviewers to list the people living in the household unit. Young black men are especially likely to be missed when they are not in the labor force and move from place to place. Furthermore, people who do not have telephones are disproportionately poor. And, of course, people in this telephone sample who refused to be interviewed or could not be reached despite repeated attempts may be more alienated than those who were interviewed.

We concede these sources of possible bias. All of the results presented in this book, however, come from analyses in which the major correlates of these biases (especially income and education) are controlled. Furthermore, the study did manage to reach a sample whose demographic characteristics were very similar to the 1980 census estimates for the black population. (The quality of the sample is taken up in detail in Appendix A.) Therefore, while we may have missed the economically worst off and the most disaffected, we managed to interview blacks who are generally representative of the nation's voting-age black population. By and large, this is a politically involved electorate.

PERSEVERANCE AND INDEPENDENCE

It was in the context of hope and betrayal that the impetus for independent institutions and political strategies developed. At the same time that whites were contemplating political independence from England, blacks—those both enslaved and freed—were attempting to gain some measure of independence in a nation that degraded them and made them subservient.

In seeking independence in its most basic form—freedom from slaveholders—blacks pursued independence on both the individual and institutional levels. The historian John Hope Franklin characterizes the early searches for independence as ones that necessarily took place only in the intellectual and spiritual lives of blacks. He notes the efforts of early black writers and scholars—for example, Jupiter Hammon, Phillis Wheatley, Gustavus Vassa, and Benjamin Banneker—to escape their station, if but temporarily, by engaging in pursuits thought unassumable by people of African descent. It was in the struggle for spiritual and intellectual independence that the first independent institution—the black church—emerged.[16]

In an address to the African Methodist Episcopal Church convention in 1946, Bishop Reverdy C. Ransom pointed to the parallelism between the founding of independent black churches and the founding of the independent American republic: "... We appreciate our relationship to our nation's formation and growth. ... In 1787, when the Constitution was being framed in Philadelphia, we were five or six blocks away on Sixth and Lombard, organizing the African Methodist Episcopal Church. As the first lines of the bill proclaiming independence for the United Colonies from Great Britain were struck off, we, too, floated our flag six blocks away for manhood and independence. ..."[17] Peter Paris notes that the same statement applies also to the independent black Baptist churches established in Georgia and South Carolina a few years before the Constitutional Convention.[18]

Eighteenth-century black leaders had found that white religious institutions, like the state, would not welcome blacks into the community. Franklin emphasizes that blacks did not take steps to establish separate churches "until it was obvious they were not welcome in white churches."[19] The founding of the African Methodist Episcopal Church occurred as a consequence of several racist incidents at Saint George's Church in Philadelphia. These incidents included pulling blacks from their knees while they prayed and establishing a segregated gallery for black worshipers. One of those interrupted at prayer was Richard Allen, who had often preached at Saint George's. Along with several others, Allen left that church and formed the first African Methodist Episcopal Church.[20]

The founding of independent fraternal and self-help organizations as well as independent schools for black children followed the establishment of black churches. For the most part, and for obvious reasons, these emerging institutions flourished primarily outside the slaveholding South. Commenting on the importance of this phenomenon for later black political struggle, Franklin wrote:

> It is said that this and similar organizations did much to bind Negroes together and give them experience of leadership and cooperation that was to mean much in a later day. They early sought integration into the political, social and economic life of the nation. Having been rejected, there was no alternative but to forge out of their limited background and training institutions of their own. . . . The Negro's search for independence at the turn of the century was essentially, therefore, a struggle to achieve status in the evolving American civilization.[21]

Independence in black political life would arise from similar circumstances and perform much the same function.[22] We have explored this theme of independence in our multi-method and multi-level approach to the relationship of blacks to the major political parties. In order to understand contemporary black politics better, we examined the theme of independence in the black electorate using historical, survey, and case-based analyses. We conclude that political independence is an enduring part of black politics. Continued racial polarization makes it necessary. Although other ethnic groups have used similar strategies to achieve political empowerment and make socioeconomic gains, they were able to enter mainstream party politics and the so-called American melting pot. The color line, which W. E. B. Du Bois called the problem of the twentieth century, is still an indelible feature of American politics.

The Historical Legacy

Blacks have always challenged the color line by trying to participate in the major parties. Doubtless there were moments of lost opportunity, but the general story is one of a persistent struggle for inclusion, which was met by a persistent response of exclusion. The parties responded in earlier times by trying to disfranchise the Free Negroes and keep them out of party gatherings and in more recent times with indifference to the political concerns of blacks. Shunned and rejected, blacks were forced to establish independent political forums and use protest to influence electoral and party politics. Recognizing the potential power of solidarity and bloc voting, black leaders have felt that if given the vote, the black electorate could provide the "balance of power" in close political contests.

The power of the black vote was recognized as well by the major parties during Reconstruction, when blacks acted on their newly legislated rights and began to vote and run for office. As Reconstruction came to an end, southern blacks were disfranchised through the use of restrictive clauses, literacy tests, poll taxes, and the threat of violence. Forced out of the Republican party, blacks formed satellite parties—for example, the Black and Tans—and tried to convince the Republican national organization and conventions to accept them as the legitimate local organs of the party. Failing in that goal, blacks used their independent parties to maintain some influence on the local level. These satellite parties in all but a few counties disappeared toward the close of the nineteenth century as the black vote was effectively silenced. Outside the South, black participation in parties was confined to clientage relationships on the local level. In the early part of the twentieth century, their numbers were too small to achieve a "balance of power" strategy.

Although the majority of blacks were disfranchised until the middle of this century, they used many other political devices to influence the political system. The range of political behaviors they employed encompasses newly expanded definitions of "legitimate" politics: moral suasion, litigation, political parties, pressure groups, lobbying activities, protest action (both violent and nonviolent), and the vote, when they had it, have all been part of black Americans' struggle for equality and incorporation. The separate institutions and organizations of blacks have provided an infrastructure for what might be termed parallel politics—disorderly or protest politics alongside greatly constrained orderly or regular politics.

This independent political infrastructure continues to be an important resource for black politics. Black churches, historically black colleges, and the black press have been training grounds for black leaders and settings for the political socialization of the masses. Self-help and fraternal organizations have functioned in the same manner. In Chapter One, we described the efforts of men and women in such organizations: they agitated for the abolition of slavery, for the vote, for an end to lynching and other violent acts committed against blacks, for equal rights, and for equal opportunity. Early organizations and political movements lay the foundation for later ones. The post–Revolutionary War African Society and the Black Abolitionist movement as well as the post–Civil War Afro-American League were front-runners of the early-twentieth-century Niagara movement, which led to the foundation of such organizations as the NAACP and the Urban League and, later, to CORE, SNCC, SCLC, and numerous local political groups. Black power and nationalist organizations of the 1960s and 1970s emerged in the tradition of earlier movements, such as Marcus Garvey's Back to Africa movement and Elijah Muhammed's Black Muslims. All of these organizations sought empowerment based on racial solidarity. All but a few—those that were emigrationist and separatist—existed to increase the influence of blacks and bring about political and economic incorporation.

The political movements of the 1960s and 1970s expanded this infrastructure in size and character. As a consequence of the Voting Rights Act, the number of black voters and black elected officials increased dramatically. Despite this new foothold in the electoral arena, the need to define their own political goals and to influence strategy decisions prompted black leaders to form independent caucuses and organizations in a wide range of public- and private-sector institutions. As we noted earlier, these organizations were not separatist. They maintained a sense of community among blacks and functioned to increase black influence in political life and, ultimately, to achieve incorporation into mainstream America. Beyond fostering an independent infrastructure, betrayal necessarily feeds a political ideology of independence based on distrust of whites and cynicism about the institutions of regular politics.

Since the theme of independence once again became important in the 1984 presidential campaign, our survey focused on the Jackson candidacy and a separate black party as contemporary expressions of the struggle to relate to the party system.

Independence in 1984

The 1984 presidential campaign was distinguished from all preceding campaigns by the level and breadth of black participation and the most successful bid by a black presidential candidate. Jesse Jackson relied largely on an independent political infrastructure that mobilized blacks to support him in the primaries in spite of a cool response from many key black Democrats and elected officials. Jackson's attempt to mobilize a Rainbow Coalition of locked-out groups constituted an "insider" independent strategy to exert progressive political influence within the Democratic party. There was also the possibility that he would adopt an "outsider" strategy, mounting an independent bid for the presidency. This election thus presented a unique opportunity to study the theme of black independence in presidential politics.

A number of writers have examined the Jackson candidacy, although few have done so from the perspective of the black electorate. Our study used data from a nationally representative survey of the black electorate to explore two related questions—how blacks evaluated and related to the major parties and how they viewed their political options outside these parties. Analyses using measures of support for Jackson and for a black political voice were used to explore the theme of independence from the viewpoint of the black electorate.

Our analyses demonstrated that support for Jackson and advocacy of a black party and a vote-black strategy were separate themes. Only one measure, intention to vote for Jackson had he run as an independent, was common to both. This statistical separation lent initial support to our original expectation that support for Jackson was an "insider" expression of independence and advocacy of a black political voice an "outsider" expression. Evaluations of the candidates and parties demonstrated, however, that the insider/outsider distinction was not an apt one. The supporters of Jackson and the advocates of an independent voice came from different sectors of the black community and expressed different types of group solidarity, but both were Democratic partisans. Their independence was expressed within the Democratic fold. Neither were political outsiders in the usual sense of the term. Nor did either fit the expectations many Americans developed in the 1960s of black nationalists as separatist, divisive, and dangerous.[23] On the contrary, independence in 1984 was consistent with the longer sweep of history—that, with few exceptions, black political independence has always been aimed at political incorporation.

As we have shown, Jackson was supported by a large majority of the black electorate. Eight in ten voters thought his candidacy a good idea; slightly more than five in ten said they would vote for him if he were to make a presidential bid outside the Democratic party; and two-thirds of those who voted in a primary cast ballots for him. The strongest supporters, more highly educated than others but otherwise drawn from many sectors of the black community, were internal critics of the Democratic party. As supporters of Jackson, they, of course, felt less positively toward the Democratic ticket, although they voted for Walter Mondale in November at the same rate as other blacks. They were critical of the Democratic party's treatment of Jackson and of its lack of responsiveness to issues of concern to blacks, yet they definitely were not potential converts to the Republican party. They had a low regard for Ronald Reagan, the Republican party, and its treatment of blacks. Their approval of an activist federal government and of liberal public policies stood in opposition to the conservative agenda of the Republican party. Political activists, they participated more frequently than others in nearly all activities measured in the survey: petitioning and direct-action forms of protest and both traditional and church-based campaign activities.

In brief, the strongest supporters were politically active people who were ready to support their candidate within the party and to criticize its handling of racial matters. But they were not prepared to turn away from electoral politics, support the Republicans, or leave the Democratic party. Most would surely have voted for an independent Jackson ticket, but they did not see Jackson's candidacy as a step toward an independent party.

Advocacy of a separate black party and a vote-black strategy was much rarer. Only one-quarter of the electorate approved of this kind of independence, and, on average, the strongest support was found among the most disadvantaged of the black electorate. Yet they were not alienated from electoral politics, the party system, or even the Democratic party. In fact, they felt surprisingly positive toward the Democrats. They rated the party ticket, the party itself, and blacks who voted for Mondale more positively than did blacks who were opposed to an independent voice—and also more positively than the strong Jackson supporters. More of the advocates than non-advocates thought that the Democratic party worked hard on black issues and that it treated Jackson the same as it did other candidates. These advocates appeared to be political outsiders only in the sense of being structurally disadvantaged. They were politically powerless blacks seeking to be heard by a party not likely to address their employment, economic, and social needs.

Thus we found not two forms of independence, but two expressions of the same underlying theme—willingness to use strategies of independence to try to make the Democratic party more accountable to the needs of the black population. For some, the strategies included internal criticism of the party and supporting Jackson rather than Mondale in the primaries. For others, they encompassed the apparently more extreme expression of supporting a separate black party and a policy of always voting for black candidates. For both, they involved voting for Jackson if he were to take his candidacy outside the party. Both were "insider" strategies.

Apart from structural differences, the critical distinction between blacks who expressed independence in these two ways was the type of solidarity they felt. The Jackson supporters and advocates of a black political voice were both group-identified. We delineated two types of group identity—one based on a sense of common fate, the other on an exclusive preference for being black rather than American or both black and American. Jackson supporters included people with both types of identity; advocates of an independent voice were primarily people with an exclusivist black identity. The common-fate identity was politicized; the exclusivist identity was not. Both types were pro-black. For the advocates, this pro-black sentiment was accompanied by negative sentiments toward whites. Advocates were less likely to feel close to whites and more likely to feel that most whites want to keep blacks down. A minority of advocates also felt that blacks should avoid whites. The type of solidarity that distinguished the advocates from the non-advocates emphasizes "we versus them" in intergroup relations, limits the policy concerns of the advocates to those explicitly related to race, and limits discontent with a lack of power to that felt by blacks. The politicized sense of common fate found among many Jackson supporters was not exclusivist. It did not preclude a broad political view, a generalized discontent with the relative powerlessness of all locked-out groups, and concern with policies relevant to all minorities and to the nation as a whole.

A Closer View

Our analysis revealed that the advocates of an independent black voice lacked both structural and organizational resources. The breadth and level of their political participation as well as their type of solidarity are consequences of this disadvantaged status. Their exclusivist solidarity cast everything in black and white. Although not personally alienated, the advocates lacked a sense of group political efficacy. Why, then, did they support a black party and a vote-black strategy? An in-depth examination of these advocates in Chapter Five—using quantitative and qualitative analyses—brings the nature of this segment of the black electorate into focus.

In this closer view, we disaggregated the advocates using a case-analysis approach. Although, on average, the advocates lacked the structural and organizational resources that facilitate involvement in politics, roughly one-fifth had the political resources that allowed them to be classified as potential leaders, half because they had both structural and organizational resources, the rest equally split between having one or the other. The remainder of the advocates—the vast majority—had neither.

Seven in ten of these atypical advocates who might be able to provide leadership for a black political voice were also Jackson supporters. Unlike the rest of the advocates, they resembled Jackson supporters in their sense of group efficacy and in their broader political view. The main difference between this group and the Jackson supporters who did not approve of a black party and a vote-black strategy was in the potential leaders' greater centrality of support for government intervention in racial matters and their more negative views of whites.

An examination of the interviews with these potential leaders showed that the group with both structural and organizational resources were younger and more educated than the others. They were more likely to belong to national black organizations and were more active in politics, particularly working for black candidates. Overall, this group of what we called nationally oriented advocates were the most like other Jackson supporters. The group of potential leaders with only organizational resources were older, more likely to live in the South, and especially active in local black organizations and local politics. These potential leaders with a local orientation were, on the whole, loyal old-line Democrats. We called the group with only structural resources, individualistic advocates. In comparison with the other potential leaders and the other advocates, they were opposed to an activist, federal government and in favor of self-help. They were also less discontented with power relationships and more favorable toward the Republican party. For them, advocacy of a black political voice expressed conservative political views. Not involved in the black political infrastructure or in politics generally, they were not even potential leaders but supporters of self-help in its extreme sense—going it alone.

The remainder of the advocates were truly alienated from the political system. They lacked both structural and organizational resources and thus participated minimally; they were less interested in politics and felt less politically competent; and they did not believe in the group's political efficacy. Their principal resource was their strong racial solidarity, although this race-centered solidarity was not politicized.

Our cases revealed that the advocates' strong pro-black sentiments and negative feelings toward whites grew out of the experience of being black in America—what we have called betrayal. A quotation from one of the nationally oriented potential leaders sums up the meaning of independence for the advocates: "White folks never wanted black folks to have anything and they never will. Black folks should take part in everything that goes on in American life, but they will often have to do it separately from whites. In integrated groups, whites inevitably try to take over, and they don't understand or care about policies that would help the black masses."

Continuity and Change

We have examined the development of an independent political infrastructure among blacks as a reaction to the rejection and betrayal of whites. This infrastructure, supporting engagement in both protest and electoral politics, emerged from and reinforces a sense of community and solidarity among blacks. Empowerment and advancement through racial solidarity has been a common theme of most of the institutions and organizations that make up the infrastructure. As Marable, a Marxist analyst of black politics, believes, political incorporation has nearly always been their goal:

> The majority of Afro-American social institutions, from the Black churches to civic associations, were led by Blacks who were at best neutral, and more often than not positively hostile towards any form of racial separatism, whether imposed from without or created from within their communities. Black workers created separate unions, but most labour leaders looked forward to a time when the colour line would not be drawn by the AFL.[24]

Efforts to use the party system have been but one of many political initiatives in black politics. Black leaders have persistently searched for strategies that would make the party system work for the black electorate. Historically, independent strategies included supporting the opposite party (even when it was not congenial to black interests); running independent candidates; taking part in third parties; forming satellite parties within the major parties; creating entirely separate black parties; and rejecting parties altogether. Leaders have urged the black electorate to vote for candidates with the best platform, regardless of party. Broad support for this sentiment has been found also among the electorate. Blacks have rarely exercised this independence at the polls, however. They have been extremely loyal to a single party, and for good reason. For most of the history of party politics in this country, only one major party at a time has even approximately represented the interests of the black electorate.

The historical dilemma persists. Blacks are dependent on the Democratic party, which can take the black vote for granted. Whatever the "new black conservatives" might wish, most of the black electorate does not see the Republican party as an alternative. The electorate's dominant ideology favoring an activist federal government, reduction in the range of inequality, and greater equality between groups is not congenial to the individualistic ideology of the Republican party. Given the size of the black electorate, a concerted mobilization by a separate black party has no chance of electoral success, and blacks understandably fear that support for a black party will negate the impact of the black vote. Of course, blacks now participate in both elections and the Democratic party in numbers unimaginable before the Voting Rights Act was passed in 1965. But they have not managed to turn their participation into an effective use of the party system to make government more accountable to their collective interests.

The two expressions of independence found in 1984 in support for Jackson and for a black party and a vote-black strategy must be seen in the context of this continuing dilemma. Some might ask whether either was truly an expression of independence, since both were found among Democratic partisans. We believe they both were. The strong Jackson supporters showed independence by voting in the primaries for a candidate many key black Democrats and black public officials did not endorse. Independence was most evident among those who voted in the earliest primaries, before it was clear that Jackson would become one of the three major Democratic contenders. The strong Jackson supporters also expressed an independent-minded criticism of the party's level of response to black concerns. Unless the Democratic party becomes far more committed to policies that will address the economic and educational problems of the have-nots, these politically active, policy-oriented blacks who supported Jackson will continue to be the party's critics. The distrust of whites and the race-centered identities of the black-voice advocates will continue to be fueled by a political economy that provides primarily low-wage jobs to blacks, fails to educate young black people, and tolerates racial invective. The economic and political situation will have to change if distrust and wariness are to disappear.

In our view, these sentiments could lead a large proportion of the black electorate to support an independent presidential candidate if certain political conditions were present. Both of the major parties would have to nominate candidates perceived by blacks as not noticeably different from each other with respect to concern for racial justice and poor Americans. In other words, neither of the candidates would possibly be seen by blacks as a lesser of two evils. An attractive third candidate, reacting in the same manner as the black electorate to the choices of the major parties, would have to take his or her candidacy outside the Democratic party. According to Walters, the final and most important factor would be a resocialization of both black leaders and the electorate to a strategy of independent leverage. These conditions did not exist in 1984.[25]

Despite somewhat different political conditions in 1988, four obstacles discussed throughout this book still limit the effectiveness of party politics for blacks. First, in most districts they lack the numbers to have a telling influence on the vote. Second, they are as dependent now on a single party as they ever were. Third, the racial divisions that have affected the vote ever since the 1960s are persisting features of party and electoral politics. Jackson's white support in 1988, though larger than in 1984, came from only 12 percent of white primary voters. In 1988, race was the decisive factor in Democratic voting patterns, not just in southern states on Super Tuesday but also in most northern states. Exit and other opinion polls detailed a sizable negative vote against Jackson. The final breakdown of Jackson's and Michael Dukakis's supporters showed not only a huge racial division but also that Dukakis owed a great deal to the ethnic factor. His campaign, which heavily stressed winning support from Catholics and Jews, won 60 percent of the Catholic vote, 75 percent of the Jewish vote, but just 43 percent of the white Protestant vote.[26] These figures dramatically support our conclusion that ethnic politics are alive and well in the United States, as they are throughout the world. Black solidarity is one instance; the white ethnic support for Dukakis is another; and behind these divisions are different perceptions of the causes of and solutions for group inequalities.

The fourth and most important continuing political liability for the black electorate is the nation's general conservatism. The individualism expressed by the general public limits campaign rhetoric and the government's capacity to pursue policies that blacks believe are in their collective interest. This individualism and its expression in political conservatism became a strong political force in the 1970s. Although support for a broader role did begin to increase after 1982, Americans still favor limited action by the federal government. The conservative political climate constrains the degree to which the Democratic party feels it can afford to respond to policies preferred by the majority of the black electorate and by the more progressive of the white Democrats.

The Democratic party's electoral strategy for 1988 represented the impact of the dominant political culture on the black electorate's relationship to party politics. It focused on conservative Independents and Democrats who voted for Reagan in 1984. The calculation that the Democrats could win the 1988 presidential race by courting swing groups proved incorrect. But in a choice between white defectors and

loyal blacks, the party now, as always, steers a course more sympathetic to whites than to blacks. And thus the party's strategy for 1988
symbolized the black electorate's continuing dilemma in the ongoing
story of blacks in electoral and party politics.

Notes

1. Hamilton 1973, 245–246.
2. See Shapiro and Patterson 1986; Patterson, Young, and Shapiro 1986; and Shapiro
   et al. 1987a, 1987b.
3. Glazer 1984, 2.
4. See *Public Opinion* 1984, 26–27. It is likely that Latinos would have disagreed
   among themselves had the survey assessed separately the opinions of those of
   Cuban, Puerto Rican, and Mexican origin.
5. Huber and Form 1973.
6. See Kluegel and Smith (1981) for a review of studies investigating Americans'
   beliefs about stratification and, especially, adherence to an individualistic
   ideology.
7. See Gurin and Morrison 1976; Gurin, Gurin, and Morrison 1978.
8. *Public Opinion* 1985, 2, 3, 28.
9. See Cook, Barrett, and Popkin (1987) for a report of a survey conducted in 1986
   showing differences in causal attributions. Lichter (1985), reporting on a 1985
   survey of a random sample of six hundred blacks, presents a portrait of black
   attitudes that is considerably different from that in most other surveys. It reveals
   less awareness of structural obstacles, greater approval of individualism, and an
   altogether more conservative electorate than either we or others have found. Estimates can vary, of course, depending on sampling procedures.
10. Formal schooling increases awareness of systemic sources of inequality for both
    whites and blacks, although few other demographic factors or adult experiences
    seem to be influential among whites. Running into market constraints and per-
    sonal discrimination affects the attributions given by blacks, however. (See Gurin
    and Morrison 1976.) The impact of these social factors indicates that the funda-
    mental-attribution bias cannot be entirely the result of universal, cognitive pro-
    cesses. In their own kind of dispositional bias, psychologists have overemphasized
    the significance of cognitive factors and de-emphasized the role of cultural
    ideologies and structural factors in explaining the fundamental-attribution bias.
11. See Brickman et al. 1980, 2.
12. Mark (1980) gives examples of macro-justice: "The resource allotment of the best-
    off shall not exceed three times the resource allotment of the least-off"; "no one's
    resource allotment shall fall below one half the median resource allotment";
    "resources shall be distributed normally" (pp. 6, 8). And the second principle
    offered by Rawls (1971) to provide a more egalitarian theory of justice is about the
    shape of the results of distribution: "Social and economic inequalities are to be
    arranged so that they are . . . to the greatest benefit of the least advantaged" (p. 83).

13. See Verba and Orren 1985. They declare, "Floors and ceilings, by definition, violate the sanctity of individual achievement associated with equality of opportunity. Each tampers with the hierarchy that individual effort would produce. A ceiling, however, is likely to be seen as the greater affront to the value of individual achievement" (p. 6).

14. Of course, the political demands made by the Civil Rights movement for protection of the voting rights of blacks reflected the one area where all Americans subscribe to principles of macro-justice—that regardless of property, education, or wealth, each person is to have one vote. "Americans have always been more egalitarian in the political than in the economic realm. In politics the idea is democracy and one person, one vote. . . . In economics, by contrast, the dominant norm is capitalism, a system in which income and other rewards accrue to talent and effort" (Verba and Orren 1985, 8). Drawing together comparative studies of political and economic equality, Verba and Orren show that the United States ranks first, second, or third among fourteen nations on all but one of twelve indicators of political equality but near the bottom on a ranking of indicators of economic equality (1985; see Tables 1.1 and 1.2). Hochschild (1981) also argues that arenas must be considered if we are to understand how Americans conceive of justice. Justice, she argues, involves two sets of principles: equality, an assumption that all people may legitimately make the same claims on social resources; and differentiation, an assumption that people may legitimately make varying claims on social resources. Both principles are applied in three arenas: political, social, and economic. She suggests that most Americans favor principles of equality and apply egalitarian norms in the political and social arenas but favor principles of differentiation and mainly use differentiating norms in the economic arena.

15. Differences were also found between the blacks in our study and those in the 1984 NES. These differences persist even after controlling for characteristics of the respondents affected by telephone non-coverage and non-response and for race of the interviewer. Net of the effects of age, education, income, gender, region, and race of interviewer, NBES blacks had stronger psychological resources than did NES blacks. Our estimates of the psychological resources of blacks are more reliable, since they are based on a much larger sample size than the N of 250 blacks in the NES. After controlling for age and education, blacks and whites in the NES exhibited approximately the same level of interest in politics, although blacks were more likely to feel that the system is unresponsive and to distrust government. (See Appendix B.6, Table 4.)

16. Franklin [1947] 1987.

17. Ransom, cited in Paris 1985, 107.

18. Ibid.

19. Franklin [1947] 1987, 94.

20. Ibid.

21. Ibid., 95.

22. Paris (1985) describes the independent institutions forged by blacks as surrogate worlds that maintained the spiritual, social, and political life of blacks until they could become part of the larger society.

23. Ironically, whites, who long tolerated segregation as a way to keep blacks in their place, have consistently condemned blacks' expressions of solidarity in their bid for inclusion as examples of reverse racism.

24. Marable 1985, 57.

25. Supporting an independent candidate is not synonymous with independent leverage as defined by Walters (1988). That strategy begins within the party during the primary and pre-convention phases of a presidential campaign. A candidate supported by the black electorate can have enough delegates to affect the convention's choice, the party's platform, and nominations to the party's leadership. When this kind of bargaining fails, however, independent leverage may involve supporting an independent candidate. Walters notes that the internal bargaining and especially the mounting of an independent race depend on black leaders and the electorate rejecting the strategy of dependent leverage, even as a lesser of two evils.
26. *New York Times*, July 13, 1988.

Methodological Issues in Telephone Surveys of Black Americans: The 1984 National Black Election Study

$\mathbf{T}$HE DECISION TO CONDUCT a large national study of the black electorate by telephone raised a number of methodological concerns. The overarching issue was the feasibility of such a study given that blacks comprise only about 12 percent of the national population. How could we efficiently screen and locate a representative sample of black Americans? We also faced possible biases stemming from population non-coverage, non-response, and race-of-interviewer effects. Although these concerns have to be addressed regardless of the target population, they take on special significance in studies of racial minorities.[1] Despite these problems, a national study of the black electorate was especially timely in 1984. Although the National Election Studies (NES) have been an important resource for data on the general electorate during the last forty years, there has been no large-scale study of black Americans.[2] The typical NES sample yields only 150–200 blacks, too few to allow for a study of their political attitudes, beliefs, and behavior.

In addition to the paucity of research on blacks, several other aspects of the 1984 presidential race made a study like the National Black Election Study (NBES) important. Reagan, the incumbent president running for reelection, had threatened the legal and socioeconomic gains of blacks. Jackson, a black man, was seen by some as trying to combine the protest politics of the 1960s with partisan politics in his race against Mondale, an old-line liberal, for the Democratic nomination. All of this took place in the context of recent electoral victories for black mayors in the nation's largest cities. The victory most proximate to the 1984 election was that of Harold Washington in Chicago, the third largest city in the country. Feeling the time was right for a large-scale study of the black electorate but wary of the cost of face-to-face interviews, we turned to the telephone survey.

The 1984 NBES was conducted by the Program for Research on Black Americans at the Institute for Social Research (ISR) at the University of Michigan. Following the design of the well-known NES conducted by the Center for Political Studies (CPS) at the ISR, respondents were contacted both before and after the November presidential election. Altogether 1,151 respondents of voting age were interviewed by telephone in the pre-election survey, 871 of whom were reinterviewed after the election. The response rates before and after the election were 58 percent and 76 percent, respectively (if disconnected or other untraceable numbers are excluded, the post-election response rate is 81 percent). This national sample of blacks was drawn using random digit dial (RDD) methods with a two-stage cluster design.[3]

As noted above, the methodological challenges presented by the NBES stemmed from the feasibility of conducting a high-quality yet cost-efficient RDD telephone survey of black Americans. Subsumed under the general feasibility question were questions regarding the procedures to be used for screening to find black households, the rate of eligibility (the number of telephone numbers that had to be screened to yield the desired number of blacks with working numbers), as well as the effects of population non-coverage, non-response, and race of the interviewer. In this appendix, we discuss how we addressed each concern in the NBES sample, questionnaire design, and interviewing methodology.

SCREENING FOR RACE AND RATE OF ELIGIBILITY

A pilot survey was conducted in February and March of 1984 to estimate the rate of eligibility and the feasibility of screening blacks by telephone. Pre-pilot estimates suggested that only about 2–2.5 percent of all possible primary numbers screened would be working numbers in households with blacks. (Only about 20–25 percent of all numbers are working household numbers.)[4] Although this rate was low, it was thought that black eligibility would be increased in the secondary numbers by using only primary numbers belonging to black households. We assumed that the clustering found in racially segregated residential areas would be replicated to some extent in numbers generated from these black primary numbers, since geographic location is often a factor when assigning telephone numbers.

For the pilot, all telephone exchanges in the United States were assigned to one of three "black household density" strata. These strata were as follows:

1. High black density—exchanges in all large standard metropolitan statistical areas (SMSAs; those with black density of 15 percent or more)
2. Medium black density—exchanges in small SMSAs and non-SMSAs in Alabama, Florida, Georgia, Louisiana, Mississippi, North Carolina, South Carolina, and Virginia
3. Low black density—all remaining exchanges

The pilot consisted of two parts, each with a different sample design. In the first, primary numbers were sampled from each stratum with equal probability; in the second, primary numbers were sampled with disproportionate probability from strata 1 and 2 only. The experimental design also addressed eligibility across three different number series at the secondary stage—100, 200, and 400.[5]

The result of the pilot showed that a combination of disproportional sampling of the three strata and the use of number series generated from the primaries beyond 100 significantly reduced the costs of sampling and screening. These gains were accompanied by a small loss in precision, however.[6]

Based on the pilot findings, we utilized a disproportionate probability design for the NBES. All households with at least one black occupant and a working telephone number were eligible. The selection rate for the high density stratum of primary numbers was three times that for the low density stratum. The rate for the medium density stratum was twice that for the low density stratum. Thus the appropriate weights equal the stratum number. The 200 number series was used to generate the secondary numbers. The overall Waksberg cluster size was 7.5 and included the primary number.

Given the disproportionate probability design, weighting is necessary when presenting point estimates such as proportions or means. Weighting in more complex statistical analyses is subject to debate—some argue that non-equal probability sampling schemes do not affect the underlying relationships estimated, for example through regression techniques;[7] others feel that failure to take into account the non-randomness of the sample could lead to misspecified models and thus to misleading conclusions. Regardless, weighted data should not be used to estimate significance levels, since the sample size is artificially manipulated.

DuMouchel and Duncan found that although weighted estimates can differ from unweighted ones, the differences are not significant.[8] If weighted estimates differ sharply from unweighted estimates, the model should be scrutinized for possible problems of misspecification. In the case of small differences, unweighted estimates are preferred.

The compromise we adopted for this book estimates both un-weighted and weighted models in all multivariate analyses. We found very small differences between the two. The tables summarizing multivariate analyses present results for the unweighted model. All means and percentages shown in the tables not involving multivariate analyses are based on the weighted N.

The racial composition of a household was determined by including a direct question about race in the screening process. In the pilot, two screening forms were tested, one long and one short. The long form included several attitude questions in addition to one about the household's racial composition. The short form included only the introduction by the interviewer, the standard screening questions to determine whether the number belonged to a business or a household, and the racial-composition question. The following question was used to determine whether there were eligible black adults in the household:

> Would you mind telling me your race? Are you white, black, American Indian or Alaskan Native, Asian or Pacific Islander?

After this question, we asked the number of persons aged 18 and older in the household. If there was more than one person in this age category in the household, the informant was then asked whether all of the other adults in the household were of the same race and, if not, what race they were. Households with at least one black adult were eligible for the NBES. Although interviewers did not explain why racial identity was asked, respondents answered without hesitation. Additionally, because no differences in response rate were found between the two forms, the shorter one was used in the final study.

POPULATION NON-RESPONSE AND UNDERCOVERAGE

Two other concerns, non-response and undercoverage, affected the final sample's representativeness. Both are issues in any survey, although they are particularly problematic in telephone studies. Population undercoverage results from households with nonworking phones or without phones altogether. Non-response, which includes refusals and non-interviews due to health problems, disability, language problems, or absence from the home over the duration of the study, is largely a function of respondent characteristics or behavior. Nonetheless, non-response is consistently lower for telephone surveys than for face-to-face interviews.[9] In this section, we discuss the potential bias that could result from the separate and combined effects of undercoverage and non-response and how these were addressed in the NBES. Finally, we evaluate the representativeness of the final NBES sample by comparing it with 1980 census data.

Non-response

Until recently, response rates in telephone surveys (varying from 50 to 70 percent) were consistently lower than those in face-to-face surveys. As the face-to-face rates have declined overall and particularly in urban areas, the two sets of rates have converged. Response rates, regardless of interview mode, present special problems for researchers. When as many as one-half to two-fifths of the respondents selected in a sample are not interviewed, the representativeness of the survey is threatened.

In face-to-face interviews, non-respondents are likely to be older and middle class; they also tend to reside in large urban areas and reside in the West.[10] This characterization, based on only a few studies, may not be conclusive. The characteristics of non-respondents in telephone surveys are even less well known. Thornberry and Massey have estimated response rates for different subgroups in the 1981 National Health Interview that was conducted by telephone.[11] The elderly, blacks, and persons with lower levels of education had disproportionately lower rates of response. Response rates differ not only by population subgroup and interview mode but also by the substantive content of the study. Steeh reports that election studies have higher non-response rates than other studies do.[12] For these reasons, the pilot served an additional purpose—that of assessing the degree of discrepancy in response rates between a black election survey and typical surveys conducted by the telephone facility of the Survey Research Center.

The response rate in the pilot was 57 percent (an average of 53 percent in the equal probability section and 60 percent in the disproportionate probability section). The 58 percent response rate attained in the pre-election wave of the final study was, therefore, nearly the same as in the pilot. This rate is comparable to that achieved in other telephone surveys conducted by the SRC during the same time period. The study most similar to the NBES, the 1984 NES telephone survey carried out during the primaries and up to the election (called the Continuous Monitoring Study), achieved a rate of 62 percent. The response rate for the 1984 pre-election NES conducted in face-to-face interviews was 71 percent. The NES post-election reinterview used both face-to-face and telephone interviews; respondents were assigned randomly to the two modes. Both modes achieved a reinterview rate of 83 percent. Recontact rates are generally higher than initial interview rates. Because the 1984 NES response rates are not available by race, we are unable to discern whether our response rates differed from the rates obtained for blacks in the NES.

Potential bias from non-response is a concern in all of these studies and must be taken into account during the analysis of data by controlling characteristics associated with non-response—age, income, region, and urbanicity.

Undercoverage

Like non-response, telephone undercoverage is not distributed equally across the population and thus is the source of another potential bias. Estimates of the number of households without telephones range from 6.9 to 7.4 percent of the general population.[13] Non-telephone households are more likely to be located in the South, particularly in small urban and rural areas, and occupied by persons who are under age 35, single (never married, separated, or divorced), less educated, and in a lower income bracket. Non-coverage is also greater for black households: approximately 15.5 percent of black households are estimated to be without working telephones. Thus undercoverage is potentially a serious problem in telephone surveys of blacks. Nonetheless, the demographic distribution of persons interviewed in the NBES is reasonably similar to the estimates for blacks in the 1980 census. This shows that bias from undercoverage and non-response is actually not great and can easily be adjusted in data analysis. (See below.)

We used two strategies, both involving questionnaire construction, to investigate the characteristics of blacks not covered in the NBES. One approach, replicating questions asked in the NES face-to-face interviews, allowed us to assess possible attitudinal and background differences between black respondents in telephone and non-telephone households. This is similar to using a dual-frame design, in which an RDD phone sample is supplemented with an area probability sample.[14] The second approach involved asking respondents in the NBES if peo-

ple without phones ever used their telephones and about the characteristics of anyone who did. This allowed us to estimate the similarities
and differences between people with and without telephones.

Table A.1 shows selected characteristics of the NES black respondents in telephone and non-telephone households. The presence
of a telephone was determined in the NES pre-election survey; 77
percent had telephones. This non-coverage rate is larger than the
15 percent estimated for blacks by the National Health Survey.[15] The
results in Table A.1 show, as expected, that respondents in non-
telephone households are disproportionately young, not well educated,
and poor. Consistent with their lower incomes, they are also somewhat more likely to be women. Renters are also less likely than home-
owners to have telephones.

What did our second approach reveal about undercoverage? We
asked the following question of the NBES respondents:

> We realize there are a lot of people who do not have phones in their homes.
> These people sometimes use the telephones of family, friends or neigh-
> bors. Is there someone like that who uses your telephone?

Nearly one-fifth of our respondents answered yes to this question, and
of these 59 percent said that two or more persons used their phone. The
majority said that these phone users were neighbors; the remainder
were friends or relatives. Of the persons using the phones of these
respondents, 21 percent were reported as living in the same building;
41 percent, in the same block; 28 percent, in the same neighborhood;
and only 10 percent, in areas at a greater distance from the respondents' homes.

Table A.2 shows selected characteristics of the NBES respondents
whose telephones were used by others and of those whose phones were
not used by others. The former were younger, less educated, in a lower
income bracket, single, and residing in a small town or rural area,
particularly in the South. These are the same characteristics as those
found in studies of non-coverage for persons without telephones. Thus
blacks without telephones appear to use the phones of persons who are
in circumstances similar to their own and who share with them a
number of demographic and socioeconomic characteristics.

All in all, these two approaches for estimating the characteristics of
households without telephones yielded evidence consistent with other
studies. The main difference between phone and non-phone households is socioeconomic. Therefore controlling for household income
and education in our analyses should have reduced bias from the ef-

APPENDIX A, TABLE 1

Socioeconomic and Demographic Characteristics of Phone and Non-Phone Black Households in the 1984 NES

		Phone (158)	Non-Phone (48)
A.	*Age*		
	18–29	30.1%	51.0%
	30–39	19.3	14.9
	40–49	15.4	10.6
	50–59	10.8	6.4
	60–69	12.2	14.9
	70 or More	12.2	2.2
		100.0%	100.0%
B.	*Education*		
	0–8	14.6%	12.5%
	9–11	19.5	29.2
	12	32.3	35.4
	13–15	22.2	16.6
	16+	11.4	6.3
		100.0%	100.0%
C.	*Gender*		
	Men	39.2%	27.1%
	Women	60.8	72.9
		100.0%	100.0%
D.	*Family Income*		
		38.6%	50.0%
		20.8	18.8
		16.5	8.3
		11.4	2.1
		5.7	2.0
	(Refused/not ascertained)	7.0	18.8
		100.0%	100.0%
E.	*Home Ownership*		
	Own Home	38.0%	18.8%
	Rent	59.5	79.2
	Other Arrangements	2.5	2.0
		100.0%	100.0%

APPENDIX A, TABLE 2
Selected Characteristics of Respondents Who Said Someone Not Living with Them Used Their Telephone

		Non-Household Residents Use R's Phone	
		Yes 206	*No* 925
A.	*Gender*		
	Men	33.3%	38.9%
	Women	66.7	61.1
		100.0%	100.0%
B.	*Age**		
	18–24	26.0%	18.3%
	25–34	33.2	27.7
	35–54	26.6	30.3
	55–64	5.6	10.8
	65–91	8.6	12.9
		100.0%	100.0%
C.	*Years of Education**		
	0–11	32.6%	26.7%
	12	34.2	30.1
	13–15	23.5	25.9
	16+	9.7	17.3
		100.0%	100.0%
D.	*Total Household Income**		
	Less than $10,000	38.9%	29.9%
	$10,000–19,999	36.1	29.8
	$20,000–29,999	14.6	17.2
	$30,000 and Above	10.4	23.1
		100.0%	100.0%
E.	*Region and Size of Place of Residence**		
	South: Small Towns, Rural	32.6%	23.6%
	South: Small Cities/Suburb	20.4	15.6
	South: Large City	14.4	17.6
	Non-South: Small Town, Rural	3.9	4.1
	Non-South: Small City/Suburb	8.9	12.0
	Non-South: Large City	19.8	27.1
		100.0%	100.0%
F.	*Marital Status**		
	Married	30.2%	42.9%
	Divorced/Separated/Widowed	35.5	29.3
	Never Married	34.3	27.8
		100.0%	100.0%

Note: Percentages shown are based on weighted data.
* Unweighted.

fects of undercoverage. All of the analyses presented in this book systematically used such controls.

THE SAMPLE'S REPRESENTATIVENESS

Although not perfect, one strategy for assessing the possible bias in the
NBES owing to the joint effects of undercoverage and non-response is
to compare the characteristics of the NBES respondents with census
estimates of non-institutionalized blacks aged 18 and older. (See Table
A.3.) Overall, the NBES sample is not greatly different from the 1980
census estimates. Educational differences are the largest, while differences in religion, income, gender, and marital status are quite small.
Since people with a lower education are less likely to have telephones
and more likely to be non-respondents in telephone surveys, blacks
with less than a high school education were underrepresented in the
NBES.

Some characteristics associated with non-coverage differ from those
associated with non-response. For example, telephone undercoverage
is greater among those under age 35, and non-response is greater among
both those under age 25 and those aged 65 and older. The joint effects
may compensate for each other, and this may explain why the age
distribution of the NBES sample does not differ much from that of the
census. A second example involves household income. Lower income
persons are more likely not to have telephones, while middle and up-
per income persons are more likely to be among a survey's non-respondents (at least in the face-to-face mode). This may explain why the
NBES and census income distributions are fairly similar.

Gender differences are more complicated. It could be argued that the
census is not a good gauge for estimating the gender breakdown of the
black population, since the census is criticized for undercounting
black men (despite various compensatory strategies used in 1980). The
high rates of mortality and institutional incarceration among black
men affect the census and all sample surveys. Nonetheless, the NBES
has a more discrepant sex ratio than the census. Other national household probability samples of the black population also end up with a
ratio similar to that of the NBES.[16] Indeed, the 1984 NES has essentially the same proportions of black men and women as the NBES. (See
Table A.1.) The gender discrepancy produced for blacks in household
sample surveys needs to be studied. In particular, the impact of various
methodologies for household listings and respondent selection should
be examined to ascertain what effect, if any, the increasing number of

APPENDIX A, TABLE 3
Selected Characteristics of NBES Respondents Compared To Those of Noninstitutionalized Black Population, 18 Years Old and Older in 1980 Census

		NBES (weighted)	1980 Census
A.	*Age*		
	18–24	20.1%	18.2%
	25–34	28.5	26.2
	35–54	29.4	30.7
	55+	22.0	24.9
		100.0%	100.0%
B.	*Gender*		
	Men	37.8%	43.8%
	Women	62.2	56.2
		100.0%	100.0%
C.	*Years of Education*		
	0–11	28.1%	45.8%
	12	30.9	31.8
	13–15	25.3	15.0
	16+	15.7	7.4
		100.0%	100.0%
D.	*Region*		
	South	59.4%	52.5%
	Non-South	40.6	47.5
		100.0%	100.0%
E.	*Total Household Income*		
	Less than $10,000	32.8%	40.4%
	$10,000–$19,999	30.5	26.3
	$20,000–$29,999	16.4	18.4
	$30,000–$39,999	10.8	8.9
	$40,000+	9.5	6.0
		100.0%	100.0%
F.	*Marital Status*		
	Married	40.6%	45.2%
	Widowed	11.8	9.5
	Divorced/Separated	18.7	16.9
	Not Married	28.9	28.4
		100.0%	100.0%
G.	*Labor Force Participation*		
	Working	53.8%	54.2%
	Unemployed/Not in Labor Force	47.2	45.8
		100.0%	100.0%

female-headed households among the black population has on sampling in household surveys.

In brief, the overall bias in our final sample is smaller than we had expected. Our distributions are similar enough to those of the census that the strategy of controlling for age, gender, education, income, urbanicity, and region in all data analyses should have produced reasonable estimates of distributions and relationships for the black population.

EFFECTS OF THE INTERVIEWER'S RACE

Response differences on racially sensitive items stemming from cross-racial interviewing have been found for white as well as for black respondents and in telephone as well as in face-to-face interviews.[17] Cotter, Cohen, and Coulter suggest two reasons why race may have little or no effect in telephone surveys.[18] First, the interviewer is not visible; and second, even if race is discerned, the relative distance and anonymity of the telephone mutes a respondent's need to avoid offending an interviewer. These investigators did not ask questions pertaining to racially sensitive areas, however. Moreover, it is not customary in telephone surveys to ask respondents what race they think the interviewer is. Instead, the actual race of the interviewer is used in examining its effect on survey responses. Since the psychological impact is the critical issue, it is important to know what the respondent believed the interviewer to be. We attempted to measure the respondent's perception by asking the following question, which appeared at the end of the pre-election survey:

> We'd like to find out what kinds of things people can tell just from listening to a person's voice over the telephone. During the interview did you think I was white, black or someone of another race?

Nearly all respondents (94 percent) were willing to classify the interviewer by race.

Because the NBES was a study of political attitudes, including support for Jackson's bid for the Democratic presidential nomination, most of the questions had explicit or implicit racial content. Therefore they were unusually susceptible to race-of-interviewer effects, and, indeed, Hatchett found that responses to a large number of items differed according to the perceived race of the interviewer.[20] The vast majority of these items contained material that some people might consider potentially offensive or threatening to whites. For example,

respondents interviewed by whites were less likely than those interviewed by blacks to give responses that were militant, pro-black, or
anti-white. For this reason, the results presented in this book are consistently controlled for perceived race of interviewer.

Race or Place?

Because the SRC's telephone facility was overloaded, half of the interviews were conducted by a private research firm. The SRC had both
white and black interviewers (the latter a minority); the private firm,
exclusively black interviewers. The race-of-interviewer effects may,
therefore, have resulted from differences in the training and experience
and the demographic and socioeconomic characteristics of the two
staffs. We checked this possibility, carrying out the race-of-interviewer
analyses with respondents interviewed only by the SRC interviewers
to see whether these effects would be found even in a highly trained
staff. Although there were fewer significant effects, there were still
differences between the responses of people interviewed by blacks and
those of people interviewed by whites.

SUMMARY AND IMPLICATIONS

We have discussed several methodological challenges presented by a
national RDD telephone survey of black Americans—screening for
blacks, rate of eligibility, population non-coverage, non-response, and
race-of-interviewer effects. For the most part, the small pilot study,
conducted early in 1984, was the main vehicle for addressing these
issues. Results from this pilot aided in the design of both the sample
and the questionnaires for the final study.

We found that screening for race was relatively easy, and that a
disproportionate two-step RDD sampling design that included the 200
number series in the secondary stage was a cost-efficient design with a
tolerable loss in precision. This design, however, requires the use of
weights in the presentations of percentages and means and the evaluation of the impact of weighting on estimates in more complex statistical analyses.

The social and demographic characteristics of our respondents
proved to be fairly representative of the census estimates of the nation's black population. Despite this, our assessment of potential
biases from non-coverage, non-response, and race-of-interviewer effects suggests that gender, age, income, education, urbanicity, region,
and race of interviewer should be controlled in data analyses. We have

done that systematically. Of course, the precautions we have taken should be followed in all studies. All in all, the various strategies and assessments described above produced a sample and data set whose quality is comparable to that of other studies of the American electorate.

Notes

1. See Jackson, Tucker, and Bowman 1982; Jackson and Hatchett 1986; and Tourangeau and Smith 1985.
2. Several ongoing studies of public opinion have had oversamples of blacks, most notably the National Election Studies conducted by the Center for Political Studies at the University of Michigan and the General Social Survey conducted by the National Opinion Research Center. This oversampling has not been done on a continuing basis, however.
3. Waksberg 1978.
4. Groves and Kahn 1979.
5. In Inglis, Groves, and Heeringa (1987) appears the following example: "The number series 764-4424 is a member of the 4400–4499 hundred series, 4400–4599 two hundred series and the 4400–4799 four hundred series."
6. See ibid. for a more detailed discussion of the pilot sample and the final sample for the pre-election study.
7. Draper and Smith 1966.
8. DuMouchel and Duncan 1983.
9. Groves and Kahn 1979.
10. Hawkins 1977; DeMaio 1980.
11. Thornberry and Massey 1983.
12. Steeh 1981.
13. Thornberry and Massey 1983.
14. Groves and Lepkowski 1982.
15. Thornberry and Massey 1983.
16. Jackson and Hatchett 1986.
17. Schuman and Converse 1971; Hatchett and Schuman 1975–1976.
18. Cotter, Cohen, and Coulter 1982.
19. Ibid.
20. Hatchett 1987.

APPENDIX B

Supplementary Tables

APPENDIX B.2, TABLE 1
Demographic and Structural Effects on Organizational Resources

Characteristics and Resources	Attend a Church Frequently		Attend a Church Involved in Election	
	r	B	r	B
Age: older	.145	.125**	−.007	.064
Education	.013	.057	.169	.152***
Family income	−.029	−.010	.109	.066
Employment status: full-time	−.083	−.053	.074	.041
Receiving Social Security	.110	.055	−.010	.024
Receiving other welfare	.066	.087*	−.003	.040
Gender: female	.189	.194***	.086	.116*
Region: non-South	−.107	−.095**	−.024	−.021
Urbanicity	−.068	.029	−.037	.005
R^2	—	8.7%	—	16.9%****

Note: Regressions are based on the 871 respondents who participated in both the pre- and post-election surveys.

$*p < .05.$ $**p < .01.$ $***p < .001.$ $****p < .0001.$

APPENDIX B.2, TABLE 2
Demographic and Structural Effects on Solidarity: Identity

Characteristics and Resources	Feel a Sense of Common Fate		Being Black More Important Than Having Dual Identity	
	r	B	r	B
Age: older	−.047	.023	−.102	−.082**
Education	.261	.211***	.055	.026
Family income	.242	.110**	.002	.037
Employment status: full-time	.149	.050	−.033	−.096**
Receiving Social Security	−.040	.060	−.031	−.027
Receiving other welfare	−.115	−.005	.062	.027
Marital status: married	.098	.017	.047	.040
Gender: female	−.155	−.125***	−.036	−.040
Region: non-South	.067	.067	.018	.046
Urbanicity	.025	−.041	−.024	−.042
R^2	—	11.1%****	—	2.8%**

Note: Regressions are based on the 871 respondents who participated in both the pre- and post-election surveys.

$**p < .01.$ $***p < .001.$ $****p < .0001.$

280

Characteristics and Resources	Belong to an Organization to Help Blacks	
	r	*B*
Age: older	.095	.219***
Education	.308	.262***
Family income	.296	.183***
Employment status: full-time	.130	.013
Receiving Social Security	−.066	.042
Receiving other welfare	.075	.040
Gender: female	.058	.016
Region: non-South	.050	.021
Urbanicity	.081	.005
R^2	—	16.8%****

APPENDIX B.2, TABLE 3
Demographic and Structural Effects on Solidarity: Political Consciousness

Characteristics and Resources	Discontented with Power of Blacks		Discontented with Power of Subordinates	
	r	B	r	B
Age: older	.065	.078*	−.050	−.030
Education	.108	.116**	.141	.104**
Family income	.140	.095*	.132	.088*
Employment status: full-time	−.057	−.064	.045	.008
Receiving Social Security	−.013	−.007	−.015	.040
Receiving other welfare	−.068	−.047	−.028	.003
Marital status: married	.063	.061	.057	.043
Gender: female	−.021	−.037	.070	.094**
Region: non-South	.085	.024	.119	.142****
Urbanicity	.007	.031	−.006	−.064
R^2	—	7.1%****	—	5.2%****

Note: Regressions are based on the 871 respondents who participated in both the pre- and post-election surveys.

*$p < .05$.
**$p < .01$.
***$p < .001$.
****$p < .0001$.

Characteristics and Resources	Reject Legitimacy (Blame the System)		Approve of Collective Action		Favor Black Nationalism	
	r	*B*	*r*	*B*	*r*	*B*
Age: older	.056	.067	−.063	.036	.144	.132***
Education	.025	.046	.094	.070	−.003	.079*
Family income	.026	.039	.110	.027	−.046	−.057
Employment status: full-time	−.015	−.004	.101	.054	−.047	.009
Receiving Social Security	.036	.026	−.044	.022	.123	.074
Receiving other welfare	.022	.045	−.063	−.026	.045	−.035
Marital status: married	.037	.031	.023	.021	.015	.020
Gender: female	.054	.057	−.002	.019	.003	−.004
Region: non-South	−.032	−.039	−.002	−.011	.051	−.016
Urbanicity	.067	.066	−.023	.019	−.089	−.092**
R^2	—	1.7%	—	1.9%	—	3.1%**

APPENDIX B.2, TABLE 4
Interrelationships of Measures of Group Identity and Group Political Consciousness

Identity and Political Consciousness	1	2	3	4	5	6	7
Hold an identity based on common fate (1)	1.000						
Feel collective political discontent (2)	.188****	1.000					
Feel discrimination is still a problem (3)	.255****	.244****	1.000				
Feel collective economic discontent (4)	.235****	.223****	.234****	1.000			
Reject legitimacy of racial disparities (5)	.171****	.115***	.204****	.104**	1.000		
Approve of collective strategies (6)	.146***	.244****	.087*	.094**	.037	1.000	
Hold an exclusivist black identity (7)	.064	.021	.008	.091**	.039	.054	1.000

Note: Correlations between exclusivist black identity and other measures are point-biserial; other correlations are product-moment. Point-biserial correlations were used because the measure of exclusivist black identity is dichotomous and because its formula adjusts for highly skewed distributions between the dichotomous categories.

$*p < .05.$
$**p < .01.$
$***p < .001.$
$****p < .0001.$

284

APPENDIX B.2, TABLE 5
Demographic and Structural Effects on Ideological and Party Identification

Characteristics and Resources	Liberal/Conservative		Party Identification			
			Pre-election		Post-election	
	r	B	r	B	r	B
Age: older	.059	.125**	.175	.191****	.150	.170****
Education	.123	.112**	.001	.027	.034	.046
Family income	.108	.078	.003	-.019	.004	.058
Employment status: full-time	-.032	-.002	.002	.046	.002	-.030
Receiving Social Security	-.047	-.055	-.042	-.014	-.042	-.035
Receiving other welfare	.006	.058	-.053	-.029	-.053	-.025
Marital status: married	.007	-.023	-.045	-.051	-.045	.023
Gender: female	-.012	-.014	.082	.099**	.082	.103**
Region: non-South	.067	-.004	.029	.003	.037	.004
Urbanicity	.145	.114**	.067	.058	.061	.043
R^2	—	4.9%	—	5.1%****	—	4.6%****

Note: Regressions are based on the 871 respondents who participated in both the pre- and post-election surveys.

**$p < .01$.
****$p < .0001$.

APPENDIX B.2, TABLE 6
Demographic and Structural Effects on Policy Preferences

Characteristics and Resources	Favor Spending on Community Needs (index)		Favor Spending on Crime	Favor Spending on Jobs	Favor Spending on Schools
	r	B	B	B	B
Age: older	.037	.030	.060	.002	.033
Education	.075	.078*	.022	.040	.144***
Family income	.020	−.049	.024	−.155****	.043
Employment status: full-time	.015	.021	.012	.019	.024
Receiving Social Security	.019	.032	.000	.041	.026
Receiving other welfare	.011	−.035	.056	−.003	−.006
Marital status: married	.033	.059	.039	.000	.059
Gender: female	.037	.048	.037	.007	.042
Region: non-South	.099	.067	.100**	.002	.034
Urbanicity	.122	.092**	.094**	.047	.012
R^2	—	3.0%****	2.9%****	1.4%	1.9%

APPENDIX B.2, TABLE 6
(continued)

Characteristics and Resources	Favor Government Action to Aid Minorities		Favor School Integration		Favor Pressuring Congress to Alter Policy in South Africa	
	r	B	r	B	r	B
Age: older	.019	−.008	−.072	−.073	.076	.108**
Education	−.016	.055	.013	.033	−.029	.024
Family income	−.085	−.063	−.031	−.076	.028	−.033
Employment status: full-time	−.080	−.052	−.121	−.078	.029	.029
Receiving Social Security	.066	.037	−.052	−.052	−.046	−.076
Receiving other welfare	−.049	−.013	−.021	−.035	−.054	−.033
Marital status: married	−.031	.002	.016	.013	.019	.014
Gender: female	−.021	−.041	−.145	−.158***	−.037	−.024
Region: non-South	.004	.022	−.056	−.030	.122	.092**
Urbanicity	−.034	−.042	−.059	−.046	.124	.071*
R^2	—	.015	—	4.1%****	—	3.6%****

Note: Regressions are based on the 871 respondents who participated in both the pre- and post-election surveys.

*p < .05.   **p < .01.   ***p < .001.   ****p < .0001.

Characteristics and Resources	Favor Spending on Social Welfare (index)		Favor Spending on Food Stamps	Favor Spending on Medicare	Favor Government- Ensured Standard of Living	
	r	B	B	B	r	B
Age: older	−.043	−.030	−.028	−.069	.024	−.038
Education	−.155	−.078*	−.073	−.090*	−.069	.024
Family income	−.144	−.049	−.024	−.044	−.141	−.075
Employment status: full-time	−.145	.021	−.122**	−.044	−.184	−.152****
Receiving Social Security	.119	.032	.038	.082*	.092	.028
Receiving other welfare	.108	−.037	.058	−.016	.100	.036
Marital status: married	−.091	−.034	−.056	−.036	.031	.059
Gender: female	.039	.008	.019	−.006	.097	.064
Region: non-South	.057	.079*	.141***	−.046	−.029	−.014
Urbanicity	−.041	−.053	−.101***	.034	−.054	.030
R^2	—	4.9%****	8.8%****	1.8%	—	4.9%****

Characteristics and Resources	Favor Greater Involvement in Central America		Favor Increased Defense Spending	
	r	B	r	B
Age: older	.004	.015	.062	−.024
Education	−.021	−.024	−.212	−.174****
Family income	.024	.042	−.169	−.100**
Employment status: full-time	.001	−.024	−.082	−.030
Receiving Social Security	−.017	−.024	.104	.059
Receiving other welfare	.000	.017	.011	−.051
Marital status: married	.008	.031	−.009	.030
Gender: female	−.134	−.137****	−.040	−.057
Region: non-South	−.076	−.081*	.146	.128***
Urbanicity	−.039	−.013	−.091	.001
R^2	—	2.8%**	—	7.8%****

APPENDIX B.2, TABLE 7
Demographic and Structural Effects
on Assessments of Personal or Family Economic Circumstances

Characteristics and Resources	One Year Ago		Four Years Ago	
	r	B	r	B
Age: older	.264	.251****	.231	.228****
Education	−.151	.005	−.101	.066
Family income	−.190	−.114**	−.177	−.111**
Employment status: full-time	−.242	−.141***	−.239	−.152**
Receiving Social Security	.094	−.111**	.091	−.092**
Receiving other welfare	.079	.027	.114	.079*
Marital status: married	−.059	−.003	−.056	.003
Gender: female	.072	.039	.060	.021
Region: non-South	.079	.068*	.043	.014
Urbanicity	.038	−.001	.049	.024
R^2	—	12.8%****	—	10.9%****

Note: Regressions are based on the 871 respondents who participated in both the pre- and post-election surveys. Higher scores indicate that the respondent's personal or family economic circumstances are worse now than before or are absolutely or relatively bad now.
 *$p < .05$. **$p < .01$. ***$p < .001$. ****$p < .0001$.

APPENDIX B.2, TABLE 8
Demographic and Structural Effects
on Assessments of Economic Circumstances: Group Comparison

Characteristics and Resources	Blacks Worse Off Than Whites	
	r	B
Age: older	.031	.097**
Education	.217	.214****
Family income	.169	.036
Employment status: full-time	−.050	.033
Receiving Social Security	.061	−.040
Receiving other welfare	.075	−.000
Marital status: married	.116	.084**
Gender: female	.067	.040
Region: non-South	.168	.155****
Urbanicity	.126	.031
R^2	—	9.5%****

Note: Regressions are based on the 871 respondents who participated in both the pre- and post-election surveys. Higher scores indicate that the respondent considers the economic circumstances of blacks worse now than before or absolutely or relatively bad now. The index is comprised of two judgments—that blacks are worse off than whites and that blacks are absolutely not doing well.
 **$p < .01$. ****$p < .0001$.

APPENDIX B.2, TABLE 9
Demographic and Structural Effects
on Historical Economic Assessments of Group's Circumstances

Characteristics and Resources	Blacks Worse Off Than One Year Ago		Blacks Worse Off Than Four Years Ago	
	r	B	r	B
Age: older	.206	.277****	.218	.303****
Education	.057	.137***	.112	.206****
Family income	.041	.024	.066	−.017
Employment status: full-time	−.044	−.009	−.042	−.034
Receiving Social Security	.027	−.066	.002	−.094*
Receiving other welfare	.028	.084*	−.012	.054
Marital status: married	.043	.024	.111	.098**
Gender: female	.049	.053	.042	.053
Region: non-South	.091	.075*	.153	.157****
Urbanicity	.052	−.016	.058	−.049
R^2	—	7.7%****	—	12.3%****

Note: Regressions are based on the 871 respondents who participated in both the pre- and post-election surveys. Higher scores indicate that the respondent considers the economic circumstances of blacks worse now than before or absolutely or relatively bad now.
*$p < .05$.   **$p < .01$.   ***$p < .001$.   ****$p < .0001$.

APPENDIX B.2, TABLE 10
Demographic and Structural Effects
on Assessments of Society's Economic Circumstances

Characteristics and Resources	One Year Ago	
	r	B
Age	.101	.098*
Education	−.084	−.001
Family income	−.118	−.063
Employment status: full-time	−.132	−.063
Receiving Social Security	.028	−.071
Receiving other welfare	.114	.075*
Marital status: married	−.029	.026
Gender: female	.148	.129**
Region: non-South	.052	.045
Urbanicity	.026	.012
R^2	—	5.4%****

Note: Regressions are based on the 871 respondents who participated in both the pre- and post-election surveys. Higher scores indicate that the respondent considers the economic circumstances of the society as a whole worse now than before or absolutely or relatively bad now.
*$p < .05$.   **$p < .01$.   ****$p < .0001$.

APPENDIX B.2, TABLE 11
Demographic and Structural Effects on Psychological Resources: Interest in Political Affairs

Characteristics and Resources	Pay Attention to Campaigns		Follow Government and Public Affairs		Care Which Party Wins	
	r	B	r	B	r	B
Age: older	.175	.261****	.077	.187****	.038	.055
Education	.143	.187****	.217	.196****	.098	.107**
Family income	.119	.052	.202	.072	.050	.013
Employment status: full-time	−.013	−.072	.128	.052	.004	−.050
Receiving Social Security	−.029	−.098**	−.082	−.054*	−.004	−.007
Receiving other welfare	−.094	−.006	−.108	.015	−.064	−.030
Marital status: married	.075	.008	.121	.041	.039	.026
Gender: female	.112	.099**	.122	.090**	−.092	−.009
Region: non-South	−.005	−.054	.011	−.044	−.063	−.104**
Urbanicity	.078	.043	.114	.084*	.049	.075*
R^2	—	9.8%****	—	10.6%****	—	3.1%**

Note: Regressions are based on the 871 respondents who participated in both the pre- and post-election surveys.
*$p < .05$.
**$p < .01$.
****$p < .0001$.

APPENDIX B.2, TABLE 12
Demographic and Structural Effects on Psychological Resources: Interest Aroused by Black Politics

Characteristics and Resources	Election of Black Mayors Aroused Interest		Jackson Candidacy Aroused Interest	
	r	B	r	B
Age: older	-.015	-.029	-.076	-.075
Education	-.058	-.033	-.006	-.019
Family income	-.085	-.063	-.026	-.014
Employment status: full-time	-.054	-.049	-.004	-.049
Receiving Social Security	-.004	-.045	-.049	-.047
Receiving other welfare	-.011	-.059	-.029	-.053
Marital status: married	-.055	-.039	-.029	-.039
Gender: female	-.022	-.006	.008	.015
Region: non-South	-.022	-.018	-.115	-.099**
Urbanicity	.076	.079*	-.071	-.028
R^2		1.9%		2.5%**

Note: Regressions are based on the 871 respondents who participated in both the pre- and post-election surveys.
*$p < .05$.
**$p < .01$.

APPENDIX B.2, TABLE 13
Demographic and Structural Effects on Psychological Resources: Group Efficacy

Characteristics and Resources	Blacks Can Make a Difference in Presidential Elections				
	Pre-election		Post-election		Change
	r	B	r	B	B
Age: older	.001	.046	−.072	−.074*	−.088*
Education	.083	.070	.047	.027	.003
Family income	.067	.038	.036	.034	.021
Employment: full-time	.053	.042	.041	.029	.011
Receiving Social Security	−.039	−.039	−.006	.041	.054
Receiving other welfare	−.062	−.038	.019	.026	.038
Marital status: married	.006	−.026	.024	.026	−.034
Gender: female	.026	.036	.048	.052	.039
Region: non-South	.008	.025	−.037	−.030	−.038
Urbanicity	−.025	−.057	−.030	−.011	.027
Pre-measure (for change)	—	—	—	—	.329
R^2	—	1.5%	—	1.2%	11.9%

Note: Regressions are based on the 871 respondents who participated in both pre- and post-election surveys.

*$p < .05$.

**$p < .01$.

292

| Blacks Can Make a Difference in Local Elections | | | | | Rainbow Coalition Decide How Country Should Be Run | | | | |
| Pre-election | | Post-election | | Change | Pre-election | | Post-election | | Change |
r	B	r	B	B	r	B	r	B	B
−.029	.003	−.025	.005	.004	.062	.058	.037	.056	.041
.146	.087*	.165	.129**	.105**	.011	.062	.079	.095**	.078*
.155	.073	.148	.043	.020	.026	.036	.062	.007	.017
.062	.049	.034	.018	.011	.048	.032	.051	.028	.020
−.058	−.000	−.045	.022	.023	.058	.037	.006	−.022	.012
−.117	−.062	−.083	−.013	.002	.037	.044	−.017	.029	.016
.092	.044	.128	.094*	.082	−.007	.017	.086	−.071	.068
−.065	−.035	−.091	−.065	−.055	−.008	−.018	−.055	−.049	−.041
−.006	−.023	−.004	−.023	.026	.067	.061	−.009	.021	−.039
.037	−.029	.061	.061	.053	.035	.001	.021	−.022	.020
—	—	—	—	.266	—	—	—	—	.274
—	3.9%	4.9%	—	11.7%	—	1.3%	1.9%	—	9.3%

293

APPENDIX B.2, TABLE 14
Demographic and Structural Effects on Psychological Resources: Political Efficacy

Characteristics and Resources	Feel Sense of Personal Political Competence		Believe System Is Unresponsive			
			Pre-election		Post-election	
	r	B	r	B	r	B
Age: older	-.160	-.089**	-.138	.090*	.133	.083*
Education	.304	.192****	-.206	-.114**	-.210	-.104**
Family income	.292	.209****	-.165	-.077**	-.214	-.118**
Employment status: full-time	.127	.051	-.057	-.063	-.166	-.053
Receiving Social Security	-.116	-.008	.084	-.040	.095	-.033
Receiving other welfare	-.103	-.010	.091	.023	.099	.021
Marital status: married	.040	-.047	.039	.012	.028	.006
Gender: female	-.089	-.057	.028	.003	.077	.044
Region: non-South	.075	.038	.049	.095**	-.009	.023
Urbanicity	.084	.023	-.092	-.115**	-.072	-.062
R^2	—	14.4%****	—	7.2%****	—	7.4%****

Note: Regressions are based on the 871 respondents who participated in both the pre- and post-election surveys.
  *$p < .05$.
  **$p < .01$.
  ****$p < .0001$.

APPENDIX B.2, TABLE 15
Demographic and Structural Effects on Psychological Resources: Trust in Government

Characteristics and Resources	Distrust Government			
	Pre-election		Post-election	
	r	B	r	B
Age: older	-.005	.042	.043	.069
Education	.059	.039	.068	.052
Family income	.071	.022	.068	-.008
Employment status: full-time	.056	.002	.092	.093*
Receiving Social Security	-.088	-.086*	-.070	-.067
Receiving other welfare	.017	.042	-.030	.009
Marital status: married	.024	-.056	.081	.069
Gender: female	.070	.041	.082	.108**
Region: non-South	.104	.097**	.074	.078
Urbanicity	.064	.016	.049	.006
R^2	—	2.8%**	—	4.1%*****

Note: Regressions are based on the 871 respondents who participated in both the pre- and post-election surveys.

   *$p < .05$.
  **$p < .01$.
 *****$p < .0001$.

APPENDIX B.3, TABLE 1
Demographic and Structural Effects on Thermometer Ratings of Candidates and Parties: Republican Symbols

Characteristics and Resources	Reagan		Republican Party		Blacks Who Supported Reagan	
	r	B	r	B	r	B
Age: older	-.044	-.111**	-.032	-.122**	-.002	-.068
Education	.011	-.009	-.055	-.028	-.080	-.049
Family income	-.008	-.055	-.068	-.064	-.111	-.111*
Employment status: full-time	-.016	-.048	-.066	-.065	-.043	-.018
Receiving Social Security	.036	.083*	.094	.121**	-.063	-.062
Receiving other welfare	-.033	-.039	-.010	-.043	-.029	-.067
Marital status: married	.112	.130**	.068	.073*	.014	.045
Gender: female	-.148	-.145****	-.110	-.124***	-.088	-.101*
Region: non-South	-.079	-.068	-.103	-.086*	-.081	-.058
Urbanicity	-.040	-.014	-.074	-.009	-.058	-.009
R^2	—	5.2%****	—	5.2%****	—	3.6%****

Note: Regressions are based on the 871 respondents who participated in both the pre- and post-election surveys.
* $p < .05$.
** $p < .01$.
*** $p < .001$.
**** $p < .0001$.

APPENDIX B.3, TABLE 2
Demographic and Structural Effects on Thermometer Ratings of Candidates and Parties: Democratic Symbols

Characteristics and Resources	Mondale		Ferraro		Democratic Party		Blacks Who Supported Mondale	
	r	B	r	B	r	B	r	B
Age: older	.208	.194***	.184	.207****	.165	.184****	.116	.072
Education	−.101	−.059	−.022	.023	−.041	.012	−.101	−.071
Family income	−.033	.059	.018	.091*	.004	.066	−.063	.037
Employment status: full-time	−.091	−.042	−.114	−.124**	−.082	−.065	−.110	−.083*
Receiving Social Security	.096	−.005	.029	−.084*	.048	−.039	.083	.013
Receiving other welfare	−.040	−.038	−.020	−.005	.012	.032	−.007	−.028
Marital status: married	−.005	−.029	.026	.003	.051	.024	−.027	−.025
Gender: female	.044	.044	.074	.078*	.048	.049	.024	.014
Region: non-South	−.112	−.130**	−.072	−.099**	−.109	−.114**	−.132	−.166****
Urbanicity	−.039	.004	−.009	.006	−.064	−.030	−.016	.056
R^2		6.6%****		6.4%****		5.2%****		4.6%****

Note: Regressions are based on the 871 respondents who participated in both the pre- and post-election surveys.

$* p < .05.$
$** p < .01.$
$*** p < .001.$
$**** p < .0001.$

297

APPENDIX B.3, TABLE 3
Demographic and Structural Effects on Evaluations of Parties' Relationships to Blacks

Characteristics and Resources	Feel Democratic Party Does Not Work Hard Enough on Black Issues		Feel Republican Party Does Not Work Hard Enough on Black Issues		Feel Democratic Party Treated Jackson Worse Than It Treated Other Candidates	
	r	B	r	B	r	B
Age: older	-.022	.019	.022	.100**	-.110	-.061
Education	.094	.095**	.215	.169****	.147	.117**
Family income	.071	.059	.203	.111**	.108	.036
Employment status: full-time	.065	.043	.122	.052	.087	.024
Receiving Social Security	-.041	-.011	-.081	-.031	-.067	.008
Receiving other welfare	-.013	.024	-.064	.034	.011	.060
Marital status: married	.046	.029	-.001	.003	.022	.003
Gender: female	-.095	-.087	-.061	.030	-.076	-.071*
Region: non-South	.134	.161****	.120	.094**	.055	.047
Urbanicity	.017	.065	.096	.014	.035	.003
R^2	—	4.0%****	—	7.9%****	—	3.8%****

Note: Regressions are based on the 871 respondents who participated in both the pre- and post-election surveys.

  * $p < .05$.
 ** $p < .01$.
**** $p < .0001$.

APPENDIX B.3, TABLE 4
Views of Candidates and Parties, Support for Jackson, and Advocacy of a Black Political Voice

Views of Candidates and Parties	Support Jackson			Advocate Black Political Voice		
	r	B_1[†]	B_2[††]	r	B_1[†]	B_2[††]
Thermometer Ratings of Candidates						
Reagan	-.132	-.152****	-.135****	-.095	-.112***	-.090**
Mondale	-.231	-.206****	-.197****	.060	.061*	.069*
Jackson	.464	.452****	.447****	.188	.198****	.182****
Ferraro	-.102	-.084**	-.065*	.051	.074*	.089**
Thermometer Ratings of Political Symbols						
Democratic party	.015	.039	.039	.066	.078**	.078**
Republican party	-.088	-.095**	-.078*	-.007	-.043	-.029
Blacks who supported Jackson	.318	.315****	.306****	.158	.179****	.172****
Blacks who supported Mondale	-.134	-.114***	-.102**	.125	.107**	.118***
Blacks who supported Reagan	-.099	-.096**	-.081**	.029	.007	.005
A black vice-president	.265	.255****	.239****	.114	.138****	.125****
Democratic party treated Jackson worse than it treated other candidates	.147	.173****	.152****	.197	.068*	.049

Note: Regressions are based on the 871 respondents who participated in both the pre- and post-election surveys.
† Effect for each political measure with controls for demographic variables.
†† Effect also controls race of interviewer.
  * $p < .05$.
 ** $p < .01$.
 *** $p < .001$.
 **** $p < .0001$.

APPENDIX B.3, TABLE 5
Factor Structure of Modes of Political Participation: The Black Electorate

Political Acts	Church Campaigning	Traditional Campaigning	Voting	Petitioning	Direct Protest Action
Attended a church activity to support a black candidate	.773	.141	.002	.187	.038
Worked for a candidate through church	.665	.312	.010	.041	.039
Contributed to a church collection for a candidate	.725	.056	.039	-.053	.155
Influenced people to vote for/against a party or a candidate	.027	.499	.096	.283	.039
Went to a political meeting in support of a candidate	.173	.645	.017	.266	.165
Gave money in support of a candidate	.302	.513	.037	.182	.256
Campaigned for a black candidate	.127	.745	.004	.110	.123
Helped with voter registration/got people to the polls	.113	.684	.077	-.035	-.008
Worked for a political party	.080	.481	.031	.452	-.071
Voted for					
a black candidate	-.008	-.128	.728	.128	.178
a House/Senate seat	.035	.037	.751	.228	.091
a state/local office	.031	.053	.807	.185	.036
president in 1980	.152	.123	.174	.467	-.159
Contacted a public official	.029	.202	.047	.734	.227
Signed a petition	.117	.056	.108	.621	.285
Attended a protest meeting or demonstration	.087	.101	.000	.382	.572
Picketed or boycotted	.031	.171	.044	.116	.786
Percentage total variance explained	9.9%	13.8%	10.1%	13.2%	7.6%

Note: Principal-components factor analysis. We specified that five factors should be extracted for rotation. The factor loadings are based on varimax rotation. The analysis was performed on the 871 respondents who participated in both the pre- and post-election surveys.

APPENDIX B.3, TABLE 6
Factor Structure of Modes of Political Participation: Strong Jackson Supporters

Political Acts	Participated in Protest Activity	Participated in Traditional and Church Campaigning	Voted in a State/Local Contest	Voted for President in 1980	Voted for a Black Candidate
Contacted a public official	.669	.091	.047	.321	.203
Attended a protest meeting or demonstration	.699	.160	.182	.089	-.161
Picketed or boycotted	.676	.130	-.168	-.145	-.049
Signed a petition	.555	.102	.364	.311	-.059
Helped with voter registration/got people to the polls	.137	.666	.002	-.123	.120
Campaigned for a black candidate	.244	.629	-.060	.123	.316
Worked for a candidate through church	-.107	.616	.119	.235	-.139
Attended political meetings in support of a candidate	.364	.575	-.018	.104	.033
Contributed to a church collection for a candidate	-.032	.561	-.025	.064	-.178
Attended a church activity in support of a black candidate	-.139	.557	.113	.413	-.130
Gave money to a candidate	.340	.527	.058	.091	.164
Influenced people to vote for/against a party or a candidate	.331	.417	-.052	-.023	.386
Voted for					
a House/Senate seat	.018	.088	.856	-.070	-.031
state/local office	.076	.053	.810	.063	.288
president in 1980	.083	.056	-.006	.722	.133
a black candidate	-.028	-.031	.213	.128	.795
Worked for a party or campaign	.281	.211	-.021	.615	.026
Percentage total variance explained	15.2%	15.3%	9.3%	8.1%	7.1%

Note: Principal-components factor analysis. The Kaiser criterion was used to determine how many factors would be extracted for rotation. The factor loadings are based on varimax rotation. The analysis was performed on the 297 strong Jackson supporters who participated in both the pre- and post-election surveys.

APPENDIX B.3, TABLE 7
Demographic and Structural Effects on Political Participation

Characteristics and Resources	Voted in 1980		Participated in Campaign Activities		Participated in Church Campaign Activities	
	r	B	r	B	r	B
Age: older	.365	.448****	.001	.094**	.082	.143***
Education	.115	.170****	.247	.188****	.036	.065
Family income	.146	.030	.260	.159****	.047	.054
Employment status: full-time	.039	.061	.136	−.034	.039	.038
Receiving Social Security	.048	−.042	−.069	−.003	−.023	−.057
Receiving other welfare	−.150	−.045	−.104	.015	−.056	−.024
Marital status: married	.206	.154****	.101	.008	.025	−.014
Gender: female	.010	.066	−.099	−.064	.088	.101**
Region: non-South	.090	.064*	.046	.015	−.059	−.042
Urbanicity	.002	.031	.006	.012	−.051	−.057
R^2	—	23.7%****	—	9.9%****	—	3.4%****

Note: Regressions are based on the 871 respondents who participated in both the pre- and post-election surveys.

[a] Petitioning and direct-action protest are combined in this measure of protest activities.

*p < .05.   **p < .01.   ***p < .001.   ****p < .0001.

APPENDIX B.3, TABLE 8
Relationships Between Political Participation and Support for Jackson and Advocacy of a Black Political Voice

Political Acts	Support Jackson		Advocate Black Political Voice	
	r	B	r	B
Participated in protest activity	.146	.095**	−.182	−.084*
Participated in campaign activity	.124	.087**	−.097	−.075*
Participated in church activity	.079	.086**	.034	.063*
Voted in November	.056	.046	−.064	−.002
Voted in a House or Senate race	.021	.011	−.124	−.069*
Voted in a state or local race	.000	−.023	−.139	−.073*
Voted in a primary	.019	.042	−.019	.034

Note: Regressions are based on the 871 respondents who participated in both the pre- and post-election surveys. This table summarizes fourteen separate regression analyses. The coefficients are from equations that included demographic and structural controls and one participation measure regressed on support for Jackson and black political voice.

*p < .05.   **p < .01.

Participated in Protest Activities[a]		Voted in November		Voted for a House/Senate Seat		Voted in a Local/State Contest		Voted for Black Candidates	
r	B	r	B	r	B	r	B	r	B
−.023	−.022	.104	.220****	.073	.104**	.022	.113**	.043	.070
.386	.236****	.187	.227****	.134	.115**	.177	.145***	.146**	.169****
.338	.145***	.111	.015	.164	.100**	.182	.082*	.073	.028
.219	.047	.061	.023	.029	−.028	.104	.030	.026	−.001
−.153	−.004	−.043	−.056	−.010	.005	−.094	−.063	.009	−.023
−.155	−.028	−.075	−.010	−.056	.014	.054	.033	−.073	−.028
.053	.039	.126	.093**	.126	.088**	.133	.080*	.003	−.056
.113	.001	.019	.039	−.047	−.017	−.003	.031	−.086	.020
.163	.115***	.014	.007	.089	.059	.055	.024	.089	.085*
.174	.080*	.037	−.003	.085	.037	.053	.003	.061	.102
—	2.1%****	—	7.8%****	—	5.8%****	—	6.5%****	—	3.9%****

APPENDIX B.4, TABLE 1
Change Before and After the Election
in Psychological Resources and Support for Jackson

	Support for Jackson
Psychological Resources	*B*
Attention to political campaigns	.078**
	(.032)
Group efficacy in local elections	.031
	(.033)
Group efficacy in presidential elections	.045
	(.033)
Group efficacy in the Rainbow Coalition's potential effectiveness	.080*
	(.033)
Distrust	.058
	(.031)
System unresponsiveness	.033
	(.032)
Centrality of black identity	.044
	(.033)
Power discontent	.046
	(.033)

Note: Regressions are based on the 871 respondents who participated in both the pre- and post-election surveys. This table summarizes eight regressions in which the change in each psychological resource before and after the election was entered separately, and structural or demographic factors and perceived race of interviewer were controlled. Standard errors are presented in parentheses.
  *$p < .05$.
 **$p < .01$.

APPENDIX B.5, TABLE 1
Change Before and After the Election
in Psychological Resources and Advocacy of a Black Political Voice

	Advocacy of a Black Political Voice
Psychological Resources	B
Attention to political campaigns	.011
	(.032)
Group efficacy in local elections	.036
	(.033)
Group efficacy in presidential elections	.135****
	(.033)
Group efficacy in the Rainbow Coalition's	
potential effectiveness	.096***
	(.034)
Distrust	.032
	(.031)
System unresponsiveness	.086**
	(.034)
Centrality of black identity	.111***
	(.033)
Power discontent	.036
	(.033)

Note: Regressions are based on the 871 respondents who participated in both the pre- and post-election surveys. This table summarizes eight regressions in which the change in each psychological resource before and after the election was entered separately, and structural or demographic factors and perceived race of interviewer were controlled. Standard errors are presented in parentheses.

  $**p < .01.$
  $***p < .001.$
  $****p < .0001.$

APPENDIX B.5, TABLE 2
Political Evaluations of Three Types of Potential Leaders of a Black Political Voice and of Other Advocates

Political Evaluations	Potential Leaders of a Black Political Voice				Other Advocates of a Black Political Voice (169)
	Individualistic Advocates: Those Not Active in Black Organizations (13)	Local Leaders with Organizational Experience (13)	National Leaders with Organizational Experience (25)	All Potential Leaders (51)	
Percentage who felt that					
Democrats treated Jackson worse than they treated other candidates	28%	31%	62%****	45%	5%****
Democrats work very hard on black issues	24%	77%	23%	37%	46%
Republicans don't work hard at all on black issues	48%	54%	54%	52%	24%***
Average Thermometer Ratings					
Democrats					
Mondale	67.1	85.3	56.2***	66.4	63.3
Ferraro	64.9	63.2	61.2	62.6	62.5
Democratic party	81.6	84.2	80.3	81.2	80.0
Blacks who voted for Mondale in primary	73.2	67.4	67.3	68.8	69.7
Republicans					
Reagan	32.1	19.0	18.7*	22.2	27.2
Republican party	33.4	19.1	18.9*	22.6	38.9**
Blacks who voted for Reagan	32.7	20.1	15.5*	21.1	35.6**

Percentage Voting					
Registered for the first time in 1984	19%	0%	0%	9%	20%*
Voted in the 1980 presidential race	52%	85%	92%**	80%	59%**
Voted in the 1984 House/Senate race	52%	77%	77%	73%	60%*
Voted in state/local races	62%	82%	90%	81%	62%*
Average Participation (on scale of 1–5, 5 = high)					
Traditional campaign activities	1.92	2.23	3.00*	2.53	1.76****
Church-related campaign	1.64	2.23	2.34	2.13	1.53****
Petitioning/protest	1.84	1.39	3.08**	2.33	1.05***
Demonstration/protest	.56	.31	1.23*	.82	.22**

Note: Two sets of asterisks indicate statistically significant differences: the first represents differences among the three types of leaders; the second represents differences between leaders and non-leaders. The numbers in parentheses show how many are in each group of potential leaders and in the group of other advocates.

*$p < .05$.
**$p < .01$.
***$p < .001$.
****$p < .0001$.

Average Solidarity Resource Scores of Three Types of Potential Leaders of a Black Political Voice and of Other Advocates

	Potential Leaders of a Black Political Voice	
Solidarity Measures	Individualistic Advocates: Those Not Active in Black Organizations (13)	Local Leaders with Organizational Experience (13)
Black Identity		
Sense of common fate (on scale of 1–16, 16 = high)	8.71	8.75
Exclusivist black identity (1 = being American more important than being black 2 = being both black and American is important 3 = being black more important than being American)	2.04	2.15
Political Consciousness		
Collective discontent (on scale of 1–4, 4 = blacks have far too little power)	3.10	3.31
Rejection of legitimacy (on scale of 1–2, 2 = blacks who don't do well in life are held back by race)	1.25	1.90
Approval of collective strategies (1 = blacks should work to improve personal situation 4 = blacks should be more active in black organizations)	1.02	1.80
Black Nationalism (on scale of 1–5, 5 = high)	2.30	2.50

Note: Two sets of asterisks indicate statistically significant differences: the first represents differences among the three types of leaders; the second represents differences between leaders and non-leaders. The numbers in parentheses show how many are in each group of potential leaders and in the group of other advocates.

$^*p < .05.$
$^{**}p < .01.$

Solidarity Measures	Potential Leaders of a Black Political Voice		Other Advocates of a Black Political Voice *(169)*
	National Leaders with Organizational Experience *(25)*	All Potential Leaders *(51)*	
Black Identity			
Sense of common fate (on scale of 1–16, 16 = high)	12.0*	10.33	8.69*
Exclusivist black identity (1 = being American more important than being black 2 = being both black and American is important 3 = being black more important than being American)	2.23	2.16	2.03
Political Consciousness			
Collective discontent (on scale of 1–4, 4 = blacks have far too little power)	3.96*	3.67	3.25*
Rejection of legitimacy (on scale of 1–2, 2 = blacks who don't do well in life are held back by race)	1.95	1.68	1.66
Approval of collective strategies (1 = blacks should work to improve personal situation 4 = blacks should be more active in black organizations)	1.89**	1.76	1.40*
Black Nationalism (on scale of 1–5, 5 = high)	3.10**	2.73	2.69

APPENDIX B.5, TABLE 4
Average Intergroup Attitude Scores of Three Types of Potential Leaders of a Black Political Voice and of Other Advocates

	Potential Leaders of a Black Political Voice	
Intergroup Measures	Individualistic Advocates: Those Not Active in Black Organizations (13)	Local Leaders with Organizational Experience (13)
Pro-black Feelings		
(on scale of 1–4, 4 = very close)		
Closeness to black people in Africa	1.64	2.00
Closeness to West Indians	1.63	2.00
Feelings Toward Whites		
Closeness to whites		
(on scale of 1–4, 4 = very close)	1.58	2.08
Blacks should have nothing to do with whites		
(on scale of 1–4, 4 = strongly agree)	2.33	2.61
Most white people want to keep blacks down		
(on scale of 1–3, 3 = agree)	2.42	2.31
Political Judgments of Power of Various Groups		
(on scale of 1–4, 1 = too much; 4 = far too little)		
Superordinates		
Whites	1.63	1.17
Business executives	1.89	1.39
Men	1.56	1.32
Subordinates		
Poor people	3.76	3.77
People on welfare	3.12	3.53
Older people	2.62	2.92
Women	2.80	2.39
Young people	3.08	2.69

Note: Two sets of asterisks indicate statistically significant differences: the first represents differences among the three types of leaders; the second represents differences between leaders and non-leaders. The numbers in parentheses show how many are in each group of potential leaders and in the group of other advocates.

*p < .05.
**p < .01.

APPENDIX B.5, Table 4
(continued)

| Intergroup Measures | Potential Leaders of a Black Political Voice | | Other Advocates of a Black Political Voice (169) |
	National Leaders with Organizational Experience (25)	All Potential Leaders (51)	
Pro-black Feelings			
(on scale of 1–4, 4 = very close)			
Closeness to black people in Africa	2.00	1.69	1.60
Closeness to West Indians	1.77	1.92	1.40*
Feelings Toward Whites			
Closeness to whites			
(on scale of 1–4, 4 = very close)	1.61	1.72	1.71
Blacks should have nothing to do with whites			
(on scale of 1–4, 4 = strongly agree)	2.61	2.54	2.22*
Most white people want to keep blacks down			
(on scale of 1–3, 3 = agree)	2.42	2.39	2.11*
Political Judgments of Power of Various Groups			
(on scale of 1–4, 1 = too much; 4 = far too little)			
Superordinates			
Whites	1.15*	1.27	1.64**
Business executives	1.21*	1.43	1.82*
Men	1.23	1.33	1.77**
Subordinates			
Poor people	3.62	3.69	3.47*
People on welfare	3.62*	3.47	3.14*
Older people	3.42*	3.08	2.86
Women	3.54**	3.06	2.83*
Young people	2.92*	2.90	2.94

APPENDIX B.5, TABLE 5
Policy Views of Three Types of Potential Leaders
of a Black Political Voice and of Other Advocates

Average Scores on Domestic-Policy Measures	Potential Leaders of a Black Political Voice	
	Individualistic Advocates: Those Not Active in Black Organizations (13)	Local Leaders with Organizational Experience (13)
Spending Policies (on scale of 1–3, 3 = in favor of increasing)		
Social welfare	2.52	2.58
Community services	2.70	2.73
Defense	2.09	1.54
Government Action (on scale of 1–3, 3 = in favor of more action)		
Assurance of standard of living	2.00	2.52
Aid to minorities and affirmative action (racial area)	3.09	3.43
Self-help against government action (racial area)	2.72	2.15
Centrality of Racial Policy (on scale of 1–5, 5 = extremely important)	2.95	3.40
Distance Candidates Perceived to Be from Own Racial Policy (0 = same; −6 = candidate less favorable toward government action)		
Reagan	−2.02	−3.47
Mondale	−1.35	−1.30
Foreign Policy Measures Blacks should pressure Congress to alter policy on South Africa (on scale of 1–3, 3 = very important)	2.19	2.62
Central America (on scale of 1–3, 3 = U.S. should become more involved)	1.83	1.21

Note: Two sets of asterisks indicate statistically significant differences: the first represents differences among the three types of leaders; the second represents differences between leaders and non-leaders. The numbers in parentheses show how many are in each group of potential leaders and in the group of other advocates.

*p < .05.
**p < .01.

Average Scores on Domestic-Policy Measures	Potential Leaders of a Black Political Voice		Other Advocates of a Black Political Voice (169)
	National Leaders with Organizational Experience (25)	All Potential Leaders (51)	
Spending Policies (on scale of 1–3, 3 = in favor of increasing)			
Social welfare	2.50	2.52	2.62
Community services	2.79	2.75	2.67
Defense	1.64*	1.79	1.94*
Government Action (on scale of 1–3, 3 = in favor of more action)			
Assurance of standard of living	2.37*	2.31	2.31
Aid to minorities and affirmative action (racial area)	3.31*	3.28	3.27
Self-help against government action (racial area)	2.04*	2.24	2.56**
Centrality of Racial Policy (on scale of 1–5, 5 = extremely important)	3.67*	3.42	2.85**
Distance Candidates Perceived to Be from Own Racial Policy (0 = same; −6 = candidate less favorable toward government action)			
Reagan	−3.33*	−3.13	−2.66*
Mondale	−1.30	−1.32	−.71*
Foreign Policy Measures			
Blacks should pressure Congress to alter policy on South Africa (on scale of 1–3, 3 = very important)	2.60*	2.50	2.51
Central America (on scale of 1–3, 3 = U.S. should become more involved)	1.18*	1.35	1.63*

APPENDIX B.5, TABLE 6
Psychological Resources of Three Types of Potential Leaders
of a Black Political Voice and of Other Advocates

	Potential Leaders of a Black Political Voice	
Average Scores	*Individualistic Advocates: Those Not Active in Black Organizations* (13)	*Local Leaders with Organizational Experience* (13)
Believe political system unresponsive (on scale of 1–5, 5 = unresponsive)	3.20	2.30
Distrust in government (on scale of 1–12, 12 = high)	7.50	8.88
Personal political competence (on scale of 1–5, 5 = high competence)	3.17	2.23
Group efficacy (on scale of 1–4, 4 = blacks can do the following)		
Affect local elections	2.56	2.81
Affect presidential elections	2.24	2.85
The Rainbow Coalition can affect how the country is run	2.04	2.54
Interest in general politics (on scale of 1–5, 5 = high)		
Pay attention to campaigns	2.24	3.08
Care which party wins	3.52	3.08
Interest aroused by black politics (on scale of 1–5, 5 = more interest)		
Success of black mayors aroused interest	2.80	3.08
Jackson candidacy aroused interest	3.44	3.69

Note: Two sets of asterisks indicate statistically significant differences: the first represents differences among the three types of leaders; the second represents differences between leaders and non-leaders.
    $^*p < .05.$
    $^{**}p < .01.$
    $^{****}p < .0001.$

| | Potential Leaders of a Black Political Voice | | |
| | National Leaders with Organizational Experience | All Potential Leaders | Other Advocates of a Black Political Voice |
Average Scores	(25)	(51)	(169)
Believe political system unresponsive			
(on scale of 1–5, 5 = unresponsive)	2.82**	2.78	3.06*
Distrust in government			
(on scale of 1–12, 12 = high)	9.85*	9.00	8.18**
Personal political competence			
(on scale of 1–5, 5 = high competence)	4.07*	3.37	2.23****
Group efficacy			
(on scale of 1–4, 4 = blacks can do the following)			
Affect local elections	2.93*	2.81	2.51**
Affect presidential elections	2.85	2.69	2.46
The Rainbow Coalition can affect how the country is run	2.62*	2.45	2.33
Interest in general politics			
(on scale of 1–5, 5 = high)			
Pay attention to campaigns	3.08*	2.86	2.33
Care which party wins	4.00	3.64	2.98*
Interest aroused by black politics			
(on scale of 1–5, 5 = more interest)			
Success of black mayors aroused interest	2.92	2.92	3.04
Jackson candidacy aroused interest	3.68	3.62	3.07*

APPENDIX B.6, TABLE 1
Comparison of Blacks and Whites on Spending Preferences, Aid to Minorities, and Assurance of Economic Security

Policy Preferences	Whites (NES)[a]	Blacks (NBES)[b]
Community Needs (post-election)		
Crime	50%	48%
Public schools	46%	79%
Jobs for the unemployed	34%	82%
Social Welfare (post-election)		
Medicare	41%	79%
Food stamps	−18%	39%
Defense (pre-election)	2%	−13%
Assurance of Jobs and a Standard of Living (post-election)		
(1–3 on seven-point scale)	25%	43%
Aid to Minorities (pre-election)		
(1–3 on seven-point scale)	28%	60%

Note: Entries are computed by subtracting percentage wanting a decrease from percentage wanting an increase.

[a] Percentage difference based on 1946 white respondents on the pre-election survey and 1,716 white respondents on the post-election survey.

[b] Percentage difference based on the 115 black respondents on the pre-election survey and 871 black respondents on the post-election survey.

APPENDIX B.6, TABLE 2
Average Spending Preferences of Blacks and Whites with Family Income Below $10,000 and $40,000 or Above and with Less Than a High School Education and Some College

	Family Income			
	Less Than $10,000		$40,000 and Above	
Spending Preferences (post-election) (1 = increase; 2 = same; 3 = decrease)	Blacks (NBES) (208)	Whites (NES) (276)	Blacks (NBES) (72)	Whites (NES) (306)
Community Needs				
Crime	1.53	1.53	1.47	1.50
Public schools	1.18	1.47	1.10	1.58
Jobs for the unemployed	1.16	1.48	1.27	1.84
Social Welfare				
Medicare	1.26	1.49	1.25	1.67
Food stamps	1.49	1.97	1.70	2.31
Defense Spending	2.01	2.08	2.27	1.97

Note: The means are adjusted for age, gender, and region and, in the case of blacks, for perceived race of interviewer. Respondents who participated in both the pre- and post-election surveys were included in this analysis. The numbers in parentheses show how many NBES and NES respondents are in the two income and the two education categories.

316

APPENDIX B.6, TABLE 2
(continued)

Spending Preferences (post-election) (1 = increase; 2 = same; 3 = decrease)	Education			
	Less Than High School		At Least Some College	
	Blacks (NBES) (177)	Whites (NES) (292)	Blacks (NBES) (140)	Whites (NES) (299)
Community Needs				
Crime	1.55	1.47	1.44	1.57
Public schools	1.29	1.54	1.09	1.54
Jobs for the unemployed	1.23	1.45	1.21	1.79
Social Welfare				
Medicare	1.19	1.45	1.30	1.69
Food stamps	1.40	2.06	1.67	2.19
Defense Spending	1.90	1.85	2.32	2.24

APPENDIX B.6, TABLE 3
Average Psychological Resources of Blacks and Whites
with Family Income Below $10,000 and $40,000 Above
and with Less Than a High School Education and Some College

| | Family Income | | | |
| | Less Than $10,000 | | $40,000 and Above | |
Psychological Resources	Blacks (NBES) (208)	Whites (NES) (276)	Blacks (NBES) (72)	Whites (NES) (306)
General Interest				
Paid attention to political campaigns (pre-election) (on scale of 1–5, 1 = high)	2.53	3.02	2.55	2.86
Cared which party won (post-election) (on scale of 1–5, 1 = great deal)	2.44	2.19	2.54	2.04
Followed public affairs (post-election) (on scale of 1–4, 1 = most of the time)	2.13	2.25	1.89	2.24
Sense of Personal Competence (post-election) (on scale of 1–5, 5 = high)	2.38	2.05	3.50	2.46
Responsiveness of Government (pre-election)				
Felt people have no say (on scale of 1–5, 1 = unresponsive)	3.33	3.65	3.52	3.95
Felt public officials don't care (on scale of 1–5, 1 = unresponsive)	2.72	2.99	3.11	3.71
Distrust (post-election)				
How much of time can government in Washington be trusted to do what is right? (on scale of 1–5, 5 = only some of the time)	4.34	3.98	4.54	3.96
How much attention does government pay to what people think? (on scale of 1–5, 5 = not much)	3.69	3.08	3.69	3.02
Government runs for the interests of a few or for all? (on scale of 1–5, 5 = few; 1 = all)	2.74	2.35	3.20	2.18

Note: The means are adjusted for age, gender, and religion and, in the case of blacks, for perceived race of interviewer. Respondents who participated in both the pre- and post-election surveys were included in this analysis. The numbers in parentheses show how many NBES and NES respondents are in the two income and two education categories.

	Education			
	Less Than High School		At Least Some College	
Psychological Resources	*Blacks (NBES) (177)*	*Whites (NES) (292)*	*Blacks (NBES) (140)*	*Whites (NES) (299)*
General Interest				
Paid attention to political campaigns (pre-election) (on scale of 1–5, 1 = high)	2.66	3.55	1.91	2.35
Cared which party won (post-election) (on scale of 1–5, 1 = great deal)	1.96	1.85	2.22	1.50
Followed public affairs (post-election) (on scale of 1–4, 1 = most of the time)	2.32	2.63	1.63	1.80
Sense of Personal Competence (post-election) (on scale of 1–5, 5 = high)	2.21	1.63	3.57	2.84
Responsiveness of Government (pre-election)				
Felt people have no say (on scale of 1–5, 1 = unresponsive)	3.13	3.19	4.07	4.26
Felt public officials don't care (on scale of 1–5, 1 = unresponsive)	2.48	2.83	3.32	3.64
Distrust (post-election)				
How much of time can government in Washington be trusted to do what is right? (on scale of 1–5, 5 = only some of the time)	4.49	3.97	4.43	4.03
How much attention does government pay to what people think? (on scale of 1–5, 5 = not much)	3.64	3.50	3.68	2.81
Government runs for the interests of a few or for all? (on scale of 1–5, 5 = few; 1 = all)	2.61	2.41	3.19	2.29

APPENDIX B.6, TABLE 4
Comparison of Blacks and Whites on Psychological Resources

Psychological Resources	Whites (NES) (pre-election N = 1,946; post-election N = 1,719)	Blacks (NES) (pre-election N = 250; post-election N = 215)
Interest in Politics		
Had interest in campaign (pre-election) (on scale of 1–5, 1 = high)	2.92	2.78
Cared which party won (pre-election) (on scale of 1–5, 5 = great deal)	2.16	2.05
Followed public affairs (post-election) (on scale of 1–4, 1 = most of the time)	2.21	2.35
Sense of Personal Competence (post-election) (on scale of 1–5, 1 = high)	2.16	1.89
Responsiveness of Government (pre-election)		
Felt people have no say (on scale of 1–5, 1 = unresponsive)	3.81	3.56
Felt public officials don't care (on scale of 1–5, 1 = unresponsive)	3.35	3.22
Distrust (post-election)		
How much of time can government in Washington be trusted to do what is right? (on scale of 1–5, 5 = only some of the time)	4.01	4.32
How much attention does government pay to what people think? (on scale of 1–5, 5 = not much)	3.12	3.30
Government runs for the interests of a few or for all? (on scale of 1–5, 1 = few; 5 = all)	2.73	2.31

Note: Cell means controlled for income and education.
[a] The pre- and post-election Ns are different from the totals given in other tables due to missing data on the race of interviewer.

Psychological Resources	Blacks (NBES)[a] Interviewed by	
	White Interviewer (pre-election N = 646; post-election N = 327)	Black Interviewer (pre-election N = 390; post-election N = 416)
Interest in Politics		
Had interest in campaign (pre-election) (on scale of 1–5, 1 = high)	2.39	2.41
Cared which party won (pre-election) (on scale of 1–5, 5 = great deal)	1.92	1.83
Followed public affairs (post-election) (on scale of 1–4, 1 = most of the time)	1.93	1.97
Sense of Personal Competence (post-election) (on scale of 1–5, 1 = high)	2.71	2.53
Responsiveness of Government (pre-election)		
Felt people have no say (on scale of 1–5, 1 = unresponsive)	3.51	3.54
Felt public officials don't care (on scale of 1–5, 1 = unresponsive)	2.92	2.87
Distrust (post-election)		
How much of time can government in Washington be trusted to do what is right? (on scale of 1–5, 5 = only some of the time)	4.40	4.58
How much attention does government pay to what people think? (on scale of 1–5, 5 = not much)	3.68	3.71
Government runs for the interests of a few or for all? (on scale of 1–5, 1 = few; 5 = all)	2.21	1.86

APPENDIX B.6, TABLE 5
Relationships Between Measures of Political Participation and Socioeconomic Status Adjusted for Measures of Class-Based Motivation and Resources

	Income Betas				
Political Acts	1	2	3	4	5
Took part in protest	.145	.108	.124	.099	.063
	(.039)	(.039)	(.039)	(.038)	(.038)
Voted in 1980	.030	.024	.018	.008	.002
	(.038)	(.039)	(.039)	(.039)	(.039)
Took part in campaign activities	.159	.134	.139	.102	.183
	(.042)	(.042)	(.042)	(.040)	(.041)

APPENDIX B.6, TABLE 5
(continued)

	Education Betas				
Political Acts	1	2	3	4	5
Took part in protest	.263	.221	.216	.197	.141
	(.037)	(.037)	(.036)	(.037)	(.036)
Voted in 1980	.170	.160	.143	.139	.118
	(.036)	(.037)	(.036)	(.037)	(.037)
Took part in campaign activities	.188	.158	.151	.106	.080
	(.040)	(.039)	(.039)	(.038)	(.039)

Note: $B1$ = Adjusted for socio-demographics (age, sex, and region).
$B2$ = Adjusted for socio-demographics and psychological resources.
$B3$ = Adjusted for socio-demographics, psychological resources, and solidarity (racial identity and consciousness).
$B4$ = Adjusted for socio-demographics, psychological resources, solidarity, and organizational resources.
$B5$ = Adjusted for all measures indicated in 1–4 above.
Standard errors appear in parentheses.

Bibliography

Aberbach, J., and J. Walker. 1970. "Political trust and racial ideology." *American Political Science Review* 64:1199–1213.

Abramson, P. R., and W. Claggett. 1984. "Race-related differences in self-reported and validated turnout." *Journal of Politics* 46:719–738.

Allen, W. R., and R. Farley. 1986. "The shifting social and economic tides of black America, 1950–1980." *Annual Review of Sociology* 12:277–306.

Allworth, E., ed. 1977. *Nationality group survival in multi-ethnic states: Shifting support patterns in the Soviet Baltic region.* New York: Praeger.

Andersen, K. 1990. "Women and citizenship in the 1920s." In *Women, politics, and change,* ed. L. Tilly and P. Gurin. New York: Russell Sage Foundation.

Atkinson, J. W. 1964. *An introduction to motivation.* Princeton, N.J.: Van Nostrand.

Atkinson, J. W., and D. Birch. 1978. An introduction to motivation. Rev. ed. New York: Van Nostrand.

Atkinson, J. W., and N. T. Feather. 1966. *Theory of achievement motivation.* New York: Wiley.

Azrael, J. R., ed. 1978. *Soviet nationality policies and practices.* New York: Praeger.

Banfield, E., and J. Q. Wilson. 1963. *City politics.* New York: Vintage Books, Random House.

Barnes, S. H., M. Kaase, et al. 1979. *Political action: Mass participation in five western democracies.* Beverly Hills, Calif.: Sage Publications.

Barnett, M. R. 1982. "The Congressional black caucus: Illusions and realities of power." In *The new black politics: The search for political power,* ed. M. B. Preston, L. J. Henderson, Jr., and P. Puryear, 28–54. New York: Longman.

Baron, H. M. 1985. "Racism transformed: The complications of the 1960s." *Review of radical economics* (17:3): 10–23.

Barth, F. 1969. Introduction to *Ethnic groups and boundaries,* ed. F. Barth, 1–38. Boston: Little, Brown.

Baxter, S., and M. Lansing. 1983. *Women and politics: The visible majority.* Ann Arbor: University of Michigan Press.

Bensel, R. F. 1984. *Sectionalism and American political development 1880–1980.* Madison: University of Wisconsin Press.

Benson, L. 1973. "Group cohesion and social and ideological conflict: A critique of some Marxian and Tocquevillian theories." *American Behavioral Scientist* 16:741–766.

Béteille, A. 1986. "Individualism and equality." *Current Anthropology* 27:121–128.

Blydenburgh, J. C. 1971. "A controlled experiment to measure the effects of personal contact campaigning." *Midwest Journal of Political Science* 15:365–381.

Bobo, L. 1986. "Stratification beliefs and support for racial change and social welfare policies." Paper presented at meeting of the American Sociological Association, New York.

Bobo, L. 1988. "Group conflict, prejudice, and the paradox of contemporary racial attitudes." In *Eliminating racism: Means and controversies*, ed. P. A. Katz and D. A. Taylor. New York: Plenum.

Bonacich, E. 1972. "A theory of ethnic antagonism: The split labor market." *American Sociological Review* 37:547–559.

Bonacich, E. 1979. "The past, present, and future of split labor market theory." In *Research in race and ethnic relations*, ed. C. B. Maggett and C. Leggon, 17–64. Greenwich, Conn.: JAI Press.

Bonacich, E., and J. Modell. 1980. *The economic basis of ethnic solidarity: Small business in the Japanese American community*. Berkeley: University of California Press.

Boston, T. D. 1985. "Racial inequality and call stratification: A contribution to a critique of black conservatism." *Review of Radical Political Economics* 17(3):46–71.

Bowles, S., D. M. Gordon, and T. E. Weisskopf. 1989. "Business ascendancy and economic impasse: A structural retrospective on conservative economics, 1979–1987." *Journal of Economic Perspective* 3(1):107–134.

Bracey, J. H., Jr. 1971. "Black nationalism since Garvey." In *Key issues in the Afro-American experience*, ed. N. I. Huggins, M. Kilson, and D. M. Fox, vol. 2, 259–279. New York: Harcourt Brace Jovanovich.

Brewer, M. B., and R. M. Kramer. 1985. "The psychology of intergroup attitudes and behavior." *American Psychological Review* 36:216–243.

Brickman, P., R. Folger, E. Goode, and Y. Schul. 1980. "Micro and macro justice." In *The Justice Motive in Social Behavior*, ed. M. J. Lerner. New York: Plenum.

Broman, C. L., H. W. Neighbors, and J. S. Jackson. 1986. "Racial group identification among black adults." University of Michigan, unpublished paper.

Brooks, E. 1990. "In politics to stay: Black women mobilizing the black female electorate during the 1920s." In *Women, politics, and change*, ed. L. Tilly and P. Gurin. New York: Russell Sage Foundation.

Brown, C. 1984. "Manchild in Harlem." *New York Times Magazine*, September 16, 36–77.

Brown, M. K., and S. P. Erie. 1981. "Blacks and the legacy of the Great Society: The economic and political impact of federal social policy." *Public Policy* 29(3):299–330.

Brown, R. E. 1986. "Group-based determinants of black political participation." University of Michigan, unpublished paper.

Brown, R. E., and J. S. Jackson. 1986. "Church-based determinants of black campaign participation." University of Michigan, unpublished paper.

Brown, R. E., J. S. Jackson, and P. J. Bowman. 1981. "The political state of blacks in the '80s." University of Michigan, unpublished paper.

Brown, R. E., and M. Lansing. 1985. "Church-based and campaign activity by black women in the 1984 presidential election." Paper presented at the Midwestern Political Science Association, Chicago.

Brown, R. E., and C. Tate. 1985. "Clan-based support for the national black political party." University of Michigan, unpublished paper.

Campbell, B. A. 1977. "Patterns of change in the partisan loyalties of native southerners, 1952–1972." *Journal of Politics* 39:730–761.

Campbell, B. A., P. E. Converse, W. E. Miller, and D. E. Stockes. 1960. *The American Voter*. New York: Wiley.

Caraley, D., C. V. Hamilton, A. T. Mason, R. A. McCaughey, N. W. Polsby, J. L. Pressman, A. M. Schlesinger, Jr., G. L. Sherry, and T. Wicker. 1974–75. "American political institutions after Watergate—a discussion." *Political Science Quarterly* 89:713–749.

Carden, M. L. 1974. *The new feminist movement*. New York: Russell Sage Foundation.

Cassell, C. A., and D. B. Hill. 1981. "Explanations of turnout decline: A multivariate test." *American Politics Quarterly* 9:181–196.

Cavanagh, T. E. 1984a. *The impact of the black electorate.* Washington, D.C.: Joint Center for Political Studies.

Cavanagh, T. E. 1984b. "election round-up." *Focus* 12:4–6.

Cavanagh, T. E. 1985a. *Inside black America: The message of the black vote in the 1984 elections.* Washington, D.C.: Joint Center for Political Studies.

Cavanagh, T. E. 1985b. "Black mobilization and partisanship: 1984 and beyond." Paper presented at Joint Center for Political Studies Conference, April, Carnegie Endowment Center, Washington, D.C.

Cavanagh, T. E. 1985c. "Blacks, Hispanics, and women in the 1984 elections: Trends in voter registration and turnout." Paper presented at League of Women Voters Education Fund Conference on Electoral Participation, July, Washington, D.C.

Cavanagh, T. E., and L. S. Foster. 1984. *Jesse Jackson's campaign: The primaries and caucuses.* Washington, D.C.: Joint Center for Political Studies.

Clark, H. H. 1985. "Language use and language users." In *The handbook of social psychology,* ed. G. Lindzey and E. Aronson, 179–231. 3d ed. New York: Random House.

Clark, R. 1984. "The American blacks: A passion for politics." *Dissent,* Summer, 261–264.

Coleman, M., and L. B. McLemore. 1982. "Black independent politics in Mississippi: Constants and challenges." In *The new black politics: The search for political power,* ed. M. B. Preston, L. J. Henderson, Jr., and P. Puryear, 131–156. New York: Longman.

Cone, J. H. 1970. "Black consciousness and the black church: A historical, theological interpretation." *Annals of the American Academy of Political and Social Science* 387:449–455.

Connor, W. 1978. "A nation is a nation, is a state, is an ethnic group, is a . . ." *Ethnic and Racial Studies* 1:377–400.

Connor, W. 1984. *The national question in Marxist-Leninist theory and strategy.* Princeton, N.J.: Princeton University Press.

Conover, P. J. 1984. "The influence of group identifications on political perceptions and evaluation." *Journal of Politics* 46:760–785.

Conover, P. J., and S. Feldman. 1984. "Group identification, values, and the nature of political beliefs." *American Politics Quarterly* 12:151–175.

Contee, C. G. 1976. "Edwin G. Walker, black leader: Generally acknowledged son of David Walker." *Negro Historical Bulletin* 39:556–559.

Converse, P. E. 1964. "The nature of belief systems in mass publics." In *Ideology and Discontent,* ed. D. Apter. New York: Free Press.

Converse, P. E. 1972. "Change in the American electorate." In *The human meaning of social change,* ed. A. A. Campbell and P. E. Converse. New York: Russell Sage Foundation.

Cook, F. L., E. J. Barrett, and S. J. Popkin. 1987. *Convergent perspectives on social welfare policy: Views from Congressmembers, the general public, and AFDC recipients,* unpublished manuscript, Northwestern University.

Cook, S. D. 1972. Introduction to *Black political parties,* ed. H. Walton. New York: The Free Press.

Coser, L. A. 1956. *The functions of social conflict.* New York: Free Press.

Cott, Nancy F. 1990. "Across the great divide: Women in politics before and after 1920." In *Women, politics, and change,* ed. L. Tilly and P. Gurin. New York: Russell Sage Foundation.

Cotter, P. R., J. Cohen, and P. B. Coulter. 1982. "Race of interview effects in telephone interviews." *Public Opinion Quarterly* 46:278–284.

Cox, O. C. 1948. *Caste, class and race.* Garden City, N.Y.: Doubleday.

Crotty, W. J. 1971. "Party effort and its impact on the vote." *American Political Science Review* 65:439–450.

Crotty, W. J. 1985. "The presidential nomination process and minority candidates: The lessons of the Jackson campaign." Paper presented at conference sponsored by the Joint Center of Political Studies, April, Washington, D.C.

Cruse, H. 1987. *Plural but equal.* New York: William Morrow.

Dahl, R. A. 1961. *Who governs? Democracy and power in an American City.* New Haven, Conn.: Yale University Press.

Daniels, L. A. 1981. "The new black conservatives." *New York Times Magazine,* October 4, 20–60.

Danigelis, N. L. 1982. "Race, class, and political involvement in the U.S." *Social Forces* 61:532–550.

Davis, A. Y. 1983. *Women, race and class.* New York: Vintage Books, Random House.

Dawson, M. C. 1986. "Race, class and dimensions of Afro-American political attitudes." University of Michigan, unpublished paper.

DeMaio, T. J. 1980. "Refusals: Who, where and why?" *Public Opinion Quarterly* 44:223–233.

Dillingham, G. L. 1981. "The emerging black middle class: Class conscious or race conscious?" *Ethnic and Racial Studies* 4:432–451.

Dittmer, J. 1986. "The Politics of the Mississippi movement, 1954–1964." In *Civil rights movement in America,* ed. C. W. Eagles, 65–93. Jackson: University of Mississippi Press.

Douglass, F. 1881. *Life and times of Frederick Douglass.* Hartford, Conn.: Park.

Drake, St. C., and H. R. Cayton. 1945. *Black metropolis.* New York: Harcourt, Brace.

Draper, N. R., and H. Smith. 1966. *Applied regression analysis.* New York: Wiley.

Dreyer, J. T. 1976. *China's forty millions minority nationalities and national integration in the People's Republic of China.* Cambridge, Mass.: Harvard University Press.

DuMouchel, W. H., and G. J. Duncan. 1983. "Using sample weights in multiple regression analysis of stratified samples." *Journal of the American Statistical Association* 78:535–543.

Eagles, C. W., ed. 1986. *The civil rights movement in America.* Jackson: University of Mississippi Press.

Engstrom, R. L., and M. D. McDonald. 1981. "The election of blacks to City Councils— classifying the impact of electoral arrangements on the seats-population relationship." *American Political Science Review* 75:344–354.

Enloe, C. H. 1973. *Ethnic conflict and political development.* Boston: Little, Brown.

Erikson, E. 1956. "The problem of ego identity." *Journal of the American Psychoanalytic Association* 4:56–121.

Fanon, F. 1963. *The wretched of the earth.* New York: Grove Press.

Farley, R. 1984. *Blacks and whites: Narrowing the gap?* Cambridge, Mass.: Harvard University Press.

Farley, R., and W. Allen. 1987. *The color line and the quality of life in America.* New York: Russell Sage Foundation.

Faw, R., and N. Skelton. 1986. *Thunder in America: The improbable presidential campaign of Jesse Jackson.* Austin: Texas Monthly Press.

Feagin, J. R. 1975. *Subordinating the poor.* Englewood Cliffs, N.J.: Prentice-Hall.

Fireman, B., and W. A. Gamson. 1979. "Utilitarian logic in the resource mobilization perspective." In *The dynamics of social movements,* ed. M. Zald and J. McCarthy. Cambridge, Mass.: Winthrop.

Fischer, C. 1977. *Networks and places: Social relations in the urban setting.* New York: Free Press.

Flewellen, K. 1981. "The national black independent political party: Will history repeat?" *Freedomways* 21:93–105.

Fossett, M. A., O. R. Galle, and W. R. Kelly. 1986. "Racial occupational inequality, 1940–1980: National and regional trends." *American Sociological Review* 51:421–429.

Fragier, E. F. 1957. *Black bourgeoisie: The rise of a new middle class in the United States.* Glencoe, Ill.: Free Press.

Franklin, J. H. 1943. *The free negro in North Carolina, 1790–1860.* Chapel Hill: University of North Carolina Press.

Franklin, J. H. [1947] 1987. *From slavery to freedom.* New York: Alfred Knopf.

Freeman, R. 1976. *Black elite: The new market for highly educated black Americans.* New York: McGraw-Hill.

Frye, H. T. 1975. "The rise of a black political party: Institutional consequences of emerging political consciousness." Ph.D. diss., University of California, Berkeley.

Gamson, W. A. 1968. *Power and discontent.* Homewood, Ill.: Dorsey Press.

Gamson, W. A. 1975. *The strategy of social protest.* Homewood, Ill.: Dorsey Press.

Garrow, D. J. 1986. *Bearing the cross: Martin Luther King, Jr. and the Southern Christian Leadership Conference.* New York: William Morrow.

Geertz, C. 1963. *Old societies and new states.* New York: Free Press.

Giddings, P. 1984. *When and where I enter: The impact of black women on race and sex in America.* New York: William Morrow.

Gilliam, F. D., Jr. 1986. "Black America: Divided by class?" *Public Opinion* 9:53–57.

Githens, M., and J. L. Prestage. 1977. *A portrait of marginality: The political behavior of the American woman.* New York: David McKay.

Glazer, N. 1971. "Blacks and ethnic groups: The differences and the political difference it makes." In *Key issues in the Afro-American experience,* ed. N. I. Huggins, M. Kilson, and D. M. Fox., vol. 2, 193–211. New York: Harcourt Brace Jovanovich.

Glazer, N. 1975. "The universalisation of ethnicity: Peoples in the boiling pot." *Encounter* 44:8–17.

Glazer, N. 1984. "The structure of ethnicity." *Public Opinion* 7:2–6.

Glazer, N., and D. P. Moynihan, ed. 1975. *Ethnicity: Theory and experience.* Cambridge, Mass.: Harvard University Press.

Greeley, A. M. 1974. "Political participation among ethnic groups in the United States: A preliminary reconnaissance." *American Journal of Sociology* 80:170–204.

Green, P. 1984. "The reality beneath the rainbow." *Nation,* March 17.

Griffin, W. W. 1983. "The political realignment of black voters in Indianapolis, 1924." *Indiana Magazine of History* 79(2): 133–166.

Groves, R. M., and R. L. Kahn. 1979. *Surveys by telephone: A national comparison with personal interviews.* New York: Academic Press.

Groves, R., and J. M. Lepkowski. 1982. "Alternative Dual Frame Mixed Made Survey Designs." Proceedings of the Section on Survey Research Methods, American Statistical Associated, August, 1982, Cincinnati, Ohio.

Gurin, P. 1987. "The political implications of women's statuses." In *Modern women managing dual roles,* ed. F. Crosby. New Haven, Conn.: Yale University Press.

Gurin, P., and E. G. Epps. 1975. *Black consciousness, identity and achievement.* New York: Wiley.

Gurin, P., G. Gurin, and B. M. Morrison. 1978. "Personal and ideological aspects of internal and external control." *Social Psychology Quarterly* 41:275–296.

Gurin, P., A. H. Miller, and G. Gurin. 1980. "Stratum identification and consciousness." *Social Psychology Quarterly* 43:30–47.

Gurin, P., and B. M. Morrison. 1976. *Education, labor market experiences, and current expectancies of black and white men and women.* Ann Arbor, Mich.: Institute for Social Research.

Gurin, P., and A. Townsend. 1986. "Properties of gender identity and their implications for gender consciousness." *British Journal of Social Psychology* 25:139–148.

Hacker, A. 1987. "American apartheid." *New York Review of Books,* December 3, 26–33.

Hall, W. S., W. E. Cross, and R. Freedle. 1972. "Stages in the development of black awareness: An exploratory investigation." In *Black psychology,* ed. R. L. Jones, 156–165. New York: Harper.

Hamilton, C. V. 1969. "Conflict, race and system-transformation in the United States." *Journal of International Affairs* 23(1):106–118.

Hamilton, C. V. 1973. *The black experience in American politics.* New York: G. P. Putnam's Sons.

Hamilton, C. V. 1978. "Blacks and electoral politics." *Social Policy* 9(1):21–27.

Hamilton, C. V. 1981. "New elites and pluralism." *Proceedings of the Academy of Political Science* 34(2):167–173.

Hamilton, C. V. 1982a. Foreword to *The new black politics: The search for political power,* ed. M. B. Breston, L. J. Henderson, Jr., and P. Puryear, xvii–xx. New York: Longman.

Hamilton, C. V. 1982b. "America in search of itself: A review essay." *Political Science Quarterly* 97:487–493.

Hamilton, C. V. 1986a. "Social policy and the welfare of black Americans: From rights to resources." *Political Science Quarterly* 101:239–255.

Hamilton, C. V. 1986b. "Federal law and the courts in the civil rights movement." In *Civil rights movement in America,* ed. C. W. Eagles, 97–117. Jackson: University of Mississippi Press.

Hannan, M. T. 1979. "The dynamics of ethnic boundaries in modern states." In *National Development and the World System,* ed. J. W. Meyer and M. T. Hannan, 235–275. Chicago: University of Chicago Press.

Harding, V. 1981. *There is a river.* New York: Harcourt Brace Jovanovich.

Harman, H. H. 1967. *Modern factor analysis.* 2d ed. Chicago: University of Chicago Press.

Hatchett, S. J. 1982. "Black racial attitude change in Detroit: 1968–1974." Ann Arbor, Mich.: University Microfilm.

Hatchett, S. J. 1987. "Facts and artifacts of race of interviewer effect: The case of the telephone survey." Paper presented at meetings of the Southern Sociological Society, Atlanta.

Hatchett, S. J., and H. Schuman. 1975–1976. "The effects of black and white interviewers on white responses." *Public Opinion Quarterly* 39:523–528.

Hawkins, D. F. 1975. Estimation of non-response bias. *Sociological Methods* 3:462–485.

Hayes-Bautista, D. E. 1974. "Becoming Chicano: A 'disassimilation' theory of transformation of ethnic identity." Ph.D. diss., University of California, Berkeley.

Hechter, M. 1975. *Internal colonialism: The Celtic fringe in British national development 1536–1966.* Berkeley: University of California Press.

Henderson, L. J., Jr. 1982. "Black politics and the American presidential elections." In *The new black politics,* ed. M. B. Breston, L. J. Henderson, Jr., and P. Puryear, 3–27. New York: Longman.

Hochschild, J. L. 1981. *What's fair? American beliefs about distributive justice.* Cambridge, Mass.: Harvard University Press.

Holden, M. 1972. "Memorandum on black political strategies." *Afro-American Studies,* 3(3): 143–174.

Holden, M. 1973. *The politics of the black "nation."* Peabody, Mass.: Chandler-Smith.

Holden, M. 1973. *The white man's burden.* Peabody, Mass.: Chandler-Smith.

Holden, M. 1986. *The president, Congress, and race relations.* Boulder: University of Colorado Press.

Holden, M. 1988. "Racial stratifications as fact and as issue: The last of presidential leadership." Paper presented at a symposium sponsored by the Smithsonian Institution and the Joint Center for Political Studies, March, Washington, D.C.

Holt, T. 1977. *Black over white: Negro political leadership in South Carolina during Reconstruction.* Chicago: University of Illinois Press.

House, J. S., and W. M. Mason. 1975. "Political alienation in America, 1952–1968." *American Sociological Review* 40:123–147.

Howard, V. B. 1974. "Negro politics and the suffrage question in Kentucky, 1866–1872." *Register of the Kentucky Historical Society* 72:111–133.

Huber, J., and W. H. Form. 1973. *Income and ideology.* New York: Free Press.

Huggins, N. I., M. Kilson, and D. M. Fox, ed. 1971. *Key issues in the Afro-American experience.* 2 vols. New York: Harcourt Brace Jovanovich.

Inglis, K. M., R. Groves, and S. Heeringa. 1987. "Telephone sample designs for the black household population." *Survey Methodology* 13:1–14.

Isaacs, H. R. 1975. *Idols of the tribe.* New York: Harper & Row.

Isaacs, H. R. 1979. *Power and identity: Tribalism in world politics.* New York: Foreign Policy Association.

Jackson, J. S., and S. J. Hatchett. 1986. "Intergenerational research: Methodological considerations." In *Intergenerational relations,* ed. N. Datan, A. L. Greene, and H. W. Reese. Hillsdale, N.J.: Lawrence Erlbaum Associates.

Jackson, J. S., S. J. Hatchett, and R. E. Brown. 1985. "Attitudes of the black electorate toward the candidates and issues in 1984," University of Michigan, unpublished paper.

Jackson, J. S., W. McCullough, and G. Gurin. 1981. "Family socialization environments and group identity developments in black Americans." In *Black families,* ed. H. McAdoo. Beverly Hills, Calif.: Sage Publications.

Jackson, J. S., M. Tucker, and P. J. Bowman. 1982. "Conceptual and methodological problems in survey research on black Americans." In *Methodological problems in minority research,* ed. W. T. Lui. Pacific Asian American Mental Health Research Center.

Jennings, J. T. 1985. "The current population survey of voting and registration: Summary and history." Paper presented at League of Women Voters Education Fund Conference on Electoral Participation, July, Washington, D.C.

Jones, H. M. 1978. "Black political empowerment in Atlanta: Myth and reality." *Annals of the American Academy of Political and Social Science* 439:90–117.

Jones, J. 1990. "The political implications of black and white women's work in the South, 1890–1965." In *Women, politics, and change,* ed. L. Tilly and P. Gurin. New York: Russell Sage Foundation.

Jordan, W. D. 1968. *White over black.* Chapel Hill: University of North Carolina Press.

Jordan, W. D. 1970. "Development of slavery in the United States." *America's black past,* ed. E. Foner. New York: Harper & Row.

Karnig, A. K., and S. Welch. 1982. "Electoral structure and black representation on city councils." *Social Science Quarterly* 63:99–114.

Katznelson, I. 1973. *Black men, white cities: Race, politics and migration in the U.S., 1900–30, and Britain, 1948–68.* London: Oxford University Press.

Katznelson, I. 1981. *City trenches: Urban politics and the patterning of class in the United States.* Chicago: University of Chicago Press.

Kilson, M. 1971. "Political change in the Negro ghetto, 1900–1940s." In *Key issues in the Afro-American experience,* ed. N. I. Huggins, M. Kilson, and D. M. Fox, vol. 2, 167–192. New York: Harcourt Brace Jovanovich.

Kinder, D. R., and D. O. Sears. 1985. "Public opinion and political action." In *The handbook of social psychology,* ed. G. Kindzey and E. Aronson, vol. 2. New York: Random House.

King, M. L., Jr. 1986. "I have found a dream." In *A testament of hope: The essential writings of Martin Luther King, Jr.,* ed. J. M. Washington. New York: Harper & Row.

King, R. R. 1973. *Minorities under communism: Nationalities as a source of tension among Balkan communist states.* Cambridge, Mass.: Harvard University Press.

Kleppner, P. 1970. *The cross of culture: A social analysis of midwestern politics 1850–1900.* New York: Free Press.

Klobus-Edwards, P., J. N. Edwards, and D. L. Klemmack. 1978. "Difference in social participation: Blacks and whites." *Social Forces* 56:1035–1052.

Kluegel, J. R., and E. R. Smith. 1981. "Beliefs about stratification." *Annual Review of Sociology* 7:29–56.

Kolko, G. 1963. *The triumph of conservatism: A reinterpretation of American history, 1900–1916.* Glencoe, Ill.: Free Press.

Kramer, G. H. 1971. "The effects of precinct-level canvassing on voting behavior." *Public Opinion Quarterly* 34:560–572.

Labov, W. 1972. *Language in the inner city.* Philadelphia: University of Pennsylvania Press.

Landess, T. H., and R. M. Quinn. 1985. *Jesse Jackson and the politics of race.* Ottawa, Ill.: Jameson Books.

Landry, B. 1978. "Growth, the black middle-class in the 1960s." *Urban League Review* 3:68–82.

Landry, B. 1980. "The social and economic adequacy of the black middle class." In *Dilemma of the New Black Middle Class,* ed. J. Washington. Philadelphia: University of Pennsylvania.

Landry, B. 1987. *The new black middle class.* Berkeley: University of California Press.

Lane, R. E. 1959. *Political life.* Glencoe, Ill.: Free Press.

Lane, R. E. 1986. "Market justice, political justice." *American Political Science Review* 80:383–402.

Lansing, M. 1985a. "Gender, race, and political attitudes: Impact on the vote." Paper presented at annual meeting of the Midwest Political Science Association, Chicago.

Lansing, M. 1985b. "The case for women in 1984: Voting turnout in America—an enigma." Paper presented at League of Women Voters Education Fund Conference on Electoral Participation, July, Washington, D.C.

Lauwagie, B. N. 1979. "Ethnic boundaries in modern states: *Romano Lavo-Lil* revisited." *American Journal of Sociology* 85:310–337.

Lawson, S. F. 1985. *In pursuit of power: Southern and electoral politics, 1965–1982.* New York: Columbia University Press.

Lebsock, S. 1990. "Women and American politics, 1880–1920." In *Women, politics, and change,* ed. L. Tilly and P. Gurin. New York: Russell Sage Foundation.

Leifer, E. 1981. "Competing models of political mobilization: The role of ethnic ties." *American Journal of Sociology* 87:23–47.

Lemann, N. 1986. "The origins of the underclass." *Atlantic Monthly*, June, 21–55; July, 55–69.

LeMay, M. C. 1985. *The struggle for influence: The impact of minority groups on politics and public policy in the United States.* Lanham, Md.: University Press of America.

Lester, M. 1984. "Self: Sociological portraits." In *The existential self in society*, ed. J. A. Kotarba and A. Fontana. Chicago: The University of Chicago Press.

Lewin, K. 1948. *Resolving social conflict.* New York: Harper & Brothers.

Lewis, I. A., and W. Schneider. 1985. "Hard times: The public on poverty." *Public Opinion* 8:2–7.

Lewison, P. 1932. *Race, class, and party: A history of Negro suffrage and white politics in the South.* London: Oxford University Press.

Lichter, L. S. 1985. "Who speaks for black America?" *Public Opinion* 8:41–70.

Litwak, L. F. 1970. "The emancipation of the Negro abolitionist." In *America's black past*, ed. E. Foner. New York: Harper & Row.

Logan, R. 1957. *A Negro in the United States.* New York: Van Nostrand Reinhold.

Lomax, L. E. 1962. *The Negro revolt.* New York: Harper & Row.

McAdam, D. 1982. *Political process and the development of black insurgency, 1930–1970.* Chicago: University of Chicago Press.

McCormick, R. P. 1966. *The second American party system.* Chapel Hill: University of North Carolina.

McLemore, L. B. 1965. "The Freedom Democratic Party and the changing political status of the Negro in Mississippi." Master's thesis, Atlantic University.

McLemore, L. B. 1972. "The effect of political participation upon a closed society—a state in transition: The changing political climate in Mississippi." *Negro Educational Review* 23:3–12.

Mack, A. C., M. D. Coleman, and L. B. McLemore. 1988. "Current trends in black politics: Prospects and problems." In *Contemporary Southern politics*, ed. J. F. Lea. Baton Rouge: Louisiana State University Press.

Mannheim, K. [1952] 1972. *The problems of generations: Essays on the sociology of knowledge.* London: Routledge & Kegan Paul.

Marable, M. 1984. "The paradox of reform: Black politics and the Democratic party." *Southern Exposure* 12:20–25.

Marable, M. 1985. *Black American politics: From the Washington marches to Jesse Jackson.* London: Verso, New Left Books.

Mark, M. M. 1980. "Justice in the aggregate: The perceived fairness of the distribution of income." Northwestern University.

Markus, H., and R. B. Zajonc. 1985. "The cognitive perspective in social psychology." In *The handbook of social psychology*, 2nd ed., ed. G. Kindzey and E. Aronson, vol. 1. New York: Random House.

Marvick, D. 1970. "The political socialization of the American Negro." In *Political opinion and behavior: Essays and studies*, ed. E. C. Dreyer and W. A. Rosenbaum, 161–179. 2d ed. Belmont, Calif.: Wadsworth.

Marx, G. T. 1967. *Protest and prejudice: A study of belief in the black community.* New York: Harper & Row.

Mason, W. M., H. S. House, and S. S. Martin. 1981. *Dimensions of political alienation in America: Theoretical and empirical.* Ann Arbor: Population Studies Center, University of Michigan.

Mays, B., and J. Nicholson. 1933. *The Negro church.* New York: Arno Press, New York Times.

Mazrui, A. 1975. "Ethnic stratification and the military-agrarian complex." In *Ethnicity: Theory and experience,* ed. N. Glazer and D. P. Moynihan, 420–449. Cambridge, Mass.: Harvard University Press.

Memmi, A. 1968. *Dominated man.* Boston: Beacon Press.

Merton, R. K. [1957] 1968. "Continuities in the theory of reference group behavior." In *Social theory and social structure,* 215–248. New York: Free Press.

Merton, R. K. 1987. "Three fragments from a sociologist's notebook." *Annual Review of Sociology* 13:1–28.

Merton, R. K., and A. S. Kitt (Rossi). 1950. "Contributions to the theory of reference group behavior." In *Continuities in social research: Studies in the scope and method of the American soldier,* R. K. Merton and P. F. Lazarfeld, 40–105. Glencoe, Ill.: Free Press.

Milbrath, L., and M. L. Goel. 1977. *Political participation.* 3d ed. Chicago: Rand McNally.

Miller, A. H., P. Gurin, G. Gurin, and O. Malanchuk. 1981. "Group consciousness and political participation." *American Journal of Political Science* 25:494–511.

Miller, W. 1984. "What realignment?" *Focus* 12:6–8.

Miller, W. E., and M. K. Jennings. 1986. *Parties in transition: A longitudinal study of party elites and party supporters.* New York: Russell Sage Foundation.

Miller, W. E., A. H. Miller, and E. J. Schneider. 1980. *American national election studies data source book, 1952–1978.* Cambridge, Mass.: Harvard University Press.

Mitofsky, W. J., and M. Plissner. 1980. "The making of the delegates, 1968–1980." *Public Opinion* 3:37–43.

Morris, A. D. 1981. "Black southern students sit-in movement: An analysis of internal organization." *American Sociological Review* 46:744–767.

Morris, A. D. 1984. *Origins of the civil rights movement: Black communities organizing for change.* New York: Free Press.

Morris, A. D., S. J. Hatchett, and R. E. Brown. 1987. In *Political learning in adulthood: Constancy and change,* ed. R. S. Sigel. Chicago: University of Chicago Press.

Morris, R. T., and R. J. Murphy. 1966. "A paradigm for the study of class consciousness." *Sociology and Social Research* 50:298–313.

Mydral, G. 1944. *An American dilemma.* New York: Harper & Brothers.

Nagel, J. 1982. "The political mobilization of native Americans." *Social Science Journal* 19:37–45.

Nagel, J., and S. Olzak. 1982. "Ethnic mobilization in new and old states: An extension of the competition model." *Social Problems* 30:127–143.

Nelson, W. E., Jr. 1982. "Cleveland: The rise and fall of the new black politics." In *The new black politics: The search for political power,* ed. M. B. Preston, L. J. Henderson, Jr., and P. Puryear, 187–208. New York: Longman.

Newsweek. 1981. "The black conservative." March 9, 29–33.

Nielsen, F. 1985. "Toward a theory of ethnic solidarity in modern societies." *American Sociological Review* 50:133–149.

Norton, M. B., D. M. Katzman, P. D. Escott, H. P. Chudacoff, T. G. Paterson, and W. M. Tuttle, Jr. 1982. *A people and a nation: A history of the United States,* vol. 2. *Since 1965.* Boston: Houghton Mifflin.

Oberschall, A. 1978. "Theories of social conflict." *Annual Review of Sociology* 4:291–315.

Olsen, M. E. 1970. "Social and political participation of blacks." *American Sociological Review* 35:682–697.

Olzak, S. 1982. "Race and ethnicity: Residual or explanatory concepts." Paper presented to the Sociological Studies of Social Problems, San Francisco.

Olzak, S. 1983. "Contemporary ethnic mobilization." *Annual Review of Sociology* 9:355–374.

Paige, J. M. 1971. "Political orientation and riot participation." *American Sociological Review* 36:810–820.

Parenti, M. 1967. "Ethnic politics and the persistence of ethnic identification." *American Political Science Review* 717–726.

Paris, P. J. 1985. *The social teaching of the black churches.* Philadelphia: Fortress Press.

Park, R. 1913. "Racial assimilation in secondary groups with particular reference to the Negro." *Publication of the American Sociological Society* 8:66–83.

Patterson, K. D., J. T. Young, and R. Y. Shapiro. 1986. "Economic status and other influences on public opinion toward social welfare policies." Paper presented at the Annual Meeting of the Northeastern Political Science Association, Boston, Mass.

Patterson, O. 1977. *Ethnic chauvinism: The reactionary impulse.* New York: Stein & Day.

Pease, W. H., and J. H. Pease. 1971. "The Negro convention movement." In *Key issues in the Afro-American experience,* ed. N. I. Huggins, M. Kilson, and D. M. Fox, vol. 1, 191–205. New York: Harcourt Brace Jovanovich.

Pinderhughes, D. 1986. "Political choices: A realignment in partisanship among black voters." In *The state of black America,* ed. J. D. Williams, 85–113. New York: The National Urban League.

Pollock, B. H. 1984. "The Depression and the New Deal." *UCLA Historical Journal* 5:5–23.

Powell, G. B., Jr. 1986. "American voter turnout in comparative perspective." *American Political Science Review* 80:17–43.

Prestage, J. L. 1977. *Black political scientists and black survival: Essays in honor of a black scholar.* Detroit, Mich.: Balamp.

Preston, M. B. 1982. "Black politics and public policy in Chicago: Self-interest versus constituent representation." In *The new black politics: The search for political power,* ed. M. B. Preston, L. J. Henderson, Jr., and P. Puryear, 159–186. New York: Longman.

Preston, M. B. 1985. "The 1984 presidential primary campaign. Who voted for Jesse Jackson and why?" University of Illinois. Unpublished paper.

Public Opinion. 1984. Ethnicity in America, Opinion roundup 7:17–31.

Public Opinion. 1985. Poverty in America, Opinion roundup 8:2–28.

Quarles, B. 1969. *The Negro in the making of America.* New York: Collier Books.

Ragin, C. 1977. "Class, status and 'reactive ethnic cleavages': The social bases of political regionalism." *American Sociological Review* 42:438–450.

Ranney, A., and W. Kendall. 1951. *Democracy and the American system.* New York: Harcourt Brace.

Rawls, J. 1971. *A theory of justice.* Cambridge, Mass.: Harvard University Press.

Redkey, e. s. 1971. "The flowering of black nationalism: Henry McNeal Turner and Marcus Garvey." In *Key issues in the Afro-American experience,* ed. N. I. Huggins, M. Kilson, and D. M. Fox, vol. 2, 107–124. New York: Harcourt Brace Jovanovich.

Reed, A. L., Jr. 1986. *The Jesse Jackson phenomenon.* New Haven, Conn.: Yale University Press.

Reynolds, B. A. 1975. *Jesse Jackson: The man, the movement, the myth.* Chicago: Nelson-Hall.

Rice, M. F., and W. Jones, Jr., ed. 1984. *Contemporary public policy perspectives and black Americans: Issues in an era of retrenchment politics.* Westport, Conn.: Greenwood Press.

Rokkan, S. 1970. *Citizens, elections, and parties.* New York: Rand McNally.

Rosenstone, S. J., R. L. Behr, and E. H. Lazarus. 1984. *Third parties in America: citizen response to major party failure.* Princeton, N.J.: Princeton University Press.

Rosenstone, S. J., J. M. Hansen, and D. R. Kinder. 1986. "Measuring change in personal economic well-being." *Public Opinion Quarterly* 50:176–192.

St. Angelo, D., and P. Puryear. 1982. "Fear, apathy and other dimensions of black voting." In *The new black politics: The search for political power,* ed. M. B. Preston, L. J. Henderson, Jr., and P. Puryear, 109–130. New York: Longman.

Salamon, L. M., and S. Van Evera. 1973a. "Fear, apathy, and discrimination: A test of three explanations of political participation." *American Political Science Review* 67:1288–1306.

Salamon, L. M., and S. Van Evera. 1973b. "Fear revisited: A rejoinder to comment by Sam Kernall." *American Political Science Review* 67:1319–1326.

Schewel, M. J. 1981. "Local politics in Lynchburg, Virginia, in the 1890s." *Virginia Magazine of History and Biography* 89(2): 170–180.

Schlozman, R. L. 1990. "Representing women in Washington: Organizations of women in pressure politics." In *Women, politics, and change,* ed. L. Tilly and P. Gurin. New York: Russell Sage Foundation.

Schuman, H., and J. Converse. 1971. "The effects of black and white interviewers on black responses in 1968." *Public Opinion Quarterly* 35:44–68.

Schuman, H., and S. Hatchett. 1974. "Black racial attitudes: Trends and complexities." Ann Arbor, Mich.: Institute of Social Research.

Schuman, H., C. Steeh, and L. Bobo. 1985. *Racial attitudes in America: Trends and interpretations.* Cambridge, Mass.: Harvard University Press.

Sears, D. O., J. Citrin, and R. Kosterman. 1985. "The white response to Jesse Jackson in 1984." Paper presented at annual convention of the American Psychological Association, August, Los Angeles, and the annual meeting of the American Political Science Association, August, New Orleans.

Sears, D. O., R. R. Lau, T. R. Tyler, and H. M. Allen, Jr. 1980. "Self-interest vs. symbolic politics in policy attitudes and presidential voting." *American Political Science Review* 74:670–684.

Shanks, M. J., and W. E. Miller. 1985. "Policy direction and performance evaluation: Complementary explanations of the Reagan election." Paper presented at the annual meeting of the American Political Science Association, August, New Orleans.

Shapiro, R. Y., and K. D. Patterson. 1986. "The dynamics of public opinion toward social welfare policy." Paper presented at the annual meeting of the American political Science Association, Washington, D.C.

Shapiro, R. Y., K. D. Patterson, J. Russell, and J. T. Young. 1987a. "The polls: Public assistance." *Public Opinion Quarterly* 51:120–130.

Shapiro, R. Y., K. D. Patterson, J. Russell, and J. T. Young. 1987b. "The polls: Employment and social welfare." *Public Opinion Quarterly* 51:226–281.

Sheffield, J. F., Jr., and C. D. Hadley. 1984. "Racial voting in a biracial city." *American Politics Quarterly* 12:449–465.

Shingles, R. D. 1981. "Black consciousness and political participation: The missing link." *American Political Science Review* 75:76–91.

Shingles, R. D. 1986. "The black gender gap: Double jeopardy and politicalization." Paper presented at meeting of the Midwest Political Science Association, Chicago.

Sigelman, L. P., W. Roeder, M. E. Jewell, and M. A. Baer. 1985. "Voting and nonvoting: A multi-election perspective." *American Journal of Political Science* 29:749–765.

Silver, B. D., B. A. Anderson, and P. R. Abramson. 1986. "Who overreports voting?" *American Political Science Review* 80:613–624.

Sitkoff, H. 1978. *A new deal for blacks: The emergence of civil rights as a national issue. Vol. 1, The Depression decade.* New York: Oxford University Press.

Skowronek, S. 1982. *Building a new American state: The expansion of national administrative capacities, 1877–1920.* Cambridge, England: Cambridge University Press.

Smith, A. D. 1981. *The ethnic revival.* Cambridge, England: Cambridge University Press.

Smith, P. G. 1985. "History of the black political movement." *Dollars and Sense* 11:82–89.

Smith, R. C. 1981. "Black power and transformation from protest to politics." *Political Science Quarterly* 96:431–443.

Smith, R. C., and J. P. McCormick, II. 1984. "The challenge of a black presidential candidacy." *New Directions,* 38–43.

Steeh, C. G. 1981. "Trends in non-response rates, 1952–1979." *Public Opinion Quarterly* 45:40–57.

Stephan, W. G. 1985. "Intergroup relations." In *The handbook of social psychology,* 2nd ed., G. Lindzey and E. Aronson, vol. 2, 599–658. New York: Random House.

Sumner, W. G. 1906. *Folkways: A study of the sociological importance of usages, manners, customs, mores and morals.* New York: Ginn.

Tajfel, H. 1974. "Social identity and intergroup behavior." *Social Science Information* 13: 69–89.

Tajfel, H. 1978. "Social categorization, social identity, and social comparison." In *Differentiation between social groups,* ed. H. Tajfel, 61–76. New York: Academic Press.

Tajfel, H., and J. C. Turner. 1986. "The social identity theory of intergroup behavior." In *Psychology of intergroup relations,* ed. S. Worchel and W. G. Austin. Rev. ed. Chicago: Nelson-Hall.

Tate, K. 1985. "Ideological self-identification among blacks." Paper presented at the Annual Meeting of the American Political Science Association, August. New Orleans.

Terborg-Penn, R. 1983. "Discontented black feminists: Prelude and postscript to the passage of the Nineteenth Amendment." In *Decades of discontent: The women's movement, 1920–1940,* ed. L. Scharf and J. M. Jensen. Westport, Conn.: Greenwood Press.

Thornberry, O. T., and J. T. Massey. 1983. "Coverage and response in random digit dialed national surveys." Paper presented at meeting of the American Sociological Association, Detroit, Mich.

Thurman, H. 1945. *Deep river.* New York: Kennikat Press.

Tilly, C. 1978. *From mobilization to revolution.* Reading, Mass.: Addison-Wesley.

Tilly, C. 1981. Introduction to *Class conflict and collective action,* ed. L. A. Tilly and C. Tilly, 13–25. Beverly Hills, Calif.: Sage Publications.

Tilly, L., and P. Gurin, ed. 1990. *Women, politics, and change.* New York: Russell Sage Foundation.

Tomlins, C. L. 1985. *The state and the unions: Labor relations, law and the organized labor movement in America, 1880–1960.* Cambridge, England: Cambridge University Press.

Tourangeau, R., and A. W. Smith. 1985. "Finding subgroups for surveys." *Public Opinion Quarterly* 49:351–369.

Trachtenberg, A. 1982. *The incorporation of America: Culture and society in the gilded age.* New York: Hill and Wang.

Tucker, C. 1983. "Interviewer effects in telephone surveys." *Public Opinion Quarterly* 47:84–95.

U.S. Bureau of the Census. 1985. *Current Population Reports,* ser. P-20, no. 397 (January). Washington, D.C.: U.S. Government Printing Office.

U.S. Department of Labor. 1965. *The Negro family: The case for national action.* Washington, D.C.: U.S. Government Printing Office.

U.S. Department of Labor. 1983. *Time of change: 1983 handbook on women workers.* Bulletin no. 298. Washington, D.C.: U.S. Government Printing Office.

van Den Berghe, P. 1981. *The ethnic phenomenon.* New York: Elsevier.

Verba, S., B. Ahmed, and A. Bhatt. 1971. *Caste, race, and politics: A comparison of India and the United States.* Beverly Hills, Calif.: Sage Publications.

Verba, S., and N. H. Nie. 1972. *Participation in America: Political democracy and social equality.* New York: Harper & Row.

Verba, S., N. H. Nie, and J. O. Kim. 1978. *Participation and political equality: A seven-nation comparison.* Cambridge, England: Cambridge University Press.

Verba, S., and G. R. Orren. 1985. *Equality in America: The view from the top.* Cambridge, Mass.: Harvard University Press.

Waksberg, J. 1978. "Sampling methods for random digit dialing." *Journal of the American Statistical Association* 73:40–46.

Walker, J. I. 1983. "The origins and maintenance of interest groups in America." *American Political Science Review* 77:390–406.

Walters, R. W. 1975. "Strategy for 1976: A black political party." *Black Scholar* 7:8–19.

Walters, R. W. 1980. "Black presidential politics in 1980: Bargaining or begging?" *Black Scholar* 4:22–31.

Walters, R. W. 1983. "Race, resources, conflict." *Urban League Review* 7(1): 53–64.

Walters, R. W. 1985. "Black voters." *Society* 2(4):5.

Walters, R. W. 1988. *Black presidential politics: A strategic approach.* New York: SUNY Press.

Walton, H., Jr. 1972. *Black political parties: An historical and political analysis.* New York: Free Press.

Walton, H., Jr. 1985. *Invisible politics: Black political behavior.* Albany: State University of New York Press.

Weber, M. [1922] 1946. "Class, status, party." In *From Max Weber: Essays in sociology,* ed. H. M. Gerth and C. W. Mills, 180–195. New York: Oxford University Press.

Weiss, N. J. 1983. *Farewell to the party of Lincoln: Black politics in the age of FDR.* Princeton, N.J.: Princeton University Press.

Weiss, N. J. 1986. "Creative tension in the leadership of the civil rights movement." In *Civil rights movement in America,* ed. C. W. Eagles, 39–55. Jackson: University of Mississippi Press.

Welch, S., and L. Foster. 1987. "Class and conservatism in the black community." *American Politics Quarterly* 15:445–470.

Wiebe, R. H. 1967. *The search for order, 1877–1920.* New York: Hill and Wang.

Williams, E. N. 1982. "Black political progress in the 1970s: The electoral arena." In *The new black politics: The search for political power,* ed. M. B. Preston, L. J. Henderson, Jr., and P. Puryear, 73–108. New York: Longman.

Williams, R. 1975. "Relative deprivation." In *The idea of social structure,* ed. L. A. Coser. New York: Harcourt Brace Jovanovich.

Williamson, J. B. 1974a. "Beliefs about welfare poor." *Sociological Social Research* 58:163–175.

Williamson, J. B. 1974b. "Beliefs about motivation of poor and attitudes toward poverty policy." *Social Problems* 21:634–648.

Wilson, G. 1980. *Interest groups in the United States.* Oxford, England: Oxford University Press.

Wilson, J. Q. 1965. *Negro politics: The search for leadership.* New York: Free Press.

Wilson, W. J. 1978. *The declining significance of race: Blacks and changing American institutions.* 2d ed. Chicago: University of Chicago Press.

Wilson, W. J. 1986. "Academic Controversy and Intellectual Growth." Paper presented at meeting of the American Sociological Association, New York.

Wilson, W. J. 1987. *The truly disadvantaged: The inner city, the underclass, and public policy.* Chicago: University of Chicago Press.

Wolfinger, R. E., and S. J. Rosenstone. 1980. *Who votes?* New Haven, Conn.: Yale University Press.

Woods, R. B. 1982. "C.H.J. Taylor and the movement for black political independence, 1882–1892." *Journal of Negro History* 67(2): 122–135.

Woodward, C. V. 1955. *The strange career of Jim Crow.* New York: Oxford University Press.

Woodward, C. V. 1986. "The Hustler." Review of *The Jesse Jackson Phenomenon* by A. L. Reed, Jr., T. H. Landess, and R. M. Quinn. *New Republic,* June 2, 32–34.

Wright, G. C. 1983. "Black political insurgency in Louisville, Kentucky: The Lincoln Independent Party of 1921." *Journal of Negro History* 68(1):8–23.

Yinger, J. M. 1985. "Ethnicity." *Annual Review of Sociology* 11:151–180.

Young, H. J. 1979. *Major black religious leaders since 1940.* Nashville: Abingdon Press.

Zavalloni, M. 1973. "Social identity: Perspectives and prospects." *Social Science Information* 12:65–91.

Index

blacks: African and West Indian, 218;
antebellum free, 5, 217; debates among,
24; defection of, 59*n*; differences among,
263*n*; economic circumstances of, 94,
109, 122*n*; economic division among,
225–231; economic situation of, 94;
efforts of, to gain political influence, 28;
gender differences among, 72–73; grass
root, 147; history of, 2, 4–12, 137, 243–
244, 245, 252–254; influence of, 231;
location of, **69**, 72; lower-class, 117; low-
income, 226–227; northern, 24, 25; older,
123*n*, 184, 226, 248; political culture of,
118*n*; political goals of, 3, 248; political
options of, 10; political orientations of,
87, **88–92**, 93; political significance of,
32; powerlessness of, 82–83, 109, 233;
racial consciousness of, 229; in Reagan
administration, 51–52; representative
positions for, 34; self-evaluation of, 106;
southern, 24, 25, 72, 236, 253; treatment
of, 56, 102, 236. *See also* disadvantaged
blacks; middle class blacks; whites;
specific issues
Black and Tans, 24, 253
black-white comparisons, 23, 66–67, 71,
161, 233, 239*n*; education, 66, **317**, **319**;
family income, 70, **316**, **318**; party
identification, 87; policy preferences,
316; psychological resources, 249–250,
318–321; racial differences, 245–247;
spending preferences, **316–317**; work,
67, 69
black-white disparities, 198, 201, 223–225,
231–232
black-white division, 206
black-white relations, 86–87, 161, 185, 186,
196, 199–200, 213
black women, 27, 67, 69–71, 72; club
movement, 7–8
Blues and Blacks, 6
Bobo, L., 61*n*
Boston, 6
Boston, T. D., 123*n*, 216, 238*n*, 239*n*
Bowles, S., 239*n*
Bowman, P. J., 121*n*, 209*n*, 278*n*
Bracey, J. H., Jr., 38, 59*n*, 60*n*
Brewer, M. B., 121*n*
Brickman, P., 262*n*
Broman, C. L., 121*n*, 122*n*
Brooks, E., 8, 14*n*, 27, 58*n*
Brown, R. E., 120*n*, 121*n*, 143*n*, 144*n*, 177*n*,
209*n*, 210*n*, 241*n*
Brown, Willie, 155
Brownsville, Texas, 25, 26

Brown v. *Board of Education of Topeka*, 7,
38, 41
Bryan, William Jennings, 234
Bunche, Ralph, 33
bureaucracy, 31
bus: boycotts, 39; transportation, 36
busing, 50, 95, 106, 144*n*
buy-black strategy, 84, 109, 157, 185, 233

California, 32, 36, 37, 51, 175*n*
campaign: activities, 136, 143, **302**, **322**;
activities, traditional, 139, **140**, 142, 256,
300, **301**; finance laws, 206; interest in,
101, 248–249; participation, 240*n*; questions, 138. *See also* church
campaigns, 111, 114; interest in, **116**, 249,
290; 1984, 128, 138, 254
Campbell, B. A., 60*n*, 93, 122*n*
Canada, 29
candidacy, independent, 10, 126
candidates, 190, 197, **312–313**; black, 45,
71, 101, **115**, 179, **303**; black mayoralty,
101, 110, 113, 249; choice of, 87, **131**;
Democratic, 42, 52, 143, 161; evaluation of, 87, 109, 129, 134–135, 152;
identification of blacks with, 19; independent, 129, 146, 187, 200, 210*n*, 259, 260,
264*n*; MFDP, 44; presidential, 45, 128,
129, 146, 161, 260; third-party, 57*n*, 182;
views of, **299**. *See also* ratings
Carden, M. L., 121*n*
Caribbean, 29
Carter, Jimmy, 10, 51, 52, 161
categorical treatment, 229
Catholics, 261
Cavanagh, T. E., 11, 14*n*, 15*n*, 62*n*, 120*n*,
122*n*, 176*n*, 177*n*
Cayton, H. R., 218, 239*n*
CBC. *See* Congressional Black Caucus
CBS surveys, 146–148, 175*n*
census, 274, 276; estimates, 274; 1970, 214;
1980, 66, 67, 71, 214, 226, 250, 269, 270
Census Bureau, 214, 227; surveys, 15*n*, 72
Census of Population and Housing, **69**
Center for Political Studies (CPS), 266, 278*n*
Central America, **90**, 124*n*; policy views on,
312–313; U.S. involvement in, 96, **287**;
U.S. policy in, 166, 167, 196, 228
centrality, 81
Chaney, James, 48
Chicago, 26, 28, 34, 36, 218, 236; conven-
tion, 44; mayoral election in, 163; police,
49
Chicago Citizen's Committee of 1,000, 36
China, 50